MEGA BRAIN POWER

The Book of Floating: Exploring the Private Sea

Megabrain: New Tools and Techniques for Brain Growth and Mind Expansion

The Anatomy of Sex and Power: An Investigation of Mind-Body Politics

MEGA BRAIN POWER

TRANSFORM YOUR LIFE WITH MIND MACHINES AND BRAIN NUTRIENTS

MICHAEL HUTCHISON

HYPERION
NEW YORK

DISCLAIMER

Some of the devices and procedures described in *Mega Brain Power* are experimental in nature, and conclusive studies of the long- and short-term effects of some of these devices and procedures have not been performed. None of the information contained in this book should be construed as a claim or representation that these devices are intended for use in the diagnosis, cure, treatment, or prevention of disease or any other medical condition. The use of some of these devices may be dangerous for those who are not in sound mental and physical health. Of particular note is information that the light and sound devices that use flickering light may produce seizures in those subject to photo-induced epilepsy. Anyone taking or withdrawing from drugs—prescription or other—should be aware that such drug use may affect his or her perceptions and responses to the stimuli of some of these devices. Some of the devices are restricted by law to use under medical supervision only. Before using these instruments, check with your federal, state, and local regulatory agencies and consult your physician.

See p. 463 for a list of trademarked items included in this text.

Copyright © 1994 Michael Hutchison

Library of Congress Cataloging-in-Publication Data

Hutchison, Michael.
   Mega brain power : transform your life with mind machines and brain
 nutrients / Michael Hutchison. — 1st ed.
    p. cm.
 Includes bibliographical references and index.
 ISBN 1-56282-770-7
 1. Brain stimulation. 2. Nootropic agents. I. Title.
QP388.H878 1994
158'.1—dc20   93-35576
                                           CIP

Design by ROBERT BULL DESIGN

10 9 8 7 6 5 4 3 2

To Galen and Russell Hutchison

Breathing in, I am father
Breathing out, I am son.
Breathing in, love
Breathing out, love
Son, father, grandfather
Breathing love.

Our normal waking consciousness, rational consciousness as we call it, is but one special type of consciousness, while all about it, parted from it by the filmiest of screens, there lie potential forms of consciousness entirely different. We may go through life without suspecting their existence, but apply the requisite stimulus and at a touch they are there in all their completeness. . . . No account of the universe in its totality can be final that leaves these other forms of consciousness quite disregarded.

—WILLIAM JAMES,
The Varieties of Religious Experience

ACKNOWLEDGMENTS

In the years since the publication of *Megabrain*, my knowledge and understanding of psychotechnology and the extraordinary powers and potentials of the interplay between humans and technology have been widened and deepened by the information, expertise, wisdom, and love of numerous explorers, experimentalists, and experientialists. Among these, I am grateful to Robert Austin, Henry Bloomstein, Ron Brecher, L.L. Brown, Dr. Thomas Budzynski, Dennis and Beverly Cambell, Chinmayee Chakrabarty, Jerry Simon Chasen, Dr. Jon Cowan, Dr. Les Fehmi, Ron Gordon, Rick and Lynn Henriksen, Ed Hershberger, Courtney Hoblack, Larry Hughes, Allen Hunt-Badiner, Dr. Julian Isaacs, Dr. Daniel Kirsch, Alex Kochkin, Jeff Labno, Larry Minikes, Sylvia Nielsen, Dr. Len Ochs, Dr. Siegfried Othmer, Terry and Leslie Patten, Rodijah Peters, Mary Kate Price, Dr. Michael Rosenbaum, Marvin Sams, Dr. Larry Schulz, David Siever, Holly Stults, Chuck Wilson, and T.R. Wright. Without the unfailing strength, support, and love of my mother and father, Adele and Russell Hutchison, and my sisters, Suzanne, Cindy, and Callie, this book would never have been written. I have been continually inspired, challenged, and strengthened by the thousands of individuals who have written me with kind praise and their own moving tales of how their lives have been transformed by the tools and techniques I have described. Thanks.

CONTENTS

PART FOUR

BRAIN-POWERED HEALING:
Therapeutic Uses of Brain Tools

PART FIVE

BRAIN POWER NUTRIENTS AND SMART PILLS

MEGA
BRAIN
POWER

INTRODUCTION
MAKING THE BRAIN CRICKETS CHIRP

The lawyer's desk is covered with files, her phones are jangling. She's working on a deadline. She tells her secretary to hold her calls. From her desk drawer she takes a small, black electronic device the size of a paperback book. She sits back, attaches a small clip to each earlobe, slips on earphones and what look like opaque sunglasses, closes her eyes, and presses a button on the console. An array of lights flicker inside the goggles. She feels a pleasant tingling in her earlobes that spreads through her brain. She hears mesmerizing pulsating tones. She sees a kaleidoscopic swirl of bright, unearthly colors, and sinks into a state of deep relaxation and revery. Vivid mental images begin to appear. . . .

Fifteen minutes later she sits up, removes the glasses, earphones, and ear clips. She is tingling with energy, refreshed, and deeply calm.

Her brain is now functioning far more effectively than it was before.
Her memory has increased dramatically. She has a higher IQ. Her intelligence, creativity, and ability to solve problems and assimilate new information have all expanded. Her brain's processing speed has increased, and her brain cells have forged new, richer interconnections.

Her body is now profoundly relaxed. Her blood pressure and heart rate have been reduced. Her immune system is functioning more effectively. The levels of adrenaline and other stress-related substances in her body have decreased. Her resistance to stress has now increased.

She is now smarter—and healthier—than she was fifteen minutes before.

Sounds like a science fiction movie. But it's actually a scene repeated each day in hundreds of thousands of homes, offices, and clinics. Mind machines seem futuristic, but in this case the future is here today.

These high-tech brain tools exist now, and hundreds of rigorous scientific studies have proven beyond doubt their capacity to enhance mental functioning, boost brain power, and quickly produce peak performance brain states. New evidence of the enormous powers of brain machines is emerging at an accelerating rate. As this book is being written many scientists are engaged in groundbreaking research into the effects of these brain-tech systems, and their reports reveal a growing sense of excitement, a feeling that brain technology represents something truly unprecedented.

Dr. Siegfried Othmer, a researcher and clinician who uses mind tech in his clinics to treat thousands of clients with learning disorders, recently told me:

> The results we're getting are not just unprecedented, they're *revolutionary*. The implications are incredible—our brain research can have incredible effects not only on learning disabilities but in improving human brain power across the board. We're finding that not just learning disorders, but also depression, anxiety, insomnia, epilepsy, virtually every mental disorder is basically caused by a lack of *coherence* in the brain. And by using these machines, we can restore the brain to that optimal coherent state. It sounds like hyperbole, but it has to be said—what we're finding can change the lives of everyone on the planet!

SCRATCHING THE SURFACE OF THE SNOW ON THE TIP OF THE ICEBERG

Part of the excitement on the subject of mind machines stems from the fact that brain-boosting technology is so new that while individual scientists are doing research in specific areas and applications, as yet no one has a sense of what its boundaries might be. Many scientists believe that we have only begun to scratch the surface—or as one researcher put it, "we've just begun to scratch the surface of the snow on the tip of the iceberg." So far, studies by psychiatrists, psychologists, educators, therapists, physicians, sports trainers, educators, counselors, and other researchers and clinicians have revealed that these mind machines can:

"Exercise" The Brain to Make It Healthier and More Powerful. The physical fitness revolution of the last two decades has proven that the human body requires stimulation, challenge, and exercise to remain healthy. The scientific evidence makes it clear that lack of physical exercise leads to deterioration and illness: We must "use it or lose it." Now a wealth of brain research is proving that the brain, like the body, requires stimulation and challenge to function optimally: that by "exercising" the brain, we can actually strengthen it, just as our muscles grow stronger from physical exercise. Evidence suggests that the new mind machines can provide the kind of stimulation, challenge, and novelty that can strengthen the brain, increase the actual size and health of its neurons, and produce peak performance, increased intelligence, and greater well-being.

Reduce Stress and Produce Deep Relaxation. Evidence shows that various mind machines can reduce levels of stress-related neurochemicals, dramatically reduce muscle tension, lower high blood pressure, slow heart rate, soothe jangled nerves, and quickly produce whole-body levels of relaxation so deep that one neuroscientist has called this "the most profound relaxation ever experienced."

Boost IQ. In several studies, subjects with learning disabilities have shown *average* increases in IQ of over twenty points and many raise their IQ by over thirty points. Other research suggests that the machines can also dramatically boost the IQ of normal, healthy users.

Enhance Creativity. Scores on several psychological tests that measure creativity show significant boosts in subjects using types of mind technology.

Accelerate Learning. In a variety of settings, subjects using mind technology have learned more, learned faster, and proven more adept at learning difficult and complex material than ordinary subjects.

Increase Memory. Mind machines have been proven to improve both long-term and short-term memory.

Increase Sexual Pleasure. By magnifying and intensifying sensory acuity, boosting the flow of the body's natural euphoriants and sexually arousing biochemicals, and increasing brain-wave synchrony between partners, mind technology can transform sexual experience.

Produce Peak Performance States. Laboratory evidence and reports of professional athletes, musicians, stage performers, salespeople, and business executives suggest mind machines help induce the high-efficiency, effortless "flow" states optimal for peak performance.

Eliminate Substance Abuse Problems. Stunning breakthroughs in treating addiction with mind technology are producing unprecedented recovery rates and seem on the verge of revolutionizing substance abuse treatment.

Overcome Depression and Anxiety. In a variety of studies subjects have eliminated their chronic depression or anxiety completely within a short period after beginning regular use of brain-stimulating devices.

Alleviate Pain. Mind technology has proven effective in eliminating or greatly reducing both chronic, intractable pain (in such conditions as cancer and arthritis) and transient pain (such as the pain of injuries, headaches, migraines, angina).

Boost Immune Function. Researchers are exploring the effects of mind machines on sick subjects (including those with AIDS, chronic fatigue immune dysfunction syndrome, and cancers) and on healthy subjects, and on individual components of the immune system. They have found clear evidence that these devices can increase the power of the immune system to overcome existing diseases and boost its resistance to infection.

Change or Eliminate Unwanted Habits and Attitudes. Clinical evidence suggests that mind technology can produce profound and rapid personal changes, and personality transformations. They seem to do so by facilitating the release of painful memories or traumatic experiences and enhancing users' powers to program and "rescript" their unconscious mind to eliminate negative or harmful habits or attitudes and replace them with positive attitudes and behaviors.

And this is just the beginning. Other studies suggest that we have not yet begun to understand the wide range of powerful life-enhancing benefits we may ultimately derive from brain technology. The use of mind machines, many people now suggest, may have a more profound effect on our civilization than the development of the personal computer. In fact, many people believe that the personal computer is simply one type of mind machine, with its own capacities for boosting brain power and enhancing human performance.

Perhaps the most amazing thing about mind machines is how widely available, inexpensive, and easy to use they are. The preceding paragraphs, with their talk of research, scientists, clinics, and laboratories, may have evoked images of immense medical contraptions, found only in hospitals or university laboratories. But in fact, mind machines seem more like electronic toys than medical equipment. They look and feel like small computer games. Many are inexpensive, easy to operate, small in size, and sold widely through retail catalogs and stores. Most of all, they are fun.

Millions of individuals around the world are using these brain-stimulating tools to reduce stress and expand their own mental powers. As they do so, they are finding that these new high-tech tools can quickly heighten their senses and make them smarter, more creative, more relaxed, and happier.

Are you skeptical? Doubtful that peak brain states can be produced so quickly and easily?

INNOCENT WRITER IN SEARCH OF "THE EDGE": MAD SCIENTISTS AND STRANGE MACHINES

I was too. Twelve years ago, while living in New York City, I began writing magazine articles about emerging new technologies that claimed to have profound effects on the brain. The first one was about flotation tanks. I remember the editor telling me "Remember, we don't want some flotation tank puff piece—be sure to put an *edge* on it." An edge, right. I didn't care—I thought the whole thing was great, getting paid to go have fun.

The article was well received—float centers all over the country were swamped with calls—and I began rounding up other story ideas having to do with mind-altering technologies. As I would hear of something that sounded colorful and bizarre, I'd pitch it to one editor or another, and they would laugh. You have to realize, this was New York City, and the editors were professional cynics. All this "brain machine" stuff sounded so crackpot, so bogus, like something those yo-yos on the *other* coast would dream up.

I'd told each of these editors about that first editor's admonition to "put an edge on it." So as I brought in a new story idea, the editor would laugh and shout, "Yes! Mad scientist stuff! Right up your alley! Go check it out." And they would always end by saying "Just be sure to put an *edge* on it."

At that time, most of these machines were still in the experimental stage—eccentric, alien devices that looked like props from some 1950s science fiction film. Some of them existed only in the form of a single crude prototype tinkered together in the inventor's garage. The inventors and researchers would welcome me with outstretched arms and a peculiar gleam in their eye, producing reams of arcane research data, spinning out wild theories and speculations, and claiming to me that without doubt their machine could supercharge my brain. And a voice in my head would say, Be careful, these are people with a *mission*. No problem putting an edge on this article.

"Try it," they would say, opening up the door to the black chamber, holding out the goggles and headphones, attaching the electrodes to my head, seating me just so in front of the towering null-field coils. "Try it," they would say, "you'll see."

And I would think to myself, Well, I'm a writer. This is what I do. An *assignment*. And so, sometimes laughing to myself, sometimes with a bit of trepidation, but always with curiosity, I would try it. And many times, *things would happen*.

When the lights began flickering in my eyes, I soared through a kaleidoscopic stream of unearthly colored images that soon changed into vivid and realistic visions of childhood—scenes so real that I felt I was actually there. . . . When the blue frog-eyes were placed over my eyes, I was suspended in warm Caribbean waters, floating peacefully, glowing with pure mental clarity. . . . When I climbed into the sensory deprivation chamber and floated on the waters in the total blackness, my body melted as I spun head over heels through infinite black space until a story burst into my brain in its entirety, from the first sentence to the last, and when I later went home and sat down in front of my typewriter to write that story it flowed out exactly as it had come to me in the chamber. And it was a great story.

After my sessions were over, I would feel relaxed, alert, my senses keen, filled with a tingling pleasure that would stay with me, sometimes for days. And the inventors and researchers would grin at me with that gleam in their eye and nod at me and say, "See, now you know what we mean."

So I would go home and write my articles. But often, after the articles were published, I'd find myself thinking, Boy, I'd sure like to try that thing again. In fact, I'd like to have one right here with me. So the idea arose that if I was writing not just disconnected articles but a whole book devoted to these devices, then I would be able to try them again and again. And I would have an excuse to seek out these interesting machines wherever I could find them and try them out. It would be "research" for my book.

So I began to write a book. For several years I experienced, explored, and experimented with the devices. To try to understand how they could have such mind-altering effects, I spoke with scientists, pored through hundreds of books, scientific journals, and articles, in fields ranging from neurochemistry, to psychobiology, to electroencephalography, to neuroanatomy.

At the end of it I wrote a book, *Megabrain: New Tools and Techniques for Brain Growth and Mind Expansion*. It described some of my experiences with some of these machines, provided scientific explanations for their effects, and included summaries of the existing scientific research into the effects of these machines. I was unprepared for the response it created.

IS THAT A HIGH-TECH GURU IN THE MIRROR?

Suddenly, almost overnight, I and the inventors of the devices I had mentioned in the book were deluged with thousands of letters from people beseeching us for information about where they could try them, where they could buy one for themselves. I asked a few of the inventors to bring their devices to what I envisioned would be a small "Megabrain party" in a loft in Manhattan, and I arrived to find the place jammed with news reporters, videocameras, and hundreds of people excitedly trying the various machines. A few weeks later I attended a similar low-key party at a warehouse in Los Angeles, and with no publicity except word of mouth, over a thousand people showed up, from places as distant as Thailand, Japan, and Germany, and from all over the United States and Canada. They stood in long lines in hopes of getting a few minutes on one or another of the mind machines. There seemed to be a lot of people who were hungry for mind machines.

I had ended *Megabrain* with a tongue-in-cheek vision of "Brain Gyms," sleek spas furnished with brain machines where people would come to exercise their brains. But reality quickly outstripped my imagination. Within months actual brain gyms were opening up in cities across the country and, as the book was published in other languages, in cities around the world. Suddenly articles in national newsmagazines and features on network TV were showing pictures of rows of people blissfully laid out in brain gyms, lights flickering in their eyes.

The book seemed to trigger a worldwide explosion of interest in mind machines. Reporters and newsmagazines described it as "the bible of the brain machine movement" and "the book that spawned the revolution." I became known in the media as the "leading exponent" and "chief spokesman," of mind machines, "the high-tech guru of the mind-machine revolution."

Yet I didn't feel like an exponent or spokesman, and I knew I was no guru. Something in me jeered and remained skeptical. The idea of a "movement" or a "mind-machine revolution" made me distinctly uneasy—the experiences I described in the book were mine alone, intensely personal, not the common or shared experiences of a mass movement. No doubt, the machines had interesting effects for me. But maybe I was just highly susceptible to them—or just the victim of the placebo effect and my own expectations. It was hard to believe these devices could really have the same effects on thousands of other people that they seemed to have for me.

But the evidence poured in. The paperback edition of *Megabrain* appeared with my own address in the back, and in a matter of months I was swamped with thousands of letters from people describing their own experiences with mind machines, or clamoring to try the devices for themselves. I was a writer, not a showman, and dreaded public speaking, but the demand was so great it drew me away from the book I was writing. I found myself out on the road accompanied by ten cases of mind machines, doing a series of Megabrain Workshops, in which I guided people through sessions on a variety of the machines. I watched hundreds of people experience the machines and emerge with stories of bursts of insight, profound revelations, experiences of lucidity, illumination, ecstasy. Peak experiences. There was no doubt. The things just seemed to work.

THE MAGICAL MOTHER ENCOUNTER

Over the years that followed, I spoke with, corresponded with, and observed literally tens of thousands of people who used these devices. Over and over again I was amazed to witness how the machines had transformed their lives. I met with a businessman who had made millions out of a creative idea he'd had on a table that moved him through an electrostatic field; people who had recovered from chronic pain and diseases using light and sound machines; men who had meditated daily for over twenty years who found that mind machines took them to deeper levels of meditation; world-famous bodybuilders who used mind machines to increase growth hormone and build bigger muscles; older people who had recovered mental powers and memories they thought had disappeared forever; actors, dancers, painters, opera singers, and other performers who believed mind machines had sharpened their skills and boosted them into peak performance states; and hundreds of other stories.

As I heard the tales of all these people, I felt a great distance between us. The machines were producing extraordinary experiences and creating permanent changes in their lives. Not in mine. Sure, they put me into states of deep relaxation and reverie, produced some unearthly, unforgettable experiences, and even helped me write my books. But nothing more, nothing profound. The voice of God had not spoken to me out of a whirlwind.

The authentic transforming potential of the machines was really hammered home to me during one of my workshops in Manhattan. I had helped a woman get onto a machine that revolved her gently around in circles through an electromagnetic field. A few minutes later I glanced over and saw she was crying.

I quietly asked her if she wanted me to stop the machine. "No, no, please don't," she said in a childish pleading voice, "let me go on!" So I did, and she revolved around and around for about ten more minutes, with tears pouring down her cheeks. I was afraid she was having some sort of breakdown—not the sort of thing you want to have happen in your workshop.

As the machine stopped I asked her if she was all right. She beamed at me through her tears and said she felt wonderful. *Uh-oh*, said the voice in my head, *something happened here*. I asked her to sit down for a talk.

"My mother died when I was eight years old," she told me, "but I had a long conversation with her just now." She proceeded to tell me she'd been severely depressed for most of her life, was taking antidepressants, was about forty pounds overweight, had been unable to hold a job because of her depression, and had been having suicidal thoughts. And then she'd met her mother on the machine.

Her mother had been killed in a car accident. "And when I saw her today," she told me, "I realized I had always *blamed* her for leaving me . . . that ever since then I'd just been filled with anger at her for being so selfish as to get herself killed like that and *abandoning* me." She had told her mother about her anger, and her mother had responded by saying that she loved her deeply, that she had not wanted to leave her daughter—she had not *wanted* to be killed in the car accident! "I loved you then, and I love you now," the mother told her, "and I'm sorry I died and left you, but *it's time for you to stop being angry at me. Get on with your life.*"

The mother and daughter embraced in a blaze of light and love. "I realized," the woman said, "that I did love my mother, and that my mother loved me. Mother died, but at least she'd lived before she died. I haven't even lived yet. I've got to start living."

I heard from her about six months later. She wanted to talk. When I met her at the café, she looked much younger—she had dropped about forty pounds and was glowing with energy. She told me that the same day as her experience on the machine, she had stopped taking her antidepressant medication. She had felt great. She had continued seeing a therapist she met at the workshop, who used the mind machine in her practice. She had a session on the machine every week. She had taken a new job and was doing very well there. She had met a man, they were engaged to be married. She was healthy, happy, radiant, plugged in to the cosmic power outlet.

I know, I know, the whole thing sounds so pat, corny. But it really happened. And it awakened something in me, a sense of what enormous potentials these mind machines possessed. Clearly, the machine did not create the changes in this woman's life—I have no doubt that she had gone through a long process of preparation for that breakthrough experience on the machine. But if it did not cause it, the machine at least served as a catalyst for the experience. Something profound had happened. And it made me think of all the hundreds of people who had told me stories of their own life-transforming experiences on the machines. Remarkable stories. Extraordinary. Amazing.

But most of all, not mine. Most of all, *other people's stories.* And then somewhere in there I fell into an abyss.

AWAKENING IN THE ABYSS

If you had asked me in 1991, I would have told you without hesitation that I believed these mind tools represented a breakthrough in human evolution, providing humans access to richer, healthier lives. I'd said something to that effect so many times on TV and radio shows and in interviews and speeches that the words came easily to my lips.

And yet in 1991 I found myself in hell. I emerged from a fog of exhaustion that had accumulated in the year following the birth of my son and found that my own life was filled with pain, suffering, and sickness.

I was so profoundly exhausted I could barely force myself out of bed. Every muscle and joint in my body hurt so badly it was almost impossible to fall asleep, and what little sleep I did get had no restorative effect at all. My brain felt stuffed with cotton. It was difficult to think. I was barely able to sit at my computer and type a coherent sentence—the idea of actually writing something original, creative, sparkling with energy, seemed impossible. Clearly something serious was wrong.

A friend sent me to a doctor, who ran a series of tests and found that I had a severe case of chronic fatigue immune dysfunction syndrome (CFIDS). A key factor in the onset of CFIDS, he told me, is stress. As I looked around me at the shambles of my life, stress was not hard to find. It was everywhere.

I was in a nightmare of a marriage that I had been seeking to escape from for over a year. The stresses caused by the birth of a son placed even greater pressures on the marriage. At the same time, in part because of these stresses, my own business was going down the tubes. I no longer had the energy to go out and do Megabrain Workshops and seminars. My magazine, *Megabrain Report,* sat dead in the water—I simply didn't have the strength to write the articles for it and publish it. My last book had been completed in the months just before my marriage. Now years later, my agent wondered where my next book was, but I didn't even have the energy to think about what that book might be. What this meant in real life was money problems. The already high stress levels of my marriage were intensified by economic uncertainties.

And of course I was not using any mind machines. When I had still lived in New York City, my apartment had been filled with an assortment of them, and my days had been filled with frequent mind-machine meditations. A couple of float centers were nearby, and I went in for long floats several times a week, sometimes floating for up to eight hours at a time.

But in getting married, I had moved away from New York City. To my surprise, there were no float tanks available in the area where I lived. By early 1991 it had been well over three years since I had floated regularly. I had plenty of mind machines, but I couldn't really use them at home because of the stressfulness of my domestic situation.

STARVING WRITER LOST AMONG "EMPLOYEES"

By then there was a Megabrain office, where I kept most of the mind machines. But the office was miles from home, and it was a busy place, filled with work to do and with people—*employees,* for God's sake, and what had I, poor starving writer, ever done to become the kind of person who had *employees?*—talking on phones, using faxes and copiers, doing all the tasks that had to be done to maintain a network of tens of thousands of people who were interested in mind machines.

Whenever I got up the energy to get into the office, there was always so much work to do there, and so many phone calls to be returned, that it was impossible to spend much time using any of the mind machines that were all over the place. Besides, the employees were using them.

The sad fact was that I had become like the poor little rich boy when it came to mind machines. I had written *Megabrain* because using mind machines was so much fun I wanted an excuse to keep doing it. But now I had virtually every mind machine made, with the inventors and manufacturers sending me their latest devices, and I hardly ever had the chance to use them. No time. Too tired.

I saw the irony—these were machines that were supposed to increase physical energies and mental powers, and to boost mental and physical health and well-being, and here I was—the "leading authority," the "spokesman," even the "guru" of mind technology—too sick, too tired, too mentally debilitated to even use the damned machines! It was clear what had to be done.

I moved out of the house and secured court-ordered joint custody of our son. But then my wife took my son and moved out of the state. I was devastated. My friends and my lawyer assured me that while my situation worked its way through the court system, I should get to work on a book, get healthy, and get on with my life.

I looked around me. My cozy home overlooking San Francisco Bay was cluttered with an extraordinary assortment of contraptions. Over here were several new electroencephalographs (EEGs), looking like small computers, still in their boxes. Over there, eight different machines that flicker your brain waves with strobe lights. In the closet was a box full of electrical brain stimulators. *Hey,* said the voice in my head said, *according to the guru of mind technology, these things work. Why don't you use them!*

It was as simple as that. Something changed—a subtle shift in my reality. The world smelled tangy. I was ready.

MAKING THE BRAIN CRICKETS CHIRP

I had been reading much about some exciting new breakthroughs in EEG biofeedback—startling clinical evidence that people who learned to generate brain waves in the frequency ranges called alpha and theta were experiencing sudden, extraordinary, and profound experiences that changed their lives—tests showed dramatic increases in happiness, well-being, and equally dramatic decreases in anxiety and depression. Also, intriguingly, *their immune systems got stronger. Okay*, said the voice in my head, *let's start out with the simple stuff: more happiness, less anxiety, better health.*

The EEG machines had been sitting in their boxes for weeks. Suddenly it no longer seemed such a daunting prospect to get them out, connect the wires, and set them up. Within ten minutes I had three different EEG devices set up, arranged around my head as I lay on my bed. Okay, the instructions say that if I close my eyes and make alpha waves, I will hear the sound of a cricket chirping. I closed my eyes. I waited. I waited a long time. Then, as soon as I had forgotten what I was doing . . . chirp . . . chirrrrpp . . . chrrrrrpppp chrrppp chrrp!

The instructions also say that when I start to generate enough theta waves, I will hear the rhythmic creak of a locust or cicada. So I waited . . . and waited. . . . Chirrrp, chirrp, there's alpha. . . . Then . . . *Cree-ak, cree-ak*. Theta! As soon as I said it to myself, it disappeared. So I waited again, and waited, until, just as I was ready to give up: *Chirrrrp, chirrrrrp! Cree-ak cree-ak, chirrrrrrrrrrrrp!*

Pretty soon I felt like I was out on the front porch swing on a summer night, listening to the crickets and locusts. I could almost see the fireflies. I did this for about an hour. Then I got up and went out for a run. I hadn't gone running for months—hadn't had the energy.

I came back, cooked dinner, sat down, and wrote a poem. First poem in a blue moon. Good one too.

I began doing alpha and theta training three or four times a day, for about twenty minutes or a half hour at a time. When I got into the relaxed theta state, I felt like I was watching myself from up over my left shoulder. When sudden bursts of emotions would arise—anger, frustration, and pain—they no longer seemed to overwhelm me and seize my body entirely. Instead, I simply experienced them, and observed myself experiencing them, and learned how to release them and let them go.

I found that I could work at my writing and research now without being disrupted by attacks of anger or sorrow. If sudden thoughts of my distant son arose, or grief at my wife's cruelty, my "observer" self would alert me: "Here it comes, okay, now you're feeling anger . . . now release it . . . there it goes." And back to work I'd go.

It was like recovering from a long illness. Suddenly I felt my strength flowing through me, creativity, joy, I was so happy to be alive.

MAKING CONNECTIONS

Since the EEG machines worked so well, I decided to start adding some new things. I was aware of lots of research indicating that machines with stroboscopic flashing lights (called light/sound or LS machines) could actively alter brain waves and cause the brain to produce the desired alpha or theta waves, or even the more rapid, energizing beta waves. So I began experimenting with LS machines. Sometimes I would flash myself down into the alpha and theta ranges. (I would wear the EEG electrodes, and the chirping of the crickets and locusts proved that the LS machines were indeed getting me into the desired alpha and theta ranges.) Other times I would speed up my brain waves into the energizing beta range. I found these high-frequency ranges could produce unique brain states—sharply focused, clear, hyperalert. After a while it hit me that I was feeling smarter. Could it be that somehow these alterations in my brain waves were boosting my IQ, pumping up my memory?

I seemed to recall some research suggesting that flashing light machines in the beta frequencies could improve learning. I began a voracious reading of the research, and found that clinicians were now using flashing light machines to stimulate these high-frequency brain waves and producing average IQ increases of over twenty points and in some cases over thirty points. Some of the scientists were suggesting that the IQ increases might stem from increased growth of brain cells.

This triggered my memory of studies I'd read years before proving that for memories to become permanent in the brain, there had to be a process of nerve cell growth—protein synthesis—involving RNA. If something interrupted that protein synthesis, new memories did not get formed. Hmmmm. I was reminded of some papers I'd just read suggesting that one reason CFIDS caused such cognitive problems and loss of memory was that it disrupted protein synthesis and inhibited RNA—and thus inhibited the formation of new memories—in the brain.

By coincidence, I did an interview with a leading researcher of cranial electrostimulation (CES), who told me that CES not only increased learning, memory, and IQ in human subjects, but seemed to work by *stimulating protein synthesis*. He also cited studies showing that CES stimulated the release of nerve growth factor (NGF), which protects brain cells and helps them grow, thus boosting intelligence, learning, and memory.

I pulled out a CES unit that had been sitting in my closet for months and began using it an hour a day, often in combination with light and sound devices. A scientific paper arrived in the mail from a researcher suggesting that EEG biofeedback training increased protein synthesis and the growth of nerve cells in the brain. I received word from another researcher that the flashing light machines had been proven to increase growth hormone—which would, among other things, improve protein synthesis in the brain.

Suddenly all these things began falling together. I was using flashing light, I was altering my brain-wave activity, I was using electrical brain stimulation and EEG biofeedback: My memory was improving and my brain was coming awake again. I could feel my neural pathways pulsing with nerve growth factor, my brain cells churning with protein synthesis. I was alive again, with the excitement of being in pursuit of something new—new information, new insights. Hey, I should write about this, I thought. And I began to write a book.

I called up the researchers and they told me about their work. I went to visit with some of these therapists who were having unprecedented successes in using brain machines clinically to treat learning disorders, drug addiction, dyslexia, stroke, brain damage, posttraumatic stress disorder, and much more. They taught me what they were doing, and I went home and tried out their techniques. I explored ways of combining and streamlining their techniques with new types of mind machines.

One afternoon I emerged from a deep theta state. I heard a strange noise. I pulled the flashing-light goggles off my face, removed the CES electrodes from my ears, took off the headphones through which I had been hearing binaural beats, and sat up, becoming somewhat tangled in the wires of EEG sensors still strapped around my head and noticing I was still being bathed in the red light of my Biotron Projector unit at the foot of the bed, while my negative ion generator blew tangy air across my face . . . and I realized what the odd sound was: a friend stood in the doorway, convulsed with laughter.

"I'm sorry, Mike," she said. "I'm not laughing at you, it's just that you looked like . . . like . . ." She gave up trying to describe and dissolved in laughter.

Yes, I may have looked silly, but hey, I was *really* relaxed. And my brain was cooking. I was plugged in.

I began laughing too. "These things work!" I cried, waving my arms amid the techno-rubble, while she clapped her hands and laughed. My brain was ticking like a fine Swiss watch. Nerve growth factor and protein synthesis at work. I was bursting with ideas. I had emerged from the abyss. I was alive, and filled with desires to become increasingly so.

How do they work? And how can you use them so they work for you? That's why I wrote this book.

THE SHAPE OF THINGS TO COME

In this book we will explore an enormous array of mind machines and an assortment of powerful techniques and programs for using them to tune in specific brain states and to amplify the powers of the mind.

In Part I, "Tuning in Your 'Other 90 Percent,' " we will look first at the brain. What goes on in it when we're in a "peak performance" state? What makes it possible to alter the activity of our brain using external stimuli, such as a brain machine?

In Part II, "Access to Tools," we'll investigate the most effective mind tools currently available, explain how they work, describe what it feels like to experience them, and provide a "consumers' guide." This is not a "complete" guide, since there are hundreds of different mind machines now available, but one that points out to you which machines are the most effective, powerful, and reliable, and offer the best value for your dollar.

Part III, "From Your Brain to Megabrain: The Users' Guide to Mind Machines" is the longest part and the central how-to core of the book. In it we'll explore ways the mind machines can be *used*—not just passively experienced as instruments of pleasure and entertainment, but actively applied as immensely powerful tools to attain desired goals. In this part we will focus on using the brain machines to attain peak performance brain states and on using these peak states for such purposes as accelerated learning, athletic training, enhanced creativity, and much more.

In Part IV, "Brain-Powered Healing: Therapeutic Uses of Brain Tools," we will focus on how using the machines for self-improvement and therapeutic applications, including relief of pain, weight loss, smoking cessation, and treatment of drug addiction, alcoholism, anxiety, and depression.

In Part V, "Brain Power Nutrients and Smart Pills," we will explore the rapidly advancing field of psychopharmacology: the growing array of brain nutrients and cognition enhancement pills, or "smart drugs," that are legal and, when used correctly, safe. We will describe a variety of these nutrients that have been scientifically proven to produce immense increases in brain power and explore how they can be used *in combination with brain machines* for even greater effectiveness.

PART ONE

TUNING IN YOUR "OTHER 90 PERCENT"

All bibles or sacred codes have been the causes of the following errors:

1. That man has two real existing principles: viz: a body & a soul.

2. That energy, called evil, is alone from the body: & that reason, called good, is alone from the soul.

3. That God will torment man in eternity for following his energies.

But the following contraries to these are true:

1. Man has no body distinct from his soul; for that called body is a portion of soul discerned by the five senses, the chief inlets of soul in this age.

2. Energy is the only life, and is from the body; and reason is the bound or outward circumference of energy.

3. Energy is eternal delight.

—WILLIAM BLAKE,
The Marriage of Heaven and Hell

ONE
THE BRAIN REVOLUTION

We have been living through a momentous revolution: the Brain Revolution. Scientists have discovered more about the human brain in the last few years than they had learned throughout all of previous human history.

What they have discovered is that the brain is far different and far more powerful than most of us imagine. That, given the proper type of stimulation, the human brain can perform seemingly miraculous feats with ease. That the ordinary human brain, in other words, has extraordinary or exceptional powers; that these powers are not extraordinary at all, but, for most of us, simply dormant, undeveloped; and that these powers can be activated or switched on by the right type of stimulation. And, most importantly that we can learn to activate these powers, in the same way, and almost as easily, as we can learn to ride a bicycle or play the piano.

IN SEARCH OF TOOLS FOR WAKING UP

We've all experienced it—those unexpected times when our entire being seems to shift into a higher gear and function far more efficiently and powerfully than normal. We call it lucidity, insight, mastery, waking up, clarity, wisdom, enlightenment, grace, bliss, satori, creativity, learning, peak experience. . . . It's a state in which we know with absolute certainty that our normal functioning is just a pale shadow of our actual powers and capacities; that our ordinary state is like a state of deep sleep compared to this rich awakening. And we know *this is how we should be all the time.* After all, sleep is a fine and restful state, but who among us would choose to spend our entire lives in even the most comfortable bed? Most of us would like to be in this high-gear, high-efficiency state as often as possible.

A central thread running through human history has been the quest for effective and reliable techniques for entering these transcendent, awakened states. Humans have devoted an enormous amount of ingenuity and effort to finding gateways to this realm of lucidity. They have pounded on drums, danced, chanted, fasted, tried different ways of breathing, stood on their heads, sat for years in dark caves, prayed, invented and muttered magic phrases, eaten wild herbs and plants, gazed into fires, devised odd sexual practices, contemplated symbols, created colorful rituals. At times over the millennia, they have stumbled onto something that works—pound on the drum at just *that* rhythm, breathe in just *this* way, focus the attention in this very special manner—and have passed it down from generation to generation, refining it, perfecting it.

And the ingenuity and effort paid off. Humans have devised a variety of ways of entering peak states that really do work. One example is the vast array of meditative practices. They work. But the problem is that for most people, they only work imperfectly, unpredictably. And, most difficult of all, they usually require enormous amounts of practice—hard, rigorous discipline—before they really work powerfully and reliably. Studies of Zen monks, for example, have shown that for the most part, the only monks who can get into the deepest state of Zen meditation quickly and at will are those who have meditated for over twenty years.

So throughout human history, the awakened state has been, for many, tantalizing but elusive—sometimes it comes, out of nowhere, spontaneously, and for a few moments we are there. And then it is gone again. As most of us have discovered, it's no easy thing to enter these peak performance domains at will.

MEDITATE LIKE A ZEN MONK IN 28 MINUTES!
—advertisement for a popular brain-tech product

But now, as a result of the brain revolution, new breakthroughs in neuroscience and microelectronics have permitted scientists to "map" the electrical and chemical activity of the brain in action. Scientists have used the new technology to monitor the brains of those meditators, artists, and other rare individuals who are able to enter peak domains at will and to map their brain activity during those peak states.

Their first findings were that those peak states are not mysterious and unpredictable phenomena, but are clearly linked to very specific patterns of brain activity. These include dramatic changes in brainwave frequencies, hemispheric symmetry, and rapid alterations in the levels of various neurochemicals. If we could learn to produce these patterns of brain activity, they reasoned, we should be able to produce the peak states they are associated with.

As they worked with increasing excitement, the scientists discovered that it did not require years of training or any special meditative powers to produce those unique patterns of brain activity associated with peak brain states. They found that by using types of mechanical stimulation, such as flickering strobe lights, precise combinations of pulsating sound waves, or rhythmic physical movement, they could actually produce those same "peak state" brain patterns in ordinary people with no meditative experience.

And so it has happened: Over the last few years scientists and electronics engineers have used advanced technology to design a variety of devices—*mind machines*—that trigger those desired brain patterns, quickly and safely, allowing users rapid access to peak performance brain states.

TOOLS FOR EVOLUTION?

The technology is now evolving rapidly. New, more sophisticated and effective versions of those earlier devices are emerging constantly. New tools and techniques are appearing with dizzying speed. There's a sense of constant innovation that feels very much like the excitement of the early years of personal computer development, when no sooner had one unprecedented generation of PCs reached the market than another generation of even more powerful, smaller, and less expensive computers emerged.

What these new brain machines may represent is something truly revolutionary. In fact, many scientists and others are suggesting that these machines may represent a "revolution in evolution," permitting humans, for the first time, truly to learn to control their own brain states, consciously *choosing* those brain states most appropriate for the task at hand.

Imagine being able to change your brain state with the same ease you flick the channels on your TV set. Are you studying to pass your mathematics exams? Select the proper "math-consciousness" setting on your brain machine and switch your brain waves into the proper configuration. Are you interested in listening to Beethoven? Plug into the brain state that combines heightened auditory acuity and heightened aesthetic perceptions and tweak it with a bit of synesthesia— turning up your ability to see, taste, and smell, as well as hear music. If unwanted anger threatens to disrupt your work at the office, switch to a more peaceful, relaxed brain state. When you're having sex, you and your partner set the dial to turn up your erotic powers and sensitivity to sensory stimuli. If you're going through an emergency, under a lot of stress, or feel a cold coming on, select the program for pumping up your immune system. Or, if you want to extend your life span, set your brain machine to the "rejuvenation" setting and let it repair any DNA damage and stimulate the release of growth hormone and other rejuvenating biochemicals. . . .

Many scientists and cultural analysts now believe such mind-enhancing devices may represent a historic breakthrough in human development. Think of the enormous implications: tools that will allow large numbers of humans to function consistently at levels of mental efficiency, insight, creativity, and intelligence that have in the past been attained only by the gifted few. It would be what writer Michael Murphy calls "a democratization of the metanormal." Mind machines may be the tools by which the extraordinary becomes familiar.

SUGGESTED READING

For a fascinating compendium of accounts of human peak perform-ances, see *The Future of the Body: Explorations Into the Further Evolu-tion of Human Nature* by Michael Murphy (Los Angeles: J.P. Tarcher, 1992). For insight into the nature of peak performance and "flow," see *Flow: The Psychology of Optimal Experience* by Mihali Csikszent-mihalyi (New York: Harper & Row, 1990). On our genetic program-ming to seek out heightened states, see my book *The Anatomy of Sex and Power: An Investigation of Mind-Body Politics* (New York: Mor-row, 1991); Terence McKenna's *Food of the Gods* (New York: Bantam, 1992); Stanislav Grof's *Adventures in Self Discovery* (SUNY, 1985), Ronald K. Siegal's *Intoxication: Life in Pursuit of Artificial Paradise* (New York: Simon & Schuster, 1990), and Aldous Huxley's *The Doors of Perception* (New York: Harper & Brothers, 1954).

TWO
PEAK PERFORMANCE BRAIN WAVES

The Brain Revolution has been one of the most momentous events in human history. It's still going on at a furious pace. Perhaps its most exciting development has been that for the first time scientists have been able to get right down into the brain and observe the action as it happens—and then look at it again in slow motion on the instant replay.

Like most of us, brain scientists are fascinated by extraordinary powers or peak experiences. They like to have such experiences themselves, and, of course, they're keenly aware that scientific breakthroughs have been the result of scientists like themselves having such experiences. So, for many scientists, the brain event that they have observed with the greatest curiosity—the Super Bowl, so to speak—has been the peak experience event. What exactly happens in the brains of people when they are experiencing the nonordinary brain states that we call illumination, flow, enlightenment, waking up, peak experience? Neuroscientists have observed the brains of yogis, geniuses, artists, and meditators using such high-tech equipment as the EEG (electroencephalograph), MRI (magnetic resonance imaging), PET (positron emission tomography), SPECT (single photon emission computerized tomography), and SQUID (superconducting quantum interference device), and watched in rapt attention as their subjects went through rapid state changes and entered extraordinary mental realms.

What they have found, and documented in literally hundreds of experiments, has been that these heightened states are consistently linked to certain very clearly defined events or patterns of activity in the brain. Among the most interesting of these events are changes in the brain's electrical activity.

THE BRAIN-WAVE INVESTIGATION

The brain is powered by electricity. Each of its billions of individual cells "fires," or electrically discharges, at a specific frequency. The electrical activity of the brain can be monitored by placing sensors or electrodes against the scalp, which register the minute electrical signals happening inside the brain, much the way a seismograph can detect tremors taking place inside the earth. The device that registers these signals is called an electroencephalograph, or EEG. The EEG measures not the firings of individual brain cells, but rather the cooperative or collective electrical patterns of networks or communities of millions of cells firing together—fluctuations of energy sweeping across the networks of the brain. These collective energy pulsations are called brain waves.

Since the first EEG was devised in the 1920s, scientists have found that the brain has a tendency to produce brain waves of four distinct varieties, which they have called beta, alpha, theta, and delta.

Beta Waves The most rapid brain waves, beta waves, range in frequency from about 14 cycles per second (called 14 Hertz, abbreviated Hz) to more than 100 Hz. When we are in a normal waking state, eyes open, focusing on the world outside ourselves or dealing with concrete, specific problems, beta waves (particularly those between 14 and 40 Hz) are the most dominant and powerful waves in the brain. Beta waves are associated with alertness, arousal, concentration, cognition, and—at excessive levels—anxiety.

Alpha Waves As we close our eyes and become more relaxed, passive, or unfocused, brain-wave activity slows down, and we produce bursts of alpha waves, which range in frequency from about 8 to 13 Hz. If we become quite relaxed and mentally unfocused, alpha waves become dominant throughout the brain, producing a calm and pleasant sensation called the alpha state. The alpha state seems to be the brain's "neutral" or idling state, and people who are healthy and not under stress tend to produce a lot of alpha activity. Lack of significant alpha activity can be a sign of anxiety, stress, brain damage, or illness.

Theta Waves As calmness and relaxation deepen into drowsiness, the brain shifts to slower, more powerfully rhythmic theta waves, with a frequency range of about 4 to 8 Hz. Theta has been called the twilight state, between waking and sleep. It's often accompanied by unexpected, dreamlike mental images. Often these images are accompanied by vivid memories, particularly childhood memories. Theta offers access to unconscious material, reveries, free association, sudden insight, creative ideas. It's a mysterious, elusive state, and for a long time experimenters had difficulty studying it because it is hard to maintain for any period of time. Most people tend to fall asleep as soon as they begin generating large amounts of theta.

Delta Waves As we fall asleep the dominant brain waves become delta, which are even slower than theta, in the frequency range below 4 Hz.

When most of us are in the delta state we're either asleep or otherwise unconscious. However, there is growing evidence that individuals may maintain consciousness while in a dominant delta state. This seems to be associated with certain deep trancelike or "nonphysical" states. It is while we're in the delta state that our brains are triggered to release large quantities of healing growth hormone.

INSTANT SATORI MACHINES AND THE ROYAL ROAD TO BLISS

In the 1960s many people were extremely interested in experiencing peak states. For many, psychedelics were the quickest and most reliable mind expansion technique. But drugs, while powerful and effective state-change tools, had drawbacks. They were illegal; the state changes they produced were long-lasting and durable, which made it next to impossible to change back into ordinary brain states on demand; and they also had unknown long-term effects on health. So, many people were eager to find a "drugless high," or some way to expand consciousness without the drawbacks of psychedelic drugs.

Among others, the Beatles, the most popular and influential rock group of the era, had become followers of a guru who taught them meditation. They began singing its praises as a way of reaching heightened states of consciousness without drugs. The guru appeared on the *Johnny Carson* show, wearing his white robes, giggling, and holding a flower. Meditation was In. Millions of people began trying to meditate. Millions of people were disappointed to find that meditation took practice and discipline, and did not instantly catapult them into enlightenment.

A look at EEG tracings made it clear that meditators produced a lot of alpha waves. Some young researchers developed a type of EEG that was "tuned" to respond to alpha waves by producing a beeping sound. They called this process biofeedback—that is, feeding back to the subject information from his or her own body. When people used EEG biofeedback, they could quickly learn to produce alpha waves simply by doing things that produced a beeping sound, such as sitting with their eyes closed, in a relaxed, passive state.

The researchers noticed that people who went through this alpha biofeedback training process experienced interesting changes—they became more calm and relaxed in their daily lives, they tended to give up such habits as smoking and heavy drinking, and they learned how to produce alpha waves at will, even when not hooked up to the biofeedback system.

This was exciting. Some researchers even suggested that the alpha state was synonymous with meditation. This was Big News, and the mass media soon latched onto it. Sensational stories about "instant nirvana" and "mechanical meditation" claimed that the alpha state was not only the same thing as meditation, but it could also be a quick cure for stress, one without all the mystic voodoo and spiritual trappings that most people associated with meditation. As research psychologist Joe Kamiya, who was then the pioneer investigator of alpha feedback, remembers it, "a surprisingly large number of people seemed to conclude that alpha would be the royal road to bliss, enlightenment, and higher consciousness. Nirvana now, through feedback."

Sales of "alpha machines" boomed. Thousands of people sat around learning to get into alpha. Thousands of people got into alpha and found it was calm, relaxed, passive, and, ultimately, not all that interesting. Because it was like just sitting there doing nothing, just . . . being there. And so thousands of alpha training devices went up on the shelf in the top of the closet and began gathering dust.

DISCOVERING THE TWILIGHT ZONE

Almost unnoticed amid the hoopla surrounding the alpha state was a series of EEG studies by Japanese scientists of Zen monks going into deep meditative states. They found that as monks went into meditation, they did indeed go into alpha, but the most skilled meditators sank right through alpha and began producing the slower theta waves. And, intriguingly, even in the depths of theta—for most people the gateway to sleep—the monks were not asleep but extremely alert mentally.

Interestingly, the more meditative experience monks had, the more theta they generated. And the only ones who were able to get into this deep theta state quickly and at will were those monks who had *more than twenty years of meditative experience.*

Excited by this work, biofeedback researchers Elmer and Alyce Green of the Menninger Foundation decided to explore the effects of theta. They designed a biofeedback device that enabled them to train subjects to enter theta. The Greens described their observations of many people experiencing theta in their seminal book *Beyond Biofeedback* as "associated with a deeply internalized state and with a quieting of the body, emotions, and thoughts, thus allowing usually 'unheard or unseen things' to come to the consciousness in the form of hypnagogic memory."

The Greens next designed a study in which one group learned to enter theta for a period of time every day, while another group—the control group—simply became very relaxed. They discovered that the theta subjects frequently reported vivid memories of long-forgotten childhood events: "They were not like going through a memory in one's mind, but rather like an experience, a reliving." The Greens also found that those producing theta waves frequently became highly creative, and had "new and valid ideas or syntheses of ideas."

The Greens were surprised to discover that the subjects they taught to enter the theta state reported that they had life-altering insights, or what the researchers called "integrative experiences leading to feelings of psychological well-being." They fell in love, discovered new talents, decided to change jobs and strike out in new, more satisfying directions. In essence, these people felt their lives had been transformed. On psychological tests, the Greens discovered that the theta subjects were "psychologically healthier, had more social poise, were less rigid and conforming, and were more self-accepting and creative" than the control group.

Finally, and most astonishingly, the Greens were surprised to note that those taught to enter the theta state became *very healthy*. While members of the control group (who were not producing theta waves) continued to have a normal number of illnesses, members of the theta group had almost no illness whatsoever.

The Greens felt they had stumbled onto something unprecedented. They reported that the theta state caused people to "experience a new kind of body consciousness very much related to their total well-being." Physiologically the theta state seemed to bring "physical healing, physical regeneration." In the emotional domain, the theta state was "manifested in improved relationships with other people as well as greater tolerance, understanding, and love of oneself and of one's world." In the mental domain, the theta state produced "new and valid ideas of syntheses of ideas, not primarily by deduction, but springing by intuition from unconscious sources." All in all, it seemed as if there was something magic about the theta state.

Working independently, biofeedback researcher and psychologist Dr. Thomas Budzynski, then employed at the University of Colorado Medical Center, also sensed something magic about the theta state. He conducted extensive research into the properties of theta, which he dubbed the "twilight state." People in theta, he found, were hypersuggestible, as if in a hypnotic trance. They are also able to learn enormous amounts very quickly. Theta, Budzynski suggested, is the state in which "superlearning" takes place—when in theta, people are able to learn new languages, accept suggestions for changes in behaviors and attitudes, memorize vast amounts of information. Said Budzynski, "the hypnagogic state, the twilight state, between waking and sleep, has the properties of *uncritical acceptance of verbal material, or almost any material it can process.*"

"MIRACULOUS RESOLUTIONS" AT THE CROSSOVER POINT

These findings about theta were exciting but never became widely known. Then in 1989 Dr. Eugene Peniston and Dr. Paul Kulkosky of the University of Southern Colorado (who had learned some of their techniques from the Greens at the Menninger Foundation) conducted studies in which they used EEG biofeedback to train a group of chronic alcoholics to enter first the alpha and then the theta state, while another group served as a control group. The researchers discovered that the alpha-theta group showed an extraordinary recovery rate many orders of magnitude greater than the control group. More impressively, after thirteen months members of the alpha-theta group showed "sustained prevention of relapse." (Even more impressively, a further follow-up study three years later has shown the same sustained relapse prevention.)

And, in the most intriguing findings of all, the alpha-theta group showed a profound personality transformation. Among the extraordinary changes noted in their subjects, Peniston and Kulkosky found significant increases in such qualities as warmth, abstract thinking, stability, conscientiousness, boldness, imaginativeness, and self-control, and significant decreases not only in depression but also in anxiety and other problems.

Overcoming addiction. Transforming personality. These were magic phrases. The Peniston studies emerged just when concern with addictive behaviors and personality transformation had become subjects of urgent interest to millions of people. Millions of people were going to twelve-step programs modeled on Alcoholics Anonymous to overcome their "addictions" to everything from sex, to overeating, to shopping, and were seeking to transform their current addictive personality by stripping away their false masks and communicating with their "inner child."

With its implied message that EEG alpha-theta feedback could help individuals overcome all sorts of addictive behavior patterns and find a happier, more integrated personality, the Peniston-Kulkosky work aroused enormous interest and excitement among biofeedback researchers and clinicians.

Modifying and expanding upon this work, many workers have begun using multichannel "brain-mapping" EEGs to explore in more detail what happens in the brain as the individuals undergo the personality transformations noted by Peniston and Kulkosky. What they have found is that when a subject becomes deeply relaxed, alpha brainwave activity increases through the whole brain. As relaxation increases, the subject begins to produce more and more theta activity. As theta amplitude increases, alpha seems to recede or diminish, until theta supersedes alpha.

At that point, according to some researchers—at what they are calling the crossover point or the critical point—the subjects experience important, emotionally loaded, even life-transforming moments. These frequently consist of creative insights, vivid memories from childhood, or, in the case of the Vietnam vets suffering from posttraumatic stress syndrome or adults who were abused as children, the emergence of suppressed or repressed experiences. Subjects consistently report these moments as profound, moving, life transforming, even spiritual moments. One of these clinicians, Houston therapist William Beckwith, has reported that in his clients, the crossover point is "often accompanied by spontaneous surfacing of previously inaccessible memories, often from early childhood," as well as "the seemingly miraculous resolutions of complex psychological problems."

THE MAGIC RHYTHM AND THE GATEWAY TO MEMORY

Meanwhile, other scientists, intrigued by the fact that the theta state seemed to increase learning and also seemed to produce frequent vivid memories, began investigating the relationship between theta and memory.

They found that for memories to be formed, the brain must undergo a process called long-term potentiation (LTP), which involves electrical and chemical changes in the neurons involved in storing memory. When LTP does not happen, information that enters the brain is not stored but totally forgotten. Neurophysiologist Dr. Gary Lynch and associates of at the University of California at Irvine discovered that the key to LTP is theta brain waves. "We have found the magic rhythm that makes LTP," said Lynch. "There's a magic rhythm, the theta rhythm."

Significantly, the theta rhythm is what Lynch calls "the natural, indigenous rhythm" of a part of the brain called the hippocampus, which is essential for the formation and storage of new memories and the calling up of old memories.

CHILDHOOD MEMORIES AND THETA

As virtually everyone who uses a mind machine discovers, theta seems to trigger the sudden reliving or vivid remembering of long-forgotten childhood memories. One explanation for this link between theta and childhood is that, while adults rarely produce theta, children are in a theta state most of the time—up to the age of around six, children produce mostly theta waves. The amount of theta progressively decreases as the child grows into adulthood. In other words, children spend most of their time in what we adults would call a trancelike, altered state of consciousness, and one that is extremely open and receptive, highly conducive to the learning of new information and the creation of memories.

In recent years a large number of scientific studies have explored a phenomenon called state-bound or state-dependent learning. In essence, they have found that things experienced in one state of consciousness are far more easily remembered later when we are once again in that same state. Things learned when we're happy are remembered best when we're happy; what we learn when cold is remembered best when we're cold; and so on.

These findings provide an explanation for the appearance of childhood memories to adults who are in theta. Children spend most of their time in the theta state. But as adults, we rarely experience a true theta state. Most of us have a few seconds of it as we fall asleep, and that's all. During those brief moments in theta, we may experience sudden flashes of memory, vivid images, odd disconnected ideas, but we're quickly asleep. Virtually all of our memories from childhood, then, are state dependent—they're laid down while we're in one state, but it's a state that we almost never experience as adults. To remember them, we have to get back to the state in which they were first created.

One of the characteristics of mind machines is that they are capable of putting people into the theta state and *keeping them there for long periods of time while they remain awake*. Mind machines can put us back into the childlike theta state. That means that all those memories, creative ideas, spontaneous images, and integrative experiences that occur during theta become available to our conscious mind—we become consciously aware of what had been stored in our unconscious mind, and we remember it when we emerge from the theta state. This is one of the reasons that Thomas Budzynski has called one type of mind machine "a facilitator of unconscious retrieval."

THETA AND INSIGHT

For thousands of years humans have been aware of the enormous creative values of the theta state. Budzynski notes that "Shamanistic and other primitive ceremonies often included procedures designed to produce these states. It was believed (and still is in certain cultures) that the dreamlike images elicited in the twilight state allowed the dreamer to foretell events, instruct as to healing procedures, and give important information."

The eighteenth-century mystic Emanuel Swedenborg wrote in detail about his own theta experiences and described ways of inducing them. The visionary chemist Friedrich Kekule vividly described his state of "reverie" in which he suddenly saw a mental image of atoms forming a chain, and of snakes biting their tails, which led to his discovery that organic compounds occur in closed rings—described as "the most brilliant piece of prediction to be found in the whole range of organic chemistry." There are countless stories of such moments of inspiration and creativity occurring when the thinker is nodding off to sleep, wandering lonely as a cloud, or gazing into the fire. All of them speak of the drowsiness, the relaxation, the vivid imagery appearing unexpectedly that mark these as examples of the theta state.

One of the most powerful effects of the brain machines we will explore in this book is their capacity to put us into this beneficial, productive brain-wave state virtually at will.

MAPPING THE AWAKENED MIND

Beta activity is associated with alertness, arousal, and concentration; alpha waves with relaxation; theta with creativity, memory, integrative experiences, and healing; and delta with sleep, profound rest, and the release of growth hormone. Wouldn't it be nice if we could combine all of these qualities?

One common misperception is that when we're in the "alpha state," our brain is producing nothing but alpha, when we're in theta, our brain is producing only theta, and so on. In fact, when we observe brain-wave activity on a full-spectrum EEG (one that shows the activity of all the frequencies at once), we quickly notice that the brain is constantly active to a greater or lesser degree at all those frequencies simultaneously. When we're in an alpha state, for example, the *amplitude*, or power, of our alpha waves is much stronger than the amplitude of beta, theta, and delta, but there is still (except in exceptional cases) noticeable activity in those other ranges as well.

Some twenty years ago British biofeedback researcher C. Maxwell Cade began working with an EEG specifically designed to show full-spectrum brain-wave activity. As he worked with hundreds of people who were able to function exceptionally well, who were able to enter heightened states of consciousness easily, he began noticing similarities in the patterns of brain waves they produced.

As he compared these exceptional people with his thousands of other subjects, he noticed that there was a distinct progression. In the first stage, most people could soon learn to enter the alpha state, in which beta diminished and alpha became the dominant frequency. As they progressed in their practice, many of these people learned to enter the theta state, in which beta, alpha, and delta diminished and theta became dominant. In this, his findings matched those of the EEG studies of Zen monks.

But Cade found that the exceptional people, those who were peak performers, soon moved into a different pattern. When they were in their peak state, their EEG patterns showed that their brains were producing large amounts of alpha and theta as well as strong beta and delta activity—all at the same time.

Cade called this extraordinary brain-wave pattern the Awakened Mind. He found that these peak-performance individuals could maintain this pattern even while reading, performing mathematical calculations, and carrying on conversations! Apparently these individuals were able to draw upon the relaxing, centering properties of the alpha state, the creative, memory-accessing properties of the theta state, the healing, "grounded" properties of the delta state, and at the same time still maintain the alert concentration and external orientation of the beta state. (Cade's EEG was of a unique design, so it's possible that the Zen monks studied by earlier researchers also produced this Awakened Mind pattern. In fact, it sounds very much like the "Zen mind" state that Zen monks carry with them through all their daily activities—and the researchers simply did not notice it because their EEG equipment was not designed to monitor it.)

Using his full-spectrum EEG (which he called the Mind Mirror), Cade was able to teach many "ordinary" people how to enter this Awakened Mind state. He found that by learning to produce brain-wave patterns identical to those of peak-performance individuals, these ordinary people were transformed into peak performers themselves.

As we shall see later, many of the new mind technologies have been designed specifically to stimulate the brain to operate at several frequencies at once.

MAPPING THE BRAIN PATHS TO TRANSCENDENCE

Meanwhile, other researchers have been using sophisticated EEGs with twenty or more electrodes, which permit them to monitor the activity of the entire cortex simultaneously and present it visually in the form of colored "brain maps." These investigators, including F. Holmes Atwater, of the Monroe institute, and Dr. Ed Wilson, of the Colorado Association for Psychophysiologic Research, have been able to observe the brain maps of numerous individuals as they move from ordinary waking consciousness into peak experience or transcendent brain states. They have found that in progressing toward transcendence, the brain goes through or produces several distinctive whole-brain patterns.

RESTING-STATE ALPHA

Normal waking consciousness, these researchers have found, is characterized by dominant beta activity, along with a lot of alpha activity in the rear part of the cortex. This back-of-the-head alpha is called "resting-state alpha." It seems to be an "anchor," serving as a stabilizing force, linking us with our "normal" and familiar modes of mental processing. It's like the alpha observed in the early stages of Zen meditation.

THE DISSOCIATIVE STATE

However, when subjects enter expanded states of consciousness, they lose awareness of the physical world and reach a point, as Atwater describes it, "when non-physical phenomena constitute the whole field of perception; when there is no impression of being 'normally' in the physical body; when the physical body is asleep or fully entranced." This is what Atwater calls the dissociative state.

In the dissociative state, resting-state alpha disappears and is replaced by high-amplitude theta and delta activity, centered at the top of the head (the median of the central cortex). Interestingly, this high-amplitude theta and delta activity is synchronous. This dissociative state seems to be essentially what earlier researchers, such as the Greens, have been describing as the theta state and is equivalent to the state reached by experienced Zen meditators as they sink downward past alpha. It also seems to offer access to what has been called the unconscious mind or the personal unconscious.

THE TRANSCENDENT STATE

Beyond theta, the personal unconscious, beyond the dissociative state, is the state Atwater calls transcendence. In this state, individuals move beyond their own ego, beyond the personal unconscious mind, into a peak state of universal awareness. As Atwater observes, "Experiences in this state are many times ineffable and cannot be explained or described in words. Experiences in this realm are more than passive diversions. Their creative power can change the very nature of the participants' reality."

As they observe the transition from dissociation to transcendence on their EEG brain mappers, these researchers have found that something very odd occurs. First, the high-amplitude and synchronous theta and delta activity of the dissociative state continues. However, it is accompanied by bursts of very high *beta* activity in the temporal regions of the brain (in the area of the temples). This, apparently, is a state similar to Cade's Awakened Mind. However, Cade's Mind Mirror EGG only measured brain waves up to 40 Hz. His Awakened Mind subjects may have been producing other brain waves higher than 40 Hz.

Intriguingly, Atwater found that not only is this temporal beta activity during the transcendent state of high frequency (ranging from over 40 Hz to at least 128 Hz), but the amplitude of this beta activity increases as it rises in frequency. Since the EEG equipment now available has been able to monitor brain-wave frequencies only up to 128 Hz, investigators have no real idea what might be happening above that level. It's conceivable that these transcendent moments may be associated with bursts of temporal beta in the range of 200 Hz, 300 Hz, or even more. At this point, no one knows. And no one knows the implications.

INDUCING TRANSCENDENT EXPERIENCES AND UFO ABDUCTIONS

These findings become even more intriguing—and lead to even wilder speculations—in light of the amazing findings of Dr. Michael Persinger of Laurentian University. He was fascinated by evidence that people who had been abducted by unidentified flying objects (UFOs) and had a variety of other sorts of extraordinary or transcendent experiences were influenced by changes in the earth's magnetic field. He began placing electromagnets on subjects' temples and pulsing them at various frequencies. To his amazement, he found that many of his subjects had transcendent or extraordinary experiences. Even when subjects knew they were seated in a laboratory, with pulsed electromagnetic fields at their temples, they would emerge with realistic reports of being abducted by UFOs, having out-of-body experiences, communicating with God, and so on. Apparently, high-frequency, high-amplitude activation of the temporal regions of the brain is linked with extraordinary experiences.

SUGGESTED READING

For a good introduction to EEG biofeedback and excellent information about theta brain waves, see *Beyond Biofeedback* by Elmer and Alyce Green (New York: Delacorte, 1977). For information about the "Awakened Mind" EEG patterns, see *The Awakened Mind: Biofeedback and the Development of Higher States of Awareness* by C. Maxwell Cade and Nona Coxhead (New York: Delacorte, 1979). For a discussion of the work of Peniston and Kulkosky and the "crossover point," see my article "At the Crossover Point," and William Beckwith's "Moving Beyond Metaphors of the Mind: Addiction, Transformation and Brainwave Patterns," both in *Megabrain Report* 1(3) (1992).

THREE
WHOLE-BRAIN POWER

All the unusual abilities that some people are able to manifest . . . are associated with changes in the EEG pattern toward a more bilaterally symmetrical and integrated form. . . . My research has led me to believe that the "higher mind," on the neuropsychological level, was what Carl Jung called transcendent function, and that it was manifested by the integration of left- and right-hemisphere function.

—C. Maxwell Cade,
The Awakened Mind

SYNCHRONY: MAXIMUM EFFICIENCY OF INFORMATION TRANSPORT

One of the ways scientists investigated peak brain states was to bring skilled meditators into the laboratory, paste electrodes all over their skulls, give them a button to press to signal when they were "there," and record the activity on an electroencephalogram (EEG). The scientists found that when meditators were in their peak state, the brain-wave activity throughout the whole brain fell into a state they called synchrony.

Now, whole-brain-wave synchrony is a very specific state. It does not mean simply that the whole brain produces dominant waves of the same frequency, such as 10 Hz alpha. If you visualize brain waves as a series of peaks and valleys, then synchrony occurs when brain waves reach their peak at the same time. When brain waves are "in sync," their power increases. (Think of two waves joining together: They produce a larger wave.) So, when researchers noted that meditators produced whole-brain synchrony, what they saw was also an enormous increase in power or amplitude throughout the whole brain.

What are the effects of synchrony? One of the leading researchers into brain-wave synchrony, Dr. Lester Fehmi, of the Princeton Biofeedback Research Institute, points out that "synchrony represents the *maximum efficiency of information transport through the whole brain."* This means that brain-wave synchrony produces a sharp increase in the effects of various brain-wave states. Fehmi notes that "phase synchrony . . . is observed to enhance the magnitude and occurrence of the subjective phenomena associated with alpha and theta" and of beta as well. Thus, for example, the phenomena associated with theta, such as vivid imagery, access to memory, spontaneous creative insights, and integrative experiences all are enhanced in "magnitude and occurrence" by whole-brain synchrony.

Some of the researchers and clinicians who have been using EEG "crossover point" training now believe that part of the extraordinary transformational powers of moving through that critical point where theta surpasses alpha is a result of brain-wave synchrony. William Beckwith observes that "The production of synchronized, coherent electromagnetic energy by the human brain at a given frequency leads to a 'laser-like' condition increasing the amplitude and strength of the brain waves." He notes that

> as clients learn to increase their alpha amplitude and produce theta waves without losing consciousness, a critical point is reached when theta amplitude begins to exceed alpha amplitude. *Cross-lateral brainwave synchronization also increases* (italics added), creating a more coherent system. At this point, there are profound alterations in client mood and behavior, [including] the seemingly miraculous resolution of complex psychological problems. . . . There is a sudden re-ordering of the entire personality in ways that cannot be readily explained by other models.

Many of the mind machines we will discuss later have been designed specifically to deliver stimulation to the whole brain in order to produce whole-brain synchronization.

BRAIN-WAVE SYMMETRY AND EMOTIONS

In addition to synchrony, there is now evidence that whole-brain symmetry (that is, the relative balance of EEG activity between the right and left hemispheres) is an important key to peak brain functioning.

Stop now and note your emotional state: Are you happy, sad, upbeat, depressed? All right, now, keeping the left half of your face motionless, vigorously contract the right side of your face several times—smile energetically and forcefully, each time contracting not only the muscles in your cheeks that draw the lip corners up but also the muscles around your right eye. Stop now and pay attention to yourself. Has your emotional state changed?

If you are like most people, contracting the right side of your face probably triggered positive emotions, joy, cockiness, a lifting of the spirits. If you had contracted the left side of your face you probably would have felt an inexplicable sadness and depression.

The clear link between activity on the left side of the face and sadness and activity on the right side of the face and happiness has been scientifically documented recently. In some studies the researchers simply asked the subjects to contract either the right or left sides of their face vigorously. They found strong evidence (in over 90 percent of the subjects) that contorting one side of the face produces emotions, with the left side of the face producing sadness and negative emotions and the right side producing happiness and positive emotions.

The research emerged from one researcher's experiences as a therapist, when he noticed that clients often began therapy with great facial asymmetries, which disappeared as their distress diminished. In another study, the scientists reversed the studies just described and worked from actual feelings toward facial expressions. They found that *stress itself could cause subjects to exhibit such facial asymmetries.*

SUN BRAIN, MOON BRAIN

But *why* does facial asymmetry affect emotions? Several groups of scientists working independently have found that people with high levels of activity in the left frontal cortex tend to have a more cheerful and positive temperament—they are self-confident, outgoing, interested in people and external events, resilient, optimistic, and happy. On the other hand, people whose EEGs show more activity in the right frontal cortex than in the left tend to be more sad and negative in their outlook—they see the world as more stressful and threatening, are more suspicious of people, and feel far more fear, disgust, anxiety, self-blame, and hopelessness than the left-activated group. These findings make it particularly exciting that mind machines have proven capable of quickly altering hemispheric dominance.

THE CRYBABY BIOMARKER AND DEPRESSION IN THE BRAIN

There is also evidence that these brain-wave asymmetries may be linked to depression. The researchers compared the EEGs of a group of normal subjects who had never been treated for depression and those of a group of subjects who had been previously depressed and later successfully treated. They found that the previously depressed subjects had far less left-frontal activity, and far more right-frontal activity, than those who had never been depressed.

A recent brain-mapping study of depressive patients by C. Norman Shealy, M.D., Ph.D., at the Shealy Institute revealed that 100 percent of the patients had abnormal brain-wave activity. The most common finding was "Asymmetry of the two hemispheres with right-hemisphere dominance."

Another study revealed that patients who had just been diagnosed with depression and were about to begin treatment had less left-frontal activity than nondepressed subjects. "You find similar brain patterns in people who are depressed, or who have recovered from depression, and in normal people who are prone to bad moods," said one of the researchers, Dr. John Davidson, of the University of Wisconsin at Madison. "We suspect that people with this brain activity pattern are at high risk for depression."

There is even evidence that these brain-wave patterns and emotional "styles" may be hereditary or genetically influenced. Davidson has studied the behavior and the EEG patterns of ten-month old infants during a brief period (one minute) of separation from their mothers, and found that "those infants who cried in response to maternal separation showed greater right-frontal activation during the preceding baseline period compared with infants who did not cry." According to Davidson, "Every single infant who cried had more right frontal activation. Every one who did not had more activity on the left." He concluded that "Frontal activation asymmetry may be a state-independent marker for individual differences in threshold of reactivity to stressful events and vulnerability to particular emotions."

These clear links between frontal activation asymmetry have led many researchers to believe that these brain patterns can be useful for diagnosis, particularly for diagnosing people at risk for depression. Says Davidson, "We believe that in the face of life stress like losing a job or a divorce," those with right-frontal activation "are likely to be particularly susceptible to depression."

TURNING UP THE JUICE IN THE JOLLY LOBE

The next step, of course, is to move from simply observing the existing brain-wave patterns and using them for diagnosis to using mind machines actively to alter the patterns. As Davidson pointed out, "If you learn to regulate your negative feelings better, it may turn out that you have also learned to turn up the activity in your left frontal lobe."

It should now be clear that the earlier exercise—in which we contorted the right side of the face to produce positive emotions or good feelings—is one technique for turning up the activity in the left frontal lobe. We know that the brain is cross-wired with the body, so that the left hemisphere is linked to the right side of the body. Thus, by forcefully activating the right side of the face, it seems we are also activating the left side of the brain, the side associated with positive feelings.

FINDING THE POINT OF BALANCE

All of this research casts new light on the well-known differences between the right hemisphere and the left hemisphere. In most people, the left hemisphere is superior in processing verbal material, while the right hemisphere is superior in handling visual/spatial information. Studies by neuroscientist David Shannahoff-Khalsa of the Salk Institute for Biological Sciences indicate that hemispheric dominance is constantly shifting back and forth from the right to the left hemisphere, with average cycles of 90 to 120 minutes.

Other scientists have reached similar conclusions by testing subjects at regular intervals on verbal (left-hemisphere) and spatial (right-hemisphere) tasks. They found that when verbal ability was high, spatial ability was low, and vice versa. This discovery, Shannahoff-Khalsa points out, "suggests we can exert more control over our day-to-day mental functioning. For example, certain cognitive functions, such as language skills, mathematics and other rational processes that are thought to be primarily localized in the left hemisphere" might be boosted by "forcibly altering" our cerebral dominance. And in the same way we might "accentuate the creativity that is thought to be characteristic of right-hemisphere dominance" through similar forcible altering. It now appears clear that mind machines are highly effective tools for "forcibly altering" hemispheric dominance.

How do you know which hemisphere is dominant at any given time? One simple technique is to simply sit quietly and breathe, and feel which nostril is more "open," which one has the most air flowing through it. If your right nostril is more open, then you are in a left-hemisphere-dominant state.

Learning how to control hemispheric dominance consciously can be a powerful tool for boosting our ability to deal most effectively with the task at hand. If you're going into a conference or a written test, or some other task that requires left-hemisphere capabilities, and you find that you are in a right-hemisphere dominant phase, for example, you might want to shift quickly into left-hemisphere dominance.

However, one key finding that has emerged from these studies is that each time dominance shifts from one hemisphere to the other, there is a point at which dominance is equally balanced between both hemispheres. Researchers have found that it is at this point, and during this short period of time, when the brain is at its most fertile and creative.

The truth is that two brains are better than one. While each hemisphere seems to have its specific beneficial capacities, each has its downside as well. The right hemisphere has been linked with visual/ spatial skills; emotional and musical sensitivities; and intuitive, time-less, imagistic thought; but also with depression, suspicion, sadness, hostility, paranoia, and negative emotions. The left hemisphere has been linked with verbal skills; orientation in time; rational, logical, analytical thinking; happiness; and positive emotions. But mere analytical thought, without intuitive, emotional, imagistic, time-free insights, is rigid and uncreative.

There is a reason why we have two hemispheres: They are both necessary and complementary, and they function best when they are functioning together, synergistically. This is an obvious point of much of the research we have looked at so far. EEG studies of meditators clearly demonstrated that peak states were characterized by increased synchrony and symmetry between the hemispheres. As the statement at the beginning of this chapter indicates, C. Maxwell Cade's research led him to conclude that peak mental functioning is associated with a "bilaterally symmetrical" EEG.

It's evident that a highly integrated brain, a brain in which both hemispheres are functioning in symmetry, synchrony, harmony, and unity, is a key to peak states and peak human performance. But throughout history, humans have found that it's not easy intentionally to bring both hemispheres to bear simultaneously. Much of our lives we spend swinging back and forth between left- and right-dominant states. By providing us with the capacity to integrate and synchronize brain hemispheres, mind machines present revolutionary possibilities. Research has shown that they can alter hemispheric asymmetry and imbalance quickly and produce more symmetrical, balanced brain-wave patterns. And, the evidence suggests, by doing so they can assist in producing the peak performance states associated with whole-brain integration.

FOUR
WORKING OUT IN THE BRAIN GYM:
THE NEW SCIENCE OF BRAIN GROWTH AND MIND FITNESS

The Brain Revolution has progressed on many fronts at once. While scientists were discovering the patterns of brain activity associated with peak performance states, other scientists, led by a group at the University of California at Berkeley, were studying the actual structure of the brain and making discoveries so astounding in their implications that they literally shook the entire scientific world. What they found was that certain types of stimulation could change not only the chemistry but the actual physical structure of the brain—could actually make the brain grow physically larger and more powerful, and dramatically boost intelligence.

BUILDING BIG BRAINS:
SMART RATS LEAD THE WAY

The series of breakthrough discoveries began innocently enough when a group of Berkeley scientists decided to try to find out why some laboratory rats were smarter than others. They designed an experiment in which a group of young rats that were genetically equal were divided randomly into three groups. Each group was raised in a different environment—a standard laboratory environment, an "impoverished environment" (one rat isolated in a cage with little stimulation), and an "enriched environment" (rats raised in play groups of ten to twelve, in a large, cage filled a variety of challenges and changing stimuli).

They found that even after a few days, the rats in the enriched environments were far smarter than the standard-environment rats, while the rats from the impoverished environments were dumber. When the brains of the rats were analyzed, the scientists were shocked to find that the brains of the enriched-environment rats were larger and heavier than the others' brains.

These findings were so astonishing that when the results were published, many scientists around the world flatly stated that they were impossible. The Berkeley researchers plunged ahead with a variety of studies that not only verified their earlier findings, but also revealed what was happening anatomically to make the brains of the enriched-environment animals grow so much larger. Under the direction of neuroanatomist Marian Diamond, they discovered that the animals raised in enriched environments showed brains that were bigger and richer in a variety of ways, including thicker cerebral cortexes (the convoluted gray matter associated with higher thinking functions); actual increases in the numbers of a special type of brain cell called glial cells that are associated with increased intelligence; increases in the size and complexity of individual neurons or brain cells, including growth of the parts of neurons called dendrites that are the key to the transmission of information between neurons; and increases in the richness, density, and complexity of the interconnections (called synapses) and networks between neurons. Diamond concluded that in response to stimulation, "every part of the nerve cell from soma [body] to synapse alters its dimensions."

These discoveries—soon replicated and verified by many other researchers—were earth-shaking in their implications. In essence, they proved that stimulating the brain could make it grow bigger, more powerful, more intelligent, healthier, and qualitatively superior.

THE PRINCE-AND-THE-PAUPER EFFECT

As the research progressed, Diamond and others found that dramatic brain growth could happen with startling speed—just a few hours in an enriched environment. Later research that placed rats, monkeys, chimps, and other animals in "super-enriched environments" showed that some types of stimulation could create brain growth virtually instantaneously.

One researcher devised a way that rats could learn how to run a maze while only one hemisphere was receiving information. (Information to the other hemisphere was blocked.) He found increased growth of neurons in the hemisphere that received the input, but no growth in the other hemisphere. The equation was clear: more information, more growth; more stimulation, more growth.

Next, the researchers were amazed to find that this kind of brain growth was not confined to young animals, but could happen *at any age*. Mature and even extremely old rats, they discovered, would respond to stimulation with brain growth and increases in intelligence. The researchers even performed experiments in which aging rats raised in an impoverished environment for much of their lives were compared for smartness at maze running with rats raised in enriched environments. The enriched-environment rats were, of course, far smarter. But then, in a sort of Prince-and-the-Pauper switch, the rats from the impoverished environments were placed in enriched environments and vice versa. Immediately the formerly dumb rats began to show brain growth and sharp increases in intelligence, while the once-brainy rats began to deteriorate, their brains shrinking and their intelligence diminishing.

In study after study, Diamond and her associates proved conclusively that when it is provided with sufficient stimulation, in the form of challenge, novelty, and exercise, brain growth and improvement can continue throughout life, *at any age.*

THIS IS YOUR BRAIN WE'RE TALKING ABOUT

While the initial studies were of the brains of animals, the work of Diamond and others has expanded in recent years to include the brains of humans. Diamond has analyzed the brains of thousands of individuals and correlated the condition of those brains with the amount of stimulation the person received. What she and the other researchers have found contradicts the belief that human brain power must decrease with age. They have proven clearly that humans who have provided their brains with an enriched environment, in the form of stimulating experiences, intellectual challenges, change, and novelty, have brains as large and powerful as those of young people.

A study at the National Institute of Aging used a brain scan to study the brains of men age twenty-one to eighty-three. Researchers concluded that "the healthy aged brain is as active and efficient as the healthy young brain."

One neuroscientist at the University of California at Los Angeles took specimens from over twenty human brains and analyzed them under his microscope. He found a clear and definite relationship between the number of years of education and dendritic length: *The more people had learned, the greater their dendritic length.* The researcher concluded that these results clearly supported the "environmental diversity" studies of Diamond and others and "indicate, for the first time in human research, that intellectual challenge may have a positive effect on dendritic systems."

Diamond has concluded that, provided with sufficient stimulation and challenge, "there is good evidence that drastic structural changes do not occur in the mammalian brain with aging." She says:

> When I lecture, I show my hand—my palm is the cell body and my fingers are the dendrites. With use, you can keep those dendrites out there, extended, but without stimulation, they shrink down. It's quite simple: you use it or lose it. . . . The main factor [that provides an enriched environment] is stimulation. The nerve cells are designed to receive stimulation."

What all this means is that whatever your age, your brain has the capacity to grow, and you have the capacity to become more intelligent. What's more, it suggests that the more you learn, the greater is your capacity for further learning. The more you challenge your brain, the more powerful it becomes; the more you put into your brain, the more open it becomes. But without sufficient stimulation, whatever our age, this capacity for growth will not be tapped.

HOW SMART CAN YOU GET?

An "enriched environment" produces rapid growth in brain structure and intelligence. "Super-enriched" environments produce even greater and more rapid brain growth. It seems that with increasing levels of environmental enrichment—that is, with increasing levels of complexity, stimulation, challenge, and novelty—the brain responds with greater growth. Surely there must be a ceiling on this enriched environment effect, but no one has discovered it yet.

How smart can the brain get? We probably can't answer that question until we discover the supreme stimulation, the absolute and optimally enriched environment—which, since every human brain is unique, will be different for each individual. I'll let you be in my enriched environment if I can be in yours. . . .

NAUTILUS MACHINES FOR THE BRAIN

In the meantime, many researchers and clinicians now believe that mind machines can create a sort of instant super-enriched environment, a brain gymnasium, providing the brain with megadoses of stimulation, novelty, exercise, and challenge. And in doing so, they believe, the mind machines can stimulate rapid, healthy growth in the brain and in its powers.

Over the last twenty years there has been an extraordinary growth in our awareness of the benefits of physical fitness. In these fitness-conscious '90s, it's hard to recall those days when joggers were rare; when people who wanted to eat healthful food were scorned as "health nuts"; when anyone who lifted weights was a "muscle-bound" narcissist; when Nautilus machines, Stairmasters, Ski-Traks, and the concept of aerobics classes had not even been invented.

Today there's widespread awareness that physical exercise is not some craze, or only for jocks or narcissists, but has benefits for everyone—benefits that include not just better health but a more productive, creative, happy, and fulfilling life. So the concept of *brain fitness* is one that makes sense to increasing numbers of people. Today, increasing numbers of people are aware that the brain, like the body, requires exercise, challenge, and stimulation to remain healthy; and that, just as exercise of the body can lead to muscle growth and increased vitality, optimal levels of mental exercise and stimulation can lead to greater mental powers. One sign of this is the proliferation of brain gyms and mind spas throughout the world. Another is the explosive growth in sales of mind machines for home use.

Many of us remember our first glimpse of Nautilus and Universal machines—they seemed strange and daunting. But it soon became clear that they were designed for a specific purpose—to provide the optimal challenge to stimulate muscle growth—and that they worked. Today some of the brain-stimulating devices we will explore in this book must appear as strange and daunting to many people. But they too are designed for a specific purpose—to provide optimal levels of stimulation to the brain. And there is a wealth of evidence that they work. Just what these machines are, and how they work, is what we will look at next.

SUGGESTED READING

For information about brain growth through enriched environments, see *Enriching Heredity: The Impact of the Environment on the Anatomy of the Brain* by Marian Cleeves Diamond (New York: Free Press, 1988).

PART TWO

ACCESS TO TOOLS

If the doors of perception were cleansed every thing would appear to man as it is, infinite. For man has closed himself up, till he sees all things through narrow chinks of his cavern.

—WILLIAM BLAKE,
The Marriage of Heaven and Hell

FIVE
TAKING CHARGE:
BIOFEEDBACK AND BRAIN POWER

CONTROL YOURSELF

Stop a moment. Now, change your brain-wave activity into an alpha rhythm. . . . The question immediately arises: How? How do I know when my brain waves are in alpha? And how is it possible to change my brain waves intentionally?

One of the central assumptions of Western physiology has been that there is a fundamental distinction between parts of the human body that we can consciously control—the so-called voluntary components—and those parts over which we have no conscious control—the "involuntary" components. These involuntary components traditionally included brain waves as well as such things as the expansion and contraction of our blood vessels, blood pressure, heart rate, the secretion of hormones, healing, and the activity of the immune system.

Then the lightning bolt hit. With the development sensitive instruments that could measure minute changes in the body, scientists found that if they monitored the activity of one of the so-called involuntary processes of a human subject and fed it back to the subject with some sort of visual or auditory signal, the subject could learn to bring that process under voluntary control. They called this process biofeedback.

DISCOVERING THE BODYMIND

In a burst of studies that caused a sensation in the scientific world, biofeedback researchers proved that subjects could take voluntary control of virtually any physiological process—even the firing rhythm of individual nerve cells. One researcher, John Basmajian, hooked up subjects so they could monitor the firing rhythm of a specific neuron (called a single-motor unit). Each time the neuron fired, the subjects would be fed back a sound like a drumbeat. Amazingly, the subjects quickly learned how to control the rhythm with which the cells fired, creating intricate drum rolls, gallops, and beats. Elmer and Alyce

Green wrote, "It may be possible to bring under some degree of voluntary control any physiological process that can continuously be monitored, amplified, and displayed."

This was a momentous discovery—it meant that the long-held belief of a clear separation between voluntary and involuntary components of the human system was not accurate. It meant such processes as the secretion of hormones and the operation of the immune system could, theoretically, be intentionally controlled. It also meant that the whole foundation of mind-body dualism upon which all of Western thought had been based—that there is a clear and necessary separation between the mind and the body—had to be tossed out the window. Clearly there was some still mysterious link between mind and body.

This research marked the beginning of a great paradigm shift that was to lead to the development of such fields as psychoneuroimmunology and psychobiology and to the emergence of a new vision of the mind and body as a single, indivisible unit, a field of intelligence, a bodymind.

PRACTICAL TOOLS FOR PROFOUND RELAXATION

Aside from the theoretical implications, it quickly became clear that the breakthroughs in biofeedback had enormous practical applications. Using temperature biofeedback, migraine sufferers learned to make their hands warmer, thus increasing peripheral blood flow and alleviating the migraine. People with heart malfunctions learned to control their heart rates. Biofeedback training was effective in helping people lower their blood pressure; control gastrointestinal problems such as ulcers, excess stomach acidity, and irritable bowel syndrome; and alleviate problems associated with muscle tension, such as teeth grinding, temporomandibular joint problems, tension headache, cerebral palsy, paralysis resulting from brain damage, and much more.

More generally, researchers found that many different types of biofeedback instruments, including those that measured muscle tension (called electromyographs, or EMGs), skin temperature, and the electrical conductivity of the skin (Gallvanic Skin Response meters), were powerful tools for teaching people to become deeply relaxed. In many cases subjects could learn to put themselves into states of profound relaxation quickly after only a few biofeedback training sessions. Using biofeedback relaxation training, researchers were able to produce a wide variety of positive psychological as well as physiological effects, including alleviation of phobias and anxiety and increases in IQ.

ON THE JOYS OF OBSERVING YOUR OWN BRAIN

Fingertip temperature monitors, EMGs, and other biofeedback instruments were proving to be powerful tools for human self-regulation. But still, one type of biofeedback instrument gripped the attention of both scientists and general public alike: the EEG. It's all very interesting to see how you can make your hands warmer or colder, but it's another universe entirely to be able to actually change your brain and to be able to observe the process as it happens. What a mysterious thing—changing what's happening inside your head. And when you do it, how exciting, what fun, and what a sudden surge of power. I had gotten my first taste of it in the early 1970s when I had overheard someone talking about an experiment going on at New York University (NYU), and wangled my way into the experimental group by claiming to be an NYU student. I learned to generate alpha waves by making a machine go click-click-click. For long delightful periods I would sit there with the machine caressing me with timeless strings of beautiful clicks. It was delightful and mysterious, and a large part of the delight and the mystery was that I was listening to the activity of my own brain and becoming aware of every subtle little change that took place within it. I learned that if I thought of certain things the clicks would stop and if I thought of other things, or stopped thinking, the clicks would start.

To me it was amazing to learn that I could, in fact, change my brain and the things that were going on inside it. What a revelation! Until then, I had always assumed that whatever was going on in my mind—sadness, anger, confusion, joy—was simply "going on" and that it would keep going on until it stopped going on and something else began. But as I sat by the alpha trainer learning to spin out lovely chains of clicks—and learning to make them stop, if I wanted to—I learned that you could change your mind. It struck me as being a process something like changing TV channels. If you don't like the soap opera that's on channel 2, change to the western on channel 4.

I was filled with a sense of power. Not the power to stop speeding locomotives or leap tall buildings at a single bound, but a much more modest and personal power—the power of being aware of my own mind and knowing that I had some control over it. I loved the sessions and would have kept going back to the lab for years, except suddenly the experiment was over. No more sessions. And so my experience of EEG biofeedback was over. Or, rather, put on hold for the next twelve years.

Meanwhile, the popular craze for alpha machines ran its course. In part, the reason personal alpha trainers didn't catch on was that the machines themselves were still too crude. (This was before the invention of the microprocessor, which would make it possible to shrink such devices down from the size of a suitcase to the size of a pack of cigarettes.) Another reason was that alpha simply wasn't all it was cracked up to be. People had exaggerated expectations. They'd heard that alpha was a mystic state, satori, bliss, and sudden illumination. So they tried it out, and found that it was . . . well . . . okay. As I say, it could give you a feeling of power, but it was a very *modest* sort of power, the usefulness of which was not immediately apparent—kind of like knowing how to wiggle your ears.

Meanwhile, ironically, as the public lost interest in EEG biofeedback, researchers began making some discoveries that were actually earthshaking and dazzling, discoveries having to do with theta and whole-brain synchrony: These states, unlike alpha, had magic and mystery and power.

Some researchers, such as Les Fehmi, began working almost exclusively with synchrony, and designed biofeedback machines that would give subjects a sound or light feedback whenever they were in synchrony. The researchers found that subjects who could learn to get into a state of synchrony experienced dramatic changes: increases in IQ and grades in school, improvements in performance by executives and athletes. And, repeatedly, the subjects who learned to produce brain-wave synchrony reported extraordinary experiences of heightened states of consciousness—emotional breakthroughs, feelings of oneness with the cosmos, ecstasy. Fehmi, himself a practitioner of Zen meditation, came to believe that the state of synchrony was in many ways identical to the state of Zen satori.

Other researchers, such as Thomas Budzynski and the Greens, developed and explored EEG biofeedback devices that enabled subjects to learn to enter the mysterious theta state. But since all this research required EEG machines that cost thousands of dollars, and were not easy to use or understand, the work aroused little popular interest at the time.

But what was being discovered was extraordinary. All the researchers investigating EEG biofeedback training discovered that it clearly increased human brain power. These increases in IQ and in other types of intelligence and achievements seemed to result not only from the altered brain-wave states that were the result of EEG biofeedback training, but also from actual physiological brain growth in response to the challenge and stimulation of learning to use the mind tools—that is, from the enriched environment effect.

Among those who found increased IQ in response to biofeedback training were professors Harold Russell, Ph.D., and John Carter, Ph.D., of the University of Houston. They concluded that:

> Learning to self-regulate one's ongoing EEG frequency and amplitude activity is a complex and time consuming task. It requires a highly focused concentration on and the awareness of the brain's activity and the repetition of the patterns of mental activity that produce the desired frequency and amplitude. . . . When the task of

control of EEG activity is adequately learned and sufficiently practiced, the functioning of the human brain improves measurably, e.g. . . . scores on standardized tests of achievements or intelligence increase by 12 to 20 points.

In other words, there seems to be something inherently brain expanding about learning to manipulate your brain waves. That's one reason for the seemingly sudden burst of interest in EEG biofeedback that has erupted in the last two years, and the arrival on the scene of a variety of new consumer-oriented EEG devices.

CONSUMERS' GUIDE TO BIOFEEDBACK TECHNOLOGY

The recent development of microprocessors and the increasing development of understanding about how the brain-mind connection works have led to the design and production of a variety of new, user-friendly, and very effective biofeedback devices. Many of them can be linked with computers and/or combined with what we might call biofeed-in devices—such as the sound and light machines we explore in the next few chapters. To purchase or obtain further information about any of these devices, write: Megabrain, P.O. Box 2744, Sausalito, CA 94966, or call 1-800-456-9887.

I have found the following biofeedback machines to be most effective.

The Mind Pyramid
(Tools for Exploration)

EEG DEVICES

The *Twilight Learning System,* devised by Dr. Thomas Budzynski, guides you into alpha and theta states and is an ideal clinical device that has proven helpful in accelerated learning and in treatment of drug addiction and alcoholism, anxiety, and much more. Cost is about $3,200.

A simpler, less scientifically accurate, consumer-oriented variant is *The Mind Pyramid,* which gives sound signals indicating when the user is in alpha and theta. Cost is about $1,400.

The *Mind Mirror III,* developed by C. Maxwell Cade, provides a full-spectrum visual image of the activity of both hemispheres, permitting the user to learn how to increase or decrease the activity of various brain-wave frequencies. Cost is about $3,500.

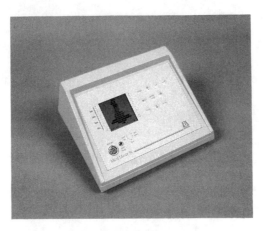

The Mind Mirror III
(Tools for Exploration)

The *Interactive Brainwave Visual Analyzer* monitors brain-wave activity and sends it to a Mac computer, which provides a variety of images of brain-wave activity. Cost is about $1,200 for one channel, $2,400 for two channels (right and left hemispheres).

The *Biofeedback Brainwave Synchronizer,* designed by Dr. Les Fehmi, provides audio and visual feedback when the user enters a state of whole-brain synchrony. Most other machines are not "phase sensitive," that is, they do not provide information about synchrony. This is a superb clinical tool for learning to enter a state of whole-brain synchrony. Cost is about $3,200.

The *Light Link* allows you to "tune in" to specific brain frequencies, by providing visual (and optional audio) feedback when your brain waves are at the desired frequency. Cost is about $950.

The *BE-200 Brain Exerciser* is phase sensitive and thus can pro-

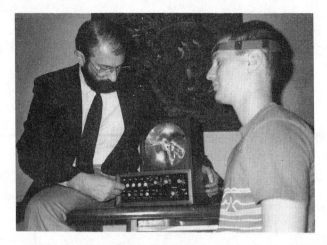

Dr. Les Fehmi with his Biofeedback Brainwave Synchronizer
(Dr. Les Fehmi)

vide feedback for states of brain-wave synchrony. It is small, links to your IBM-compatible computer, and is expandable to up to eight channels of EEG activity. Cost is about $1,600.

The *Neurosearch 24*, produced by Lexicor, is a sophisticated brain mapper. With twenty-four electrodes, it gives you a visual colored topographic map of your brain activity as it changes from moment to moment. This superb research device operates through your IBM-compatible computer and costs about $16,000.

New on the market is the *Brain Tracer*, produced by Dutch technicians who have used the circuitry and programs of a medical-

The Neurosearch 24
(Lexicor Systems)

The Brain Tracer
(Tools for Exploration)

grade brain-mapping system to produce a phenomenal, low-priced system that links to your PC and provides both audio and visual feedback of whole-spectrum brain-wave activity. It has the capacity to produce Mind Mirror–like images of both hemispheres or to shift into a variety of other display modes, such as compressed spectral array or raw EEG tracings. Cost is about $1,100.

GSR SYSTEMS

Currently the best GSR system on the market is the deceptively simple *GSR 2*. About the size of a bar of soap, you simply hold it in your hand,

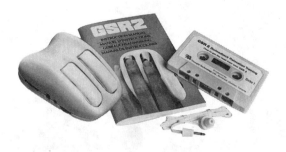

The GSR 2 Biofeedback System
(Tools for Exploration)

and it gives you audio feedback—the tone rises as you become more tense and falls as you become more relaxed. It comes with a variety of options, such as a system that plugs into your PC to give you a moment-by-moment graph of your level of arousal. Cost of the basic unit is about $60.

EMG SYSTEMS

The *Antense* straps around your forehead and measures the electrical activity of your forehead muscles (a reliable indicator of your overall muscle tension), giving you audio feedback—as your tension decreases, the tone falls. It is an excellent tool for training you to reach states of deep relaxation quickly. Cost is about $100.

The Antense EMG relaxation system
(Tools for Exploration)

SUGGESTED READING

An excellent introduction to EEG biofeedback that captures the excitement of research and discovery is *Beyond Biofeedback* by Elmer and Alyce Green (New York: Delacorte, 1977). See also *The Awakened Mind: Biofeedback and the Development of Higher States of Awareness* by C. Maxwell Cade and Nona Coxhead (New York: Delacorte, 1979); *Mind/Body Integration: Essential Readings in Biofeedback* by Erik

Peper et al (New York: Plenum, 1979); *From Ghost in the Box to Successful Biofeedback Training* by Robert Shellenberger and Judith Green (Greely, Co: Health Psychology, 1988); and my *Megabrain* (New York: Ballantine) rev. ed. 1991, chapters 10 and 11.

SIX
SOUND:
THE HEARTBEAT OF LIFE

MOMMY SOUNDS

Humans have always been enthralled by the effects of rhythmic sounds and aware of the mind-altering and brain-wave entrainment effects of rhythmic noises. After all, the first sound any of us hear, and perhaps the most powerful and evocative memorable sound, is the rhythmic booming of blood through our ears as we rest inside our mothers.

Humans were quick to find ways to duplicate this evocative rhythm and many others. In fact, it could be argued that the rhythmic use of sound to produce heightened states of consciousness may have been humankind's first great development in mind technology. Think of the first proto-hominid who picked up a stick and pounded it on a hollow log. Boom. Then he or she did it again, and again and again, while the other tribe members turned, stared, sat, listened, and joined in, awed and amazed. What a mesmerizing power.

ENTRAINING BRAIN WAVES

One clear explanation for the powers of rhythmic sounds is that they dramatically alter brain-wave activity. Researchers have found that rhythmic clicks produce clear brain-wave entrainment throughout many parts of the brain—not just in those parts associated with hearing. According to anthropologist Michael Harner, scientists studying shamanic rituals have "found that drum beat frequencies in the theta wave EEG frequency range . . . predominated during initiation procedures." So, simply by making a noise at a specific frequency, and making it rhythmically and repeatedly, you can alter your brain waves. With a simple drum, in other words, you can draw listeners downward from their waking beta rhythms into the relaxed alpha state, and even deeper, into the mysterious theta state—an ideal state for producing profound effects, through the telling of stories, the singing of songs, the casting of spells.

BINAURAL BEATS

Listen to a record of chanting: Tibetan monks, Gregorian chants. If you listen carefully, you will begin to feel the voices become one and create a single pulsating tone. One of the most noticeable effects of several instruments playing or human voices chanting at approximately the same pitch is that you will tend to hear a *wah wah wah* vibrating effect, or "beat," as the voices or instruments come into unison and then drift slightly apart. As the tones come into unison, the beat slows down; as the tones drift farther and farther out of key, the beat speeds up.

The frequency of the beat produced by two separate tones equals the frequency of the difference between those two tones. Thus, for example, a frequency of 200 Hz and one of 204 Hz would produce (among other overtones) a "beat frequency" of 4 Hz. Players of guitars, violins, and other stringed instruments use this beat phenomenon when they tune one string to a second string: When the beat slows to zero, the two strings are in tune.

This phenomenon might have remained of little interest to non-musicians were it not for the work of an intrepid explorer of inner spaces named Robert Monroe. Monroe first came to wide notice in the 1960s with his book *Journeys Out of the Body,* in which he describes a series of extraordinary experiences that took place while his physical body was asleep. Monroe became interested in finding some way of inducing this out-of-body experience. As he knew that his own experiences had something to do with a feeling of vibrations, he set about to create similar physical vibrations using sound.

Monroe discovered that while scientists had known about "beats" for years, they had not really explored the effects of beats when played over stereo headphones. He found that when the separate sounds were played through separate ears, they created what was called a binaural beat. When pure audio signals of different frequencies are delivered to the brain through separate ears—for example, when a signal of 200 cycles per second enters one ear and one of 204 cycles per second enters the other ear—the two hemispheres of the brain function together to "hear" not the actual external sound signals but a phantom third signal—a *binaural* beat—which is the difference in frequency between the two actual sound frequencies. This beat frequency is not an actual sound, but an electrical signal that can be created only by both hemispheres of the brain working together simultaneously.

And, as Monroe found, when precisely controlled tones are combined in the brain, a part of it—the olivary nucleus—begins to become "entrained to" or resonate sympathetically to this "phantom" binaural beat, like a crystal goblet vibrating in response to a pure tone, in what is known as a frequency following response. As the olivary nucleus becomes entrained, it sends signals upward into the cerebral cortex that mix with the existing patterns of brain activity there to produce noticeable state changes. As Monroe continued his investigations, he found that by using certain frequencies, he could produce a unique and coherent brain state—a state he called hemispheric synchronization.

What binaural beats can provide, then, is a very simple but powerful way of altering brain-wave activity. Combining a signal of 200 Hz in one ear with a signal of 210 Hz in the other produces a very subtle, gentle vibrating effect, yet it is stimulating the listener's deep brain at a 10 Hz frequency state. This gentle technique is far less intrusive or irritating than simply banging a drum in the listener's ear ten times per second. Thus binaural beats can provide a method for rapidly, subtly (even subliminally) altering brain-wave activity into a more organized or coherent brain state and boosting listeners into specific altered and expanded states of consciousness.

What's more, as electroencephalogram (EEG) researchers have found, these carefully tuned binaural beats can be superimposed, layer upon layer, producing complex sound matrices with powerful state-changing effects. Certain frequency combinations, for example, can produce powerful alpha activity, while other combinations effectively suppress alpha and increase synchronous theta and beta. Other combinations produce a state that combines profound relaxation with heightened alertness—a state Monroe calls "mind awake/body asleep."

There's no doubt these beats have profound brain-altering effects. A large body of research has proven their effectiveness in a variety of applications ranging from accelerated learning, to pain reduction, to boosting immune function. One recent study at Memphis State University by Dale Foster, Ph.D., used EEGs to measure the amount of alpha brain-wave production in subjects using biofeedback EEG training, subjects hearing alpha binaural beats, subjects using a combination of biofeedback and binaural beats, and a control group. Foster's conclusion: "An interactive effect was found in which the group with both alpha binaural beats and alpha biofeedback produced more treatment alpha than the group with alpha biofeedback alone." Additionally, a majority of the subjects receiving both binaural beats and feedback reported "being able to control alpha production via their focus on the alpha binaural beats." Foster concluded that "the combination of alpha frequency binaural beats and alpha brain wave feedback resulted in significantly more alpha production than alpha brain wave feedback alone."

Other evidence is emerging from Washington state educator Jo Dee Owens that for older people, the combination of delta binaural beats with high beta beats can have an extraordinary vitalizing effect.

RECORDING THE BEAT

Binaural beats are used on a variety of widely advertised audio tapes and compact discs (CDs). You may have seen ads for the best-known of these tapes, which describe the process as "ultra meditation," "high-tech meditation," and so on.

While some of these tapes are effective, many are not, because they assume that, simply by creating binaural beats at a certain frequency and sending them to the brain through the ears, they can directly trigger brain-wave activity at the same frequency. But as EEG researchers such as F. Holmes Atwater have noted, this "classical evoked potential" concept is "flawed from the onset." Binaural beats simply do not work that way.

EEG research shows that binaural beats do not directly alter EEG activity; rather they actually are "heard" in the lower auditory centers—in the olivary nucleus of each hemisphere, deep inside the brain. There the actual oscillations in response to binaural beats can be measured directly. To produce the desired state-change effects throughout the cortex, binaural beats must be combined in a highly specific mix that makes use of what Atwater calls the "audio-encephalographic interferometry effect." In essence, the binaural beat oscillations must be mixed via the olivary nucleus with existing brain-wave patterns to create "interference" patterns or wave combinations that produce higher-order patterns, out of which emerge the expanded states of consciousness.

BEYOND HEARING: SUPERCHARGING THE BRAIN

Rhythmic brain-wave entrainment, such as clicks, drum beats, and the more subtle binaural beats, have obvious effects on the brain. Another type of sound—high-frequency sound—may have even more profound effects. The first to explore the effects of high-frequency sounds systematically was the French eye, ear, nose, and throat specialist Alfred Tomatis, M.D. He found evidence that brain development is powerfully influenced by the sounds we hear while in the womb. During this time, we are suspended in amniotic fluid, with the fluid filling our ears. Since sound travels through water five times more efficiently than through air, our sense of hearing would be five times more acute. Tomatis covered microphones and speakers with membranes and submerged them in water to produce and record the type of sounds infants hear filtered through amniotic fluid—the sounds of the mother's pulse, respiration, voice, intestines, heart, and all the sounds of the external world filtered through the mother's taut belly. He found that these sounds were predominantly high-pitched squeaks, hisses, swishes, and whistles in the frequency range above 8,000 Hz.

When he recorded mothers' voices and other sounds at the high-frequency range and played them back to children with learning disabilities—autism, dyslexia, hyperactivity—he noticed immediate and dramatic improvements in learning and behavior. This high-frequency sound, Tomatis theorized, "awakens a sense of our most archaic relationship with the mother." Such sounds seem to touch our most ancient and primordial memories—the bliss of the womb, oneness with the mother—and provide listeners with a memory and whole-body experience of oneness and wholeness. Tomatis also found that these sounds seemed to boost brainpower, energize the body, and reduce stress-related problems of all sorts.

SUPERCHARGED MONKS

Tomatis's research and clinical experiences led him to conclude that the ear is a primary organ of consciousness. Until then, most people, including scientists studying the ear, thought of the ears as having only a single function: hearing. They were not aware that hearing is only one aspect of a larger, dynamic process, a process that involves every cell in the body.

Tomatis discovered that the ear not only "hears," but the vibrating waves it hears also stimulate sensory nerves in the inner ear, where they are transformed into electrical impulses that travel along several routes to the brain. Some travel to the hearing centers, where they are translated into sounds. Others send a charge of electrical potential into the cerebellum, which controls physical motion and sensations of balance and equilibrium; and from there into the limbic brain, which controls emotions and the release of hormones and other biochemicals that influence the entire body. The electrical potential created by sounds is also transmitted to the cortex, which controls the higher functions of consciousness. Thus sounds provide nourishment for the brain and the entire body in the form of electroneural stimulation to the brain. They seem to charge up the brain in the same way batteries are recharged.

And, Tomatis surmised, since sound nourishes the body and brain, then it is possible that insufficient sound, particularly in the crucial high-frequency ranges, can have similar effects as insufficient food nutrients, depleting our resources and leading to sickness.

At one point Tomatis was called in to treat all the monks in a Benedictine monastery for fatigue and listlessness. Tomatis found that a new abbot had eliminated their normal practice of chanting for six to eight hours every day. With its high echoing overtones, chanting is a rich source of high-frequency sound. After Tomatis instructed the monks to resume their chanting, all quickly recovered their vigor.

According to Tomatis, "Some sounds are as good as two cups of coffee. Gregorian chants are a fantastic energy source."

As Tomatis monitored the process by which sound was translated into nerve energy in the inner ear, he found that high frequencies—8,000 Hz and over—accelerated the recharging process. Sadly, while most humans are born with the ability to hear sound waves between about 16 and 20,000 cycles per second, noise pollution and physical and psychological stress have dramatically diminished the hearing range of most people. In these noisy, stressful days, even children show stress-related hearing loss in the high-frequency ranges. This means that many people in modern society have become deaf to the energizing, healing nutrients of these sounds. We are, in a real sense, in a state of *sound deprivation.*

PUMPING SOUNDS WITH THE EAR MUSCLES

Tomatis developed a sound recording process called the "Electronic Ear" that filters out ordinary sounds while reproducing and emphasizing the high-frequency ones. With this "fitness center for the inner ear," he could switch between the high- and low-frequency sounds, alternately tensing and relaxing tiny muscles in the listener's ears. Just as repeatedly pumping weights builds muscles, Tomatis found that this repeated contraction and expansion exercised and strengthened the ear muscles, and the ears slowly regained their ability to hear the higher frequencies again. Once the ears had been "opened," he found, the brain could recharge quickly by absorbing the nutrients of full-frequency sounds.

One key discovery by Tomatis was that "the voice can only produce what the ear can hear." Since our hearing range is so diminished as a result of stress and noise, our verbal expression has been stripped of richness. Most of our verbal communication and our hearing is limited to a narrow frequency range between 300 and 3,000 Hz—something like eating a diet limited to meat and potatoes. But Tomatis found that when ears are "opened" by high-frequency sounds, they not only regain their ability to hear high frequencies, they produce a whole-body healing and energizing effect, a dramatic increase in mental powers from the increased ability to "hear" and be aware of external reality, and a noticeable opening and enriching of the vocal range.

Think of the narrow, lifeless, wooden tones of people who are sick, depressed, or under severe stress, and compare them to the rich tones and sweeping vocal range of vital and vigorous singers, political orators, or religious leaders. People whose vocal and auditory range is wide are clearly more open, aware, and responsive to others, as a result of their highly sensitive ability to hear others. This may explain why orchestra conductors are among the longest living people in the world. And the direct link between stress and vocal range casts light on why professional singers are notoriously subject to laryngitis and other vocal problems when under stress.

Tomatis began using the high-frequency sounds of his Electronic Ear for therapeutic purposes and achieved extraordinary success in treating a wide variety of disorders. What is now called the Tomatis Effect has been scientifically tested and confirmed by researchers and therapists around the world. The technique, which involves progressively introducing more and more high-frequency sounds and alternating them with low-frequency and full-frequency sounds is now used in over 180 centers throughout the world to alleviate deafness, emotional disturbances, hypertension, insomnia, speech defects, epilepsy, hyperactivity, dyslexia, autism, depression, and more. Many performing musical artists claim the technique has increased their musical abilities and sensitivities by expanding their abilities to hear and sing. Other documented results from the Tomatis method include heightened creativity and mental capacity, improvement of memory and concentration, deep relaxation, weight loss, and much more.

SOUND THERAPY FOR THE WALKMAN

However, since the Tomatis method requires patients to sit for several hours a day wearing headphones, listening to music through the sophisticated Electronic Ear equipment in the therapist's office, the cost in both time and money was too great for widespread use. The development of the Walkman changed all that. In 1984 Canadian writer Patricia Joudry wrote a book explaining the Tomatis technique, *Sound Therapy for the Walkman*, and produced a series of "filtered" classical music tapes, also called "Sound Therapy for the Walkman." What had formerly required over $20,000 in equipment, or thousands of dollars in treatment fees, was now available at a cost of about $235 (for four ninety-minute cassettes), and could be listened to over an inexpensive cassette tape player. This enabled users to hear the brain-charging music while they went about their daily lives, instead of having to sit in a therapist's office for hours each day.

What they hear is classical music recorded in the normal full-frequency range alternating periodically with the same music recorded through high-pass filters, which record only the sounds between approximately 8,000 Hz to over 15,000 Hz. These high frequencies sound like hisses and extend into ranges that are not really "heard" but nevertheless have a stimulating effect on the ear. This switching between high-frequency and full-frequency music expands and contracts the tiny ear muscles and opens up hearing to progressively wider ranges.

Since Joudry released her tapes, newer techniques have emerged to deliver high-frequency sounds. Joudry recorded her series on metal tapes. This increases the life span of the tapes, but it also sharply decreases the life span of your cassette player. The metal tapes played hour after hour over the sensitive playback head of the cassette player have the effect of sandpaper, wearing it down and quickly reducing its sensitivity to the very same high-frequency sounds you want to be hearing.

SILENT STIMULATION?

Newer techniques avoid this pitfall. These include the Klangtherapie (Soundtherapie) CDs from the German company Lambdona that are now widely used in European clinics with impressive results. Perhaps the most important breakthrough in the delivery of high "sound therapy" frequencies is a newly patented Silent Stim process. Recent tests have shown that it can produce sound therapy tapes and CDs that are over 75 decibels stronger in the high-frequency ranges (which translates mathematically to about 12 million times more powerful) than the Joudry cassettes.

The process gains much of its power by sweeping (frequency modulating) the high-frequency end of the audio program from about 6,000 to 18,000 Hz. It also sweeps the low-frequency end from about 20 to 200 Hz. Both ends are then swept in rhythmic alternations, forcing the ear muscles to exercise by expanding and contracting between the high- and low-frequency sound groupings. Since these sounds are partially outside the normal human hearing range, they can be played on the tapes or CDs 100 percent of the time as "silent" background to music or other sounds, (the high-frequency sounds of the Sound Therapy tapes appear about 10 percent of the time). They can thus have profound brain-stimulating effects without even being audible.

CONSUMERS' GUIDE TO SOUND THERAPY TECHNOLOGY

One of the most powerful "sound therapy" techniques, of course, is music. Pure music, without high-tech add-ons, has been proven in recent scientific studies to boost immune function; reduce pain, anxiety, and depression; treat mental, neurological, emotional, and physical disorders (including autism, learning disabilities, and stroke); and much more. Evidence suggests that certain types of music seem to have the most powerful positive effects—among them are baroque, classical, romantic, types of jazz, chants, and the relaxing, spacious, meditative sounds of much "new music," including the mind-altering music of composer/musicians such as Constance Demby, Iasos, Marcey, Jim Oliver, and Boris Mourashkin.

All good music is, in this sense, mind altering. However, a number of new audio programs or products make use of advanced technology, such as the binaural beats and high-frequency effects just described, or other advanced-state change techniques to directly influence brain waves and brain chemistry, increase mental powers, and produce heightened states. The following are some of the most effective of these "psychoacoustic" programs. While they are effective alone, I have found them to be especially powerful when used in combination with other types of mind technology, such as light/sound devices, flotation, ganzfelds, motion, and sound tables, etc. To purchase or obtain further information about any of the tapes and CDs described below, write Megabrain, P.O. Box 2744, Sausalito, CA 94966, or call 1-800-456-9887.

Acoustic Brain Research tapes use a variety of psychoacoustic techniques, including binaural beats, to produce states ranging from deep relaxation to "Mind Gymnastiks."

Brain/Mind Research tapes and CDs, created by Dr. Jeffrey Thompson, use state-of-the-art acoustic techniques along with "primordial sounds" and evocative "new age" music to induce trancelike states of deep relaxation.

Brain/Mind Resonance tapes use a combination of psychoacoustic techniques to produce specific states such as "up" (maximum productivity), "down" (relaxation), "now" (centering), and "forever" (consciousness expansion).

Changeworks tapes by Ericksonian hypnotherapists Tom Condon and Carol Erickson use a "double-induction" technique, with two voices reciting poetic monologues and stories through separate ears— they cause you to drop quickly into a relaxed, trancelike state during which you unconsciously assimilate many of the hidden suggestions contained in the stories.

Hemi-Sync tapes, devised by Robert Monroe, use binaural beats. Many use spoken hypnotic inductions to guide you to heightened states or instruct you in learning to "imprint" certain states so that you may recall them later using "cues" or signals you create yourself.

Hypno-Peripheral Processing tapes, by Dr. Lloyd Glauberman, use a "double-induction" technique—you hear two separate fairy-tale–like stories, one through each ear, that contain imbedded suggestions for behavioral change. The process is enhanced by binaural beats.

Neurosonics tapes are the brainchild of Dr. Richard Bandler, co-creator of Neurolinguistic Programming (NLP). They combine psychoacoustic techniques along with Bandler's mastery as a hypnotist—he is a compelling and unique vocalist—to guide you through a series of dynamic, supercharging experiences.

Paraliminal Tapes fuse Neurolinguistic Programming techniques with psychoacoustic sounds to guide you through a variety of behavior-changing experiences, ranging from changing belief systems to generating a "new history."

Sound RX tapes and CDs are created by the pioneering and multitalented Steven Halpern, using binaural beats and other brainwave–altering techniques, enhanced by his own spacious, mysterious musical compositions.

Gregorian Chants have been recorded by the monks of Solesmes and the nuns of St. Cecilia's, and are available in a variety of tapes and CDs. They provide the rich high-frequency overtones that Tomatis's research has found to charge the brain.

My own *MegaBrain* tapes use a unique combination of psychoactive sounds and binaural beats at bioactive window frequencies combined with brain-charging high-frequency sounds and powerful infrasonic or subaudible sounds as well as clicks, phasing effects, and other brain-expanding techniques to produce a variety of specific brain states ranging from deep relaxation, to transcendence, to high-energy exercise tapes.

The Binaural Signal Generator
(AWI Electronics)

The *Binaural Signal Generator* plugs into your home audio system and permits you to create your own binaural beats, so you can record personalized audio tapes or play binaural beats through your own system, alone or in combination with your favorite music. Cost is about $390.

SUGGESTED READING

For a good introduction to the healing and mind-enhancing powers of music, see *Healing Sounds: the Power of Harmonics* by Jonathan Goldman (Rockport, MA: Element, 1992) and two thought-provoking anthologies edited by Don Campbell: *Music: Physician for Times to Come*

(Wheaton, IL: Quest, 1991) and *Music and Miracles* (Wheaton, IL: Quest, 1992). See also *Sound Health: The Music and Sounds That Make Us Whole* by Steven Halpern and Louis Savary (New York: Harper & Row, 1985).

For more information about the sound explorations of Dr. Tomatis, see *Sound Therapy for the Walkman* by Patricia Joudry (St. Denis, Saskatchewan: Steele & Steele, 1984); *About the Tomatis Method* by Tim Gilmour, Paul Madaule, and Billie Thompson; and Alfred Tomatis's own *The Conscious Ear* (Barrytown, NY: Station Hill Press, 1991).

For binaural beats, see "Auditory Beats in the Brain" by Gerald Oster, *Scientific American* 229 (1973): 94–102.

S E V E N
LIGHT POWER

The light of the body is your eye; when your eye is clear, your whole
body is clear, your whole body is also full of light; but when it is bad,
your body is full of darkness.

—Luke 11:34

•

The sun, my dear, the sun is God.

—Joseph Mallord William Turner, dying words

•

More light . . . more light!

—Goethe, dying words

•

All matter is frozen light.

—David Bohm, physicist

All life on our planet has evolved in and is dependent on light from the
sun, which is carried to the earth in the form of electromagnetic waves,
including the narrow band of visible color and invisible ultraviolet
wavelengths. We evolved as creatures who live much of our waking
lives in the light of the sun, using that specific balance of wavelengths
to see, to guide our bodies' production of neurochemicals and hormones, to organize our bodies' natural rhythms.

Today many of us spend most of our time indoors, or behind
eyeglasses, automobile windshields, glass windows, and sunglasses. All
of this glass blocks out natural ultraviolet and other wavelengths,
ensuring that only distorted forms of light enter our visual tract. Yet
a growing body of research makes it clear that natural, balanced full-
spectrum light is an essential nutrient for the brain and body.

Many of us, including scientists, have long believed that the eye
had only one purpose: seeing. But a series of extraordinary studies in
the 1970s have proven that seeing is only one aspect of a dynamic
process that influences every cell in our body. As light waves strike the

eyes—which are actual extensions of the brain—they stimulate the photoreceptor nerves and are translated into electrical impulses. Some impulses travel to the visual cortex, where they create the images of eyesight, and affect the cerebral cortex, which controls motivation, speech, reasoning, learning, memory, and so on. Other light-created electrical impulses travel directly to the brain's hypothalamus, the master gland, which controls and coordinates most of our life-sustaining functions. Through the hypothalamus the light energy impulses affect the autonomic nervous system. Through the pituitary they regulate every significant gland in our endocrine system. Light current also travels directly from the eye to the brainstem, which controls such functions as equilibrium and cardiovascular and gastrointestinal activities. In other words, light directly influences all of our body functions and mind states. As Albert Szent-Gyorgyi, Nobel Prize winner and discoverer of vitamin C, concluded from his work in bioelectronics, "all the energy which we take into our bodies is derived from the sun."

OUR APPETITE FOR LIGHT

Light is a nutrient, and without this nourishment we become imbalanced and depressed, and our immune systems decline. Just as we speak of a minimum daily requirement for various vitamins and other nutrients, we have a minimum daily requirement for light. Scientists have studied the effects of insufficient light on individuals and whole countries (such as the northern European countries during the months of winter darkness) and found a direct correlation to irritability, fatigue, illness, insomnia, depression, alcoholism, suicide, and other mental illnesses. On the other hand, light researchers have proven that exposures to sunlight will produce decreases in resting heart rate, blood pressure, blood sugar, and lactic acid in the blood following exercise; and increases in strength, energy, endurance, stress tolerance, and the ability of the blood to absorb and carry oxygen.

Just as we can suffer from malnutrition, insufficient sunlight causes a state of light deprivation that can be called malillumination. If we want to operate at our peak, mentally and physically, it's absolutely essential that we find a healthy source of full-spectrum light. Since our society is organized to keep us out of the light for most of our lives, a variety of healthy full-spectrum light sources have been developed and are seeing increasing use. (Full-spectrum light has the same balance of visible color and invisible ultraviolet wavelengths as sunlight.)

THE COLOR OF LIFE

In addition to the natural full-spectrum light provided by the sun, our species evolved seeing and being influenced by various natural colors created by narrow bandwidths of the full-spectrum light. Our minds, brains, and bodies respond naturally and instinctively to the colors such as the green of the jungle, plants, grasses; the blue of the sky and water; the reds and violets of sunrise and sunset; the yellows of summer sun and dry grass. We speak of "royal purple," "seeing red," feeling "green with envy," "blue" and "in the pink," and seeing the world "through rose-tinted glasses." New evidence suggests that colors by themselves can trigger a flood of specific neurochemicals and hormones, can alter our mood and cause us to become aroused or serene, can serve as trigger mechanisms for memories. Certain colors, for example, have been proven to produce arousal of the autonomic nervous system, while others have calming effects.

Researchers have recently discovered that our body's enzyme systems are so sensitive to light and colors that certain colors can activate or deactivate enzymes, alter the flow of chemicals across cell membranes, and cause some enzymes to be as much as *500 percent more effective*. New research by neurologist C. Norman Shealy has revealed that short exposure to specific colors leads to sharp increases in the production of norepinephrine, serotonin, beta-endorphin, cholinesterase, melatonin, oxytocin, growth hormone, luteinizing hormone, and other hormones and neurochemicals. Color is a powerful regulator of many key biological systems and functions.

Just as natural full-spectrum light is an essential nutrient, we now know that colors too serve as nutrients. Living in a world of artificial light delivered into our brains and bodies in distorted unnatural wavelengths and colors is clearly as toxic to our health as the synthetic and distorted forms of foods we consume. To operate at our peak, we need to obtain our minimum daily requirement of colors. Since many of us cannot "consume" natural colors outdoors, new color systems have been developed that are proving to be powerful tools for delivering color nutrients to the hungry brain.

BRAIN BENEFITS OF A GOOD TAN

Dr. John Ott has been studying the effects of light on living things for decades. His books, such as *Health and Light* have been filled with eye-opening discoveries about the crucial importance of full-spectrum light. A key finding is that, contrary to all the alarms and warnings about the dangers of exposure to ultraviolet (UV) light, UV light is in fact a key part of the full spectrum of natural light and is absolutely essential to human health. Other scientists have verified Ott's findings.

We now know, for example, that UV light: activates the synthesis of vitamin D, a prerequisite for the absorption of calcium and other minerals from the diet; lowers blood pressure; reduces cholesterol; increases levels of sex hormones; is an effective treatment for diseases such as psoriasis, tuberculosis, asthma, and many others; and activates a key hormone in the skin that influences many of the body's regulatory systems as well as the immune system.

The recent and ongoing scares about the dangers of UV light, particularly its link with skin cancers, have created a climate of "fear of sunlight" and led many people to cut themselves off entirely from this essential nutrient. As Ott points out, too much oxygen at birth can blind a baby. However, "It would be foolish to jump to the conclusion that oxygen is hazardous to your health and that you should live without oxygen. Yet this is exactly the conclusion that is drawn with ultraviolet light. . . . The public has to understand that light is a 'nutrient' just like a vitamin or a mineral."

Contradicting the current prevailing beliefs about UV light and skin cancer has been a continuing stream of studies showing that skin cancers are much higher in office workers than in individuals regularly exposed to sunlight. Additional research has shown that fluorescent office lights emit radiation and can cause mutations in skin cells. The key seems to be moderation. The new field of photobiology has developed from John Ott's work. Among the findings in recent years:

Cholesterol. Insufficient light can interfere with endocrine functions, such as calcium absorption, and lead to increased levels of cholesterol.

Depression. Seasonal affective disorder (SAD), a cyclic mood disorder characterized by fall/winter depressions, is caused by insufficient light. An estimated 5 million Americans suffer from SAD. Studies at the National Institute of Mental Health have shown that the cure is exposure to full-spectrum lighting for two to six hours per day.

EM Radiation. Full-spectrum lights can actually avert damage from electromagnetic (EM) pollution. Our computers, for example, emit EM radiation that can cause the iron in red blood cells to become polarized and "clump" together, inhibiting blood flow and oxygen supply. Complaints from this include headaches, nausea, eyestrain, and fatigue, and it is thought to be a contributing cause to many degenerative conditions, including Alzheimer's disease. Increased levels of miscarriages occur in women who work in front of computers. But Ott has found that when these "clumped" blood cells are exposed to full-spectrum lighting, the clumping is broken up; and his research suggests that exposure to full-spectrum lighting can help our bodies resist the negative effects of exposure to EM radiation.

Health and Productivity. Full-spectrum light (with ultraviolet light) has been proven to increase productivity while decreasing absenteeism caused by illness and to improve visual acuity, easing eyestrain and fatigue.

Learning. Non–full-spectrum lighting may be a key cause of learning disabilities. Numerous studies in public schools comparing full-spectrum lights with ordinary fluorescent lights have shown that students receiving full-spectrum light showed higher academic achievement, less absenteeism, far less hyperactivity, and fewer dental cavities.

Strength and athletic performance. Full-spectrum light increases strength and athletic performance. In a study at the University of Illinois, a physical education class was divided in two. The half that was given light with ultraviolet light included increased their performance by 20 percent, while the half that didn't receive the light improved by only 1 percent.

Stress. Artificial non–full-spectrum light has been found to increase stress biochemicals such as adrenocorticotrophic hormone (ACTH) and cortisol, and to make students irritable, reduce production among factory workers, and make office workers sluggish and add to their stress levels.

As a result of Ott's pioneering work, a variety of full-spectrum lights have been developed and are now available. I describe them at the end of this chapter.

LIGHT AND COLOR THERAPY

Though it is little known today, the systematic therapeutic, healing use of light and color has a history that stretches back several thousand years. In the late nineteenth century a number of medical doctors had great success with the use of various colors for healing, using sunlight filtered through colored glass, and later using colored filters with artificial light. Niels Finsen of Denmark won the Nobel Prize in 1903 for his medical use of light, including a treatment for tuberculosis. He gained recognition for his use of light in seemingly miraculous cures of thousands of patients. In the early twentieth century, Dinshah Ghadiali and Dr. Harry Riley Spitler furthered the science of light therapy by developing more effective systems for applying color to the human body.

Their scientific light therapy systems were reaching increasing numbers of people when, in 1939, sulfanilamide was discovered, and its discoverer won the Nobel Prize. The development of pharmaceutical treatments quickly overshadowed the proven effectiveness of noninvasive light therapy. World War II, with its demand for fast and power-ful pharmaceuticals, led to an era of total pharmaceutical dominance. Light therapy was ignored by the medical establishment that had previously seen it as a miracle cure.

However, students of Dinshah and Spitler continued their re-search in the 1950s, '60s, and '70s. Then the breakthroughs of the Brain Revolution enabled scientists to see and measure the extraordinary impact of light on the human system. This stimulated increasing inves-tigations of light and color and, in recent years, the development of new techniques and devices for delivering light and color into the brain.

THE LUMATRON

Among the recently developed light-color therapy devices is the Luma-tron. Invented by John Downing, O.D., Ph.D., the Lumatron uses xenon gas as a full-spectrum light source. The light is passed through one of eleven color filters that can be changed easily during viewing, producing eleven different colors, ranging from violet, indigo, and blue on one end of the spectrum, to red-orange, red, and ruby on the other. The colored light is then delivered to the user's eyes through a circular lens about the size of a half dollar. According to Downing:

> The proper color stimulus will precisely reset the biological clock and entrain more balanced hypothalamic discharge rates. This in turn helps balance the neuroendocrine system. . . . It also increases the efficiency of the optic nerve and associated nerve pathways allowing the brain to naturally assimilate more vital light energy from the environment. The brain reacts to this additional photoelectric en-ergy by forming new synaptic connections and increasing its effi-ciency.

Another device, the Color Receptivity Trainer (discussed at the end of this chapter), seems to have effects equivalent to the Lumatron.

The Lumatron and the Color Receptivity Trainer deliver the colors in rhythmic pulsations and they are seen as flickers. As re-searcher Steven Vazquez, Ph.D., observes, "the flicker rate often has as profound an effect as the different colors." The flicker rate can be varied from 1 Hz to over 60 Hz. In practice, each different color is delivered at an appropriate frequency.

A short series of tests determines what color will be most effective for each subject. Once this determination has been made, the subject sits in a darkened room or under a special hood and stares into the device as it emits the proper waveband of colored light, which is focused directly on the retina.

Most users report profound perceptual, mental, and emotional experiences during sessions. In my own experience, the round bright flickering lens seems to change sizes and shapes, the colors flow and shift, emotions arise and can be discharged, and the mind seems to operate with extraordinary clarity and power.

For therapeutic purposes, Downing has found that most people require about three to five twenty-minute sessions per week, for a total of twenty to sixty sessions, to effect a long-lasting and perhaps permanent change in the hypothalamic set-point. However, the effects can be rapid and dramatic, as C. Norman Shealy discovered in a recent study.

PUMPING OUT HORMONES

Shealy measured levels of neurochemicals and hormones in subjects before and then ten minutes after a single twenty-minute exposure to violet, green, or red lights, at a frequency of 7.8 Hz. He found that the exposure produced "significant increases of 25% or more" of such key hormones as growth hormone (which promotes growth and increases fat metabolism), luteinizing hormone (which stimulates male and female sexual hormones and organs, and increases sexual arousal), and oxytocin (which promotes affection, love, and bonding behavior) as well as significant increases of serotonin, beta-endorphin, and other biochemicals. Shealy tested one individual at a frequency of 31.2 Hz (4 times 7.8) and found that the increases in growth hormone (GH), luteinizing hormone (LH), and oxytocin "were significantly more substantial than they had been in the same individual at 7.8 cycles."

Shealy concluded, among other things, that his findings "unequivocally suggest that the *color of light significantly* affects the neurochemical axis."

While Shealy's study shows immediate neurochemical changes, the most dramatic effects seem to take place cumulatively, over a period of twenty or more sessions. One woman I spoke to had suffered from a lifelong learning disability—her brain seemed to rattle along at such a rapid clip she found it impossible to slow her thoughts down enough to focus attention on printed words. After undergoing a series of sessions on the Lumatron, staring at violet light at a frequency of about 8 Hz, she became progressively more calm and focused. Most important to her, she became able to read. She was soon devouring books. "It's like a whole new world," she told me. "I keep thinking that this world of books and reading is one I've been missing my whole life."

This woman had clearly been suffering from a chronic overarousal of her autonomic nervous system. Many subjects suffering from *under*arousal, experienced as depression, chronic fatigue, learning disabilities, have experienced increases in energy and IQ and elevations in mood after receiving light stimulation in such colors as yellow, yellow-orange, orange, red-orange, red, and ruby at frequencies from 12 to 15 Hz or higher.

One recent controlled clinical study by psychotherapist Jill Ammon-Wexler, Ph.D., has produced strong evidence that light-color therapy is effective in the treatment of phobias. Clinically, she found that "some remarkable resolution of the subjects' phobic systems had occurred over the process of the twenty experimental sessions. There was also 'across the board' evidence for enhanced self-concept, and clinically-significant reductions in both anxiety and depression."

Another recently completed study by Carol J. Rustigan, a learning disability specialist at California State University, Sacramento, has produced evidence that twenty sessions on the Lumatron boost memory, reading speed, reading comprehension, and other cognitive abilities in adults with learning disorders.

A study by Houston EEG researcher Robert Boustany found that the Lumatron improved synchrony and brain-wave amplitude in both hemispheres.

Reports by scores of medical professionals around the world indicate that the Lumatron has an extraordinary range of effects. It has been used with repeated success in treating such varied conditions as allergies, anxiety, asthma, color blindness, deafness, depression (including manic-depression), epilepsy, fatigue, insomnia, migraine, pain, premenstrual syndrome, skin problems, stroke, and much more.

While the use of the Lumatron for therapeutic purposes is important, the device produces dramatic improvements in cognition and mind-body coordination in relatively healthy individuals. I have received reports of improvements in learning ability, reading speed and comprehension, mathematical ability, memory, attention span, concentration, creativity, visual memory, color and depth perception, peripheral vision, night vision, immune response, hand-eye coordination, athletic performance, balance, and much more.

INTO THE DISCOMFORT ZONE

Jacob Liberman, O.D., Ph.D, author of the excellent book *Light: Medicine of the Future,* has found that specific colors can act therapeutically by triggering the release of "toxic" memories or past experiences. Liberman has developed a technique to discover what colors his patients find most disturbing or uncomfortable, noting that "the disturbing colors seemed to represent, or in some way be related to, painful experiences in patients' lives." Liberman arranges the colors for treatment from the least disturbing to the most disturbing, and then moves the patient gently into progressively more disturbing colors. As he does so, deeper and more painful issues surface and are released.

CONSUMERS' GUIDE TO LIGHT AND COLOR TECHNOLOGY

LIGHT-ONLY SYSTEMS

To purchase or obtain further information about any of the devices and lights described below, write: Megabrain, P.O. Box 2744, Sausalito, CA 94966, or call 1-800-456-9887. As a result of his discovery of the crucial importance of full-spectrum light, John Ott began work in the 1960s to develop effective full-spectrum light systems. After helping create the *Vita-lite full-spectrum fluorescent*, he went on to devise the current *Ott Energy System* lights. These full-spectrum fluorescent lamps include a separate ultraviolet lamp, which can be easily replaced when it burns out. (In other full-spectrum lights on the market, the UV source burns out after a limited number of hours while the bulb continues to function. This leads users to think they're still getting full-spectrum light, when in fact a key component is absent.)

All fluorescent lights emit radio waves, and the cathodes (at each end of the fluorescent tube) emit low-level X-rays. Ott has solved this problem by shielding the ends of the cathodes with lead and screening the radio waves with a silver, silk-screened grid of ultraviolet-transmitting plastic. The entire system is then fully grounded back into the fixture. The Ott lighting systems come in a variety of sizes, ranging from portable one-foot by two-foot light boxes you can keep by your

The Ott Full Spectrum Light System, desk model
(Ott Light Systems, Inc.)

computer or as reading or work lights, to large recessed ceiling fixtures. The table unit costs about $295. Newly developed are the smaller Ott Task Lamp ($99) and the Ott Capsulite (which replaces 100 watt incandescent bulbs but uses less energy, lasts ten times longer than ordinary incandescents, and is shielded against cathode radiation; the cost is about $40).

Other full-spectrum light systems include the *Verilux* fluorescents, *Medic-Light*, and the *Vita-Lite*. Full-spectrum fluorescent tubes can be installed in your existing fluorescent fixtures. Be sure the light is not shielded behind glass diffusers (which cut off UV waves)—use UV-transmitting diffusers or no diffuser at all. These fluorescent fixtures emit X rays, but you can eliminate that problem very simply by covering the cathodes (at the ends of the tubes) with plain lead-impregnated tape (available from 3M Corp.). Jacob Liberman also recommends converting your system from AC to DC to eliminate the 60 Hz flicker of fluorescent lights or, if that's not possible, using an electronic ballast. This increases the cycles from 60 to 25,000 and reduces the flickering.

LIGHT AND COLOR SYSTEMS

The Lumatron, developed by John Downing, has been the subject of a substantial amount of research, some of it explored in the text. Currently it's available only in clinical models that cost $6,000 and over, though a portable unit is under development. A worldwide network of therapists, educators, and health professionals use the Lumatron. Jacob Liberman, who has designed the *Color Receptivity Trainer* (CRT), says, "I have designed the Color Receptivity Trainer as a non-medical, educational tool to assist the user in becoming equally receptive to all the different portions of the visible spectrum." The CRT is portable (it weighs under ten pounds and its dimensions are nine by nine by eight inches), but provides fourteen clinically researched and evaluated color filters, so that you can project color on an entire body or parts of the body, or view the color directly with your eyes. It has a variable flash rate with a digital display, so the colors can be projected with or without the flicker effect. Much of what I have written about the Lumatron is applicable to the CRT. It costs about $1,800.

The Stress Shield is an inexpensive (under $150) if limited color system. It consists of a pair of goggles with adjustable foam eyecups that fit over each eye, blocking out external light, while they envelop each eye with a field of diffused, uniform color (limited to red, green, or yellow). You simply put on the goggles, switch on the light, and relax with your eyes open, gazing into a field of unvarying color. This diffuse color field produces a ganzfeld effect, which is described at greater length in Chapter 12.

The Color Receptivity Trainer
(Jacob Liberman, O.D., Ph.D.)

The *Relaxmate* was designed by Dr. Shealy after extensive clinical tests. It's extremely simple—everything is contained in the goggles. They look like heavy sunglasses, with a single LED over each eye. You adjust the frequency with a dial on one corner of the glasses. No sound component. Cost is about $50.

Shakti Lights consist of seven light bulbs, each one producing a pure color with all-natural pigments (red, orange, gold, green, blue, indigo, violet). The bulbs can be used in ordinary fixtures and are excellent for color therapy, meditation, and mood alteration. The bulbs also can be used in the *Infinity Lamp*, which employs a flat, rounded screen to diffuse colored light for subtle effects in room lighting. The set of seven lights costs about $40; the Infinity Lamp $38.

SUGGESTED READING

An excellent introduction to light is *Light: Medicine of the Future* by Jacob Liberman, O.D., Ph.D. (Santa Fe: Bear & Co. 1991). See also *Health and Light* by John Ott (Devin-Adair Co., 1981); *Let There Be Light* by Darius Dinshah (Malaga, NJ: Dinshah Health Society, 1985); *The Medical and Biological Effects of Light* by Richard Wurt-

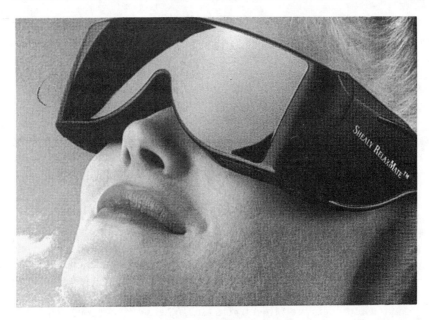

The Relaxmate
(Tools for Exploration)

man, Michael Baum, and John T. Potts, Jr. (New York: New York Academy of Sciences, 1985); and *The World of Light, Color, Health and Behavior*, a multitape and book combination by Gary Trexler, Ph.D. (Boulder, CO: 1985).

EIGHT

THE TECHNICOLOR SYMPHONY:
ORCHESTRATING YOUR BRAIN WITH LIGHT AND SOUND

Anthropologists tell of how chimpanzees trek long distances to sit gazing entranced at sunlight flashing off a waterfall. These tales suggest to me that from our most ancient origins, humans have enjoyed exploring the way a flickering light can cause mysterious visual hallucinations and alterations in consciousness. Humans have probably attempted to control these flickers since the discovery of fire. Ancient shamans and poets used the powers and images of flickering flames to enhance their magic.

Ancient scientists explored the practical applications of flickering light. In A.D. 125 Apuleius experimented with the flickering light produced by the rotation of a potter's wheel and found it could be used to diagnose a type of epilepsy. Around A.D. 200 Ptolemy noted that when he placed a spinning spoked wheel between an observer and the sun, the flickering of the sunlight through the spokes of the wheel could cause patterns and colors to appear before the observer's eyes and could produce a feeling of euphoria. At the turn of the century, French psychologist Pierre Janet noticed that when patients at the Saltpêtrière Hospital in Paris were exposed to flickering lights, they experienced reductions in hysteria and increases in relaxation.

Modern scientific research into the effects of rhythmic light and sound began in the mid-1930s when scientists discovered that the electrical rhythms of the brain tended to assume the rhythm of a flashing light stimulus, a process called entrainment. For example, when they flashed a strobe light at a frequency of 10 Hz into the eyes of a subject monitored by an electroencephalogram (EEG), the subject's brain waves tended to fall into a 10 Hz frequency.

During World War II a radar technician named Sidney Schneider was fascinated by the effects of the rhythmic light flashes on radar operators, who tended to drop into altered states while gazing at the radar screen. He then went on to develop the first commercial/medical device specifically designed to entrain brain-wave activity. First manufactured in the late 1940s, this device, called the Brainwave Synchronizer, was essentially a variable-frequency strobe. It is still marketed and in wide use around the world as an aid to hypnotherapy.

Research shifted into high gear in the late 1940s when the great British neuroscientist W. Gray Walter used an electronic strobe and advanced EEG equipment to investigate what he called the "flicker phenomenon." He found that rhythmic flashing lights quickly altered brain-wave activity, producing trancelike states of profound relaxation and vivid mental imagery. He was also startled to find that the flickering seemed to alter the brain-wave activity of the whole cortex instead of just the areas associated with vision. Wrote Walter: "The rhythmic series of flashes appear to be breaking down some of the physiologic barriers between different regions of the brain. This means the stimulus of flicker received by the visual projection area of the cortex was breaking bounds—its ripples were overflowing into other areas." The subjective experiences of those receiving the flashes were even more intriguing: "Subjects reported lights like comets, ultra-unearthly colors, mental colors, not deep visual ones."

Walter's research aroused the attention of many artists, including the American novelist William Burroughs, who put together a simple flicker device called the Dreammachine. As Burroughs described it in the 1960s:

> Subjects report dazzling lights of unearthly brilliance and color. . . . Elaborate geometric constructions of incredible intricacy build up from multidimensional mosaic into living fireballs like the mandalas of Eastern mysticism or resolve momentarily into apparently individual images and powerfully dramatic scenes like brightly colored dreams.

A flood of subsequent scientific research in the 1960s and '70s revealed that such flicker effects at certain frequencies seemed to have amazing powers. Various scientists discovered that such photic stimulation could have a variety of beneficial effects, such as increasing IQ scores, enhancing intellectual functioning, and producing greater synchronization between the two hemispheres of the brain. Other researchers found that the addition of rhythmic auditory signals dramatically increased the mind-enhancing effects. In Chapter 7 we explored some of the wide range of clinical benefits produced by flicker devices, such as the Lumatron.

THE LIGHT FANTASTIC: FROM SHAMAN'S FIRE TO LASER WHEELS

In the last chapters we discussed sound and light separately. However, humans have always been intrigued by the possibilities for influencing mental functioning that emerge from combining rhythmic sound and rhythmic light stimulation. Ancient rituals for entering trance states often involved both rhythmic sounds in the form of drum beats, clapping, or chanting and flickering lights produced by candles, torches, bonfires, or long lines of human bodies passing before the fire and chopping the light into mesmerizing rhythmic flashes. From Greek plays to Western opera, our most popular entertainment forms have made use of combinations of lights and sounds. Some composers, such as the visionary Scriabin, actually created music intended to be experienced in combination with rhythmic light displays.

Technological advances made possible even more powerful combinations of sound and light. Moving pictures developed soundtracks, and moviemakers exploited the potentials of sound to enhance the power of the flickering images onscreen. Movies from *Gone With the Wind* and *The Wizard of Oz,* to the *Star Wars* epics became true audio-visual experiences in which the rhythmic soundtrack was fused with the flickering light and the rhythmic flickering of montage editing techniques to create alterations in the audience's consciousness that would have been impossible using only sound or only light. The interplay of electronically amplified musical instruments with stroboscopic psychedelic light shows that what took place in the rock concerts of the 1960s could produce rapid and profound alterations in consciousness.

In the early 1970s Jack Schwarz, known for his feats of self-healing and self-regulation, began selling a device known as the ISIS, which used variable-frequency lights mounted in goggles combined with rhythmic sounds to produce heightened mental states. Since then increasingly sophisticated variable-frequency light and sound (LS) devices, have been developed.

LIGHT AND SOUND BREAKTHROUGHS

By the 1980s the time was right for a breakthrough in the combination of sound and light. The catalyst was the revolution in microelectronics, a revolution that allowed home electronics buffs and garage inventors to put together astonishingly sophisticated and complex LS devices using microchip technology. These computerized devices incorporated sound synthesizers to produce a rich assortment of tones, chords, and even beat frequencies. They developed computerlike "programming" capacities that permitted the user to choose one of a number of preset "sessions" designed to produce specific states of consciousness, ranging from sleep, to meditation, to extreme alertness, at the push of a button. By 1990 these devices had emerged as popular consumer electronics items, sold through catalogs and stores such as Sharper Image and Hammacher Schlemmer.

As with personal computers (PCs), new advances, new machines, and new generations of older devices appear almost constantly; and as with PCs, the advances have included smaller size, greater versatility and power, and steep reductions in price. As this is written, there are well over forty LS machines in commercial production around the world, and a new generation of devices is emerging. These new devices can "download" programs into the system's memory from some external source or to link the system to a compact disc (CD) player, so that sounds embedded in the compact disc activate complex LS sessions. They also can combine LS stimulation with EEG biofeedback capabilities. In the new LS-EEG devices, the machine reads the user's dominant brain-wave activity and then provides the optimal frequency of LS to entrain brain-wave activity toward the "target" frequency. Several such devices are now on the market and seeing increasing clinical use for treatment of learning disorders, anxiety, depression, and drug addiction, among others.

Another significant development is the advent of LS systems on a simple board that can be plugged into your computer's expansion slot or serial port. These boards permit users to program hundreds of sessions of almost any length and complexity.

Still other LS systems are being packaged in combination with cranial electro-stimulation (CES), so that the user receives pulsed electrical microcurrent stimulation at the same frequency as the LS stimulation.

These developments point the way toward the future. Soon we will have a fully *interactive* system that will allow the user to put on a few electrodes to monitor EEG as well as other physiological indicators and display them on the computer screen in real time. The system will monitor and analyze this information constantly to provide as feedback the optimal type of LS stimulation (as well as CES and appropriate digitized binaural beats, high-frequency signals, music selections or preprogrammed audio subliminal or peripheral suggestions, hypnotic inductions, information for accelerated learning, and so on). The system will store thousands of sessions, with individual users able to select desired mind states or experiences as easily as selecting a TV channel, or play back and reexperience past sessions. The technology for such a system is already available. That means it is already outmoded, at least in the mind of the inventors. The *real* future LS system will surely move in directions outside my ability to predict.

SOUND AND LIGHT RESEARCH

It has been well established over the last fifty years of research that these LS devices rapidly can produce states of deep relaxation, may increase suggestibility and receptivity to new information, and may enhance access to subconscious material. Recent evidence from around the world indicates that the machines are beneficial in the treatment of migraine headaches and learning disorders, alleviation of pain, enhancement of immune function, and much more. Here's a summary of some of the most interesting work done in the last decade.

BRAIN-WAVE ENTRAINMENT

California psychologist Julian Isaacs, Ph.D., working with a private research group called The Other 90 Percent, studied the brain-wave effects of LS devices using an advanced brain-mapping EEG. They found "very clear evidence of brainwave driving" as well as a very strong correlation between the intensity of the lights used (whether red light emitting diodes [LEDs] or incandescent bulbs) and the brain entrainment: the brighter the lights, the more entrainment.

STIMULATING NEUROCHEMICALS

Research by Dr. C. Norman Shealy and others shows that light stimulation alone (with the Lumatron and simple red LED goggles) and LS devices can increase levels of a variety of neurochemicals and hormones, including endorphins and growth hormones. This may explain many of the benefits noted by users, ranging from alleviation of stress, anxiety, depression and pain, to increased mental alertness and memory.

GATEWAY TO THE UNCONSCIOUS

Dr. Thomas Budzynski has made extensive clinical use of LS devices, and notes that the effects range "from production of drowsy, hypnagogic-like states (with theta frequency used), to vivid, holograph-like images. At times, images from childhood were experienced." This leads Budzynski to speak of the device as a "Hypnotic Facilitator" and a "Facilitator of Unconscious Retrieval" that has immense therapeutic value, since the device seems "to allow the subject to recall past childhood events with a high degree of 'being there' quality." He also finds LS devices effective for accelerated learning, since they can put users in the theta (or "twilight state") of hypersuggestibility and heightened receptivity to new information.

DEEP RELAXATION

Dr. Norman Thomas and his associate David Siever, at the University of Alberta, gave a group of experimental subjects LS stimulation at an alpha frequency for fifteen minutes, while they were being monitored for muscle tension, using an electromyograph (EMG), and for finger temperature. A control group, similarly monitored, was asked simply to relax, without any LS devices, for the same fifteen minutes. Significantly, both the experimental group and the control group were what the researchers called "resistant" or "non-hypnotisable" subjects.

While the control subjects stated that they believed they were very relaxed, the EMG and finger temperature monitors showed that they were actually experiencing *increased* amounts of muscle tension and decreases in finger temperature (associated with tension or stress). On the other hand, the LS group showed dramatic increases in relaxation, reaching profound relaxation states that continued for long periods after the fifteen minutes of LS. The researchers wrote: "It appears that audio-visual stimulation offers a simple hypnotic device in otherwise resistant subjects."

RELAXATION FOR SEDATION

In 1988 anesthesiologist Robert Cosgrove Jr., Ph.D., M.D., undertook preliminary studies of LS. In his initial evaluations, Cosgrove, an authority in pharmaceutics and biomedical engineering, noted that LS was "clearly very powerful in its ability to cause deep relaxation in most subjects. Its effectiveness has been so great that we are very enthusiastic about the prospect of evaluating the [device] for its sedative properties in patients prior to, during, and immediately following surgery. We are also undertaking studies to prove [its] utility in chronic stress."

NEURO-PATHWAY EXERCISER

Cosgrove noted that LS

with appropriately selected stimulation protocols has been observed by us to be an excellent neuropathway exerciser. As such we believe it has great potential for use in promoting optimal cerebral perform- ance. . . . Furthermore, the long-term effects of regular use of the device on maintaining and improving cerebral performance through- out life and possibly delaying for decades the deterioration of the brain traditionally associated with aging is very exciting.

INCREASED CREATIVITY AND MENTAL FLEXIBILITY

Medical researcher Dr. Gene W. Brockopp has speculated that LS could "actively induce a state of deactivation in which the brain is passive, but not asleep; awake, but not involved with the 'clutter' of an ongoing existence. If this is true, then it may be a state in which new cognitive strategies could be designed and developed." Brockopp also suggested that

If we can help a person to experience different brain-wave states consciously through driving them with external stimulation, we may facilitate the individuals' ability to allow more variations in their functioning through breaking up patterns at the neural level. This may help them develop the ability to shift gears or "shuttle" and move them away from habit patterns of behavior to become more flexible and creative, and to develop more elegant strategies of functioning.

MIGRAINE RELIEF

Light stimulation (through red LED goggles) was used to treat seven sufferers of migraine headaches—none of whom had been able to find relief with drug treatments. Out of fifty migraines studied, forty-nine were rated by subjects as being "helped" and thirty-six were stopped by the photic stimulation. Significantly, brighter lights were found to be more effective.

CHRONIC PAIN

Frederick Boesma and Constance Gagnon of the University of Alberta's Department of Educational Psychology studied the effects of regular LS on three chronic pain patients over periods of nine to seventeen months. At the outset of the study all three individuals experienced much pain and stress caused by the disabling and psychological effects of their pain, to the point that two of them were seriously contemplating suicide. But over the course of the study each subject showed significant reductions in pain and required less medication. The effect of LS did not diminish with time but actually improved in effectiveness with use. Consistent LS usage seemed to be associated with lower pain levels, easier sleep, and improved handling of stress. Long-term usage seemed to reduce and then abolish the incidence of suicidal thoughts. The patients also reported that learning how to use LS gave them greater control over their lives.

RELIEF OF ANXIETY AND STRESS.

Dr. Juan Abascal and Dr. Laurel Brucato have conducted several LS studies (including studies of officers of the Metro-Dade Police Department) at Mindworks, a Miami psychotherapy and stress reduction center. Results indicate that LS significantly reduces stress symptoms such as heart rate, blood pressure, muscle tension, and both state and trait anxiety (state anxiety measures the level of anxiety experienced at the time the research is conducted, while trait anxiety measures the disposition of individuals to experience anxiety, and is generally fairly stable over time).

ENHANCED IMMUNE FUNCTION?

William Harris, M.D., director of the Penwell Foundation, an organization for the investigation, research, and application of different modalities for the treatment of those with AIDS/HIV, has experimented with LS devices and found them extremely effective. He speculates that LS devices may boost immune function by producing states of deep relaxation, by enhancing the patients' receptivity to suggestions for healing and improving their ability to visualize and the clarity of their visualizations. "At this point it's conjecture," says Harris, "but I think that this type of machine may actually be stimulating . . . the body to produce its own chemical substances," and that these natural substances may enhance immune function and healing.

LEARNING DISORDERS

A variety of research and clinical work has demonstrated beyond doubt that by speeding up brain-wave activity into the beta range, LS machines can produce dramatic increases in IQ and in fact affect the entire personality. For a discussion of this work, see Chapter 30.

ECSTASY AND SAMADHI

In 1990 Bruce Harrah-Conforth, Ph.D., of Indiana University, found that compared to the control group, which listened to relaxing sounds with eyes closed, a group receiving LS stimulation showed dramatic alterations in their EEG patterns responding to the frequency of the LS device and also showed evidence of hemispheric synchronization. Harrah-Conforth suggests that LS devices may cause simultaneous *ergotropic arousal,* or arousal of the sympathetic nervous system and the cerebral cortex, associated with "creative" and "ecstatic experiences," and *trophotropic arousal,* or the arousal of the parasympathetic system, associated with deep relaxation and "the timeless, 'oceanic' mode of the mystic experience." In humans, Harrah-Conforth concludes, "these two states may be interpreted as hyper- and hypo-arousal, or ecstasy and samadhi."

CONSUMERS' GUIDE TO
LIGHT/SOUND DEVICES

Is there ever too much of a good thing? It's hard to imagine. But for many potential purchasers of light/sound machines, it may seem that way. It's a bit like purchasing your first (or your next) computer—there are so many of them out there! But most buyers find that they are able to select the right machine for their purposes using virtually the same criteria as computer purchasers: size (is portability important?), cost, power, capacity for running a variety of programs, ease of operation.

Today LS devices are the most popular of the new brain tools.

They consist of a console about the size of a paperback book (some as small as a deck of cards), into which are plugged stereo headphones and goggles that position tiny lights (in most cases they are red LEDs) in front of each eye. When the machine is turned on, the user hears sound patterns that pulse in rhythm with the stroboscopic flickering of the lights.

The machines range in sophistication from devices that permit you to create and store hundreds of intricate sound and light programs, to simple goggles that flash at a rate you adjust by turning a dial. The prices similarly vary from over $600 for the most advanced versions to under $100. Here I list the devices I've found to be the most effective. Because they range widely in cost and complexity, one key to my evaluation is which devices deliver the most bang for the buck. To purchase or obtain further information about any of the devices described below, write: Megabrain, P.O. Box 2744, Sausalito, CA 94966, or call 1-800-456-9887.

The DAVID Paradise combines the best features of small portable devices with the sophisticated programming options of the most costly systems. Cost is about $595. Less flexible and less programmable, but also good, are the *DAVID Paradise Junior* (cost about $495) and the *DAVID 2001* (cost about $295), in which all the controls are integrated into the headphones.

The *MindsEye Synergizer* is the best computer-linked system. Plug it into your PC, and you can use a mouse with a Windows-like graphical interface to create and store hundreds of sessions of almost

The DAVID Paradise
(David Siever)

any length and complexity. The capacity for creating complex binaural beats allows you to play it almost like a musician would play a keyboard. The cost is about $595.

The *Photosonix Galaxy* offers superb preset programs (just press a button and the machine does the rest) and also permits the creation and storage of personalized sessions. This is the best in this price range—cost is about $295.

The *MindLab DLS with PolySync* is simple, attractive, and very user-friendly. It's superb for technophobes. The "download" feature allows you to feed numerous custom-designed sessions into the device from an audiotape. It costs about $295. An identical system without the download capacity, the *Mindlab DLS*, goes for about $230.

The *Mind Gear SLX* is unique among inexpensive systems in providing both manual control and sixteen preset programs playable at four different time settings (giving you in effect sixty-four different presets). This system gives maximum flexibility at a minimum price—cost is about $150.

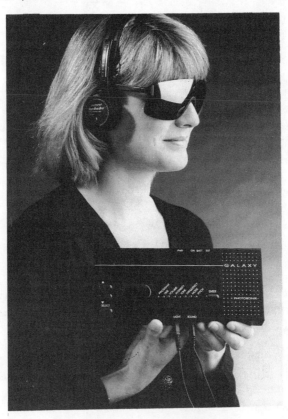

The Photosonix Galaxy
(Tools for Exploration)

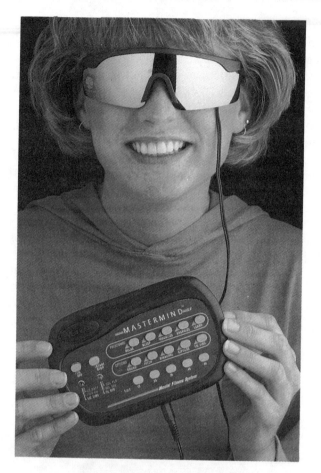

The Mastermind DLS
(Tools for Exploration)

SUGGESTED READING

A good introduction to LS is *Megabrain Report: Special Light and Sound Issue* 1 (2) (1991), which includes reviews of over twenty devices, interviews with leading manufacturers and researchers, and a survey of LS research. For creating sophisticated LS programs, see *Awakening Mind: Programming Advanced Light & Sound Sessions* by James Mann (Enlightened Enterprises, 1992). Therapists and others interested in using LS for therapeutic applications should see *Clinical Guide to Light and Sound* by Thomas Budzynski, Ph.D. (Seattle, WA: Synetic Systems, 1991).

NINE

ELECTRIC BRAIN POWER:
RECHARGING THE BATTERIES

Beth was given anesthesia when she gave birth to her first baby and later found that she had lost part of her memory. She was forced to give up her job in an aerospace plant. Years later a friend gave her a small cranial electrostimulation (CES) device and she began using it. "Almost overnight," she said, "all my memories started coming back, including everyone's telephone extensions at the plant. It was uncanny—all these old extension numbers of people I hadn't thought of in years."

This story, told to me by researcher Bob Beck, Ph.D., provides graphic evidence of a key fact: We have electric-powered brains. Each of the billions of neurons in our brains is a tiny electrical generator, as complex as a small computer, firing an electrical signal that triggers the release of various neurochemicals and links it with thousands of other neurons. Consciousness itself is now thought to be a product of the synchronous electronic firing of complex networks of neurons. "The brain is like a Christmas tree with 10 billion electric candles," says Dr. Christof Koch, a neuroscientist at the California Institute of Technology. "When we pay attention, 10,000 synchronize and flicker all at once for 100 milliseconds. Then they desynchronize and the next 10,000 come on." In addition to the neurons, the brain contains glial cells—perhaps ten times as many as neurons—that are organized and communicate by generating, transmitting, and amplifying electrical signals.

Since all our thoughts and perceptions consist of the interactions of complex networks of electrical currents that stream across the brain, it makes sense that electrical stimulation of the brain can have powerful effects on our mental state and on brain functioning.

We have already discussed how stimuli such as light and sound can act as nutrients to the brain. We have already seen how light and sound can have profound energizing, healing effects by stimulating the brain's electrical activity. Light, falling on the photoreceptors of the eye, is translated into electrical impulses, which then stimulate the entire brain via the visual cortex and the hypothalamus. Sound, stimulating the nerve endings in the ear, is translated into electrical impulses, which then stimulate the brain via the vestibular system, cerebellum, limbic system, and cortex. But there is a more direct way to send electrical impulses into the brain: Use the same rhythmic pulsations of electricity that power the brain cells themselves. If light and sound are nutrients that enrich the brain with their electrical impulses, then surely the electrical impulses themselves, if delivered in the proper form and at the proper intensity, must be like the purest nutrient.

There is evidence that this kind of direct stimulation of the neurons has a profound optimizing and normalizing effect on brain functioning. Or, in the words of leading CES researcher Dr. Ray Smith, "I think CES probably just puts the brain back to normal homeostasis—the way it was born to be."

For many years CES has been widely used as a treatment for alleviating anxiety, depression, insomnia, and the anhedonia (or inability to experience pleasure) and discomfort that accompanies withdrawal from drugs or alcohol. But recent breakthroughs have revealed that CES seems to have even more profound benefits.

BETTER LEARNING THROUGH ELECTRICITY

CES can dramatically enhance *cognitive* functioning in a variety of ways. One recent study by Dr. Daniel Kirsch and Dr. Richard Madden of the City University of Los Angeles showed that subjects receiving CES while given a learning task learned more and showed more concentration and alertness than a control group.

Other studies of subjects suffering cognitive deficits caused by brain damage showed that CES treatments not only improved cognitive functioning but in fact *reversed* the brain damage that caused the cognitive deficits in the first place. Dr. Smith, who conducted this research, believes it suggests that CES can increase brain functioning for all of us by selectively stimulating parts of the brain that are not functioning at peak capacity.

In recent studies of patients suffering from "attention-to-task deficits," impaired short-term memory, and other learning disabilities as a result of head injuries, those receiving CES treatment had "striking and significant improvement" in such areas as mental speed, visual and auditory perception, concentration, and short-term memory.

PERSONALITY TRANSFORMATION

Even more fascinating is the increasing evidence that CES, when used systematically over several weeks, can produce *personality transformations*. In one controlled study, subjects receiving CES as part of therapy for drug addiction showed dramatic personality changes. These subjects more than doubled and in some cases even tripled their scores in such areas as self-sufficiency, ego strength, and dominance or assertiveness. (Members of the control group, which didn't receive CES, showed no such changes.)

Scientists are still uncertain exactly how CES increases memory, learning, and other cognitive functions and influences personality, though they propose a number of mechanisms. CES seems to act directly on the neurons to stimulate the release of neuropeptides, such as the endorphins, and other neurochemicals, such as norepinephrine and dopamine, associated with memory, learning, and other cognitive functions.

ATTENTION AND CONCENTRATION

CES also seems to increase alertness and concentration—perhaps through its effect on the reticular activating system (the part of the brain that determines our arousal level and our state of alertness and attention). In the study by Kirsh and Madden, human subjects given a learning task improved when stimulated with CES. Over repeated trials, the control group showed decreases in learning, probably as a result of loss of concentration and boredom. The group receiving CES, however, continued to learn more and more with each trial, maintaining concentration and alertness. Perhaps the electrical stimulation acted on the reticular activating system in such a way that it continued to maintain alertness and direct attention to a task that it would otherwise have soon become habituated to and directed attention away from. This suggests that CES may help increase concentration and alertness by gently turning up the volume control knob in the brain and adjusting the fine-tuning.

Researchers also point out that CES directly stimulates the autonomic nervous system, activating the parasympathetic nervous system where necessary to trigger the "relaxation response" electrically.

Increasingly, investigators believe CES has pronounced effects on the whole-body bioelectric system, the "body electric" that has been illuminated by researchers such as Robert O. Becker. This still little-understood semiconducting DC communication system links and regulates every cell in the human body, functioning independently of the better-understood, nerve-impulse–operated "central" nervous system.

OPTIMIZING BRAIN FUNCTIONS

Smith suspects that CES has its wide variety of benefits not by stimulating specific parts of the brain, but by a more general optimizing effect on the whole brain. Smith compares the effects of CES to recharging a battery that has six cells in it, with one of them nearly dry. "If you put water in it and then let it sit, it can take forever for it to come back up to charge, if it ever does come all the way back up. On the other hand, put water and a trickle charge in there, and you simply get it functioning up to its normal level again. It's just as good as any of the others, even though it was totally dead or nearly so when you began. . . ." The electrical charge stimulates only the cell that is not functioning well, Smith suggests, while it has no effect on the other cells that are still charged. "Parts of the brain typically control each other in the homeostatic relationship. When one part of the brain is not functioning well, another part can become too strong and the whole thing's out of balance. My thought is that CES goes in to the weaker part, picks it back up and makes it as healthy and strong as the one that had the upper hand before."

PUMPING BRAIN CHEMICALS

A variety of studies have shown that CES has immediate and powerful effects in increasing levels of beta endorphin, serotonin, adrenocorticotropic hormone (ACTH), norepinephrine, and cholinesterase. Researchers have found CES effective in the treatment of depression, and suspect that its strong influence on these neurochemicals may be one explanation for its antidepressant effect. One researcher, Dr. C. Norman Shealy, has used the CES for the treatment of chronic depression and found it effective in 45 to 50 percent of all his cases when used alone. When used in combination with other brain-stimulation techniques, Shealy has found "we can increase that resolution of depression up to 70%."

Shealy's research also suggests the CES is extremely effective in the treatment of insomnia and jet lag. Other CES research has shown it to be effective in treatment of pain, headache, migraine, spasticity reduction and parkinsonism, treatment of learning disabilities, facilitation of sensory integration and fine-motor coordination, and treatment of children with cerebral palsy.

CONSUMERS' GUIDE TO CES DEVICES

CAVEAT. Is CES truly safe enough to be used by healthy people for mind-enhancement purposes? Proponents point out that CES has been scientifically studied for over forty years. They state that it has been used by millions of people without apparent ill effects. Opponents argue that in light of evidence that some kinds of electromagnetism can be harmful, there's still not enough known about how CES works, what it does to the brain and body, to pronounce such devices harmless. NOTE: Ordinary TENS (transcutaneous electro-neural stimulation) devices, used widely for the treatment of pain, are not meant for CES. To purchase or obtain further information about CES or any of the devices described below, write: Megabrain, P.O. Box 2744, Sausalito, CA 94966, or call 1-800-456-9887.

I have found the following devices most effective.

The Liss Cranial Stimulator has been the subject of much research and has been proven effective in treatment of pain, anxiety, insomnia, and depression and in producing profound alterations in such neurochemicals as serotonin, beta-endorphin, norepinephrine, and dopamine. It has a complex waveform, containing a 15,000 Hz square-wave carrier modulated by a 500 Hz signal and a 15 Hz signal. This medical device is available by prescription or to any licensed health care practitioner. If purchased with a prescription, it may be covered by medical insurance. (Insurance reimbursement code is 00740; 07685 for P.I.P./ Worker's Compensation.) Cost is about $795.

The *Alpha Stim 100* is the latest of the Alpha Stim line created by Dr. Daniel Kirsch. It provides a variety of frequency settings with a complex waveform, is very easy to use (simply clip one electrode to

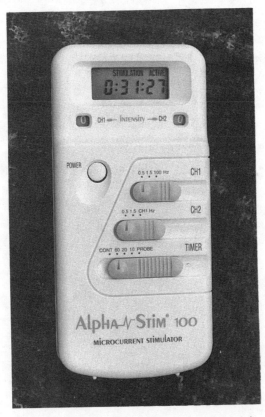

The Alpha Stim 100
(Electromedical Products International, Inc.)

each earlobe), and has proven effective in a variety of clinical tests. Like the Liss Cranial Stimulator, it is a medical device. (See the above information about prescription and medical insurance requirements.) Cost is about $599.

The *CES 100HZ* is the least expensive medically approved CES device. It delivers a 100 Hz frequency. Cost is about $399.

The *Nustar II* functions by sending electrical signals through the brain that entrain brain-wave activity to the desired frequency. Cost is about $399.

The *Brain Tuner (BT-6)* was devised by Dr. Bob Beck. It uses a complex waveform that, according to Beck, produces over 250 frequency harmonics simultaneously—"all known beneficial frequencies for the natural stimulation of the brain's neurotransmitters." Cost is about $350.

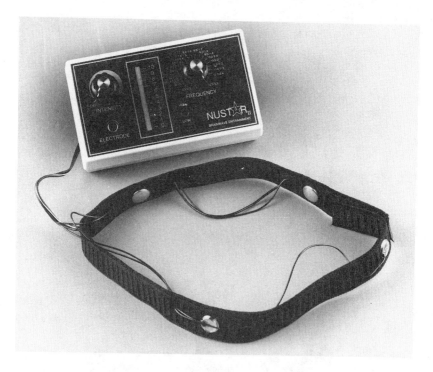

The Nustar
(Nustar)

SUGGESTED READING

A fine exploration of bioelectricity is *Cross Currents: The Promise of Electromedicine, The Perils of Electropollution*, by Robert O. Becker,

M.D. (Los Angeles: J.P. Tarcher, 1990). For a good introduction to CES, see my *Megabrain* Chapters 8 and 9. For a wide-ranging and in-depth discussion of CES, see "High Voltage: The Bioelectric Interviews, Part One—Interviews with Bob Beck, Robert O. Becker, Daniel Kirsch, and Others," *Megabrain Report* 1 (1) pp. 1–3, 10–17, 29–34, (1991), and "Supercharging the Brain: The Bioelectric Interviews, Part Two—Interview with Ray Smith," *Megabrain Report* 1 (3), (1992). Margaret Patterson's *Getting Off the Hook* (London: Harold Shaw Publishers, 1983) describes her work using CES for the treatment of drug addictions.

TEN
MOTION AND THE BRAIN

The president of a Wall Street new-technology firm—a man known for his sizzling intelligence and creativity, and who had designed some of the innovative IBM computers that helped NASA put the first men on the moon—accompanied me to a small office were he lay down on a device that revolved him steadily round and round through an electrostatic field. After fifteen minutes he called out to me. "This is wonderful! My brain is tingling! I feel like light is swirling through my brain." A few minutes later, as we rode down Riverside Drive in his limousine, he seemed deeply relaxed, his attention directed inward. Suddenly he pulled out a pencil and scribbled wildly on a sheet of paper. After a few minutes he sighed with satisfaction and turned to me. "I've just solved a problem that I have struggled with for weeks. But just now the solution came to me in a flash." Months later when I spoke with him again he assured me his insight truly was an innovative solution—one that had transformed his company, sending it into a new and profitable direction, with the development of an entirely new product.

EXERCISING THE BRAIN WITH MOTION

Another technique for supercharging the brain is physical movement, particularly spinning. Research with laboratory animals kept motionless and humans who have been immobilized has provided dramatic evidence of the crucial importance of movement to human development and mental-physical well-being. From the time of our conception, movement is an essential nutrient: Without it, the brain does not develop fully. As babies we are rocked; as kids we roll down hills and spin until we're dizzy; as adults we scuba dive, skydive, drive fast around turns, dance, and, when tired, sit in rocking chairs. This movement is not only pleasurable, but it stimulates our body and nervous system. Like light and sound, motion is a nutrient for the brain and body, and if we consistently fall short of meeting our minimum daily requirement, we become susceptible to chronic health problems.

Unfortunately, today many people are suffering from motion

deprivation. They spend most of the day with heads held upright and become couch potatoes in the evenings. Compared to healthy children and our ancestors, who were free-roaming hunters and gatherers, spending much of their time in vigorous motion, today's sedentary workers are virtually motionless, and rarely move enough to satisfy even the minimum daily requirement of motion.

One major effect of movement is that it stimulates the fluids of the inner ear, known as the vestibular system. This stimulation sends a flood of electrical impulses into our cerebellum and from there into the rest of the brain, including the pleasure and learning centers of the limbic system. This may explain the beneficial effects motion has on learning and intelligence: Motion directly stimulates learning.

MOTION SMARTNESS: BETTER GRADES THROUGH DANCING

Electroencephalograph (EEG) and other evidence has shown that the use of spinning has a profound optimizing effect on the *neuro-efficiency quotient* (NEQ), a measure of how rapidly electrical signals are transmitted by the brain's neurons and pass from one part of the brain to another—a characteristic that has been shown to correlate very closely with IQ. Recent research at Berkeley, in fact, suggests that the NEQ is directly related to IQ. Some users of motion systems have shown increases in NEQ that are statistically equivalent to increases in IQ of an astonishing thirty points or more.

This kind of evidence suggests that next time you have a test or material that requires peak mental performance, you might want to take a study break and spin around and around in your desk chair for a few minutes every half hour or so. Or get up and dance. Or, most effective of all, keep your brain in peak condition by providing enough motion to far surpass your minimum daily requirement.

Motion also affects the fluids that compose some 90 percent of our body, including cerebrospinal fluid, blood, and lymph. In other words, what vigorous or repetitive motion is doing is "massaging" the body from the inside as the fluids move about and providing an efficient form of neurological "exercise" for the nervous system.

Just as our separation from natural sounds and light has spurred the development of technological ways of producing concentrated or enhanced types of sound and light stimulation, so our sedentary lifestyle has led to the development of a variety of "motion systems" that keep the user moving constantly, providing vestibular and motion stimulation—and brain exercise—in a concentrated form.

MOVING PAST BRAIN DAMAGE

My own interest in motion systems emerges from numerous firsthand experiences of their extraordinary potential. I have described several in the introduction to this book, such as the depressed young woman who had a life-transforming encounter with her mother while on one of the systems. Others include the woman in one of my workshops who had suffered chronic back pain for twenty years and had it disappear after a session on a motion system.

When I was first doing research for the book that became *Megabrain,* I met a couple whose son was paralyzed from the neck down from carbon monoxide brain damage. On my recommendation they purchased a motion system and put him on it twenty-four hours a day. Their son was soon able to lift his head and move his arms. Recently I received a letter from the mother, with a photo of her son, who has gone through a remarkable recovery.

I have witnessed several other remarkable improvements from severe brain damage using motion systems. I'll just describe one of them. One system was installed in the hospital room of a young man who had been in a coma for many months. As he was placed on the device, his family was in the room. The change was so noticeable and rapid that his grandmother broke into tears. In the coming weeks, the young man was on the system for twelve hours a day or more. The lung congestion he had been suffering from improved dramatically. His muscle tone improved. Most interestingly, he now has his eyes open during much of the day and is capable of focusing on or watching people and movements and objects around him. As this is written, he is still improving.

CONSUMERS' GUIDE TO MOTION SYSTEMS

A number of "motion systems" are now on the market, including reclining chairs that revolve (at about 2 to 3 revolutions per minute [rpms]), and beds that gently tilt, revolve, and rock. There is evidence that these motion systems alter brain-wave activity (greatly increasing the relaxing alpha and theta waves, and enhancing hemispheric synchronization).

They are being used clinically for such purposes as treatment of brain damage, learning disabilities, and drug addiction, and are popular in brain-mind gyms around the world. Several new models at relatively low prices now make it possible for individuals to purchase such motion systems for home use.

The *Integrated Motion System* (IMS) is a moving bed that tilts gently as it revolves through a 360-degree circular rocking motion.

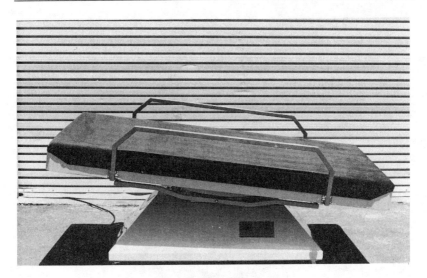

The Integrated Motion System
(Integrative Motion Systems, Inc.)

(The bed moves through a pattern 8 degrees above and below the horizontal in all four quadrants; when the head of the bed is 8 degrees below horizontal, the foot of the bed is 8 degrees above; when the right shoulder is 8 degrees below horizontal, the left foot is 8 degrees above, and so on.) The motion is fluid and slow. The bed revolves between one and six times per minute, though about 3 rpms seems to be the most effective rate. When you stretch out on it, the effect is like lying on a raft that is gently rocking on ocean waves.

Personally, I find the IMS extremely relaxing and conducive to deep trancelike states. Most users also find that for many hours, even days after a session on it, they feel energized and a sense of enhanced physical awareness. Many people find that when used in combination with a light/sound (LS) machine, cranial electrostimulation device, or a beat-frequency tape, the IMS adds a whole new kinesthetic dimension to the experience. The IMS is available on a customized basis; cost is $5,500.

Created by Dr. Larry Schulz, who also designed the Integrated Motion System, the *Symmetron* consists of a comfortable leather contour chair coupled with a variable speed "orbital platform" that revolves the chair through a "multiphase wave experience." The chair moves through a six-inch horizontal orbit (seen from above the chair remains facing in one direction while it traces a six-inch-diameter circle) while it gently tilts between 0 and 5 degrees on the vertical plane.

The movement is small but the effect is huge—most users are plunged into states of profound relaxation within minutes. One writer has called the effect "tidal weightlessness." Users who have combined

The Symmetron Chair
(Integrative Motion Systems, Inc.)

the Symmetron with a LS device have found that it intensifies the effects dramatically. Says designer Schulz, "adding the kinesthetic dimension to the LS makes it a whole new experience." The Symmetron takes up less room than the IMS (it requires no more space than any reclining chair) and costs much less. (Suggested retail is $3995.)

The name of the *Sams Potentializer* is an acronym for Sensory and Mind Stimulation, but it's also the name of the designer, medical professional Marvin W. Sams. Sams has many years of experience in clinical and research EEG and is the inventor of a variety of EEG, electrocardiograph, and other biomedical equipment.

Sams spent years monitoring the brain-wave activity of subjects using the Graham Potentializer, using a variety of EEG equipment, including the Ertl Brainwave Analyzer, that measures the neuro-efficiency Quotient (NEQ). At the same time Sams was monitoring the brain-wave pattern of advanced meditators, noting such characteristics as hemispheric dominance and brain-wave "coherence." He then designed his own device, using careful EEG analysis to determine what produced the desired physiological state—that is, the same brain-wave patterns as evidenced by highly experienced meditators.

What he came up with is a comfortable recliner chair that rotates (spins) at an almost imperceptible 1 to 3 rpms. (Sams says he tested units that rotated much more rapidly, but that the optimal brain-wave effect seems to be in this rpm range.) He combines the vestibular stimulation of spinning with what he calls "Silent Audio Frequency Electronics," an inaudible tone that is projected across the body as it rotates.

I have seen some of the EEG readings of subjects who have used the Sams Potentializer, and it's clear that the chair can produce rapid, dramatic, and long-lasting changes. Most subjects seem to show increases in slow brain-wave activity (particularly in the alpha range, associated with relaxation), enhanced NEQs and, interestingly (in light of our investigation of brain-wave synchrony in Chapter 2), *a higher degree of brain-wave coherence.* (Says Sams, coherence is "a highly desired brain-wave state that is seen only in highly experienced meditators.")

LS machines, binaural-beat tapes, and CES devices seem to gain in effectiveness when used synergistically with the Potentializer.

I recommend each of these devices, and suspect they will be especially valuable to chiropractors, physical therapists, therapists, athletes and athletic trainers, physical fitness centers, educators specializing in learning disorders, corporate relaxation programs, drug and alcohol treatment centers, brain-mind gyms, and those interested in using vestibular stimulation for the treatment of brain damage.

SUGGESTED READING

For further information about motion and motion systems, see chapter 14 of my *Megabrain* (New York: Ballantine, revised edition, 1991).

ELEVEN
SUPERCHARGING YOUR SENSES:
ACOUSTIC FIELD GENERATORS

Increasingly popular as "the ultimate mind machines" are systems that combine a variety of stimuli to provide a whole body multisensory experience, generally including lights, sound, and physical vibration. The devices are known as Whole Body Acoustic Field Generators, Sound Tables, Music Beds, and Vibro-Tactile Stimulators. As the names suggest, the key stimulus is sound—sound that is not just heard through the ears, but felt as vibrations through the whole body.

The devices range from relatively simple massage tables with powerful speakers or transducers built into them, to vast state-of-the-art computerized domelike structures that use complex and sophisticated sound-processing systems to resonate the body with optimal psychophysical impact, and incorporating music-modulated light goggles or color field video display systems that flash in sync with the music, so that you can "see" the music as well as hear and feel it, creating a state of "sensory resonance."

Some of the sound tables incorporate optional extra transducers, which can be placed under the soles of the feet, laid across the abdomen, or placed under the neck touching the shoulders, vibrating more and more of the body's surface area. The most sophisticated systems (at prices ranging from $15,000 to over $50,000) incorporate biofeedback capabilities: The system continuously monitors and "senses" your emotional-physical responses and alters the quality, loudness, and configuration of the light/sound to intensify the experience. Thus you "create" your own multisensory experience through your own mind-body state and your responses to the ongoing experience.

Researchers and practitioners who use these devices with clients report extremely powerful results, and users frequently report life-transforming or cathartic experiences while using the systems. I know by experience the profound effects such multisensory stimulation can have. I had one of these units in my office for over a year. During that time scores of visitors used it, and invariably they would emerge from their session expressing astonishment, even awe. So many people exclaimed that it was "better than sex" that the remark became an office joke.

CLINICAL REPORTS

Dr. George Fritz, biofeedback researcher and clinician who has a biofeedback clinic in Bethlehem, Pennsylvania, has conducted over 3,000 sessions on several such devices with biofeedback capabilities (including the Genesis and the Betar units) and has found them extremely effective in clinical pain control as well as for other therapeutic purposes. According to Fritz, "In my experience thus far, bioacoustic field effects feedback is the most potent and practical" of all the new technologies. "My brain-mapping data," says Fritz, "show strict correlation between brainwave changes, attentional strategy shifts, and energetic field-effects during bioacoustic feedback. With Betar the field of biofeedback can move into magnet-EEG biofeedback using bioacoustics—very powerful stuff." He concludes that this type of acoustic field effects feedback represents "the future of biofeedback interventions."

Dr. Juanita McElwain, director of music therapy at Phillips University, conducted a pilot study involving sessions on the Somatron and reports 100 percent success with complete elimination of migraine, sinus, and tension headaches.

Beth Denisch, music therapist with the Massachusetts Association for the Blind, who has used a sound table with severely developmentally delayed multihandicapped children, reports that its "ability to relax and comfort as well as enrich and enliven has made it an indispensable tool."

The Children's Cancer Center of Tampa, Florida, uses a Somatron table during painful procedures such as spinal taps and bone marrow aspirations. The bed soothes the children before and after such procedures by reducing their anxiety and distracting them from the unpleasant experience, reducing the pain medication required.

Composer David Ison of Harvard has created several types of therapeutic music—what he calls "Vibro-Tactile Software"—for use with acoustic field generators. According to Ison:

> The body holds trauma in specific areas. Usually a specific memory of a particular trauma is stored in a particular place in the body. Through my work with vibro-tactile music, I know what areas store what kinds of trauma and how to reach them. I help the body to come into resonance with an external sound source. Breathing slows down and the traumatic memories surface so they can be released.

Charles Wilson, co-creator of Discovery Sound Tables, recently created a two-week certification program for sound table operators. He offers sound table therapeutic sessions in partnership with a psychologist practicing in Marin County, California. According to Wilson:

[Using music and the sound table] I can help the client enter into a deep experience faster than any other way I know of. Most therapists spend a lot of their time getting people "in state." This technology can help them get in touch with their feelings and emotionally available to work deeply in 15 minutes or so. State specific memories and traumas surface. The client needs to re-enter certain psycho-physical states to do his or her work, and I can help re-create those states, and I can do so quickly and powerfully because the sound table accesses so many senses.

GOOD VIBRATIONS, THRILLS, AND ENDORPHINS

One way these devices may work is by stimulating the release of pleasurable neurochemicals. Dr. Avram Goldstein, head of the Addiction Research Center in Palo Alto and professor of pharmacology at Stanford, has found a link between "musical thrills," those shudders of ecstasy produced by emotionally moving music, and increased endorphin production.

Dr. Jeffrey Thompson, a sound researcher whose extensive work with the Somatron led him to design his own PSI Sound Table, has pointed out

A huge section of the brainstem and nervous system is devoted to sensing and processing vibration. The spinal cord is composed of nerve bundles carrying different kinds of sensation such as heat and cold, pain, pressure, vibration, et cetera. Two entire columns sense vibration and take up almost the whole posterior half of the spinal cord. Large portions of the deep, primitive portions of the brain near the brainstem are devoted to vibration-processing. So when you are lying on a sound table, powerful emotional information, in the form of musical vibrations, gets processed right in the part of the brain where our most deep-seated emotional programs reside. This is one reason sound tables produce such powerful effects.

SENSORY RESONANCE

Don Estes, the creator of the Vibrasound, credits the powerful effects of his device to what he calls the principle of "sensory resonance." In a state of sensory resonance, the senses provide the brain completely congruent information.

According to Estes:

Sensory deprivation such as you experience with a floatation tank is a form of sensory resonance. All the sensory inputs are simultaneously, congruently quiet. On the Vibrasound, all the senses get convergent, simultaneous stimulation. Normally, in order to focus on a single stimulus, your reticular activating system has to screen out countless "background" sensations. When the Vibrasound "drowns out" the background distractions, the attention and mental energy that would otherwise be used up by the task of sorting inputs is freed up. This in itself is highly unusual, and it means you have much more consciousness available than you would ordinarily.

And what is presented to consciousness? *Music.* And great music is profound. Communication can be boiled down to frequency, amplitude, and waveform. Music results when those elements are combined together in the most beautiful, powerful ways possible. Music is the greatest form of communication man has ever created. Music can be emotionally powerful, aesthetically powerful, mentally pleasurable, physically healing, deeply relaxing. And consciousness is uniquely freed up. No wonder the result is so profound.

While still a teenager, Dr. Patrick Flanagan a private researcher invented a unique device called the Neurophone, which communicated sound to the brain via the skin. Now, having studied the effects of sound on the body for over thirty years, he observes, "Each cavity in the body is a Helmholtz resonator; it has a specific frequency to which it resonates like a tuning fork. Thus, if the body is resonated by music, certain parts of the body will resonate particularly strongly to each frequency."

Whole-body acoustic stimulation is so powerful, Flanagan believes, in part because the human skin is itself such a powerful sense organ.

Our skin is not just a covering; it is an enormously sensitive organ with hundreds of thousands of receptors for temperature and vibrotactile input. Every organ of perception develops ontologically and phylogenetically out of skin. In the embryo skin folds and then forms our eyes and our ears. Our skin may contain the latent capacity to perceive light and sound. I think by stimulating the skin with energy in the right way, you can potentially repolarize the brain and charge it with energy.

CONSUMERS' GUIDE TO ACOUSTIC FIELD GENERATORS

The *Vibrasound* system looks like a waterbed attached to an imposing sound console equipped with a light/sound (LS) device. The user dons goggles and stretches out on the waterbed, which inventor Don Estes says is filled with a special gellike colloidal solution and which rests on a huge speaker system that is as large as the bed itself. The colloidal solution is thicker than water, and its sound-propagating properties are similar to those of the soft tissue within the human body. It thus permits a more direct, effective, and accurate transmission of sound waves into the body.

The liquid is vibrated by powerful speakers and sound-processing equipment, including a sophisticated sound equalization system. Estes says hundreds of vibrational measurements at different frequencies taken with highly sensitive accelerometers (microphones which sense vibration) allow him to program the equalization process so the experiential result is nearly perfect—and fully efficient.

Light goggles display flickering lights modulated by the music, so that the user can "see" the music in the form of brilliant light patterns dancing before his or her eyes. The total effect is a sort of sensory saturation, and users report that they rapidly dissociate from the physical environment and enter rich internal or "out-of-body" states. Cost is about $10,000.

The *Genesis* system consists of a table suspended from a futuristic tubular octahedron frame equipped with six powerful transducers "aimed" at the user's body. It uses what inventor Michael Bradford calls "biostatic field biofeedback." Sensors under the subject (half of them analog, half digital), process signals from the body and pass them through signal processor that can modify the sound signals of each transducer in a variety of ways (by changing volume, separation, reverberation, and so on). In essence, the machine can use feedback

The Vibrasound
(Tools for Exploration)

from the subject to "teach itself" to produce the maximum levels of relaxation.

The user lies at the maximum energy and sound focal point of the domelike structure. As the user relaxes, the music become fuller, louder, deeper, richer, denser. As the sensors learn from the changes in the user's energy field, the system can create a self-reinforcing feedback loop, in which the more the user relaxes, the more the music increases relaxation, leading to states of profound openness and expansion.

I have found that the biostatic field feedback of the Genesis can produce extraordinary effects. It was always a remarkable and liberating sensation when, at the instant I felt myself release and drop into a deeper level of relaxation, the quality of the music would simultaneously alter, seeming to become denser, vibrating through my entire being, producing a feeling of euphoria and wonderful "letting go." Cost is about $25,000.

Betar is an acronym for "Bio-Energetic Transduction Aided Resonance." Like the Genesis, the Betar system consists of a geodesic dome structure from which a bed/table is suspended, at the focal point of twelve transducers. Sensors measure changes in brain activity, and the device responds to these changes.

The Betar also uses more esoteric technology to produce time-

The Genesis
(Bio-Logic Systems, Inc.)

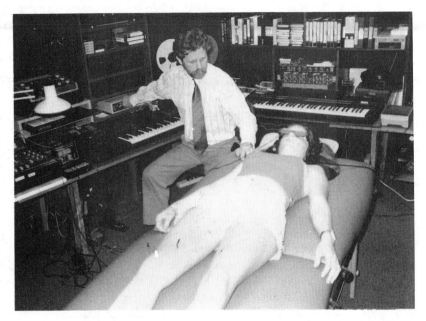

Dr. Jeffrey Thompson with a client on his Pro Sonic Induction (PSI) System
(Jeffrey D. Thompson, D.C.)

reversed sound waves, using "phase-conjugate wave" technology. According to inventor Peter Kelly, "Inputs of opposing complex sound waves produce a variety of standing scalar sound-waves in the body tissues." Kelly claims that "The mechanism . . . specifically targets stress, reaches the deepest and most minute levels of the body, and possesses an automatic self-regulation mechanism to prevent any harm to the tissues." The "Baby Betar" is a free-standing table with speakers that vibrate the Naugahyde-covered foam bed. Cost is $4,200 to $45,000.

The *Pro Sonic Induction System*, a "psycho-sensory integration acoustic table," was created by Dr. Jeffrey Thompson. It consists of four separate sealed, air-tight chambers, which Thompson claims are each scaled to exact dimensions to manipulate and tune the vibration frequency patterns within the chamber spaces "to amplify rather than interfere with one another." The top wood surface of each chamber (the surface on which the user rests) becomes a giant sounding board (like the body of a violin), and each of the four chambers is under one of the quarters of the body—right and left upper body, right and left lower body. As the chambers resonate with the subwoofer driver in the speaker housing, according to Thompson, it "drives the sound vibrations forward through the top of the table into your body on a column of air pressure wave . . . so that one's body is floating on a cushion of sound frequency vibrations."

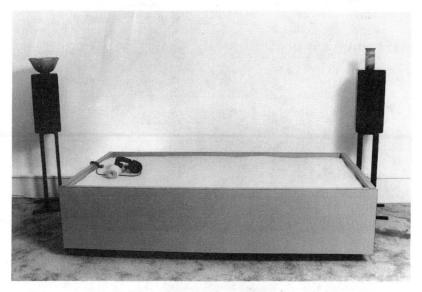

Discovery Sound Bed
(Charles Wilson)

This relatively inexpensive system offers higher power and more sound separation than any other unit in its price range. It can be used with any stereo system, though at least 100 watts per channel is recommended. Cost is $1,500 and up.

The *Discovery Sound Table* is available either as a waterbed-based unit or a massage table unit. The waterbed unit was refined by speaker-designer Paul Hughes using big ten-inch speakers. It produces a superb sound resonance experience. The massage table unit uses powerful, specially designed transducers, which developer Charles Wilson believes outperform the speakers used by his competitors while resulting in a very low priced system. Cost, $1,500 to $3,900.

There are probably more *Somatron* units in existence than all other sound tables combined. Users lie on a surface with a patented "resilient support system," which allows it to vibrate too, becoming, in effect, a second diaphragm. Developer Byron Eakins believes this enables it to provide the most intense ride with the least room noise and the lowest power (20 watts). Models include quality massage tables and reclining chairs. Deluxe models include the audio console and even a sliding cover to eliminate external stimuli and produce an intensified sound experience. Models range in cost from $3,200 to $6,000.

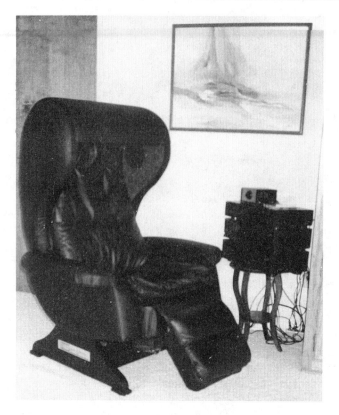

The Somatron is available in this chair model as well as a variety of sound bed systems
(Somasonics, Inc.)

TWELVE

SOUNDS OF SILENCE, VISIONS FROM THE VOID:

REDUCED STIMULATION

Repose, tranquillity, stillness, inaction—these are the levels of the universe, the ultimate perfection of the Tao.

—Chuang Tzu

•

All of human unhappiness comes from one single thing, which is not knowing how to remain quietly in one room.

—Pascal

At the opposite end of the spectrum from the sensory overload of the acoustic field systems is the sensory restriction produced by flotation tanks. For many, the float tank is the ultimate relaxation and sports training device. The user floats weightlessly, in total darkness, in twelve inches of body-temperature water saturated with 1,000 pounds of epsom salts, producing what one neuroscientist has called "the most profound relaxation available on this planet."

Without the usual external stimulations of light, sound, motion, and gravity, the "chattering monkey" in the floater's mind soon becomes silent, permitting states of extraordinary lucidity, calmness, and peace and producing an unsurpassed hypometabolic state that permits natural homeostatic mechanisms to repair and regenerate the body and mind.

FINE-TUNING THE BRAIN

One of the ways flotation seems to produce such profound quieting effects is through the actions of the brain's reticular activating system. This nerve center at the top of the brainstem controls our level of arousal and directs our attention. The attention control system is like the "tuning" knob on a radio—it selects or tunes in certain stimuli it has determined are meaningful or important, while letting us ignore the flood of sensations that are pouring into our brain every moment.

Thus we can focus on reading a book in the midst of a busy airport, or ignore the pressure of our clothes against our body but become quickly aware of a mosquito settling on our skin.

The reticular activating system is a product of evolution, and it seems to function on evolutionary principles to ensure survival. Thus it pays attention to things that are new or novel in the environment, while ignoring unchanging things, since new stimuli are potentially life-threatening.

The second component of the reticular activating system, the arousal control system, is like the volume control on a TV or radio: as sensations pass from our senses into the brain, the reticular activating system turns them up, turns them down, or turns them off. When the system turns up the levels, even a minimal stimulus, such as the dripping of water from a faucet in a distant room, can become thunderingly loud and dramatically increase our level of arousal. When it turns them down or off, even huge jet planes flying directly overhead cannot increase our arousal.

What seems to happen in the float tank is that the arousal control system of the reticular activating system receives unchanging external sensations—no light, little sound, and minimal physical sensations because the water is warmed to body temperature, so that the floater quickly loses a sensation of where the body surface ends and water begins. Thus, since there is little or no external stimulation to respond to, the system turns our arousal level down—electroencephalograph (EEG) activity slows down from the beta of arousal, into the alpha, theta, and even delta ranges.

At the same time, the attention control system perceives that the sensations that are arriving from outside the body are unchanging, unvarying. Since the reticular activating system directs attention to change and novelty, it finds nothing of interest in the external sensations and quickly shifts attention to the internal world. With no information coming in from outside, the internal sensations seem far more powerful and distinct. Images, ideas, memories, emotions that would have been drowned out by sensations coming in from the outside now become clear and vivid, just as the stars, which are rendered invisible by sunlight during the day, shine brightly on dark moonless nights.

RESEARCH SUMMARY

Flotation has been subjected to the most intense and wide-ranging scientific research of any of the mind technologies (with the possible exception of cranial electrostimulation, or CES). There are literally hundreds of studies documenting its powerful psychobiological effects. What follows is a brief summary of some of floating's proven benefits.

Stress Reduction Levels of stress-related biochemicals (cortisol, adrenocorticotropic hormone [ACTH]) are dramatically decreased, as are blood pressure and heart rate; this reduction happens while floating and persists for days, and sometimes weeks after.

Increased Tolerance for Stress Researchers have found that floating can "alter the set points in the endocrine homeostatic mechanism so that the individual would be experiencing a lower adrenal activation state"—that is, the individual would have a greater tolerance for stress.

Deep Relaxation Muscular tension, oxygen consumption, skin conductivity (GSR), or Galvanic Skin Resistance), and other measures of arousal and tension decrease to unprecedented levels; as a result of dilation of blood vessels, including the capillaries carrying blood to all parts of the brain, floating increases the flow of blood and oxygen to the brain.

Increased Brain Power and Health Increased blood flow to the brain enhances functioning, increases protein synthesis, and helps build new brain tissue and nourish neurons, leading to greater dendritic growth. By increasing protein synthesis, blood enrichment of the brain also enhances memory formation.

Altered Brain Waves Brain waves shift from the beta waves of normal consciousness to lower-frequency and higher-amplitude alpha and theta waves. In one study researchers measured elevated levels of theta activity as long as *three weeks* after a single one-hour float. As brain waves slow down, there is also increasing synchrony between different hemispheres and different areas of the brain, indicative of a more open focus of attention.

Increased Powers of Attention EEG tests measuring the habituation of subjects to stimuli such as clicks show that normal subjects quickly become habituated to clicks, while floaters maintain high levels of alertness and attention—a pattern shown by experienced meditators.

Heightened Suggestibility Because the reticular activating system turns up the brain's volume control knob and the brain becomes "hungry" for stimulation, it accepts fully whatever information that is delivered to it in the tank. Subjects who are normally poor hypnotic subjects become "hypnotic virtuosos" in the tank. Studies show that suggestions made in the tank have a "maintenance effect," retaining their power for months and, in several studies, for years.

Heightened Mental Imagery Over 90 percent of the brain's energy is expended processing external stimuli. Freed of these responsibilities in the tank, the mind turns inward, and our powers of creating and manipulating mental imagery increase dramatically.

Increased Learning Perhaps because of the lower levels of stress and distracting "noise" and because of the "stimulus hunger" effect in which the reticular activating system ensures floaters are extremely aware of information that is provided to them in the tank, floaters learn much more and at a higher level of complexity than nonfloaters.

Increased Sensory Acuity Users report that after floating, the world seems fresher, the colors more intense, sensual pleasures more delightful. Tests show dramatic increases in visual acuity and auditory acuity.

Increased Creativity Creativity is linked to mental imagery, which floating intensifies. It also frees the brain from habitual operating patterns and permits it to function in new ways more conducive to creative insights.

Increased Pleasure Floating increases levels of pleasurable neurochemicals such as endorphins.

Boosted Immune Function Floating increases a variety of immune components, including immunoglobulin A.

As a result of these benefits, floating has proven enormously effective in a wide variety of applications, ranging from sports training, to treatment of drug addictions. I have explored much of this research and its implications in *The Book of Floating*. There are also several collections of remarkable and highly readable scientific papers specifically devoted to float research. I urge interested readers to explore further.

FLOATING MIND WORK, FLOATING MIND PLAY

The flotation tank is a superb place for learning, self-exploration, and mental work of all sorts. There is abundant evidence that it increases mental powers, memory, and creativity. (See Chapter 19.) I personally find the float tank a wonderful place to get writing done—ideas flow freely, and I have an expanded ability to "see" how everything fits together at once in a book or article. Frequently entire passages have appeared to me in a flash, and I have been able to recall them clearly after I emerge from the tank and sit down in front of my notebook or computer. Many lawyers, choreographers, architects, musicians, painters, doctors, actors, and others who must do much of their work in their head have told me that they too find flotation tanks unsurpassed for pleasurable, relaxed but focused and creative work.

Floating is also an ideal place for personal growth, because it increases suggestibility as well as receptivity to information. The absence of external stimulation also seems to "unfreeze" what have been intractable beliefs, habits, attitudes, and behaviors, so that they can be eliminated, replaced, refrozen, rescripted, or reimprinted in new, more desirable patterns. This makes the tank a perfect place for self-exploration, self-hypnosis, self-suggestion, and listening to audio programs (through underwater speakers) for personal growth and transformation.

FLOATING WITH MIND TOOLS

Many of the other types of mind technology gain enormous power when used in conjunction with floating. Some, such as binaural beats, sound therapy, and other audio programs, can be used during the float. Intrepid explorers will discover that it is also possible to use CES (with the correct electrode placement) and light/sound (LS) machines while in the tank. Effects of some devices, such as motion systems, LS devices, and CES, are amplified when used prior to or after a float. Ultimately, however, floating is at its best when you use the absence of stimulation to let go of external connections; increase your awareness of physical, emotional, and spiritual states; and then let go of even that increased awareness to enter the timeless zone of pure being without consciousness.

I personally believe flotation is the most powerful tool for deep relaxation and enhanced brain functioning that has yet been devised.

GAZING HARD INTO THE VOID

In the float tank, all external light is shut off: You can open your eyes wide and still see nothing but total blackness. This has a number of powerful effects. First, it boosts sensory acuity dramatically, as the reticular activating system turns your attention from external visual stimuli to your other physical sensations. Then it intensifies psychological awareness, as your awareness, lacking any external visual input to process, continues to turn inward. Ultimately, without any external distractions, you tend to fall into an altered state of consciousness characterized by slow, synchronous brain-wave activity, hypnagogic imagery, free association of ideas, and profound relaxation.

Scientists have discovered another technique for turning off external awareness, shifting attention inward, and attaining profound relaxation. Instead of working actively to shut off external visual input, as with the float tank, they simply provide the eyes with a stimulus that is monotonous and unvarying: that is, vision without any information. As research psychologist Robert Ornstein of the Langley Porter Neuropsychiatric Institute reports, "One consequence of the way our central nervous system is structured seems to be that if awareness is restricted to one unchanging source of stimulation, a 'turning off' of consciousness of the external world follows."

BLANK-OUT AND THE CLOUD OF UNKNOWING

When there is an unvarying visual input, your reticular activating system again has the tendency to shut down your visual sense and direct your attention to other senses. With nothing to look at, the system soon decides that there is no important information coming in visually and directs awareness to other senses, creating what is known as a blank-out. Researchers have traced the course through the brain of a continuous, unvarying visual stimulus and found that it is definitely received and passed into the brain by the retina, but that at a certain point it simply "disappears" somewhere in the central nervous system: The reticular activating system has decided it is of no importance and shifted the brain's conscious attention elsewhere.

In his research, Robert Ornstein discovered that blank-out "was not merely the experience of seeing nothing, but one of not seeing, a complete disappearance of the sense of vision. . . . During 'blank-out' the observers did not know, for instance, whether their eyes were open or not." Other researchers have concluded that periods of monotonous stimulation "indicated a functional similarity between continuous stimulation and no stimulation at all."

Humans have been aware of this effect for thousands of years. One ancient meditation technique consists of simply staring at the blue cloudless sky until there is no sky. A common yogic meditation practice is *tratakum,* or "steady gaze," in which concentration is fixed on some unchanging external object, such as a rock or a mandala. The repetition of a single word or phrase to reach a state of blank-out through monotonous stimulation has been practiced by all spiritual traditions. Those traditions described the blank-out state as an experience of the "void," "emptiness," "nothingness," or "the cloud of unknowing."

The blank-out effect seems to be a key to many of the well-documented benefits of meditation, ranging from stress reduction, to increased sensory acuity and mental clarity, to increased immune function. However, as practitioners of meditative techniques attest, it's not easy to achieve this effect reliably.

PING-PONG BALLS AND PSYCHIC POWERS

Modern researchers have tried to find ways of inducing and investigating this blank-out effect in the laboratory, using techniques ranging from dense, uniform fog, to translucent goggles. One simple but effective technique used by many scientists is to cut Ping-Pong balls in half, put the split halves over the eyes of subjects, and direct a beam of light at the white hemispheres, while subjects gaze at the white field before their eyes. This technique for intentionally providing an unvarying, featureless visual input is what scientists call the *ganzfeld*.

Thoroughly researched, the ganzfeld has become a favorite laboratory research tool for scientists investigating the brain and consciousness, since has been found to be an extremely effective and reliable technique for producing blank-out and quickly inducing deeply internalized, meditative states of consciousness.

The experience is quite interesting. Looking into a ganzfeld, with eyes open in a relaxed "soft-eyed" gaze, you see only a uniform, evenly illuminated and colored but completely featureless visual space. This is a very unusual situation, which we normally never experience—just as we normally never experience the total blackness and lack of sensory stimulation of the float tank. Since the reticular activating system is designed to detect change, supplying an *unchanging* visual input creates some powerful and unique effects.

First, the color drains out of the visual field—the field becomes gray and progressively seems to disappear from your peripheral vision. A misty space seems to open up, and soon it becomes hard to tell if your eyes are open or not. At this point, EEG studies show strong alpha—which is normally not produced when eyes are open.

The monotony of the featureless visual field causes the reticular activating system to decrease your arousal, and you become lulled deeper and deeper into lower and lower stages of arousal, becoming deeply relaxed and producing lots of theta waves. Awareness of the visual field disappears completely—you experience blank-out. Subjects using ganzfelds usually report profound relaxation, revery, imagery, and altered states of consciousness. This is an ideal time for total mental stillness, for self-suggestion or recorded suggestions for behavior change, for accelerated learning. When people emerge from the ganzfeld, it seems as if the volume knob on their senses is turned way up—colors are vivid and saturated; sounds full, rich, and intense; their skin is exquisitely sensitive.

Intriguingly, numerous controlled statistical studies by parapsychologists indicate that use of the ganzfeld significantly increases the psychic abilities of subjects in such areas as telepathy, psychokinesis, and remote viewing. Says parapsychologist Julian Isaacs, of John F. Kennedy University in California, "coupled with a pair of headphones supplying 'pink noise' [a gentle shushing sound], the ganzfeld shuts down the busy sensory processing which normally drowns out the whisper-soft ESP [extrasensory perception] signals, allowing much better reception of ESP." One of the world's foremost researchers of parapsychological phemenona, Charles Honorton, formerly director of the Psychophysical Research Laboratories in Princeton, New Jersey, found that the ganzfeld was the most single most effective tool for enhancing psychic performance he had encountered.

The effects of the visual ganzfeld are enhanced by the addition of a featureless or monotonous audio field—such as surf, pink noise, or binaural beats—which effectively cuts off distracting external sounds and also, after several minutes, seems to "blank out" or disappear as attention turns inward.

For most users the ganzfeld serves as a sort of "portable flotation tank," facilitating a rapid "escape" from external stimuli into profound tranquility. The ganzfeld can thus produce—to a somewhat lesser degree—all of the benefits produced by floating.

CONSUMERS' GUIDE TO SENSORY REDUCTION TOOLS

Tanks range from inexpensive do-it-yourself kits (you can make your own tank, including pumps and filters, for under $1,000); to simple no-frills models; to deluxe versions with marine fiberglass hulls, built-in stereo systems, and video monitors (ranging in cost from $5,000 upward). There are also a variety of "dry" flotation tanks that use a gellike mattress instead of water—the effects are similar to but not quite as dramatic and powerful as those of true floating.

FLOTATION TANKS

The tanks by *Samadhi, Floatarium* and *Oasis* are excellent. All of them are stand-alone systems (no external water connections necessary), including pump, filter, water heater with temperature control, and such. Optional accessories include built-in speakers for stereo sound while floating (ideal for listening to music, suggestions, or learning tapes) and ultraviolet and ozone water sterilization (to reduce the need for chlorine). The Samadhi tank is rectangular, with a beveled end, and is easy to ship and assemble. Both the Floatarium and Oasis tanks are larger than the Samadhi, vaguely egg shape, and made of molded fiberglass. The Samadhi-tank is less expensive; prices begin about $4,000 for the basic Samadhi tank and range upward toward $10,000 for the deluxe models.

Other excellent systems include small saunalike wood-paneled "float rooms" from *Tank Alternatives,* a company that also consults

The Floatarium Tank
(Tools for Exploration)

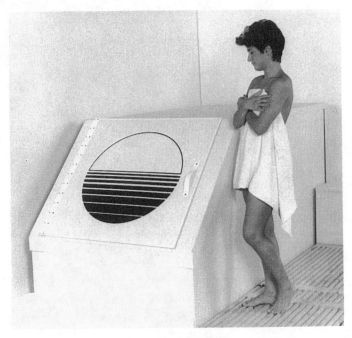

The Samadhi Tank
(Samadhi Tank Co.)

and/or provides a do-it-yourself kit. The Tank Alternative systems range from custom-designed spa/float rooms costing up to $25,000 to do-it-yourself kits, containing pumps, filters, and other parts, costing about $1,500. You can purchase simple plans for about $50.

GANZFELD SYSTEMS

One of the simplest ways of creating a ganzfeld is simply to cut a Ping-Pong ball in half, place one half over each eye like a cup, and keep your eyes open as you stare at a bright light source through the shell of the ball. Theoretically, as you gaze into the brightly lighted field that covers each eye, you see a featureless field—no details, no visual information for your mind to stare at. In practice, Ping-Pong balls work, but imperfectly. It's hard to get a comfortable fit without having light leaking around the edges and without variations or "hot spots" of higher light intensity.

Most attempts to design effective portable ganzfelds have used goggles or face masks of some sort. The *Tranquilite*, which I wrote about in *Megabrain*, is still in the prototype stage. The *Theta One*, which I also wrote about earlier, used an electroluminescent strip set inside sunglasses frames. Lots of ambient light and peripheral visual information kept it from being a true ganzfeld.

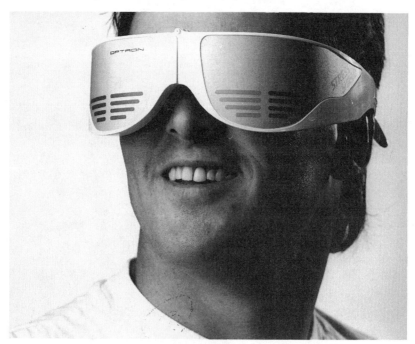

The Stress Shield produces a ganzfeld effect in several colors
(Tools for Exploration)

The best ganzfield to emerge yet is the *Stress Shield*. These goggles have adjustable soft foam eyecups that are comfortable but still effective at blocking out ambient light and providing a uniform visual field. The Stress Shield adds to the powers of the ganzfeld the powers of color (explored in Chapter 7). You can select a visual field of red, green, or yellow light. Many users find that red increases their energy, while yellow seems to enhance mental and creative abilities, and green is deeply relaxing, reducing anxiety and stress. The goggles are powered by 2 AAA batteries. Cost is under $150.

BIOCIRCUITS

One other type of "passive" device that has shown to have profound effects is what the manufacturers call *Biocircuits*. They are nonmechanical tools (flat plates or pads made of copper or silk, connected by copper or silk cables) that introduce no external electrical or magnetic energy to the body, but simply connect different body parts.

First developed over sixty years ago, biocircuits had been used by thousands of people, and there were a lot of compelling reports that the devices produced states of profound relaxation, balancing and energizing of the system, and much more. Recently, evidence has emerged in a rigorously conducted double-blind study by Dr. Julian Isaacs that biocircuits are dramatically effective in producing the "theta state," in lowering electromyographic muscle tension, in subjective estimates of

Biocircuits
(Tools for Exploration)

depth of relaxation, in sensations of warmth and "non-ordinariness" of the experience, and in the perceived benefit and perceived overall effectiveness of the session. Isaacs reports that "the results obtained were surprisingly strong and consistent, despite [my] initial scepticism regarding biocircuits." Cost for the basic unit is $59.

SUGGESTED READING

For more information about floating, see *The Book of Floating: Exploring the Private Sea* by Michael Hutchison (New York: Morrow, 1984). Also, *The Center of the Cyclone* by John Lilly (New York: Julian, 1972), and *The Deep Self* by John Lilly (New York: Simon & Schuster, 1977).

The best compendiums of scientific research are *Restricted Environmental Stimulation: Research and Commentary* edited by John W. Turner and Thomas H. Fine (Toledo, Ohio, Medical College of Ohio, 1992); and *Restricted Environmental Stimulation: Theoretical and Empirical Developments in Flotation REST* edited by Peter Suedfeld, John Turner and Thomas Fine (New York: Springer-Verlag, 1990).

For more information about ganzfelds, see my *Megabrain* (New York: Ballantine, 1986, 1991), Chapter 15.

PART THREE

FROM YOUR BRAIN TO MEGABRAIN:
The Users' Guide to Mind Machines

Most people live . . . in a very restricted circle of their potential being. They *make use* of a very small portion of their possible consciousness, and of their soul's resources in general, much like a man who, out of his whole bodily organism, should get into a habit of using and moving only his little finger.

—WILLIAM JAMES,
The Varieties of Religious Experience

INTRODUCTION

MEGABRAIN SOFTWARE: PROGRAMS, APPLICATIONS, TECHNIQUES

There are intriguing parallels between the emergence of brain machines today and the advent of the personal computer (PC) over a decade ago. Back in the 1970s, most people who were aware of computers at all considered them to be huge, enormously expensive, immensely complicated machines used by scientists. Most computers were in scientific labs or universities. Where else would they be? Why in the world would anyone want one in his or her office or home? What would you do with one even if you had one? Today computers have transformed virtually every aspect of our lives, and it's hard for many of us to imagine how we ever lived without them.

What happened over the last decade that made PCs into mass-market consumer-electronics items? The first thing was that the hardware went through a series of extraordinary and rapid transformations: Each new generation was smaller, easier to operate, vastly more powerful, and far less expensive.

The second key to the mass popularity of PCs was the development of a huge variety of *software*—programs that enabled users to apply the massive computing power of the hardware toward specific tasks, ranging from word processing, to spreadsheets, to design, to publishing, to game playing. Without such software, the hardware would have remained virtually inaccessible to most users. Think now: How often would you use your computer if you had to create your own programs?

The parallels are obvious: Brain machines, which first were unwieldy, expensive, complex, and bore the weird-scientist aura of the laboratory, have now gone through a rapid evolution and emerged miniaturized, easy to operate, inexpensive, and as sleekly designed as miniature coffee grinders.

Today the brain machine hardware exists. It's effective and innovatively designed. In addition, as increasing amounts of scientific evidence indicate, when used skillfully these brain machines can produce peak performance brain states, heightened mental powers, and enhanced mind-body interaction. All brain machines are sold with short manuals explaining their operation: how to turn them on, change the batteries, adjust the controls. What each mind-machine hardware package lacks, in most cases, is the software—the programs, systems, techniques, or operating environments that will allow users to apply the machine's sophisticated circuitry and advanced potentials and capacities toward specific tasks and applications.

Yes, you've purchased the machine. But how do you use it as an accelerated learning machine to help you study for your English lit exam? How can you use it as a sports training aid, to help you cut strokes off your golf game, to increase your endurance or improve your backhand? How can you use the machine to help you reduce stress, lower blood pressure, reduce pain, lose weight? Because of this lack of application programs, many mind-machine purchasers end up putting the devices on a shelf in the back of their closets once the novelty of the experience has worn off.

Chapters 13 to 31 form a compendium of mind-machine programs, or what I'm calling *Megabrain software*. In Parts III and IV I will present a variety of strategies/systems/applications/techniques that I have found to be extremely powerful and effective when used in combination with mind machines. The techniques have emerged from my experimentation with and observations of thousands of people in Megabrain Workshops, from the work of skilled therapists and clinicians who have made extensive use of mind machines in their practices, from my conversations and correspondence with thousands of explorers and experimentalists around the world, and from my own personal experimentation and explorations. I have been trying different sorts of brain machines under an immense variety of conditions for well over a decade. My use has ranged from just-for-fun test drives of new machines, to systematic and analytical investigations of single devices over long periods of time, to urgent use of the machines under conditions of extreme stress and pain.

In the chapters that follow, I will describe a large assortment of programs and applications. In general, and except where otherwise noted, the techniques are effective with virtually all of the brain technologies now available, including light/sound (LS), binaural beats, cranial electrostimulation (CES), movement devices, acoustic field systems, flotation tanks, ganzfelds, and electroencephalograph (EEG) and Galvanic Skin Response biofeedback. What's more, they're also effective with various combinations of brain technology used synergistically (that is, LS stimulation while on a motion system, CES with a ganzfeld, binaural beats and hypnosubliminal audiotapes while floating, and so on). For convenience and brevity, I will usually refer to all these types of mind-enhancing, performance-boosting systems and machines as mind tools or mind technology.

THIRTEEN
CHANGING CHANNELS:
BRAIN TUNING AND STATE CHANGE

Our research involving nonordinary states of consciousness thus supports the concepts of C.G. Jung, who suggested that in our dreams and visions we can experience myths that are not from our own cultures and that were previously unknown to us from our readings, viewing of art, or conversations with others. This is the world of the "collective unconscious," an infinite ocean of knowledge from which we can each draw. In this age of advanced technology, we might compare the collective unconscious to a transmitting station that constantly broadcasts every bit of program material and information ever transmitted by radio and television. At any time we can "switch channels," changing from the channel of everyday life to which we normally stay tuned, to an infinite number of other channels, crossing the boundaries of time, space, and even species. It is virtually impossible to imagine that we are always surrounded by this information and that we are able to tap into it whenever we wish. But our analogy of the radio waves gives us an approximation of the immensity of information we can access through the collective unconscious.

—Stanislav Grof, M.D.,
The Holotropic Mind

THE POWER OF CHANGING YOUR STATE

The first step toward making active, systematic, and productive use of your mind tool is to learn to use it to change your state.

It was a classic subway rider's nightmare: rush hour in Manhattan on a sweltering summer afternoon. On the downtown IND we stood sweating, squeezed together so tightly no one was able to move an arm. Suddenly the train stopped. The hum of the motors died. The train had shut down. A collective groan went up. Then the lights went out. The groan became louder. From somewhere down the car came screams of terror. A voice shouted, "Hey, some guy's having a heart attack here!" Voices shouted to punch out the windows, and others cried out that they couldn't breathe. "I need air, I need air!" Cries of panic were heard. I felt my own chest constricting, my breathing becoming tight. The conductor's voice came over the loudspeaker system to tell us someone had jumped onto the tracks at the 34th Street station and we would have to wait until the situation was cleared up. So, while some continued to shout in panic, most of us settled back in the darkness into that common New York City state you could call Ordinary Emergency.

I was in the midst of writing a book about the use of the flotation tank and had been floating several times a week. The thought appeared that maybe I could treat this situation like being in a float tank. After all, like the tank, this was a place of total darkness. So I took a breath, let it out slowly, and pretended I was floating peacefully in a flotation tank. I remembered the heavy lightness that filled my limbs while in the tank, the feeling of release, the sensation of floating, free of gravity, in black, infinite space. And it happened—within a few seconds I felt the tension flow out of my body. It had been hard to breathe, but now my chest relaxed and I breathed deeply and easily. The tension on my face flowed into a smile. I was floating. . . . After a moment of peaceful rest, I remembered where I was and began laughing. The whole scene had a macabre comical air. I was relaxed.

This was one of my first experiences of intentional *state change*. By changing my mental state, I changed my body state. By changing my mind/body state, I was able to change my behavior and attitudes. In a very real sense, I was able to alter my reality. It was a direct result of my experience of mind technology—the float tank.

EMPOWERING AND INHIBITING STATES

All of us know what *states* are, since we're in states every moment of our lives. Some of the states we get into are very nice: joy, pleasure, confidence, belief, love, concentration, ecstasy, energy, lucidity, clarity, courage, determination, and so on. These are *empowering states*, since when we are in these states we have the power to act positively, to get things done, to enjoy our lives. These states sustain our most elemental power, the existential *power to be*. These empowering states are essential to achieving excellence, peak performance, and peak experiences.

Other states we get into are not so nice: fear, anxiety, depression, sadness, frustration, helplessness, anger, confusion, weakness, futility, loneliness, guilt, boredom, exhaustion. These are *inhibiting states*, since they have the effect of hindering, obstructing, restraining, suppressing, repressing, thwarting, blocking us from achieving excellence, peak performance, and peak experiences. At times they can threaten to undermine or destroy our power to be.

STATE-DEPENDENT MEMORY

As I mentioned earlier, scientists have discovered that memory is "state dependent": Things you learn when you're happy you remember best when you're happy; what you learn when you're sad is remembered best when you're sad. According to Dr. Gordon Bower, of Stanford University, one of the pioneer explorers of state-dependent memory, states are like "different libraries into which a person places memory records. A given memory record can be retrieved only by returning into that library."

We've all had the experience of trying to find our misplaced car keys. After a period of frantic searching we stop and think, "What did I do the last time I came in and put those keys down?" If we're successful in "reliving" the last time we had the keys, we will generally suddenly remember where the keys are in a sudden whole-body flash of "knowing." In other words, we're trying to get back into the state we were in the last time we had the keys: We're accessing state-dependent memory.

To look at this in another way, the current state we're in acts like a magnet to memories that are linked to that state. When you're in a sad mood, you tend to attract sad memories, recollections, and associations. For example, there are streets of New York City that are forever linked in my mind with a former love and the events of our relationship. When I am melancholy and I walk through those streets, every place I look I see things that stir up melancholy and sad memories. Yet when I am happy and I walk through those same streets, the things I see remind me of moments of joy and love—all that I see makes me glad. It all depends on the state I'm in.

STATE-DEPENDENT BEHAVIOR

Many of us live with the attitude that these states are something that *happen* to us, that they are like weather fronts that pass over us, bringing sunny days, rainstorms, or pressure inversions, all beyond our control. "Hey, I'd like to go to the beach today, but it's rainy." "Yeah, I should probably go play with my children, but I'm too angry right now." "I'd like to be loving and affectionate with my spouse, but right now I'm tired and depressed. Maybe later I'll feel more like it." We behave in certain ways because we're in certain states.

What we're talking about here, then, is something more than

state-dependent memory—it's *state-dependent behavior*. To an extraordinary degree, our states control our behavior. Think of being in one state—fear—and entering a room full of people, or having to deliver a lecture to a strange audience. What would your behavior be? Now, think of being in a different state—happy self-confidence—and entering that same room, or delivering a lecture to that same audience. Your behavior would be quite different from your fear-state behavior. To that degree, your behavior is state dependent.

Think of other behaviors. When we are in calm, centered, relaxed, and happy states, our tendency to engage in certain behaviors—such as smoking, drinking, eating excessively, taking drugs—is markedly different from our tendency to engage in those behaviors when we are in states such as anger, depression, or anxiety. To that degree, these unwanted behaviors are state dependent. What this means is that *if we could change our state, we could change our behaviors.*

EXCEPTIONAL STATES

And just as unwanted behaviors are state dependent, so are those much-desired exceptional behaviors. Think of the last time you hit that perfect drive that flew off the head of your golf club and shot 300 yards straight down the fairway. . . . Or the time you had that breakthrough creative insight when you suddenly solved a problem that had been bothering you for ages. . . . Or that time when you and your partner had a sexual experience that was sizzling, sublime, and perfect ecstasy. . . . What state were you in? If you could recall that state in its fullness and totality, and reenter it the next time you addressed the golf ball, wanted to learn or understand something new, or had sex, then you could make another perfect drive, have another breakthrough insight, have another peak experience.

Athletes know this intuitively and go through what might seem to be bizarre rituals in their attempts to reenter their peak state. Watch the high jumper as he pulls his shorts up just so and then spits just so, puts his head down, swings his arms, and places his foot forward, then backward, then forward, then backward, then pauses before he begins his run toward the bar. Watch the baseball batter as he pounds his bat twice on the plate, swings it around three times, spits, tugs on his shirt at the right shoulder, tugs on his shirt at the left shoulder, puts his hand on top of his helmet, swings the bat around twice more, pounds the plate once, spits once more, and then draws back the bat and stands ready to take the pitch. Unconsciously or consciously, athletes are always trying to remember themselves as they were at their remembered moment of perfection, trying to reenter the state they were in the last time they made a perfect high jump, the last time they made a perfect swing. They understand that if they can once again truly enter the state they were in during that past peak performance, then they can deliver another peak performance.

To the degree that behavior is state dependent, then, if we could somehow put ourselves into the same states exceptional performers are in when they perform their extraordinary acts, we should be able to perform exceptionally ourselves. In their book *Supermemory* Sheila Ostrander and Lynn Schroeder ask:

> How do we access what we know, but don't know any more? Why do we only use a smidgen of what is adjudged innate human ability? Perhaps we don't enjoy the exceptional functioning of the super-memory star, of the Olympic high jumper, the brilliant business strategist, even the miraculous self-healer, because *we don't know how to get into the state where these abilities live.* If we should get there by accident, we don't know how to recall those states again when needed.

LIFE HAPPENS

States control behavior. But as I pointed out earlier, many of us feel that, to a great extent, our states happen to us. We are in a sad mood, so we will be sad until we stop being sad. And since we are sad now, we will behave in certain ways that are different from the ways we would behave if we were happy. So since our states control our behavior, then so long as we believe our states happen to us, like weather, to a great degree we must believe *our behavior happens to us.*

That's the way it feels a lot of the time. Hey, Wally, why did you insult the boss like that? Well, gee, I don't know, I was just angry and he kept talking on and on and I kept getting more and more angry and . . . it just *happened.* Hey, Karen, I thought you said you were going to quit smoking. Yes, well, the phone rang and it was an important sale I had to make and, suddenly, the cigarette was just there in my hand and I was taking a drag. It just happened.

To say our behavior happens to us is another way of saying we're *not responsible* for our behavior, any more than we're responsible for the weather. Well, I know I'm eating too much/smoking too much/drinking too much, but I'm sad and depressed right now because my relationship has broken up. The implication is that sooner or later the weather will change, the sadness and depression will lift, and the problem with eating, smoking, or drinking will disappear. Stuff happens to us. And then things change and *other* stuff happens to us. And thus we see the philosophical underpinnings of the great T-shirt and bumper sticker motto of our era, SHIT HAPPENS. To which we are meant to add the unstated but implied AND I'M NOT RESPONSIBLE.

DYSFUNCTIONAL STATES

The belief that we aren't responsible for our behavior has led in recent years to a peculiar cultural phenomenon, blaming unwanted
behaviors on *addiction*. Addiction, it is argued, is a disease. Just as
we don't blame someone for incurable diseases such as diabetes or
sickle cell anemia, which can disrupt and destroy lives, so we can't
blame individuals for addictions to drugs or alcohol or cigarettes,
which also disrupt and destroy lives. The best way to treat the disease of addiction, it is believed, is by going through the twelve-step
process, pioneered by Alcoholics Anonymous (AA). The first step and
most essential step in this process is for the addict to admit and accept completely that he or she is "powerless" over alcohol or drugs.
It is also essential for the addict to accept that his or her disease is
incurable. After the admission of total powerlessness and the acceptance that the disease is incurable, the addict calls upon God or a
Higher Power to change the unwanted behavior. This twelve-step
program has seemed to work, at least for many alcoholics or drug
addicts. And for over forty years, these programs were strictly limited to dealing with alcohol or drug addiction.

Then in the 1980s came the explosive growth of the idea that we
could become addicted not just to the classic addictive drugs but to a
variety of behavior patterns. Since the "disease model" and the
twelve-step method had seemed helpful in treating alcohol and drug
addictions, many people began to believe that the disease model and
the twelve-step method should be equally helpful in treating other
types of "addictions." This expansion process began with those whose
lives had been influenced by alcohol or drugs: husbands, wives, and
children of addicts—members of what came to be known as the "dysfunctional family." In twelve-step and support groups such as Al-Anon
and Adult Children of Alcoholics (ACOA), husbands, wives, and children of addicts and alcoholics used the twelve-step program to admit
their own powerlessness over addictive behavior and to admit their
own "addiction" to their addict mates.

And suddenly, within just a few years, there had emerged an
astonishing variety of step programs and support groups based on the
AA model, for people who wanted to overcome their "addictions" to
sex, food, dieting, money, shopping, anger, romance, men, work, lazi-
ness, exercise, food binging and vomiting, TV, savings coupons, and
much more. And from these emerged other support groups for relatives
of people who were addicted to food, money, anger, and so on. Today
virtually any behavior that might lead to unwanted consequences has
now been classified as an addiction and spawned a network of step
programs and support groups.

The addiction model is enormously seductive. If these unwanted
behaviors are addictions, then they are, by the accepted definition,

diseases, and we're not responsible for our diseases or the diseases of our parents or spouses or lovers. And of course the first step toward overcoming these addictions, as counseled by the twelve-step groups, is to accept and admit that we are *powerless* over our addiction. If we are powerless, we are not responsible. In fact, we are *victims* of our disease. And those who are members of dysfunctional families, "adult children" of addicts, are doubly victims, because they are "trapped" in unwanted behaviors not of their own making, but imposed on them by their addictive parents or their dysfunctional family. All these harmful behaviors are the result of addiction, which is a disease, which means they're not our fault. We're not responsible. Our behavior "happens" to us. It is the result of our mental states, and our states are the result of our dysfunctional family life. Our dysfunctional behavior is the result of our dysfunctional brain states that are the product of our dysfunctional family life of our dysfunctional childhood. We must accept we are powerless. Shit happens.

CHANGING CHANNELS ON THE LIFE TV

But a central finding of the Brain Revolution, and the central message of this book, is that our brain states (and thus our behavior) are *not* beyond our control. We are *not* powerless, we are *not* victims of our past or our environment. The neuroscientific evidence is absolutely clear: *We can change states intentionally, quickly, at will.*

It's a discovery many people make naturally in the course of growing up. It's a discovery that most of us must make over and over and over, in different states and different contexts, until it becomes no longer a surprise, but evident and dependable. I believe making that discovery is an essential part of becoming a healthy adult.

One of the first times I made the discovery was, as I described it earlier, when I wormed my way into a biofeedback research project at New York University and discovered I could make the alpha clicker go by doing certain things with my brain, and that by making the clicker go—by increasing my alpha activity—I could change my mood. I found that I didn't have to keep experiencing the emotions flowing through me if I didn't want to. What I was learning, in my own plodding way, was the process of state change. What I was learning is that to the degree that behavior is state dependent, behavior doesn't happen to us—we choose our behavior.

One way we choose our behavior is by choosing our state. If there are certain behaviors we want to change, then to change them we must change our state. And state change is not only possible, it is easy to learn. Just like changing the channel on the TV, we can learn to switch from inhibiting states to empowering states: changing channels on the life TV.

Learning to change states is, I believe, a key to becoming a functional healthy adult. A central driving force of human evolution and a key to human history has been the search for and exploration of techniques for changing states. Humans have been tireless and determined in their attempts to devise reliable techniques for changing state. The methods they have explored and invented are countless, ranging from self-flagellation to masturbation, from waging war to taking drugs, from sticking needles in acupuncture points to skydiving, and include various types of breathing, dancing, chanting, fasting, ritual, meditation, prayer, reading, storytelling, hypnosis, visualization, sex.

Using technology to help produce state changes is nothing new. Humans have always used the latest technological or scientific developments to assist them in their quest for reliable state-change tools. When the big breakthrough in technology was grasping a stick or stone in the hand and applying it to something else, you can be sure that one of the first uses to which this technology was put was rhythmical pounding, or drumming—still a highly effective state-change technique.

The great technological breakthrough of printing quickly spread throughout the world one of the most powerful and far-reaching state-change techniques of human history—reading.

In our century, a variety of technological developments were combined to create a state-change technology of remarkable richness— the cinema, epitomized by the Hollywood movie. You walk in off the street in one state and reemerge on the street in a different state several hours later, having been catapulted through a variety of intense state changes—from fear and horror, to love and joy, anger or grief. Sometimes the state change produced is long-lasting—I can still vividly remember entering the movie theater as just one of hundreds of kids in T-shirts and Keds, and emerging two hours later as a swashbuckling pirate captain, running wild through the city streets, leaping over garbage cans with cutlass slashing, and seeking buried treasure with my shipmates through the back alleys of Pittsburgh.

STIMULATING STATE CHANGE

A central discovery of the Brain Revolution has been that all states are linked to and determined by physical conditions in the brain. Using electrical probes, scientists discovered, for example, very small but distinct "pleasure centers" in the brain, as well as nearby centers associated with such states as fear and rage. They discovered that certain neurochemicals, such as the endorphins, could produce pleasure states, while others, such as oxytocin, could produce states very much like love. They discovered, as we saw earlier, that high levels of activity in the right frontal regions of the cortex were associated with depression and negative emotional states, while high levels of activity in the left frontal cortex were associated with happiness and positive emotional states.

Even more important, the scientists of the Brain Revolution have discovered that by changing the physical conditions of the brain, they can change the states. With a mild electrical stimulus in one area of the brain, they could produce such pleasure that a subject would do virtually anything—including going without food, sleep, or sex—to continue to experience it. By moving the electrical stimulus to a nearby area of the brain, they could produce utter terror. In some of the research mentioned earlier, scientists found that by actively inducing releases of beta-endorphin, they could produce feelings of euphoria. They also found that by causing subjects to change the amount of brain-wave activity of a certain frequency, they could produce trance-like states and feelings of oneness with the universe. That is, scientists found that they could produce rapid and dramatic state changes using simple and safe technologies.

The next step was to take these simple and safe laboratory techniques for state change and package them in a way that made them accessible to large numbers of people. These mind technologies are now widely available. We have explored the best ones in Part II.

To return to the metaphor of weather: Many of us used to think our states were like weather. When a storm swept over us, we just had to wait it out. Now we know that we can change our states. The mind technology for state change is widely available. So now we have a new question, and a new responsibility: What state do we want to be in? If we have the capacity to select our states, then we have the responsibility to select the states that will help us to reach our goals.

And so another question arises: What are our goals? Do we want wealth? Love? Creativity? Power? Happiness? Peace on earth? We now have the capacity to switch ourselves out of inhibiting states into empowering states, out of destructive behaviors into constructive behaviors—states and behaviors that will help us accomplish the things that are important to us. But what is important?

Mind technology opens up new possibilities for human achievement. These state-change tools can be "labor savers" by helping us quickly to get out of inhibiting states and into empowering states, and to change from unwanted behaviors to desired behaviors—something that might have taken us hours or days or months before the development of mind technology.

Because mind tools seem to offer such rapid and powerful effects, some have accused them of being "too easy." But this is like accusing cars or airplanes of being "too easy." Yes, just as cars and planes get us places far faster than we could get there by walking, mind tools can produce state changes and get us into productive empowering states far faster than we could get there by years of disciplined work at "self-control" or "willpower."

But mind tools, like cars and planes, are neither bad nor good in themselves. They are simply tools to help us do things more rapidly than we could otherwise do them, helping us get places faster than we could through ancient techniques. The fact remains: Whether we walk or fly by jet, whether we meditate or use a mind machine, we still have to decide on our destination.

Mind machines exist; the possibility of rapid state change exists. Each of us still must answer the difficult questions: What states do we seek, what behaviors do we desire, what are the goals of our lives, and how can we use these state-change devices to help us reach those goals? Once you have purchased a mind tool, you must decide what to do with it.

Throughout this book you are going to learn an assortment of state-changing techniques that will permit you to switch into the states that are best suited for helping you to perform at your peak and to reach your goals most effectively. But perform at your peak to what purpose? And reach what goals?

I believe that mind tools themselves offer the most effective techniques yet devised for the kind of contemplation and self-exploration that will be required to answer these questions.

Of course, there's no reason whatsoever that using mind tools has to involve the slightest bit of introspection. Many people are interested in using mind tools for very straightforward and self-evident state-change purposes: to reduce stress, relax, lower blood pressure, increase sexual pleasure, alleviate insomnia, increase memory, and so on. And it goes without saying that mind machines can be used simply for fun—put them on, flip the switch, and see what happens. Humans love to change states: Just about everything we do—watch TV, take drugs, have sex, eat, work, sleep—is either to change our state or earn enough money to change our state. Since we do it anyway, why not do it more safely, quickly, and healthfully with mind tools?

BICYCLE-TRAINING-WHEELS EFFECT

Some critics and skeptics have raised the objection that, while it's important to learn how to change states, mind machines are simply too "easy" and, like drugs, can become a crutch, keeping us from learning how to change states by our own powers. The answer is that in my experience, these machines seem to have quite the opposite effect—they stimulate and help people to learn.

It's what I've called the bicycle-training-wheels effect. Some children use training wheels to help them learn how to ride their bicycles. But once they have learned how to ride, they quickly discard the wheels—who needs training wheels when you can whiz along on two wheels?

In a similar way, mind technology helps many people get into mental states they could not easily, or would not ordinarily, enter by themselves. Mind tools get us there quickly and reliably. We learn what that state feels like. We learn that we can, for example, go from a state of normal consciousness into a deeply relaxed theta state, or a highly aroused and focused beta state, or a synchronized, open-focus alpha state, and do so in a matter of seconds—and then return back to normal consciousness again.

By repeatedly going through such rapid state changes with the assistance of mind tools, we learn that such state changes are not only possible but easily accomplished. By repeatedly entering heightened states, we can learn what those states feel like and learn to associate them with physical sensations (such as feelings of lightness or heaviness, tingling in the fingertips) or imagery (visions of deep blackness or being filled with light).

Having learned what those states feel like, and having gone through the transition between normal states and heightened states numerous times with the assistance of mind tech, we can learn how to get into those states ourselves, without assistance. We have learned to ride without the training wheels. At that point we can apply the lessons of state change in every aspect of our lives. By that time we've made the discovery: State change is possible. State change can lead to behavior change. We are responsible for our behavior. We make shit happen.

SUGGESTED READING

An excellent exploration of state-dependent learning and behavior is *The Psychobiology of Mind-Body Healing* by Ernest Lawrence Rossi (New York: Norton, 1988).

F O U R T E E N
DEEP RELAXATION ON COMMAND

Whether you use the state-change tools to explore the meaning of life, reach important goals, change deep-seated behavior patterns and attitudes, or simply relax and have fun, you will get the most out of mind technology if you begin by learning to use your mind tools to reach a state of deep relaxation quickly.

But wait, you say, isn't that the responsibility of the machine? After all, many of these devices claim in their literature to be "relaxation" devices, and many of them, such as light/sound (LS) machines, offer a variety of preset "relaxation" sessions.

It's true that numerous scientific studies have shown that mind tools can induce deep relaxation states in untrained subjects; some studies have found mind tools even produce relaxation states in untrained subjects as deep as or deeper than the relaxation attained by subjects with extensive training and practice in relaxation techniques such as Progressive Relaxation. Speaking generally, put on your mind tool (such as an alpha binaural-beat tape or an LS machine that slows down from beta into into alpha) and within ten to fifteen minutes you should be more relaxed.

The problem is that qualifier "more." Many of us start from such a high level of stress, muscular tension, and/or nervous arousal that even though we become more relaxed in relative terms, we're still, in absolute terms, not in true deep relaxation. True relaxation is a highly beneficial hypometabolic state in which muscular tension throughout the whole body is dramatically decreased (users describe it as feeling their body "go to sleep" or "melt away," or as simply losing all awareness of having a physical body), and in which the beta brain-wave activity of active consciousness diminishes, while alpha and theta activity increases and becomes dominant.

One odd finding that has emerged from recent research is that most people don't really know when they are truly relaxed. For example, in some experiments, subjects have listened to "relaxing" music or been given instructions to relax while lying in a dark and quiet place, while their brain-wave activity, muscle tension, galvanic skin response, fingertip temperature, and other measures of actual relaxation are being monitored. At the end of the session, when asked to describe their state and even measure how "deep" their relaxation is, the subjects frequently estimate that they became very deeply relaxed. But their bodies tell a different story: During the session their levels of tension have not decreased at all, and in many cases they actually have risen! That is, many people believe themselves to be relaxed when in fact they are in a state of arousal or tension.

Also, many of us have had the experience of being so tense or agitated that we know we would benefit from relaxing, we know that using our mind machine would help us relax, but we're simply too wound up to put it on, or if we do put it on, we're unable to let go sufficiently for it to carry us into a relaxed state. In fact, one of the main problems with popular relaxation and stress reduction techniques of all kinds—including biofeedback, "relaxation response" meditation techniques, and systematic relaxation procedures—is what the researchers call "lack of transference." They may be highly effective in a training seminar, during a quiet evening at home, or at a doctor or therapist's office, but they still remain extremely difficult to use effectively in the midst of the pressures and urgencies of the everyday world.

And finally, even though the brain tools are effective in producing relaxation for most of us, in many cases it can take fifteen or twenty minutes or more to let go of muscle tension and mental chatter and reach a truly relaxed state. If we have set aside twenty minutes for our session, then we have little or no time to pursue active strategies (described later) before we're back into our busy schedule again. Clearly, mastering a relaxation technique that can reliably get you into a deeply relaxed state in just a few moments can be helpful.

Deep relaxation is a key and a prerequisite to most of the various strategies applications and techniques that you will learn in the rest of this book, from accelerated learning, to visualization, to problem-solving, to self-healing, to attaining a state of hypersuggestibility. If we want to fill our cup with fresh juice, we first have to pour the stale stuff out of the cup.

To return to the metaphor of state change as a sort of switching channels on our consciousness TV, a new image cannot appear on the screen before the old image is erased. In this case, deep relaxation is one way of erasing from our screen the image of our current state—thoughts, worries, stress, tensions. Once all these images, static, and other interference have been erased, we have a blank screen, what I call state zero, on which we can then project our new state.

Fortunately, since the mind tools themselves are helping induce deep relaxation, they speed up the learning process enormously: Relaxation techniques that might take weeks of disciplined practice to master without the use of mind tools can now be mastered in just a few sessions. In fact, research suggests that all methods of relaxation or mental or physical self-regulation work more powerfully and effectively in combination with mind machines than in any other environment.

ACCESSING STATE ZERO

No matter what mind tool we use, and no matter what our levels of stress, tension, and arousal, all of us can profit enormously, and amplify the power of our mind-tech tool, by learning and practicing a relaxation technique that we use in conjunction with it. I suggest that you begin each mind-tech session by using your relaxation technique: Get yourself down to state zero quickly. Soon this will become almost automatic, and the relaxation process will accelerate. A technique that at the start might allow you to reach deep relaxation in ten minutes will soon take just seconds. Over time, your relaxation technique will become linked with your mind tool, so that simply by putting it on you will find yourself returning almost instantaneously to a relaxed state.

Dr. Herbert Benson of Harvard Medical School has studied the beneficial effects of the way our body and mind move toward state zero—what he calls the "relaxation response"—as well as many of the techniques, ranging from ancient meditative disciplines to modern systems, used to reach this state or trigger this response. He found that they all worked by using certain specific techniques or elements in combination. The key elements he identified are:

Mental Device. There should be some sort of constant stimulus, such as a word or phrase repeated silently or audibly or fixed attention on an object or process. Attention to this mental device or technique shifts you away from logical, externally oriented thought.

Passive Attitude. Let the process happen, do not attempt to force it or control it. If distracting thoughts arise, simply observe them, let them go, and return to the process.

Decreased Muscle Tonus. Get into a comfortable position so that minimal muscular tension is required.

Quiet Environment. Try to use your mind tool where you won't be interrupted or distracted by external stimuli.

In many cases, your mind tool provides the first element, the constant stimulus, whether in the form of rhythmic tones and flashing lights, or by repeated phrases or tones on an audiocassette. However, you can increase the relaxation effect of your mind tool by adding your own mental device, whether it is the silent repetition of a word, such as "Relax," "Calm," or "Zero," or focusing attention on your breath. By using these elements in combination with your mind tool, you can quickly reach your state zero. Following are some of the relaxation techniques that can be used to enhance your brain-tech sessions.

BREATH AWARENESS

Abdominal Breathing. Relax your abdominal muscles, so that when you inhale, your belly expands, and when you exhale your belly contracts. As you inhale, let your diaphragm drop, so your lungs fill from the bottom up. Shallow breathing (expanding and contracting the chest and rib cage) is physiologically linked to the fight-or-flight response; thus chest breathing causes the autonomic nervous system to remain in a state of arousal and inhibits relaxation. In all the breathing and other relaxation practices that follow, breathe abdominally. Do not force your breathing, but simply *let it happen by itself*. As you become more and more deeply relaxed, you will find that your breathing becomes slower: One important physiological effect of the relaxation response is a decrease in your body's oxygen consumption as your metabolism slows down. Your body undergoes a shift and uses oxygen more efficiently; since you need less oxygen, your breathing rate slows. As your breathing diminishes, it can become so slow as to be almost imperceptible. This can produce a feeling of delightful effortlessness that many describe as "floating," or "lightness," or the body "breathing itself."

Nose Breathing. One effective technique is simply to focus attention on the breath as it passes in and out of the nose. Continue your abdominal breathing. As you inhale, feel the air streaming in, the coolness at the tip of your nose. As you exhale, feel the air flowing out, the warmth at the same spot. If you wish, count your inhalations, numbering each from one to ten; when you reach ten begin with one again. Should thoughts rise into your awareness, don't resist them but allow them to pass, and then return all attention to your breathing.

Moving Around the Body. With each breath, direct your total attention to a particular spot in your body. Move systematically through your body. (You may begin at the top of your head, and move breath by breath downward through your head, neck, chest, right arm and fingers, left arm and fingers, torso, right leg and foot, left leg and foot, and back up again to end at the top of your head. Some people find it more effective to count each spot, beginning at the top of the head with one, and ending up back at the top of the head at a count of sixty or so.) As your attention moves from place to place, it creates and is accompanied by strong body sensations—feelings of melting, warmth, brightness, growing "softer." By the time you have made a full cycle, you should be deeply relaxed.

Visualization of Light. The nostril breathing practice described earlier can be combined with visualization: See the air entering your nostrils as pure white light. As you inhale, follow the flow of light through your nasal passages, into your abdomen; visualize it radiating to every part of your body. Then as you exhale, see the light flow back out of your body—now somewhat darker, dirtier, smudged, carrying with it some of the tiredness or toxins from your system.

There are many variations. For example, use visualization of light in combination with the moving-around-the-body technique—with each count, as you focus your attention on another part of the body, see the light flow to that part, see it glowing warmly. Move the light around your body.

The White Cloud. This technique is derived from the ancient Chinese practice *Qigong*. (*Qi* or *chi*, pronounced "chee," is a Chinese word for breath or air, and can be interpreted as "life energy" or "vital breath.") Visualize the air entering your nostrils as a cloud of intense and pure white light. This is *qi*, the "vital breath," the energy of life. As you inhale, observe the cloud flow through your nasal passages, downward into your abdomen, and down farther to the base of your spine. There, the white cloud enters your spine as if the spine were a tube, and moves upward. Feel and see the white cloud moving up your spine, past your upper back, your neck, until it pours out of the top of your spine like thick white smoke from the top of a tube. The glowing white cloud pours into your head, circulating and filling your skull. As you exhale through your mouth, the cloud is expelled, now somewhat darker, dirtier, smudged, carrying with it some of the tiredness or toxins from your system. Repeat this breath several times. Focus on your breathing entirely.

MINDFULNESS

Breath awareness is one element of a practice called mindfulness that can not only be an effective relaxation technique but, if practiced regularly, can lead to profound transformations in your life. On the most basic level, mindfulness involves simply *being aware*, witnessing, observing patiently, with detachment and without judging, what you are doing. You begin by becoming a spectator of your own stream of consciousness. Ultimately, with practice, mindfulness can lead to "waking up" from ordinary consciousness into a state in which each moment is a peak experience and in which one has direct and immediate access to one's full powers.

The first step to mindfulness is breath awareness. As in the Nose Breathing exercise, simply focus your attention on your breathing and hold it there. Be aware of the sensations that accompany your breathing as it comes and goes through your nostrils, your lungs, your abdomen. Any thoughts or perceptions apart from the sensation of breathing are distractions. If your mind becomes distracted, just bring it back to your breathing. Don't attempt to *do* anything; don't attempt to control your breathing; don't attempt to *think about* your breathing. Simply be aware, and sustain your awareness through the entire inhalation and exhalation.

People who are very active mentally often find that their racing thoughts, mental chatter, and concerns about daily activities and unfinished business seem to distract them from their mindfulness. Their first impulse often is to attempt to suppress these thoughts. Suppressing thoughts, however, is just another type of mental activity. Instead, simply become aware of what is going on your mind, with a detached, observing attitude: You are the witness, the observer, not the actor. Let the racing thoughts pass through your mind without focusing on them, as you might let a freight train roar past you without focusing on any of the individual boxcars, and return your awareness to your breathing.

As thoughts arise, don't fight against them, don't judge them, simply be aware of them and then release them and return your attention to your breathing. As you continue to attend gently to your breathing in and breathing out, you will, over time, notice a subtle shift in awareness. As Zen master Thich Nhat Hanh describes the process: "As we breathe in, we know we are breathing in, and as we breathe out, we know we are breathing out. As we do this, we observe many elements of happiness inside us and around us. We can really enjoy touching our breathing and our being alive."

You will find this practice calms the body and mind. Very quickly you become aware of your thoughts and feelings, and by observing them and returning your attention to your breathing, you learn that "you" are not your thoughts and feelings, that you can detach yourself from them, observe them from a distance. In time this practice can lead to feelings of inner stillness, clarity, and centeredness.

Body Scan. As your mindfulness practice progresses, and you find you can maintain sustained periods of continuous attention to your breath, you may want to practice other types of mindfulness. One technique is the body scan. As you become relaxed, turn your attention from your breath to your body, moving in a step-by-step fashion around your body, focusing attention on each part in turn, being aware of sensations, feelings, thoughts, whatever arises into consciousness, and then returning awareness to that part of the body. Feel each region fully, breathe to that region, *be* in that region, and then let go, *feel* all the tension and fatigue in that part of the body flowing out, and finally move on to the next region.

Mindfulness also can be directed at music: Use a music tape in conjunction with your mind tool, and as you become relaxed, turn your attention from your breath to the music, not thinking about it or listening to it judgmentally, but simply being aware of the music, moment by moment, as pure sound, hearing each note. If thoughts arise or your attention is drawn away, simply return awareness to the music.

As your practice progresses, you may want to focus your attention on the thoughts that flow through your awareness. Be aware of their content and the emotional charge that may accompany them, but don't judge them; simply observe them as "events," and let them go. Notice what thoughts keep coming back to you, what feelings and moods; don't get drawn into thinking about your thoughts, simply notice them and let them go.

Mindful Breathing Exercise. The following exercise, created by Thich Nhat Hanh, demonstrates how mindfulness can lead to deep peace and insight. I have found it works superbly in combination with mind tools to eliminate tension, stress, and anxiety quickly and put you into a state of profound calmness and relaxation.

Breathing in, I know I am breathing in.
Breathing out, I know I am breathing out.
In/Out.

Breathing in, I see myself as a flower.
Breathing out, I feel fresh.
Flower/Fresh.

Breathing in, I see myself as a mountain.
Breathing out, I feel solid.
Mountain/Solid.

Breathing in, I see myself as still water.
Breathing out, I reflect things as they are.
Water/Reflecting.

Breathing in, I see myself as space.
Breathing out, I feel free.
Space/Free.

To do the exercise, say the words of the first verse to yourself as you breathe in and out. Repeat it five or ten times, until you feel yourself, in Hanh's words, "stopping, calming, and returning to your true home in the present moment." Then move on to the succeeding verses, repeating each until you feel ready to move on to the next. As Hanh observes, "Breathing in and out consciously helps you become your best—calm, fresh, solid, clear, and free, able to enjoy the present moment as the best moment of your life."

MINDFULNESS AND ENHANCED PERCEPTIONS

Mindfulness is a practice that can be carried beyond your mind-tech session into the rest of your daily life. This practice of being fully conscious of each moment can have profound effects, ranging from boosting your immune system, to enhancing your mental functioning, to heightening your awareness, to intensifying the pleasure and the quality of your life. One series of studies done at Harvard Medical School tested a group of subjects who practiced mindfulness and a control group of nonmeditators, and compared their abilities to perceive millisecond flashes of light on a device called a tachistoscope. The mindfulness group's perceptions were extraordinarily keen: While the control group was barely able to see the flashes or separate one flash from the next, the mindfulness group perceived the flashes so clearly that they could observe the instant the flash started and the moment it reached its peak, began to cease, was gone, and so on, throughout the entire rising and falling of the flash.

Such studies are a clear indication that the practice of mindfulness can have dramatic effects on brain functioning and consciousness. Fortunately, reports from users suggest that mind technology can be a powerful adjunct to mindfulness, not only helping novices learn mindfulness, but actually increasing powers of mindfulness and attention.

SUGGESTED READING

A number of relaxation techniques are included in my *Book of Floating* (New York: Morrow/Quill, 1984). See also two books by Herbert Benson, M.D.: *The Relaxation Response* (New York: Morrow, 1975) and *The Mind/Body Effect* (New York: Simon & Schuster, 1979). See also *The Relaxed Body* by Daniel Goleman, et al (New York: Doubleday, 1986), *Open Focus Handbook* by Lester Fehmi and George Fritz (Princeton: Biofeedback Computers, 1982), and *Quality of Mind: Tools for Self Mastery and Enhanced Performance* by Joel and Michelle Levey (Boston: Wisdom, 1991).

Perhaps the best introduction to mindfulness meditation is *Full Catastrophe Living* by Jon Kabat-Zinn, Ph.D. (New York: Delacorte, 1990). I highly recommend any of the books of Thich Nhat Hanh including *The Miracle of Mindfulness: A Manual on Meditation (Boston: Beacon, 1984)*, and *Touching Peace: Practicing the Art of Mindful Living* (New York: Parallax, 1992). Other excellent works are *Seeking the Heart of Wisdom: The Path of Insight Meditation* by Joseph Goldstein and Jack Kornfeld (Berkeley, CA: Shambala, 1987), Stephen Levine's *A Gradual Awakening* (New York Anchor/Doubleday, 1979), and Shunryu Suzuki's *Zen Mind, Beginner's Mind* (New York Weatherhill, 1986).

FIFTEEN

BEYOND RELAXATION:

SELF-HYPNOSIS AND SUGGESTION

MASTERING YOUR MIND

One of the most direct and powerful ways to use the mind-technology experience to effect changes in your attitudes and behavior is by using suggestion while you are in an open, highly receptive, *suggestible* state—a trance state. This is just another way of saying self-hypnosis.

One of the characteristics of the theta or twilight state that we have discussed is hypersuggestibility. (In other words, suggestions or statements enter directly into your brain or unconscious mind, and are accepted as being true, bypassing the mental filters and critical defense mechanisms by which we usually judge such statements.) In theta, as Thomas Budzynski points out, our minds uncritically accept verbal material or almost any material they can process. Our subjective experience of theta, however, is one of a drowsy, largely unconscious state. As soon as we become conscious, or begin actively paying attention to something, we pop out of theta and are no longer hypersuggestible, since our critical screening defenses are operating once again. For that reason, the best way to use the hypersuggestibility of theta is with audiotaped suggestions (or suggestions spoken by someone else). That way we can stay in theta and let the suggestions wash over us without paying any attention to them or the process.

Self-hypnosis, on the other hand, permits us to enter a hypersuggestible state and *actively* to offer ourselves suggestions for personal action and change even while monitoring ourselves to be certain we remain in a trance state and while remaining in conscious control of the process. Self-hypnosis is not a difficult or arcane procedure. It is quite simple, and can be easily learned from any of the popular how-to books available. It consists mainly of three elements: deep relaxation, focused attention, and suggestions. Ultimately, as you'll see, even deep relaxation is not necessary. Hypnotherapist Milton Erickson defined the deep trance or hypnotic state as simply "a limited focus of attention inward."

ON BECOMING HYPNOTIC VIRTUOSOS

We know that mind tools are highly effective at producing states of profound relaxation. As for focused attention, I've suggested that mind tools, in part by effectively blocking out external stimuli, provide an unparalleled environment for calming, clarifying, and focusing the mind. Some research with brain tech and hypnosis has been done; as you might expect, it shows that people using mind tools go into a deeper state of hypnosis than they do when hypnotized without them. In addition, there's evidence that mind tools significantly increase hypnotizability—that is, people who ordinarily can't be hypnotized can go into deep hypnosis when using mind tools. One study of flotation, for example, concluded that some of the subjects who initially were virtually unhypnotizable "became hypnotic virtuosos" in the tank.

The first step toward self-hypnosis is called induction. Without mind technology, this process can be lengthy, with much of the time spent in becoming progressively more deeply relaxed and mentally focused. However, mind tech speeds this process up enormously. Simply use one of the techniques described earlier to access state zero and then quickly move to induction.

Once you've reached state zero, you can proceed with your induction by using some sort of sequence that takes you progressively deeper into hypnosis. One popular induction is the countdown. In your mind, count backward from ten to zero, moving slowly, one count with each exhalation. As you count, give yourself suggestions that you are moving into trance. For example, you might say in your mind:

> Ten . . . with each number I count downward, I am becoming more relaxed, more suggestible, more focused. Nine . . . by the time I reach zero, I will be in a deep, relaxed, focused, hypersuggestible trance. Eight . . . with each count I am becoming more suggestible, more receptive. Seven . . . with each breath I am releasing tension, my entire body is coming to a state of deep rest, comfort, peace, and heightened suggestibility. . . . At the count of zero, I am in a state of trance, open, receptive, suggestible. Six . . . with each count I am going deeper . . .

and so on, until you reach zero.

"I SEE," SAID THE BLIND MAN: USING YOUR PRIMARY SENSORY MODALITY

There are countless ways of inducing trance. Examples of full-length inductions can be found in any book on self-hypnosis. (I recommend those found in the "Suggested Reading" section for this chapter.) The secret is finding an induction or selection of inductions that work for you. One key to this is discovering and learning how to use your primary *sensory modality* (to use the phrase created by neurolinguistic programming [NLP] creators Richard Bandler and John Grinder, who were students of Milton Erickson).

Whatever the true nature of "reality" may be, each of us experiences that reality by processing it or interpreting it in some way. Scientists have found that most humans tend to process or interpret reality by reference to one or more of their senses. What's more, most of us represent reality to ourselves by reference to one or more of three major senses: sight, hearing, and feel. That is, most of us tend to experience reality in predominantly *visual, auditory,* or *kinesthetic* ways. These are our "representational systems," or sensory modalities.

What is your primary sensory modality? What sense(s) do you use to represent your experiences or feelings to yourself? In what way are you most *aware?* One way to find out is to listen to yourself—and to others—talk. Your language mirrors your primary sensory modality: The words you use reflect the sensory modality you favor at that time. Notice how differently people respond when they have something explained to them. "I *see,*" says one person. "I *hear* you," says another. A third might say, "I got it," or "I can *feel* where you're coming from."

Listen especially to the words you and others use—those words will suggest which portion of sensory experience you or others are primarily aware of while you're speaking. They can reveal to you which modality or representational system(s) you or they favor.

Visual Modality This modality is at work when people use such verbs as: see, view, look, examine, find, read, show, observe, glimpse, envision, peek, gaze. Visual descriptions make use of such categories (or *submodalities*) as color, location, focus, shape, brightness, movement or speed, size, contrast, direction, distance, clarity, and depth.

Auditory Modality This modality is expressed in such verbs as: listen, hear, tell, describe, overhear, sound, quiet, ask, yell, sing, speak, talk, call, shout; or in such submodalities as sound or words, pitch, tone, voice, rhythm, volume.

Kinesthetic Modality Common kinesthetic verbs include: go, grasp, catch, fight, grab, hold, hit, climb, run, struggle, throw, walk, push, feel, grip, handle, get, hang on, fly, spin. Submodalities include weight, pressure, shape, temperature, movement, intensity, texture.

When you have a memory from childhood, does it spring to mind most vividly as mental images, sounds, or physical sensations? When you think of a delicious meal, is it a kinesthetic feeling (the actual tastes of different foods, happiness, warmth, a full stomach), a series of images (sparkling crystal, colorful vegetables, steam rising from a baked potato, the color of the wine, white linen, flickering candles), or sounds (tinkling crystal, laughter of friends at the table, clatter of silverware, crunch of raw carrots)? Most of us tend of have one primary sensory modality, a secondary modality that we use frequently but less often than our primary modality, and one that we use rarely.

Discovering your primary and secondary sensory modalities opens up a world of information about yourself and about others. For example, by consciously exploring sensory modalities you don't normally use, you often will find yourself seeing reality in a new way—this is truly a way of "expanding" your self by using an expanded array of sensory experiences. In your use of mind tech, you might find it valuable intentionally to explore sensory modalities you don't normally use. For example, people who are primarily visual might find that use of mind tools that focus on auditory or kinesthetic stimulation might open up new areas of awareness. Or, if you tend to experience your mind-machine sessions primarily in one modality, try changing to a different modality: The experience will seem new and will reveal new information, uncover new feelings.

Another approach I recommend is using your primary sensory modality to open you up to your least developed sensory modality. For example, some people are highly visual but have very little kinesthetic awareness. Such people might use a visual mind tool—such as the flickering lights of lights and sound (LS)—to help them enter a state of relaxed awareness, and combine that experience with some kinesthetic experience—motion devices, massage, physical movement, the vibration of sound transmitted to the body through a sound table or a water mattress. By doing so they may find themselves awakening to a new awareness of the powers of the kinesthetic domain. Or, primarily kinesthetic people with a low auditory awareness might use kinesthetic tools, such as motion systems, sound tables, or cranial electrostimulation (CES) to get themselves into relaxed and receptive states, and then using primarily auditory mind tools—such as binaural-beat tapes, spoken word hypnotic inductions, or verbal learning material.

SENSORY MODALITIES FOR TRANCE INDUCTION

For the purposes of learning to move into trance, I suggest you explore your sensory modalities by trying a variety of inductions, each one using a single primary modality. Once you have found your primary sensory modality, you can use the language of that sensory modality as the most effective way to move yourself into a trance state. For example, you might try inductions such as the following (expanded by your own imagination, creativity, and intuition, and stated to yourself):

Visual. See yourself walking down stairs or moving down a series of escalators, each one a different color, each one taking you deeper into hypnosis.

Kinesthetic. Feel yourself somersaulting backward in slow motion, head over heels, through black infinite space, with each somersault taking you deeper into trance.

Auditory. Hear a voice counting backward from 100; with each count it grows more distant; with each count you are becoming more relaxed, more focused, more suggestible, until by the time the voice has reached the count of zero, it has disappeared into the distance, and you are in a deep trance.

MULTISENSORY INDUCTIONS

Many people find that the most effective inductions combine several sensory modalities and operate by engaging their attention and suggestibility on a variety of sensory levels. Here's one example of a multisensory induction.

Imagine yourself floating downward through clear tropical waters. You can see the small boat floating on the surface growing smaller and smaller as you sink deeper. You see your bubbles floating gently upward toward the surface. As you sink deeper you see coral cliffs rising above you. You feel the water pressure grow with a pleasing heaviness around your body as you float downward. You feel your arms, legs, your entire body, floating, deeper and deeper, suspended by the water. With each breath you can hear your bubbles flowing upward toward the surface. You hear your voice counting backward, slowly. As you sink deeper and deeper you are sinking deeper into a relaxed, suggestible trance. . . .

MAKING SUGGESTIONS

Once you are deeply relaxed and focused, you are in a state of hyper-suggestibility: You know you are, because you have suggested this to yourself. In this trance state, you can offer yourself suggestions for personal change, and they can have profound and long-lasting effects. A few general principles will enhance the effectiveness of suggestion.

Suspend Judgment. Believe your suggestions. There is strong evidence that believed-in suggestions—suggestions that the subjects believe are possible—are most powerful and have the highest success rates. So turn off that censor in your head, try to feel that the suggestion is true, experience it as real in your imagination.

Be Concrete and Specific. Brain research indicates that right-hemisphere speech comprehension is simple and concrete. It doesn't process abstract material well, if at all. Many hypnotherapists have found that suggestions act on the brain in the form of concrete images. Thus, the suggestion "I will win" will be less effective than suggestions such as "I will keep my head down and follow through." Also, the word "not" is neither concrete nor an image: thus, when you make a suggestion such as "I will not smoke," the brain automatically produces an image of you smoking (how do you present a concrete image of "not smoking"?), and the suggestion reinforces your image of yourself as a smoker. So . . .

Be Positive. Direct your suggestions toward what you want rather than against what you don't want—positive suggestions have more force than negative ones. Instead of "I am not afraid . . ." you might say "I am bold . . ."; instead of saying "I will not smoke," you might say "I love my body and enjoy acting in healthy ways"; instead of "I won't be late for appointments," you might suggest "I enjoy arriving early for appointments."

Use the Present Tense. Suggest "I am healing," not "I will heal," for future-tense suggestions by definition take effect only in the future, which of course never arrives.

Use Your Primary Sensory Modality. Don't simply use a verbal suggestion, but appeal to your primary sensory modality. If you are strongly visual, provide visual suggestions using visual submodalities, such as colors, brightness, contrast. Actually see yourself successfully performing the activity.

Use Many Senses. Strengthen the message by communicating it in your nondominant sensory modalities. If your suggestions are primarily visual, add some auditory and kinesthetic elements too; make yourself really hear and feel the suggestion as well as see it.

Repeat. Repetition is perhaps the most widely used suggestion technique, used by everyone from political leaders to TV commercials. Repeat your suggestion several times using various wordings, images, sensory modalities, and submodalities.

Use Rhythm. Suggestions are more effective when stated rhythmically and linked to your own rhythms of breath and voice. Researchers have found that voice intonation and rhythm are processed through the right brain (the emotional hemisphere) and thus can have greater emotional impact. Compare the powerful rhythms and changing voice intonations of gospel preachers or Jesse Jackson with the monotonous, unrhythmic speech patterns of a Henry Kissinger or George Bush.

Be Authoritative. A key to the power of suggestion is that we listen to and believe information that comes from authorities: Research has proven that suggestions from a person wearing a white coat and perceived to be a doctor are far more effective than the same suggestions from the same person but without the white coat. Put forth your suggestions with command power, and the assurance of authority.

While in trance you will want to offer yourself several types of suggestions, ranging from general to very specific.

GENERAL SUGGESTIONS

These broad affirmations are useful in producing a positive state while in your trance and at any time in your life. Some examples: *I like myself. I'm happy to be me. I respect and appreciate myself. I enjoy great vitality and health. I am in control of my mind, body and emotions now. My body heals itself at all times. I am a good person. I am relaxed and at peace.*

PERSONAL SUGGESTIONS

These suggestions and affirmations are directed toward your specific goals, problems, and skills. You can suggest them now in your trance state, but also repeat them in specific situations when needed and throughout your day. For example: *I praise my children at every opportunity. I breathe deeply through my abdomen. I am burning away excess fat and flattening my belly. I eat only when I am hungry. Whenever I want a cigarette I breathe deeply.*

ACTION SUGGESTIONS

A third type of suggestion you may want to use are short self-talk phrases that you can use later to trigger specific actions. These might include: *Power now. Push off. Focus. Follow through. Release. Let go. Think thin. Quick.*

You can visualize the situations under which you want to use each of these suggestions. You can then implant the suggestion so that each time you repeat that word or phrase, it will serve as a trigger for the desired action you have just visualized.

REINFORCING SUGGESTIONS

You will also want to strengthen these general, personal, and action suggestions by repeating them to yourself frequently in all areas of your life so that they will become not simply conscious suggestions or affirmations but *habitual thought patterns*. Do so by implanting reinforcing suggestions.

IMPLANTING HYPNOTIC CUES

One way of strengthening both general and personal suggestions is to capitalize on the hypersuggestibility of your trance state to implant suggestions that certain external signals will cause you to repeat certain affirmations. For example, you might suggest that opening the refrigerator door will trigger in your mind the suggestion "I eat only when I'm hungry." Or you could suggest that each time your phone rings, the suggestion "I am relaxed and breathe deeply" will be triggered.

IMPLANTING QUICK HYPNOSIS CUES

Another way of using suggestions is to implant a trigger that you can use in the future to help you reenter the hypnotic state quickly and easily. Many people like to use a signal or cue word: For example, you might suggest to yourself that when you are in a relaxed state and say "Shazam" to yourself, it is a signal for you to go directly into a deep hypnotic trance, relaxed, focused, and hypersuggestible. In this way you may learn to shorten your induction procedure dramatically or, with repeated practice, bypass it completely and go directly from waking consciousness into a hypnotic state.

IDEOMOTOR SIGNALS

While in a trance state, people have more direct access to hidden or unconscious material. One effective way of learning information that is hidden away in your unconscious mind is to use ideomotor finger signals: Suggest to yourself that you will ask yourself questions, that you will respond to those questions truthfully, and that if the answer to a question is yes you will respond by moving your right forefinger; if the answer is no, you will move your left forefinger (or allow your own unconscious to suggest to you which signals to use). This is a valuable technique for everything from uncovering past (and long-suppressed) traumas, to making decisions, to remembering where you put the car keys.

A procedure for dealing with a problem might begin by questioning yourself whether this problem has its roots in some occurrence in your past. If the ideomotor signal is yes, you might then ask if this occurrence took place in the first twenty years of your life. If yes, then narrow down the period of time further, by focusing in on a specific occasion. Another method is to ask specific questions that your ideo-motor signals can answer either yes or no.

Using ideomotor signals also can be a powerful tool for examining your current physical and mental states. For example, many competi-tive athletes are constantly on the edge of overtraining, which leads to sickness or injuries. So many use ideomotor signals to ask themselves questions such as: Should I work out hard today? Should I take it easy today? Is today right for upper-body weight work?

The method is equally effective for uncovering your own uncon-scious attitudes and beliefs. Do you really want that new job? Is goal X more important to you right now or goal Y? These are the kinds of questions that you really know the answers to—you just have to know how to ask yourself in the right way. Often ideomotor signals are the right way.

ANCHORING

One of the most remarkable features of being in a trance state is that you can plant suggestions to take effect at some later point, when you're no longer in trance. We're all familiar with the concept of *posthypnotic suggestion,* usually in the "magic show" setting: For exam-ple, the hypnotist plants the suggestion that when the subject receives a certain signal or stimulus, he or she will then feel compelled to bark like a dog. A recent variation of this technique permits individuals in trance to give themselves a trigger mechanism called an anchor. When the anchor is employed later, it can automatically activate specific desired behaviors or states.

All experiences are made up multiple components: While you're going through an experience you are hearing, seeing, feeling, tasting, and smelling numerous things. *Anchoring* refers to the tendency for any one of the components of an experience to bring about recall of the entire experience. We've all had the experience of smelling something that suddenly takes us back to an experience years before. For Proust, the taste of a piece of madeleine dipped in tea served as an anchor that re-created an entire world, which flowed out in an immense flood of memory that became the massive novel *A la Recherche du Temp Perdu.*

An anchor is basically a *conditioning* or stimulus/response mecha-nism: Pavlov conditioned dogs to salivate at the sound of a bell by teaching them to associate the bell with food. Anchors are created whenever we're in a heightened or intense mental state and we receive a specific signal or stimulus at the peak of that state. At that point a neurological link between the stimulus and the state is created. Pavlov's dogs were in a heightened state (hunger) when they were given food, and at the peak of that state the bell rang. In time the bell alone was enough to cause the dogs to salivate. In a similar way hundreds of oldies but goodies trigger a response in me: I was in a heightened state (sexual arousal) in the backseat of a car, for example, when I first heard the Beatles. The record was "I Want to Hold Your Hand," on the Cousin Brucie show, WABC radio—and now, thirty years later, when I hear the song it triggers a Pavlovian response in me. The song is an anchor for that intense psychophysiological state.

Anchors can be created under virtually any circumstances—we do it all the time, when we unconsciously link a specific slogan with a specific product ("Just Do It"), or a signal with a feeling state (a Christmas tree, the flashing lights on a police car), or a signal with an action (the stoplight turns red). Athletes anchor themselves constantly: The tennis pro goes through a serving ritual, bouncing the ball on the ground just the right number of times, to anchor himself into the state to make a perfect serve. However, we now know that *the more intense or heightened our mental state, the more rapidly and powerfully are we going to create anchors, and the longer will those anchors last.*

Mind machines, as much evidence indicates, are highly effective tools for creating intense and heightened mental states. In the self-hypnotic trance we enter a heightened and intensified condition called hypersuggestibility. The combination of hypnotic trance and mind machines is one of the most extraordinarily effective and rapid ways of creating powerful anchors that has yet been discovered. And since mastering the technique of using anchors is a key to rapid state change, and therefore a key to behavior change, the combination of trance-state suggestions and mind technology represents a profound new technique for behavior change.

How do you create anchors? The first step is to get into the state you wish to anchor. This is where self-hypnosis is so valuable. Let's say you tend to get flustered and slow-witted when in the midst of staff meetings and want to anchor a feeling of cool-headedness and verbal ease, fluency, and control. You use your mind technology, enter your hypnotic trance, and when in a hypersuggestible state, you *create the reality* of being at a staff meeting. That is, you visualize it and experience it with as much detail as possible: Create the meeting room, seeing how the table and chairs are arranged, seeing all your associates, including, for example, the clothes they're wearing, the looks on their faces, what they might be saying; hear the sounds, smell the smells, feel yourself sitting in your chair . . . all in concrete detail. And as you create this inner reality of the staff meeting, just as vividly you experience yourself speaking out, expressing yourself, being fluent, cool-headed, witty, and controlled. You experience this as intensely and powerfully as possible. Experience and enjoy fully how it feels to be confident and in control. Then, at the peak of this experience, when you are fully and intensely experiencing the exhilaration, the confidence, the sensations of mastery . . . at that point, create your anchor.

The anchor can be any distinctive stimulus. You might, for example, place your thumb against the first knuckle of your right forefinger. Evidence indicates that the best anchors are those that combine several different sensory modalities—sound, image, sensation, and so on. So you might want to create an anchor that combines the thumb against right forefinger with a verbal anchor (something like "Speak now" spoken internally); with an image (perhaps an image of bright light filling your body); with a kinesthetic sensation (a feeling of tingling energy filling your body).

Once created, the anchor serves as a sort of posthypnotic suggestion. When it's time for you to speak at the next staff meeting, you will activate your anchor: Place your thumb against your right forefinger, take a breath, and say to yourself "Speak now." See the light filling you, feel the tingle. You will find yourself experiencing the feeling of verbal mastery and cool-headedness that you experienced in your trance state, because these feelings are neurologically linked to the anchor.

If you create your anchor when you are in a highly focused and intense state, one experience of the anchor stimulus will be enough to produce a strong response when you activate it later. However, in all cases *repetition serves to strengthen an anchor*. By enabling you to create strong and effective anchors to return to your deeply relaxed, focused state quickly, consistently, and reliably, mind tools are invaluable.

BUILDING UP YOUR ANCHOR COLLECTION

Having successfully created one anchor—that is, having created your anchor and then later having tested it in real-life conditions and found it effective—the next step is to create more. Since anchors are essentially neurologically based signals or cues for specific state changes or types of behavior, you can anchor any type of state change or behavior you desire. You may want to create specific anchors for an entire repertoire of states and behaviors—one for relaxation, for example, one for a sudden burst of physical energy, one for a burst of joy, one for intense concentration, one for creativity, one for self-healing, one for pain relief, one for confidence, one for supercharging your memory, one for heightened sensory acuity and pleasure, and so on. The potential is limitless.

Earlier we posed some questions: Why do we use only a tiny part of our innate human powers? Why can't we have the extraordinary physical coordination of an Olympic athlete? Why can't we have the musical abilities of a virtuoso? Why can't we have powers of self-healing possessed by some individuals? And I cited the answer put forth by Sheila Ostrander and Lynn Schroeder: "Because *we don't know how to get into the state where these abilities live.*"

But using the state change/behavior change techniques just described, theoretically we should be able to call upon vast reserves of untapped powers. The most exciting aspect of the anchoring technique is that the state or the behavior that you anchor does not have to be one that you've already experienced. Your capacity to create and use anchors is limited only by your imagination. If you can use your mind machine to enter a trance and vividly, intensely experience the state of being, for example, an Olympic athlete, a musical virtuoso, a creative genius, a spiritual healer, and if you can securely anchor those states and behaviors, then you should be able to call upon them when you need or desire them in your life.

Of course, few of us have been given the actual physical gifts— part genetic, part a lifetime of training—required to be an actual Olympic athlete, virtuoso musician, creative genius, spiritual healer. But we all have the powers within us to be the greatest athlete, the best musician, the most creative person, the most powerful healer we can be. Using these techniques of experiencing states, anchoring those states, and later activating the anchor to reenter the desired state, we can call upon our own highest and purest powers.

ACTION SECTION—EXERCISE
ANCHORING A PEAK STATE

Select a peak performance state you would like to be able to access whenever you need it. Good states to start with are some of the ones just mentioned above—high energy, peak physical coordination, creativity, healing, mental clarity. For the purposes of this exercise I will speak of anchoring a high-energy state. Find a quiet place, use your mind technology, get to state zero, and induce a state of suggestibility.

Now remember as vividly as possible an occasion when you experienced that rush of boundless energy and enthusiasm. Childhood memories are extremely powerful and effective. You might imagine yourself riding your bike, the wind streaming through your hair, your body tingling with youthful vitality. Make your current mind and body state resonate with the memory of your youthful high-energy body mind state, like one tuning fork resonating to another. Don't just think of it—actually *be there*, experience it with every cell of your body, using every sensory modality you can—see, feel, smell, taste, hear the experience and yourself being the experience.

When you are experiencing, remembering, imagining, visualizing, being your youthful high-energy self as vividly and intensely as possible, explore your sensations. Move through your entire body. Are your fingers tingling? Is your body heavy? Light? Floating? Vibrating? Are you smiling? Is your breathing deep? Light? Moving down into your belly?

As you experience fully this bodymind memory of high energy, create your anchor—perhaps a finger signal, a signal word, a vivid image (such as white light pouring through your body), or all of these combined. Realize and tell yourself that every time in the future that you give yourself this signal (or combination of signals), you will activate these bodymind neural circuits, and you will fully experience this energy state. Suggest to yourself that *the more you use this anchor, the more powerful and effective it will become.*

End your session, sit up, and be sure you're in a waking state of consciousness. Now activate your anchor. If you have been successful in anchoring the desired state, you should reexperience it. Enjoy the experience, and remind yourself that repetition serves to strengthen the anchor.

REMINDERS TO REMEMBER:
EXTERNAL CUES

It's clear that the mind responds well to cues and anchors, which are basically just *reminders*. Unfortunately, as most of us have discovered at one time or another, the mind is not so good at generating its own reminders. For example, if we want to breathe more deeply, we will do so quickly when a friend reminds us, but often we can go for long periods forgetting to breathe deeply, until some internal or external cue reminds us. Thus the comicstrip image of tying a string around your finger.

As we've discovered in our exploration of anchors, we have an extraordinary capacity to assign virtually any deeply personal meaning to a cue or stimulus that is in itself without inherent meaning. So we can assign the meaning "relax" to a finger signal, and whenever we give ourselves that signal, we automatically activate a complex relaxation response. In this case, the cue is a self-generated cue. But, as we've noted, while we can be great at responding to cues, we can be lousy at remembering to give ourselves the cues. Using external anchors or cues is one solution.

One type of external cue is something in the external world. We can, while in our hypersuggestible trance state, arbitrarily assign the meaning "relax" or "breathe deeply" to the ring of a phone or a car horn. When we hear the cue, we automatically relax or breathe deeply.

GOOD VIBES

However, there is an even more effective technique for generating cues, and that is by carrying with us an "onboard" cue generator. One such tool that I have found extremely valuable is a small and very inexpensive "intention-arousing device" called the MotivAider. I did not describe this tool in Part II, because it doesn't fit under any of the "mind machine" categories, though it is in fact one of the most powerful tools for boosting brain power that I've encountered. The device looks like a small pager and is worn on a belt or waistband or carried in your

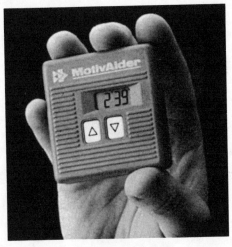

The MotivAider
(Behavioral Dynamics)

pocket. It is user-programmable, and works privately and automatically, by periodically sending you a brief, silent vibration. You can adjust the timing, so that the machine will give its brief, tingling vibration from once every minute to once a day. Or you can set it to deliver its vibrating reminder on a random rather than a regular basis.

The brainchild of Minnesota clinical psychologist Dr. Steve Levinson, the MotivAider was originally developed to help motivated patients follow through with medically prescribed self-care. The device is now being used for everything from sports training (reminding athletes at intervals throughout the day to relax or visualize themselves executing a perfect play), to quitting smoking, to alleviating teeth grinding.

Simply by creating a message ("breathe deeply") and "attaching" the message to the vibration of the MotivAider, the vibration quickly *becomes* the message. By using the MotivAider in combination with mind-tech tools, you can not only attach the message to the MotivAider much more tightly, but you can attach a far more powerful message to the device: You can, in fact, turn it into a powerful anchor for peak states or dramatic state changes.

ACTION SECTION—EXERCISE
ANCHORING AN EXTERNAL CUE

Here's how it works. First, decide what state or meaning you want the device to anchor for you. If you're a teacher, you might want the signal to remind you that "praise works." If you have a temper, you might want it to remind you to smile. Cancer patients use the device to remind them to do a healing visualization or experience a feeling of healing.

Once you've decided on what you want the device to anchor, adjust the timing so the MotivAider vibrates once every minute. Now put it off to one side, near your hand, as you use your mind tool to become relaxed, reach state zero, and go into your hypnotic or suggestible state. Once there, anchor the state, as suggested earlier. Don't just think of it—actually *be there,* experiencing it with every cell of your body, using every sensory modality. As you experience fully this bodymind state, place your hand on the MotivAider or place the MotivAider on your stomach. Now attach or anchor your state to the vibration of the MotivAider. Suggest to yourself that every time in the future that you feel the vibration, it automatically will trigger a verbal message (such as "high energy," "relax," "speak up," and so on), and activate these bodymind neural circuits, causing you to reexperience this energy state fully. Now let the device vibrate once, twice, three times or more while you're in your trance state, each time intensifying the fusion of the state with the vibrating stimulus.

After you've emerged from your mind-tech session, you can adjust the MotivAider to vibrate every five minutes, every half hour, or randomly. By controlling how frequently the vibration is delivered, you can control how prominent the intention or the state will be in your own awareness—whether you want it on the front burner or a back burner. In practice, you'll experimentally and experientially arrive at a level of awareness of a state, thought, or intention that produces the most favorable results for you.

While the MotivAider is the best thing I've found for the purpose, you can create anchors with other onboard cue generators, such as digital watches with alarms, hourly chimes, and so on. Whatever you use, I strongly suggest you experiment with this technique. We will be using mind tools in combination with anchors for such varied applications as accelerated learning, sports training, releasing emotions, pain reduction, and much more in the chapters that follow.

SUGGESTED READING

For an introduction to self-hypnosis, see my *Book of Floating,* (New York: William Morrow/Quill, 1984). Three more detailed manuals include *Self-Hypnotism* by Leslie LeCron (New York: Prentice-Hall, 1964), *Self-Mastery Through Self-Hypnosis* by Dr. Roger Bernhardt and David Martin (Indianapolis: Bobbs-Merrill, 1977), and *Healing with Mind Power* by Richard Shames and Chuck Sterin (Emmaus, PA: Rodale Press, 1978). An excellent resource for hypnosis and self-suggestion is *The Psychobiology of Mind-Body Healing* by Ernest Rossi (New York: Norton, 1988). Neuro-linguistic programming techniques can be used for all aspects of self-hypnosis and self-suggestion, as well to explore the sensory modalities and anchoring techniques described in this chapter. The best introduction to NLP techniques is *Using Your Brain for a Change* by Richard Bandler (Moab, Utah: Real People Press, 1985). Also filled with brilliant insights and techniques are other books by NLP creators Richard Bandler and John Grinder: See especially *Frogs Into Princes: Neuro- Linguistic Programming* (Moab, Utah: Real People Press, 1979); *Trance-formations: Neuro-Linguistic Programming and the Structure of Hypnosis* (Moab, Utah: Real People Press, 1981); and *ReFraming: Neuro-Linguistic Programming and the Transformation of Meaning* (Moab, Utah: Real People Press, 1982). A useful compendium of NLP techniques is *Unlimited Power* by Anthony Robbins (New York: Fawcett, 1986).

SIXTEEN

SEEING IN THE MIND'S EYE:

VISUALIZATION

The words or the language, as they are written or spoken, do not seem to play any role in my mechanism of thought. The psychical entities which seem to serve as elements in thought are certain signs and more or less clear images which can be "voluntarily" reproduced and combined.

—Albert Einstein

•

The ability to think in sensory images instead of in words is an absolutely essential first step toward the mastery of higher states of consciousness, self-control of pain, etc.

—C. Maxwell Cade,
The Awakened Mind

As you will have noticed by now, one of the keys to becoming deeply relaxed, to entering a focused trancelike state, to providing effective suggestions, and to creating powerful anchors is the capacity to use *mental imagery*. As our discussion of sensory modalities suggested, people tend to respond most to visual, auditory, or kinesthetic modes. But even though the word imagery suggests a visual image, for the sake of convenience I will follow the practice of psychologists and describe as imagery any of these nonverbal modes of cognition—whether it's an actual visual image (someone's face, for example), a clear mental "hearing" of sounds (such as the voice of your mother or a bell clanging), a clear mental kinesthetic sensation (the feeling of cat's fur or spinning around), or a remembered smell (grandma's house, the attic). For our purposes, then, all of these modes are ways of using mental imagery.

SEEING IS BELIEVING

The scientific evidence is very clear: What our mind perceives in the form of vivid mental imagery our body tends to believe is actually true. The simple act of vividly imagining a scene makes it a real experience. Dr. Edmund Jacobson, a physiologist and the developer of Progressive Relaxation therapy, established this link many years ago by having people visualize themselves running. He then measured their minute muscular contractions and found they were exactly like those that would have been produced if they had actually been running. Later experimenters with much more sensitive instruments also have found that the body responds to such visualizations—when the brain perceives something as happening, it tends to generate organic changes in the body.

VISUAL PRACTICE

In one of the most famous experiments in psychology, a researcher divided boys randomly into three groups and measured their skill at shooting basketball free throws: One group actually practiced shooting free throws every day; one group just visualized themselves shooting free throws; one group didn't practice or visualize. At the end of the study, the boys were tested again. As expected, the nonpractice nonvisualization group showed no improvement. Also as expected, the group that practiced every day improved—by 24 percent. But unexpectedly and astonishingly, the group that only visualized shooting improved by 23 percent, almost as much as if they had actually practiced every day!

Numerous other studies have confirmed the power of visualization. One intriguing study of dart players showed that the scores of those who imagined themselves throwing nothing but bull's-eyes improved by 28 percent while the scores of a second group that visualized themselves throwing at the bull's-eye but missing actually deteriorated by 3 percent! Another study proved that one group of dart players that visualized themselves throwing bull's-eyes improved, but a second group, which not only saw but actually felt, heard, smelled, tasted—experienced with all senses the entire physical process of throwing bull's-eyes—improved far more than the simple seeing group.

SEEING OUR BODIES, OUR SELVES

Mental imagery is not just some inner movie that might have an influence on our behavior through simple positive thinking or making us feel good. This fact is made clear by the increasing examples of ways mental imagery can produce dramatic and profound organic changes in our own bodies.

Numerous meticulously documented studies have proven, for example, that women using mental imagery can produce rapid and significant growth in the size of their breasts. In one study, the women in the mental imagery group were told to visualize themselves as they would like to be, with larger breasts. In another study, the subjects visualized blood and energy flowing into their breasts. In still another study, it was suggested that the women visualize a warm towel over their breasts, with a heat lamp shining down on them. In each of these studies the increase in breast size was surprisingly large and took place rapidly—in just a few weeks. In one study, average increase in breast size was two inches; in another, just under one and a half inches. One carefully controlled twelve-week study showed an average increase in breast size of 2.1 inches. It's clear that the increase in breast size was not a result of putting on extra pounds—the women who increased breast size reported that they had lost weight during the twelve-week period. Interestingly, in each case the breast enlargement through visualization took place when the women were placed in a hypersuggestible state through some type of hypnosis. This has important implications for the potential effectiveness of mind technology.

Whatever your thoughts about the positive value these women placed on larger breasts, these studies clearly demonstrate the power of mental imagery to produce rapid changes in our body. If we can change the size of our breasts through mental imagery, then there is no reason why we cannot produce other organic changes, ranging from boosting our immune systems to increasing muscle growth or triggering the release of desired neurochemicals such as growth hormone.

In fact, recent studies have proven this body-altering effect of mental imagery. In one study one group was hypnotized and a control group was not. Both were told to visualize one component of their immune system increasing in size and number. Within just a few minutes, their blood was tested. The hypnotized visualizers showed sharp increases in these white blood cells, while the control group did not. Again, the fact that hypnosis seemed to be the key to the power of visualization has important implications for the use of mind tools.

Perhaps the most widely known proponent of the medical powers of visualization is Dr. O. Carl Simonton, formerly director of the Cancer Counseling and Research Center in Fort Worth, Texas. Simonton has written several popular books and numerous scientific studies of his work teaching "terminal" cancer patients to visualize their bodies successfully resisting and overcoming cancer. He counsels patients to visualize white blood cells as "a vast army," powerful polar bears, or white sharks tearing apart and devouring cancer cells. Statistical studies of his patients have shown that those who use visualization live twice as long after the diagnosis of cancer as those who do not. Many of his patients recover completely through spontaneous remission. Significantly, Simonton teaches his clients to first enter a state of deep, focused, trancelike relaxation before beginning their visualization. He has found that this trancelike state enhances the powers of the mental images.

VISUALIZERS AND VERBALIZERS

Research suggests that about 15 percent of us are "visualizers," who have almost constant, rich, vivid mental imagery—those who talk about having "mind movies" playing in their heads most of the time. Another 15 percent of so of us are what the researchers have called "verbalizers," whose inner world is one of verbal thoughts, ideas, and structures. The other 70 percent of the population are on a spectrum between those two extremes.

There is evidence that learning to increase our powers of visualization can be valuable. Research has proven that visualizers breathe more regularly than verbalizers, and verbalizers breathe more regularly than normally when they are performing spatial tasks that require visualization. Science writer Gordon Rattray Taylor cites studies showing that "high imagers are more relaxed, more creative, more mature, and more flexible than low-imagers. . . . We have a clue in the fact that absence of imagery is correlated with strong defences against impulse."

Strong visualization is not only linked to producing changes in the body, such as boosting immune function and changing breast size, but also to powerful memory. Visualization is also, as Taylor notes, a key component of creativity. By "seeing" things that have never been, we can invent the future, just as we can invent a work of art or a new machine. In a study that compared the effects of one type of mind tech (flotation tanks) on learning and thinking, Thomas Taylor of Texas A & M found first that "When the same learning records are analyzed on the basis of persons who are basically 'visualizers' versus those who are primarily 'conceptualizers' [nonvisual thinkers], a greater degree of learning occurred in the visual than in the non-visual group." He also noted that the float group visualized better than the nonfloat control group and produced significantly higher amounts of theta waves. So there is reason to believe that mind tools can help people increase their own visualization powers.

According to psychologist Robert Sommer:

> There is virtual unanimity among imagery researchers that everyone has the capacity to think visually. This is as innate a potential as drawing or building or the use of language, or any other skill that develops through practice. If the potential is there, there is the possibility of improvement through training. Not all people can become superimagers, any more than they will be able to sketch like Leonardo . . . but everyone has the potential to improve the pungency of his or her thinking over what it presently is.

MIND MACHINES AND VISUALIZATION

In light of studies such as those just described, it's clear that mental imagery becomes far more powerful when it takes place in a deeply relaxed, trancelike state. Since the most typical and reliable effects of mind tools seem to be putting the user into a deeply relaxed, hypersuggestible trancelike state, it makes sense to assume that mind tools can enhance the power of mental imagery.

In fact, in my own experience and from the reports of others, there can be no doubt that mind technology dramatically amplifies and intensifies mental imagery. Mental imagery experts have found that there's a direct correlation between relaxation and visualization: The deeper the relaxation, the more vivid and controllable are the mental images.

CHANGING BRAIN STATES

Virtually all the methods of visualization practiced throughout history—from yogic meditation, to the monk's silent cell or the hermit's cave—have worked by shutting off or altering external stimuli and by altering the workings of the brain—changing brain waves, brain chemistry, patterns of hemispheric activity. By cutting off or providing optimal external stimuli and by quickly altering brain states, mind tools produce the kind of internal focus that can enhance mental imagery and increase the user's ability to practice creating and manipulating mental imagery.

We know, for example, that mind technology can promote strong theta brain-wave activity, producing the "twilight state," which is associated with the production of powerful mental imagery. It's also proven that brain tools can shift our hemispheric dominance quickly, enhancing the activity of the right hemisphere, which is associated with mental imagery. Clearly by practice and providing the right environment, the ability to create and manipulate mental images can be improved. Here are some techniques for practicing visualization using brain technology.

ACTION SECTION—VISUALIZATION
ACTIVE VISUALIZATION

We know that visualizations or mental images are accepted by our unconscious mind as being as "real" as events or experiences that have actually occurred. The way external reality is transmitted to the unconscious, in other words, is in the form of mental images. This is what we might call active visualization. Here are a some ways to strengthen your powers of visualization, your control of mental imagery, and, ultimately, your creativity.

Colors. As you use your mind tool to relax into state zero, imagine a set of oil paints or crayons. Look at each color. Visualize your face in that color. The face of your mother. How does that color affect you? How does changing the color change your own emotional responses? Imagine a pyramid, a cube, a sphere, or a cylinder. Color it red. Now change the color. . . . What changes do you feel? What effects do different colors have on you?

Cartoons. Visualize familiar cartoon figures—Donald Duck, Goofy, Roadrunner. Visualize them running, dancing, acting out scenes from your favorite plays or movies.

Memories. Visualize a familiar scene from long ago—perhaps your first-grade classroom. See it clearly—notice the chalkboards, the chalks, each desk. Who is sitting next to you? Can you see the rubber streaks on the floor? Walk around the room. See all the familiar faces. Visualize them dancing, acting out a play. What happens when the President of the United States walks into the room? What happens when you as an adult walk into the room? What do your old classmates say to you? How does this scene make you feel?

Visualize the face of someone you love. See the texture of the skin, the eyes, the hair, the movement of the lips as the person speaks to you. What is the voice saying to you? Pay attention—it's probably something important.

Take a visual tour through the house you grew up in. . . . Imagine climbing up the old sycamore tree to your treehouse. . . . See yourself in a full-length mirror. . . . Now begin dancing, singing, making gestures. What do you see?

Practicing active visualization will not only strengthen your skills in using mental imagery, it will increase your awareness, your sensitivity to visual information, and your creativity. It also will provide you with interesting and important information about what's going on in your own mind. In addition, active visualization is the foundation for a variety of athletic training, peak performance, healing, pain reduction, and other self-regulatory techniques we will explore in later chapters.

RECEPTIVE VISUALIZATION

Just as we can transmit information about "reality" to our unconscious mind in the form of images, the unconscious mind transmits its reality to our conscious mind in the form of images. We experience these visual messages from the unconscious in the form of dreams, fantasies, imagination, mental flashes. Imagery, that is, seems to be the "language" by which our conscious and unconscious minds communicate. Paying attention to this spontaneous inner imagery is what could be called receptive visualization.

So, just as we can communicate powerful peak performance messages to our unconscious by means of active visualization techniques, we can gain access to the most important thoughts and ideas of our unconscious by paying attention to the images that emerge from it. One of the most effective ways of doing this using mind technology is simply to use your brain tool to reach deep relaxation, or state zero, and then simply observe what mental images arise. Don't actively try to create images, and don't try to change the images that do arise. Simply observe them, without judging or commenting mentally on them, and permit them to drift away. A whole chain of images or scenes may emerge. Simply be aware of them and let them drift away.

After a certain period of time, you may want to move from a state of effortless observation to a state of more active analysis. Remember the images that arose. See what meaning they might have for you. Are the various images linked together in some way? What is the message your unconscious mind is sending you?

VISUAL ANSWERS FROM THE UNCONSCIOUS

Another valuable technique begins with active visualization and leads into receptive visualization. The first step is to formulate a question or define a problem to which you want your unconscious mind to provide a creative solution. This can be done either before or after you use your mind machine to reach state zero. Once the problem or question has been stated clearly, address it to your unconscious. Then simply wait in a state of mindfulness—calm, observing, effortless—and allow the answer to emerge in the form of a mental image. Often the answer will be a very specific image that provides a clear answer or solution. Other times the images that arise may seem irrelevant or unclear. Don't ignore seemingly irrelevant images—further analysis or thought may reveal that they contain significant messages.

SETTING THE SCENE

Many people find it useful to stimulate their unconscious imagery by creating rich visual scenarios. For example, having reached a deeply relaxed state, you may imagine yourself stretched out on the warm sand of a deserted beach. Experience it with all your senses. Soon you see a distant figure walking toward you along the beach. Who is it? Allow the scene to unfold spontaneously and see what emerges. Or you may visualize yourself walking along a beautiful path through the forest. You come to a fork in the road—one road leads deeper into the forest, the other up the hill. Choose one of the paths and continue on your journey. Where do you go? Whom do you meet?

In coming chapters we will explore other techniques for improving your powers of visualization. These will include shifting your visualizations into different sensory modalities, using different submodalities, shifting point of view, using *associative* imagery and *dissociative* imagery, and much more.

SUGGESTED READING

An excellent introduction to mental imagery is *Seeing with the Mind's Eye* by Mike Samuels, M.D., and Nancy Samuels (New York: Random House, 1975). *Creative Visualization* by Shakti Gawain (New York: Bantam, 1988) offers a wealth of visualization techniques. The technique of psychosynthesis, developed by psychiatrist Roberto Assagioli, uses many extraordinary and powerful visualizations as tools for self-transformation. See Assagioli's *Psychosynthesis* (New York: Viking, 1971) and *The Act of Will* (New York: Viking, 1973).

S E V E N T E E N
DEEP SELF:
EXPLORATION AND TRANSFORMATION

DISCOVERING AND LETTING GO

Once you have learned a few of the simple techniques outlined in the last chapters, a whole new universe of ways to use mind technology opens, and your mind tool becomes not simply a way to relax and passively entertain and enjoy yourself, but a versatile agent for actively transforming your life. In this chapter I will briefly touch on a few of the ways you can use brain tech for self-exploration, problem-solving, and personal growth.

RELEASING

One technique that I have found profoundly effective when used in combination with mind-tech tools is a process of consciously and intentionally releasing emotions or desires as they arise, developed by Lester Levenson. A successful, hard-driving businessman, Levenson suffered a massive heart attack that left him with what doctors said was only a few weeks to live. He went through a period of deep self-examination and concluded that his own feelings—not the world around him or the people in it—were the cause of all his health problems. He also realized that his struggle against those feelings was what had destroyed his health and caused him to suffer in many ways. Levenson discovered that he had within himself the ability to discharge completely all his negative feelings. As he did so, this health and his life blossomed.

As he began teaching his insights to others, Levenson found that all humans have an innate ability to discharge completely negative emotions. He developed his insights into a system that can be used by anyone and applied in any area of life, from self-exploration, to interpersonal relationships, to health, to business. He called this the Sedona Method, or the Release Technique.

SUPPRESS

In essence, Levenson found that most people have three usual ways of handling a feeling. The first way is to suppress the feeling. This, Levenson found, is the worst, most destructive thing you can do with feelings, because suppressed feelings don't go away—they build up and fester inside, causing anxiety, tension, depression, and a host of stress-related problems. The repressed energy these suppressed feelings create eventually drives you to behave in ways you don't like and can't control.

EXPRESS

The second usual way of handling a feeling is to express it or vent it. By "blowing up," or losing our tempers, we relieve the pressure of the accumulated emotions. This can feel good, since it puts the feeling into action. But it doesn't get rid of the feeling: It simply relieves the pressure of it temporarily. Also, expressing our negative emotions can be unpleasant for the person who is on the receiving end. This in turn can cause more distress on our part because we feel guilty about having hurt someone else by expressing the original feeling.

ESCAPE

The third common way to cope with feelings is by attempting to avoid dealing with them through distractions—talk, television, food, smoking, drinking, drugs, movies, sex, and so on. But despite our attempts to escape them, the feelings are still there—and still take their toll in the form of stress. So escape is really just another form of suppression.

RELEASE

But there is another option for handling a feeling. That is, you can let go of the feeling: release it, *discharge* it. We've all had the experience of being in the midst of some emotional explosion—an argument, an outburst of anger—and suddenly beginning to laugh at ourselves, realizing how silly or useless our behavior is. It's something like pressing the reset button on your computer, dumping all the jumbled programs and rebooting.

From the viewpoint of evolutionary biology, this capacity to quickly release emotions that block useful behavior certainly has a survival value—it would increase the "fitness" of the species having this capacity. An animal that is able to let go of irrational fears and angers and act in useful (survival-oriented) ways will have an evolutionary advantage over similar animals that are controlled by their emotions. Thus, for humans, the capacity to release has over millions of years become innate—a natural, instinctive ability.

Levenson found that this letting go was the healthiest way to handle a feeling. He developed a technique that teaches people to consciously use their innate capacity to release emotions whenever they want. His simple technique has been found to have a cumulative effect: Each time you release an emotion, you discharge or eliminate some of the suppressed energy of the feeling, leaving you more calm and clear-headed—more capable of acting in productive, healthy ways. With time, as you discharge more and more suppressed energy by releasing more and more feelings, you may be able to reach a state of *imperturbability,* in which nothing—no person or event—can throw you off balance or disrupt your calm clarity.

Many people who practice this technique find that, very quickly, their sense of purpose and direction become more positive and clear, resulting in better decision making and higher productivity. Insurance giant Mony, Inc., for example, commissioned a study of the effects of the Sedona Method on the sales of a group of field underwriters. Mony found that in the six months following the training, the trained group outperformed a control group in sales commissions by 33 percent.

THE PSYCHOBIOLOGY OF RELEASING

Subjectively, the experience of releasing produces feelings of relaxation, calmness, even pleasure. Often a strong release is accompanied by physical sensations—a sigh or outbreath, a ticklish feeling inside that can blossom into laughter.

Scientific research suggests that the Release Technique is an extraordinarily powerful stress-reduction tool. A study by Dr. Richard Davidson of the Laboratory of Cognitive Psychobiology at the State University of New York at Purchase, in collaboration with Dr. David McClelland of the Department of Psychology and Social Relations at Harvard University, compared the effects of the Release Technique and of another proven stress-reduction technique (Progressive Relaxation, or PR), with a control group that received no training. All three groups underwent various stressful events (such as watching a gory film of industrial accidents, generating emotional imagery associated with extremely negative experiences, and word association to stimuli related to the themes of death, violence, and sex) and experienced stressful emotions while their heart rate, blood pressure, muscle tension, and other stress indicators were monitored. The subjects were measured before any training (or no training for the control group), two weeks after training, and three months after training. The findings were impressive.

As expected, both the Release Technique and Progressive Relaxation produced sharp decreases in stress indicators such as heart rate, muscle tension, and blood pressure, when baseline or resting measurements were taken, and those same indicators during peak stress experiences. However, *in virtually all the indicators, the Release Technique was far more powerful and effective than Progressive Relaxation.*

Most interestingly, during the situation that posed the greatest "stress challenge" to subjects, the Release Technique group showed the greatest decreases in heart rate and (diastolic) blood pressure. Both training groups showed significant reductions in muscle tension while they watched the stressful film: 28 percent reduction for the PR group, 26 percent for the Release group. Although the former group was specifically taught a muscle-relaxing technique, the latter group had a nearly equal reduction in muscle tension—*even though releasing it is not aimed at reducing muscle tension but is rather an internal mental technique.*

Some of the other key findings:

- The Release group showed a decrease in baseline heart rate almost twice as great as those of the PR group. (The control group showed no decrease.)
- The Release group showed a drop in heart rate in response to stress (watching a film of bloody industrial accidents) more than double that of the PR group.
- The Release group showed a drop in diastolic blood pressure (BP) (the measure of blood pressure most directly implicated in cardiovascular damage) over three times greater than those of the PR group. (The control group actually increased diastolic BP.)
- The Release group also showed significantly higher scores in tests of ability to concentrate under stress.
- Both the Release and the PR groups showed significant reductions in anxiety.
- Significantly, these dramatic reductions in stress were still present in the three-and-a-half-month follow-up, showing that the Release Technique had long-term effects.

Davidson concluded that "the Sedona Method is indeed a highly effective stress antidote procedure."

ACTION SECTION—RELEASING

As the preceding evidence suggests, the Release Technique is powerful even without any technological aids. Yet mind tech facilitates and accelerates the process in numerous ways.

STEP ONE: Focus. One approach is to first think of some problem area in your life—something that is of great urgency and concern to you. It may be your relationship with a loved one, a parent, a child; it might be your job, your health, your fears. Or you may simply want to ask yourself, "What is my *now* feeling? What emotion am I feeling now?" You can do this focusing either before or after you begin your brain-tech session. Either way, once you know what problem area you want to deal with or what your now feeling is, use your brain tool to go to state zero or get into a deeply relaxed state.

STEP TWO: Feel. Once you're relaxed, consider the problem area you want to deal with. Having focused on that area, determine your *feeling* about it. You may want to short-circuit the first step of consciously deciding on a problem area and go directly to your now feeling. Ask yourself, "What am I feeling now?"

Lester Levenson found that all our emotions and feelings can be divided into nine major categories of feeling.

Apathy. Many other feelings or emotions are related to or are a result of apathy. When we ask ourselves what we're feeling, we may use such words as: bored, careless, cold, cut off, dead, defeated, depressed, discouraged, disillusioned, drained, forgetful, futile, hopeless, humorless, indecisive, indifferent, lazy, loser, lost, negative, numb, overwhelmed, powerless, resigned, shocked, spaced out, stuck, tired, unfocused, useless, wasted, worthless. All of these, according to Levenson, are subtypes of apathy.

Grief. We may use such words as abandoned, abused, accused, anguished, ashamed, betrayed, blue, cheated, embarrassed, helpless, hurt, ignored, left out, longing, loss, melancholy, misunderstood, neglected, pity, poor me, regret, rejected, remorse, sad, unhappy.

Fear. Subtypes of fear include feeling anxious, apprehensive, cautious, cowardly, doubt, dread, foreboding, inhibited, insecure, nervous, panicky, scared, shaky, shy, skeptical, stagefright, suspicious, tense, trapped, worried.

Lust. This is the "I want" emotion. We may feel: anticipation, craving, demanding, desiring, devious, driven, envy, frustrated, greedy, impatient, manipulative, needy, obsessed, pushy, ruthless, selfish, wicked.

Anger. We may feel: aggressive, annoyed, argumentative, defiant, demanding, disgusted, fierce, frustrated, furious, hatred, impatience, jealous, mad, mean, outraged, rebellious, resentment, rude, spiteful, stern, stubborn, sullen, vengeful, vicious, violent.

Pride. We may feel: aloof, arrogant, boastful, clever, contemptuous, cool, critical, judgmental, righteous, rigid, self-satisfied, snobbish, spoiled, superior, unforgiving, vain.

Courageousness. Subtypes include feeling: adventurous, alert, aware, centered, competent, confident, creative, daring, decisive, eager, happy, independent, loving, motivated, open, positive, resourceful, self-sufficient, strong, supportive, vigorous.

Acceptance. We may feel: balance, beautiful, compassion, delight, empathy, friendly, gentle, joyful, loving, open, receptive, secure, understanding, wonder.

Peace. We may feel: calm, centered, complete, free, fulfilled, perfection, purity, quiet, serenity, tranquility, wholeness.

STEP THREE: Identify Your Feeling. Now, with this list in mind, decide: What do you really feel? Open yourself up, become aware of your physical sensations—do you feel a tightness in the chest? Tension in your stomach? A sense of heaviness? A rapid heartbeat? As you become aware of your physical sensations, use them as clues to help you discover your feeling. What word comes to mind?

As a word comes to mind, try to determine what major feeling category it falls under. Levenson has found that *the process of releasing feelings is much more powerful if you can release the feeling in its most distilled or pure form, that is, as one of the nine feeling words just listed.* If, for example, you are examining a problem area and decide that what you're feeling is "hesitant" or "worry," then you can release your hesitancy or your worry and feel some relief. However, if you trace these feelings to their source, you find they fall in the category of fear. If you perform your releasing operations on fear, rather than hesitance or worry, you will find the results are much more dramatic and powerful. It is like attacking a problem at its roots rather than simply trimming away some of the upper branches.

STEP FOUR: Feel Your Feeling. Once you have found out your true feeling about your chosen problem area and traced that to its source feeling, feel the feeling. Let it inhabit your entire body and mind. If your feeling is a grief feeling, you may find yourself breaking into tears or deep sobs. If your feeling is anger, you may feel your blood begin to boil and your entire body become rigid. That's good: Now is the time to really feel the feeling.

STEP FIVE: Could You? Now that you really feel your feeling about the problem area, ask yourself: Could I let this feeling go? In other words, would it be physically and emotionally possible for you to let that feeling go at this moment? Think about it. Become aware of the difference between your self, your "you," and what that self is feeling. Sometimes you can feel your feeling like an energy charge that is in about the same place as your body but is not really your body, or like a shadow image that is slightly out of focus with your actual self. In one way or another, you will at some point have a clear sensation that *your feeling is not you.* Once you've become aware of the difference between your now feeling and your self, you should notice that it would be possible for you to let go of your now feeling. If it's not possible for you to let the feeling go, feel it some more. Sooner or later you will reach a point where you can truthfully answer: "Yes, I *could* let this feeling go."

STEP SIX: Would You? If you *could* let it go, then the next question to ask yourself is: *Would* I let it go? Again, think about it. Many times we are quite capable of letting feelings go, but we'd really rather hang onto them. You may find yourself thinking "No, I'd rather keep feeling what I'm feeling right now." If so, then keep feeling what you're feeling. Sooner or later you will reach a point where you can truthfully answer: "Yes, I would let this feeling go."

STEP SEVEN: When? If you would let your feeling go, the next question to ask yourself is: When? Think about it. At a certain point you will answer, "I am willing to let this feeling go *now.*"

STEP EIGHT: Release. Once you say to yourself the word "now," let the feeling go. Simply release it. In most cases you'll actually feel the physical and emotional release as you let the feeling go. You may break out in laughter. You may feel as if a heavy burden has been lifted off your chest. You may feel a wave of chills sweep over you. Such a reaction is one sign of the release of all the built-up energy that you've been holding in your body as a result of the feeling you've just released. It feels good to let it go.

STEP NINE: Repeat. Once you have released the feeling, you will want to check yourself out: Do you still feel any of the feeling? If some of it is still there, then go through the process again. Often, releasing is like opening up a well—you release some and more arises. Some of our emotions are so deep that they require a number of releases. Release as often as is necessary until you can truly say that you can't detect any more signs of the feeling in yourself.

Most people who begin releasing notice very quickly a decrease in nervous and physical tension: They feel more relaxed, calm, centered. By linking emotions to a physical felt sense and then releasing that physical feeling, they blow off a lot of physical tension. That leads to a quick decline in stress of all sorts.

Once you've learned to release by asking yourself the questions, you'll find that simply becoming aware of a now feeling is often enough to trigger a natural, spontaneous release. You may notice, for example, that simply by becoming aware that you feel, say, grief, you automatically release it. Once you learn to release using your mind technology, you will carry the ability over into your everyday life.

RELEASING WANTS

After practicing releasing emotions for a period of sessions, moving from specific emotions up to their source emotions and releasing those, you may find it helpful to become aware of even deeper sources of discontent—the desires of your ego, or the "wants." According to Levenson, all the dissatisfaction that we experience as the nine major categories of emotions can be traced back to *wanting*—particularly two basic types of wanting, wanting approval, or wanting control. And the very act of wanting indicates not having; in Levenson's words, *wanting implies lacking.*

FIRST-PERSON ACCOUNT

To explore and release these wants, use your mind technology, go into a state of relaxation, find out what your now feeling is, and then ask the question: Is this now feeling a result of my wanting? Is it linked to my wanting approval? Wanting to control? For example, as I write this book I am going through a painful, protracted divorce and child custody battle.

In the early months of this struggle, I found myself swept again and again by huge waves of grief, anger, fear, and longing for my son, who was 1,000 miles away. As I began to practice the Release Technique, I found that releasing my now feelings whenever they arose enabled me to remain more calm, strong, and confident. Releasing alone, without the assistance of mind technology, was calming and effective. However, when I began releasing in combination with mind tools, the effectiveness of the technique was boosted dramatically.

My own use of releasing has been in combination with a variety of mind tools, including light/sound (LS), cranial electrostimulation (CES), flotation, ganzfeld, electroencephalograph (EEG) biofeedback, and a series of psychoactive tapes I created myself using advanced sound generation techniques. Feelings clearly arise more easily and can be discharged or released more effectively when you're deeply relaxed and when your brain waves are in a more coherent state, such as alpha or theta. In fact, I now believe that much of the effectiveness of the Peniston-Kulkosky Technique of alpha-theta feedback training emerges from the natural "release" of emotions that takes place in theta.

As I learned to release using mind technology, I found that by discharging the energy of my emotions, I had more energy to put into my own life. The feelings would arise, I would feel them, release them, and the energy would be discharged. The release carried over beyond my mind-tech sessions, and I found myself moving through my days no longer savaged by the intensity of my emotions, able to work at my writing more energetically.

Releasing my emotions clearly had a calming, centering, and energizing effect on me. At that point I felt ready to move on to the next step of releasing: letting go of wants. I saw now that the source of much of my anger, grief, and fear was my wanting: I wanted the courts to do what was right and just, I wanted my son and I to be together, I wanted my former wife to obey the court-ordered joint custody agreement, I wanted my son to be safe, I wanted to be able to control my own emotions more effectively . . . As I traced these wants back, I found that they were all one type or another of wanting *control*.

When I recognized the root cause of my discontent, I was able to release my wanting control. Each time a wave of emotions swept over me, I was able to see that much of what I felt came from my wanting. By releasing it, I felt a more profound sense of peace and confidence.

You may be thinking, Well, it feels good to be in control of things, it feels good to be accepted. What's wrong with *wanting* those things? As Levenson points out, there is a difference between wanting something and having it. When we say that something is wanting, that means it is lacking: *To want is to lack*. We may want to have an ice cream cone, but as soon as we have it, our wanting of it ends, and we are more occupied with the actual having of it: tasting, experiencing, enjoying. As long as we are wanting control, that is a sure sign that we don't have it. If we are filled with wanting approval, we can be sure that we don't have it.

Often, in fact, it seems that the very wanting of something keeps us from actually having it. For example, as long as we want wealth, our wanting acts on us in such a way that it paralyzes or hinders our capacity to attain or have wealth. If we are filled with longing for someone else, that very longing makes us the kind of person the one we long for will never want to be with. By giving up or releasing our wanting of approval and control, we have taken the key steps toward actually *having* approval and control.

My own agonizing suffering, I saw, was rooted in a powerful wanting: my wanting for safety and happiness for my son that grows out of my inexpressible love for him. It was a wanting to control, a desire to be able to be with him and protect him from harm. But the wanting, which I could feel gnawing at every nerve, was clearly linked to my not having. My wanting, I understood, was in some way keeping me from having what I wanted. My wanting to protect my son from harm was causing me so much anguish that it was keeping me from actually doing what needed to be done to truly protect him. If I could release that want, then without the burden of wanting bearing down on me all the time, I would be more able to act with energy and courage to do what needed to be done to save him.

THE BIG WANT

We have traced all our emotions back to nine emotional roots, and traced those emotions back to their source in two types of wanting. Now, according to Levenson, we can ultimately trace those two wantings back to a single proto-want: wanting security or survival.

Behind each emotion, every want for control, every wanting of approval, is our deep wanting of security or survival, the voice of our ego crying out "I want! I want!" Again, this is a situation where too much wanting undermines the very thing we want. It is nice to have a sense of security. But people who are preoccupied with *wanting* security often invest so much energy and attention toward fulfilling that want that they sabotage their actual security, like a packrat busy stashing objects away in the attic of a burning house. There's a paradox here: You must let go of wanting safety and security to attain true security, you must let go to truly have, you must give up to be saved. It is, of course, an old paradox. To be born, you must die.

By discovering your now emotion or want, seeing its source in a deep wanting of security, in the desires of the ego, and then releasing that want, really letting go, you will find yourself filled with an exhilarating lightness and sense of freedom, as if a massive burden has been lifted from your shoulders.

In my own life, my releasing enabled me to let go of emotions that were disrupting my life. I continued writing this book, lecturing, conducting workshops, creating audiotapes, releasing, and doing whatever I could to bring the struggle for custody of my son to a conclusion that insured his happiness and well-being. Ultimately, after many months, it now seems that such a conclusion is in sight.

IMPERTURBABILITY

Security is not in itself a bad thing; nor are control or approval. And you will have noticed that some of the nine major feeling categories included feelings that are quite positive, particularly under the categories of courageousness, acceptance, and peace. You may be wondering if we are supposed to release these feelings. Aren't these the kind of feelings we would like to have?

The answer is that, yes, it's good to feel good. However, Levenson has found that it is important to release on even very good feelings, such as peace, serenity, wonder, love, and courage. For behind these feelings are hidden wants, desires of the ego. When you release these good feelings, you feel a physical and emotional release, just as when you release negative feelings. And what lies beyond the good feelings is *something even better*, something Levenson calls imperturbability.

Imperturbability is that quality possessed by many of the great spiritual masters, the ability to look on good and evil and let them go; it is the wisdom that life goes on. It is not so much a feeling as a state. "Everything arises and passes away," observed Gautama Buddha. "When you see this, you are above sorrow. This is the shining way."

As you practice releasing, you may find yourself having moments in which you experience imperturbability. The moments are, at first, fleeting. But, according to Levenson and thousands of people who have practiced this technique, releasing has a cumulative effect. At first, as you discharge more and more of the negative energies, you will find yourself experiencing more and more of the positive feelings. Your life will improve in every way. But sooner or later you will see the wisdom in discharging the positive feelings as well. At that point, you will see that all along you have been moving toward the peak state, imperturbability.

EXTERNAL CUE

Releasing is extremely useful and powerful when applied and practiced frequently, in all life circumstances. Thus, it's helpful to have an external reminder to signal you to release. As described in Chapter 15, you can use a mind-tech session to program yourself to link the signal from your timer, watch, or MotivAider, to a visceral reminder to release. In the early days, trigger the cue frequently—every few minutes. You'll find the release process quickly becoming an automatic part of your life.

RESOURCES

The Releasing Technique, also called the Sedona Method, is now available on an eight-videotape course that includes workbooks and other materials. The makers, the Sedona Institute, have such confidence in it that they offer a money-back guarantee. It costs $395. In addition, the technique is taught throughout the country in four-day seminars spread out over two weekends—highly recommended.

EIGHTEEN
RESCRIPTING

SCRIPTS AND IMPRINTS

All of us have certain chronic or recurrent states and behaviors that we would like to change. Some of these may be harmful, self-defeating, self-destructive, or habitual states and behavior patterns. Or they may simply be states or behaviors that we have found to be unfulfilling, or unrewarding, or that keep us from living up to our full human potential.

These unsatisfactory states or behaviors are often the result of experiences that have been imprinted on our psyches in moments when we were highly receptive or suggestible—particularly in childhood. Knowing what we do about mental imagery, and how our mind tends to work in terms of a progression of mental images, and being raised as we have been in a world of movies and television shows, it makes sense to speak of these internally guided behaviors as *scripts*.

Since rescripting or altering these internally guided behaviors is such a powerful therapeutic tool for changing harmful or unwanted behaviors, I had initially thought about presenting it in Part IV of the book, which deals specifically with *therapeutic* applications of mind tools. However, rescripting is so useful for nontherapeutic uses—such as enhancing athletic skills, learning abilities, creativity, and helping people attain peak performance states—that I felt it was important to present the techniques now.

Let's take for an example the scripts having to do with the expression of sexual energies. As sex researcher John Money of Johns Hopkins notes, "Perfectly nice, reasonable mothers and fathers go berserk when they encounter the first appearance of normal sexual rehearsal play in their children." The scene might seem to be innocuous: The infant begins to do something that is perfectly natural, perhaps playing with its genitals. A parent notices the child's sex play and immediately threatens or punishes it in some way, by shouting at it in an angry voice or by slapping its hands or shaking it. At that point an imprint is created. Perhaps the parent shouts, "You're bad!" or "You're naughty!" At that point a *script* has been laid down. As a result, the child's feelings about sex are altered in a way that will influence its behavior for the rest of its life. Thereafter sex is linked with feelings of guilt, fear, or being bad or naughty.

Or a young girl is scolded and spanked by her father for disobeying him. He shouts at her that she must learn to obey him. A script is laid down. Years later in her adult life, the woman finds herself acting out that script, in which pain, fear, humiliation, rebellion, and anger are activated automatically any time a male says something to her in a disapproving tone of voice, or from a position of authority, and she responds with inappropriate rage.

Many of our unwanted, harmful, or negative states and behaviors are the result of *conditioning*. If we could remember those childhood experiences when the scripts were created, we could rationally go back and expose the script as the false creation it is. "Oh yes, I remember it well, I was three months old and I was just touching my penis. Well, Mommy was simply tired and became angry; that doesn't mean I'm *really* bad; that doesn't mean it's *really* naughty to experience sexual pleasure." However, it's extremely difficult to remember those childhood experiences. They usually remain unconscious, because they are state dependent—or, even more resistant to memory, what the scientists call *state bound*.

WHY SCRIPTS REMAIN UNCONSCIOUS

The experiences are state bound because, to begin with, as children, we spend much of our time in a dominant theta brain-wave state, while as adults we spend most of our time in a dominant beta brain-wave state and pass through theta only fleetingly, usually as we nod off to sleep. That means that very little of anything that really happened to us in childhood is accessible to our conscious adult minds: We're simply not in the same state. We might *think* we remember what happened to us in childhood, but it is like trying to remember the true reality of a dream while we're wide awake.

In addition, most of the childhood experiences that create our harmful or unwanted states and behaviors happen when we, as children, are in an even more dramatically altered state of consciousness— fear, shock, or trauma. This, as biofeedback therapist Dr. Thomas Budzynski points out, tends to put a child into a trancelike state by shifting hemispheric dominance to the right hemisphere, which functions in a highly emotional, largely nonverbal way. In this theta, right-hemisphere–dominant, trancelike state, the child's mind is totally exposed, open, receptive, suggestible. What is "learned" during that state is learned in the most direct and intense way possible. Says Budzynski, "If you slap a child, or in any way get it into an altered state . . . and then say something to the child, you're going to be laying down a *script* in the right hemisphere, which may not have access later on to consciousness in the left hemisphere, but nevertheless will alter the behavior and attitudes of that child as an adult."

The script remains unconscious for several other reasons. Since the child is often still in a preverbal state when the script is laid down, when it grows up it cannot approach or remember this experience or imprint verbally—it is only a *feeling*.

It is also inaccessible to the conscious mind because, as recent discoveries in neuroscience have revealed, the script has been coded into memory via the limbic system, the part of the brain that controls and generates our emotions, and regulates our innate biological drives, below the level of conscious awareness. Thus it cannot be approached through logical, verbal, or intellectual analysis, or the other "higher" mental faculties of the neocortex, but only through the preverbal, emotional, primitive awareness of the limbic brain. (This provides one explanation for the inability of the various types of "talk therapy" to deal with such early experiences—how can one talk about something for which one has no words?)

The script is also unconscious because it is not simply a memory but a *state of being*—something that happens all over the body simultaneously. It is imprinted not just as certain words, images, emotions, or ideas but as a whole-body state of muscular tightness, rigidity, and respiratory tension.

Most important, the script is unconscious because it has been *intentionally forgotten*. The experiences that create these inappropriate scripts are traumatic experiences; thus, like victims of war, disasters, car or plane crashes, or other traumas, victims of childhood traumatic experiences tend to have amnesia about those experiences. It is as if the mind, having had such powerful and painful information pierced into its deepest, most sensitive areas, attempts to heal itself, burying the memories away, in an attempt to spare the victim further pain. The script or imprint becomes hidden, or, as psychiatrist Wilhelm Reich would say, it becomes *armored*.

But while the experience and the script are hidden and forgotten, they continue to operate in the individual's life. Budzynski points as examples to scripts such as "You're no good!" and "You'll never learn!" as particularly powerful and insidious. The parent rages; the child is terrified and goes into a trancelike hypersuggestible state; the angry parent shouts "You'll never amount to anything!" And like an actor unconsciously but dutifully following the script under the watchful eye of a tyrannical movie director, the child grows into an adult and wonders why he or she continues to engage in self-destructive or self-sabotaging behavior. In fact, he or she is simply obediently following the script that has been laid down in the unconscious, proving over and over to Mommy or Daddy that "I'll never amount to anything."

THE MIND-MOLECULE CONNECTION:
BODY AS A WEB OF THOUGHT

These scripts are so insidious and deeply imbedded that they become "wired" not only into our brains but into our very cells, where they manifest themselves as chronic or recurrent physical conditions. In this way state-dependent learning becomes a mechanism for transmitting and creating chronic mental and physical illness.

Psychologist Ernest Lawrence Rossi explores this "mind-molecule connection" in *The Psychobiology of Mind-Body Healing*. In this book he describes how "languages of the mind," such as words, ideas, sensations, are communicated to and integrated in the limbic system of the brain. There they are translated into the "languages of the body," in the form of neurochemical messenger molecules called neuropeptides, which flow throughout the entire body, communicating directly with the organs and cells.

These neuropeptides, we now know, carry messages that are the physiological equivalents of mental experiences. That is, they are like molecular emotions and thoughts, or pieces of intelligence, circulating and carrying mental experiences throughout the body. The body, then, must be seen as a *field of intelligence*. Mind is not located in the brain but circulates throughout the body: The body is a web of thought, a network of mind.

And in turn, each part of the body communicates its own information, thoughts, and emotions in neurochemical form to other parts of the body and to the limbic system, where the body's language is translated into the words, ideas, emotions, and sensations that are the language of the mind. Mind is a network of molecules, a web of body.

In the sample scripts we've been exploring, negative scripts or imprints enter the limbic system and become molecular emotions that change the body on a cellular level while the child is in a right-hemisphere–dominant theta state. This is a state in which the mind is extraordinarily receptive to new information, in which it learns and incorporates behaviors that continue to operate throughout life. That is, the response to the script or imprint is "learned"—becomes a habitual pattern—by entering our field of intelligence as molecular information that transforms our body on cellular and even subcellular, genetic (and most of all *unconscious*) level.

Theoretically, we could detect our own unwanted habitual scripts and patterns and intentionally try to alter them. However, the "learning" that has created the patterns is very much state dependent. The only way to correct or undo the negative pattern, then, is to enter a mind-body state like that in which the original learning (or mislearning) took place.

This explains how and why many body-centered psychotherapeutic techniques (such as Rolfing, rebirthing, Holotropic breathing, Bioenergetics) work: They encourage the subject to become deeply relaxed or highly charged emotionally, so that theta waves and right-hemisphere and limbic system activity all increase. This allows the subject to reenter or reaccess the original bodymind state, where the trauma, imprint, or script can be experienced, articulated, and replaced by new learning, imprints, or scripts.

Another effective technique for reaching these buried scripts and imprints is hypnosis. Like the body-centered therapies, it too moves beyond the limitations of logical, verbal, or intellectual analysis, or the other "higher" neocortex faculties, to work through the preverbal, emotional, primitive awareness of the limbic brain, activate the mind-molecule connection, and provide access to the self-interacting field of intelligence, the bodymind.

ACTION SECTION—RESCRIPTING

Seen in this light, the new mind technologies clearly provide the most effective tools yet developed for counteracting these deeply imbedded scripts. Like the body-centered therapies, mind tech works directly on the bodymind to slow brain-wave activity, activate the right hemisphere, and alter limbic activity such as breathing patterns. But new mind tools go far beyond the body-centered therapies by directly entraining and slowing brain-wave activity into the appropriate theta frequency range, effectively blocking out the distractions of normal life and the reminders of adult consensus reality. In the case of LS, acoustic field generators, flotation, and ganzfeld, brain technology actively disrupts logical and customary adult thought patterns and injects the user into a whole-body nonlinear unpredictable experience. This experience triggers the emotional limbic brain to resonate and activate the mind-molecule web of information, and permit access to state-dependent and even state-bound childhood experiences.

In addition, brain technology permits the user or an associate to make use of the powers of hypnosis to, in Rossi's words, "access and reframe state-dependent memory." It is a process that is called "rescripting." Budzynski, who uses LS for rescripting in his own practice as a therapist, describes the process: "The technique involves, first, the uncovering of the scripts, second, the creation of counter-scripts which present a more positive outcome, and third, the repeated presentation of the counter-script, preferably while in a deeply relaxed or hypnotic state. The L/S is used both to facilitate the uncovering and the rescripting itself."

It's important to point out that while Budzynski refers specifically to LS, the rescripting techniques he describes can be applied just as effectively using other types of brain technology.

STEP ONE: UNCOVERING

The first step toward rescripting, after using your mind tool to relax and access state zero, is *uncovering*. As the word implies, the process is something like taking the cover off a boiling pot and watching what bubbles to the surface. Though not essential, you may find that having a specific question you wish to deal with during that session facilitates the process—some particular state or behavior that causes you problems, perhaps. You may want to state clearly to yourself: I want to use this session to investigate my anger (my smoking, my back pain, my mother). In this way your unconscious mind has a context in which to work and reveal itself.

On the other hand, some of the most powerful and life-transforming uncovering experiences have happened spontaneously, and in un-predictable ways, when users simply let go to find out what was going on in their unconscious. Whichever approach you take, the most important thing is that you enter the session with a conscious commitment to release, let go, give up control, and let yourself be carried along on the currents of your unconscious.

Making Notes. During the session you may find suppressed or long-forgotten memories surfacing spontaneously in the form of visual flashbacks or images. If a friend is there, he or she can facilitate the uncovering process by gently and unobtrusively asking you what you are seeing and feeling. Many users have found that an inexpensive tape recorder (voice-activated is preferable though not necessary) is the most effective way of recording spontaneously arising material. Simply place the recorder beside you, and whenever possible—without disrupting the flow of imagery and without becoming so conscious of speaking that you cause yourself to "pop out" of state—describe your experiences. You'll find that a sort of verbal shorthand is the most effective way of doing this. Just a few words (for example, "summer nights . . . seven years old . . . boys in trees . . . great sadness . . ." and so on) can act as touchstones later, bringing to consciousness complex and detailed scenes and ideas. Whether speaking to a recorder, a friend or therapist, or simply using your memory, the intention, of course, is to observe what is happening, note what is being revealed, yet permit it to continue without disrupting the whole process by pulling yourself out of state.

Ideomotor Finger Signals. You may want to expedite the process of uncovering by using ideomotor finger signals. Once you are in a deep trance, you may ask, for example, if the problems you want to deal with are the result of a single traumatic experience. If so, you may continue using your ideomotor signals to narrow in on the date (how old were you when the experience occurred?), the location, and so on. You may combine this with suggestions that you can visualize the experience. Again, a friend or a therapist can facilitate this process by asking questions and observing your ideomotor finger signals.

Dealing with Emotions. No matter what technique you use, you can be sure you are getting close to the original scripting experience when you begin to experience intense emotions, such as grief, rage, fear. Budzynski points out that "Uncovering is a very sensitive and potentially anxiety-evoking process" and recommends it be attempted only by trained mental health professionals. However, you may feel confident that you can confront these past experiences. Working with a friend may give you the confidence that you will not be alone. Knowing and using the Release Technique also is extremely useful.

STEP TWO: RESCRIPTING

Once the harmful script has been uncovered, the next step is to develop a counterscript.

While in your deeply relaxed state, you should re-create the original traumatic experience or unwanted scripting experience, using as much concrete detail and as many sensory modalities as possible. However, as the scene is re-created, you should alter it in such a way that it produces a positive outcome. Budzynski describes a case of a woman who had an inexplicable pain in her arm. Upon going into hypnosis and using ideomotor signals, she revealed that once she had been hospitalized and unconscious after a fall from a horse. While a nurse was inserting an IV needle in her arm, a visiting relative remarked, "Gee, that looks like it would sting!" The woman's unconscious mind, in an altered state, apparently took this as a command. "The rescription was simple," says Budzynski. "An old but wise 'Dr. Welby' type physician was introduced to the scene. When the triggering remark was made, the wise physician said, 'Oh, sure, it stings for a few seconds, but then it feels as good as new.' When the client awakened, the pain was gone!"

RESCRIPTING WITH SUBMODALITIES

It's clear the mental images we use influence how we feel. One way to change the mental images is to do a whole-scene rewrite, changing the content of the mental image. But another powerful way to alter the meaning and influence of our mental images is to change the submodalities of the image. Submodalities, according to neurolinguistic programming (NLP) co-creator Richard Bandler, are "universal elements that can be used to change any visual image, no matter what the content is." There are visual, kinesthetic, and auditory submodalities, but I will focus on visual submodalities here.

For example, suppose you have a very unpleasant memory you would like to rescript. As you look at that unpleasant memory, see it as a black-and-white movie, and make it get dimmer and dimmer, so that it almost fades away. Turn it down entirely. Now see how that scene makes you feel. You may find that much of the emotional contents of the scene—your unpleasant feelings—have faded away with the image. Think of a very pleasant scene. Now turn up the brightness and the colors on that scene, and see how that makes you feel. Usually increasing the brightness and color of an image will increase the intensity of the feelings it causes.

As Bandler points out, we're all aware of this link between mental imagery and behavior:

> People talk about a "dim future" or "bright prospects." "Everything looks black." "My mind went blank." "It's a small thing, but

she blows it all our of proportion." When someone says something like that, it's not metaphorical; it's usually a literal and precise description of what that person is experiencing inside. If someone is "blowing something out of proportion," you can tell her to shrink that picture down. If she sees a "dim future," have her brighten it up. It sounds simple . . . and it is.

Experimentation is the best way to find out what changing submodalities can do to change your experience and help you in your rescripting process. Take an image and go through each of the following submodalities and see how it changes your experience. At first, change just one submodality at a time, so you can learn what its effect is, without mingling it with the effects of other submodalities. Here are some of the visual submodalities that Bandler suggests. Try them out on a pleasant experience before unleashing them on unpleasant ones.

Clarity. What's the difference in experience between a fuzzy, soft-focus image and a hard-edged, crystal-clear one?

Color. Change color intensity from vivid brightness to black and white.

Depth. Vary your image from three-dimensional to a flat two-dimensional surface.

Distance. Move the image from very close to very far off.

Duration. See the difference between a quick flicker of an image to a long-lasting one.

Forward/backward. What happens when you take a scene and run it backward, from the end to the beginning? Many of us find it funny. That's a great way to deal with unpleasant experiences—run them backward and make them ridiculous and laughable. Or run the unpleasant scene backward to its beginning, then run it forward again, but this time with the content changed to make it very pleasant. You can also put the scene into the "erase" mode, so that as it runs backward it's being erased. This is a good way to get rid of unpleasant scenes.

Movement. Vary the mental image from a still photo or slide to a slow-motion movie to lickety-split fast time.

Scope. Explore the difference between an image on a screen in front of your eyes to an expanded image, to a fully encompassing image that surrounds you, so that if you turn your head to either side you can see more.

Performing similar experiments and changing one kinesthetic submodality (weight, size, pressure, shape, temperature, movement, balance, texture, rhythm, and so on) or auditory submodality (pitch, tone, timbre, tempo, volume, duration of sounds, distance, voice, words, and so on) at a time is also valuable.

Once you've discovered the effects of these various submodalities singly, you can combine them and apply them to rescripting past experiences. Doing so can prove to be a life-transforming power. As Bandler remarks,

> What's amazing to me is that some people do it exactly backwards. Think what your life would be like if you remembered all your good experiences as dim, distant, fuzzy, black and white snapshots, but recalled all your bad experiences in vividly colorful, close, panoramic, 3-D movies. That's a great way to get depressed and think that life isn't worth living. All of us have good and bad experiences; how we recall them is often what makes the difference.

CHANGING YOUR POINT OF VIEW

Another powerful technique for changing the impact of past events is to change the way you choose to experience them. Filmmakers pay extremely careful attention to what they call POV, or point of view, because they know that the POV of a scene can determine its entire impact and significance to the audience. Do we view a scene from the POV of one of the actors in the scene, or do we see the scene from a distance, with a frame around it? Imagine how different the shower scene from *Psycho* would feel if it had been filmed from the POV of some objective observer.

POV has the same powerful determining influence in the mind movies that make up your memories. Remember some horrible thing that happened to you—really experience it as it happened. Now try to fully experience an extremely pleasant memory. Is there a difference in the point of view? Perhaps you see one of the memories exactly as you did when it happened, as if you are actually inside your body looking out through the eyes that are seeing the events happen. This is called being *associated*. Perhaps you see one of the memories from a point of view other than through your own eyes—maybe you see the scene from above, as if you're perched in a corner of the room by the ceiling; perhaps you see it as if you're watching a movie. This is called being *dissociated*.

Now, take the good and the bad memory, whichever way you experienced them, and go back and experience them from a different point of view. If you were associated in your happy memory, now recall it in a dissociated way, seeing yourself from a distance, or as if in a movie. If you were dissociated, step into your body, experience the scene in the same multisensory way you did when you were truly in it. How does it change your memories?

For most people, recalling an event in an associated way causes them to reexperience the feeling response they originally had. Most people who recall an event in a dissociated way can *observe* themselves having the original feelings without actually reexperiencing them. This can be immensely valuable. You can choose to recall your happy memories in an associated way, feeling all the pleasurable emotions and feelings that accompany them, and recall all the unpleasant memories in a dissociated way, with all the information about what happened, but without the negative feelings. As Bandler points out, "Why feel bad again? Wasn't it enough to feel bad once?"

But many people go about it in exactly the opposite way, and associate with all their unpleasant memories, while storing their pleasant memories as distant, dissociated images. Then they feel hurt and angry about unpleasant events that are long past, while not feeling any of the pleasure out of what should be their best memories.

Since mind tech can increase enormously your powers of memory and visualization, you will find it useful to go back through your most unpleasant memories and run through them from a dissociated POV. Experience a variety of good memories by being fully associated, soaking in the pleasure and good feelings of each one. In essence, you're teaching yourself to associate with good memories and dissociate from bad ones. Bandler points out that learning how and when to associate or dissociate is "one of the most profound and pervasive ways to change the quality of a person's experience, and the behavior that results from it. Dissociation is particularly useful for intensely unpleasant memories." Dissociation can be extremely valuable for victims of rape, child abuse, and experiences of war or other traumatic experiences, such as posttraumatic stress syndrome.

RESCRIPTING FOR INCREASING LIFE SATISFACTION

These techniques for rescripting and changing memories by changing point of view need not be limited to dealing with clearly traumatic childhood experiences. Even the most healthy and well-adjusted individuals have areas in which their lives are unsatisfying and their life strategies are unproductive, or in which they feel they are not living up to their fullest potential. One friend of mine I'll call Ed, for example, is a successful businessman with a rewarding and fulfilling personal and family life. However, he found that he had a nagging dissatisfaction with his own inability to loosen up, let go, and express himself in front of an audience. As he explored this in a series of sessions on an LS machine, he found that there was part of him that would have liked to have been an entertainer. He began recalling experiences from his own childhood that had to do with performing. He had vivid memories in which he had tried out or wanted to try out comedy acts and song-and-dance routines in front of his father. His father had been a hard-driving business executive, who had little time to sit down and let himself be entertained by his six-year-old son. Ed remembered one time when he did a slapstick comedy routine for his father, who sat watching impatiently without laughing. The result was that Ed, receiving no encouragement or praise from his father, had felt early on that he was not particularly skilled as an entertainer, and soon he stifled this aspect of his personality.

Ed began a rescripting process by going back to those childhood experiences in which he tried out his act on his father. Now, however, Ed created a counterscript in which his father explained to Ed that he was sorry he was too busy to pay attention, that it was his fault, not Ed's, and it had nothing to do with Ed's intrinsic talents or worth. In the counterscript, Ed was once again his six-year-old self. His father sat down and Ed did his magic tricks, slapstick gags, soft-shoe and tap-dance routines, and his father laughed uproariously, applauded often, and ended by giving Ed a bearhug, telling him how much he loved him and what a talented boy he was.

Ed also found that while his memories of performing for his father were vivid associative experiences, his memories of some of his experiences of performing in school plays or singing in a school vocal group were dim and dissociative—he saw himself as if from the back of the auditorium. He began reexperiencing those memories in an associative way, fully enjoying them.

Predictably, Ed felt a sense of release and change in his own adult life. He became more self-confident and found he had a great desire to perform. He sat down at the piano, which he had not played seriously for over twenty years, and began playing again. Soon he had joined a small band and had tremendous fun playing gigs around town. He is now considering trying out for a part at the local playhouse.

Like anchoring, rescripting gains in power with repetition, and the more vivid the rescripted experience (engaging several senses and with concrete details), the more power it has to counter the old script. Rescripting requires sensitivity and imagination. As the name implies, you must become a scriptwriter, taking old scripts that don't work, looking at them with a creative eye, and turning them into scripts that work. As in all the techniques in this book, with practice you will become better at this process.

THE SWISH

One powerful rescripting technique developed by Richard Bandler and widely used by practitioners of NLP is called the swish pattern. NLP teaches you how to do a swish pattern while in ordinary waking consciousness. However, I've found that using this (and other NLP techniques) in the midst of the deep relaxation and state zero brain-tech experience boosts it to a higher order of effectiveness. I have used this technique in many of my Megabrain Workshops and have found that it can produce rapid and dramatic effects.

In essence, a swish pattern takes something unpleasant or un-desired—a memory, an image, a behavior or habit, a state—and causes it automatically to trigger something pleasant or desired. Or, as Bandler says, it "directionalizes the brain," by making use of the human tendency to avoid unpleasantness and move toward pleasantness. Here's how it's done.

IDENTIFY CUE IMAGE

Let's say you want to change bad habit X (smoking, biting your fingernails, overeating, and so on). Once you have used your mind tool to get into a deeply relaxed, trance state, or state zero, the next step is to identify the *cue image*, that is, what you actually see as you begin to engage in habit X. For smokers, it may be your hand moving toward your pack of cigarettes, or the pocket or purse where you keep them; for nail biters, it may be the image of your hand moving toward your mouth. Since this is the cue for a habit you don't like, you should make something about this image unpleasant—the more unpleasant the better.

CREATE DESIRED OUTCOME IMAGE

The next step is to create a second picture—an image of yourself as you would be if you had already made the desired change in your behavior. This image should be very attractive and pleasant. You may have to try several images, or make several adjustments in your image, until you get something that you really like.

SWISH

Now switch the two images by "swishing" them. Start with the first cue picture big and bright. Then put a small, dim, and dark version of your desired outcome image in the bottom right-hand corner of your visual field. Then, in a flash, actually see the small, dim image growing larger and brighter and covering up the first image, which is simultaneously getting smaller and dimmer. As this happens, say to yourself "Swish!" with excitement and enthusiasm. Having done this, blank your image screen for a second, then do it again. Repeat the swish. Do it several times.

TEST

One way of testing is to try to call to mind that first image. If the swish has been effective, it will be hard to create this first picture—as soon as it comes into your mind it should fade out and be replaced by your desired outcome image.

The key to the swish technique is speed, vividness, and repetition.

Once you're in your theta state, or your trance, perform the swish pattern over and over, taking only a second or so for each repetition. If you experience this swish pattern intensely enough, you should find that whenever you begin to act out your old, harmful habit, you will immediately find yourself switching to your new behavior. In a very real sense, you will feel compelled by your old behavior to act in a different way. As Bandler observes, "You could call this pattern 'trade compulsions.' "

EXTERNAL CUES

At the end of Chapter 15 we explored ways of externally generating cues and discussed how to use a signal to anchor a peak state or a behavior-changing reminder. In the same way, you can program yourself automatically to activate a swish pattern. If the behavior you want to alter has to do with eating, you may want to suggest to yourself during your mind-tech session that opening the refrigerator door will be a cue for you to activate a swish pattern.

During the initial stages of rescripting behavior, frequent repetition of the swish increases its power. Use your onboard cue generator. Set your timer or MotivAider to activate a swish every five or ten minutes, for example, and the power of the rescripting mental images will be greatly increased.

SUGGESTED READING

For rescripting, see Thomas Budzynski's excellent articles, particularly "Brain Lateralization and Rescripting," *Somatics* 3 (1–10) (1981), and "Clinical Applications of Non-drug-induced States," in B. Wolman and M. Ullman, eds., *Handbook of States of Consciousness* (New York: Van Nostrand-Reinhold, 1986). A wonderful classic is *Programming and Metaprogramming in the Human Biocomputer* by John C. Lilly (New York: Julian, 1972). See also *Software for the Mind: How to Program Your Mind for Optimum Health and Performance* by Emmett Miller (Berkeley, CA: Celestial Arts, 1987). For in-depth discussions of associative and dissociative states, changing submodalities, the swish, and other NLP techniques, see Richard Bandler's *Using Your Brain for a Change* (Moab, Utah: Real People Press, 1985), and the other works of Richard Bandler and John Grinder, such as *Frogs Into Princes: Neuro-Linguistic Programming,* (Moab, Utah: Real People Press, 1979), *Trance-formations: Neuro-Linguistic Programming and the Structure of Hypnosis* (Moab, Utah: Real People Press, 1981), and *ReFraming: Neuro-Linguistic Programming and the Transformation of Meaning* (Moab, Utah: Real People Press, 1982).

NINETEEN
YOUR TOOLS FOR SUPERINTELLIGENCE

A brain composed of such neurons obviously can never be "filled up." Perhaps the more it knows, the more it can know and create. Perhaps, in fact, we can now propose an incredible hypothesis: The ultimate creative capacity of the brain may be, for all practical purposes, infinite.

—George Leonard,
Education and Ecstasy

ACCELERATED LEARNING

One of the most often-mentioned uses for mind tools is as "superlearning" tools. Some brain-tech manufacturers even label their products "relaxation and learning" devices. But exactly how are these tools supposed to be used for learning? There is a variety of techniques, each of which has different results and can be used for different types of learning. I will summarize these accelerated learning techniques in this chapter.

But first, it's important to note that the manufacturers' claims (and the widespread perception) that mind machines are effective tools for accelerated learning are based on strong scientific evidence. I'll review a few of the most compelling studies. (For more detailed discussions, see the updated edition of *Megabrain*.)

THE CHOKE MONSTER AND THE BONEHEAD EFFECT

Above all, there's absolutely clear evidence that stress, in itself, makes you dumber and harms your ability to perform in a variety of ways. The simplest example is one that most of us have experienced firsthand in one way or another: performance anxiety or test anxiety. We've all known that feeling of being under pressure, having to perform, and suddenly discovering that our brain has congealed into porridge. This is related to a phenomenon we explored in our discussion of releasing: "Wanting" sabotages "having." By wanting to succeed too much (and fear, or performance anxiety, is simply an outward manifestation of wanting: wanting control, wanting approval, ultimately wanting security), we cripple our ability to perform at our peak.

Lots of studies show that people perform worse on all sorts of tests, ranging from IQ tests to tests of manual dexterity, when they're under severe stress than they do under less stressful situations. The same is true in sports: Studies of basketball players, for example, prove that they shoot free throws more accurately in nonpressure game situations than in pressure situations. Similar statistical analyses have been done of other sports to prove that performance deteriorates in high-pressure situations. It's called choking.

In that Great Game of Life (to coin a phrase), all of us are under varying degrees of pressure. But evidence shows that the nasty Choke Monster tends to jump harder on those under the greatest pressure. High levels of stress make us do stupid things. Not only that, but they make us dumber. To put it another way: High stress reduces IQ. One study of 4,000 schoolchildren showed that those under the greatest amount of stress experienced declines of about fourteen points on their IQ tests.

SHIFTING INTO FLOW GEAR

On the other hand, increasing amounts of research are showing that peak performance states are associated with relaxation. No one would argue that an athlete in the middle of competition is in a state of deep physical relaxation. But we all know that the greatest athletes are the ones who "make it look easy," because at their peak moments they move with a fluid ease that mirrors a deep inner relaxation. Another way of saying this is that the athletes and others in peak performance states are not "wanting" to perform well but are fully engaged in the flow of doing. They have released or let go of wanting and are immersed in pure doing and being.

Perhaps this apparent ease and effortlessness during peak performance is a result of increased brain efficiency and coherence. Brain research suggests that this is the case. At the National Institute of Mental Health, scientists studied the brain activity of people who were in various states of concentration. They found that individuals who were in true peak performance concentration states showed *decreased* activity in the cortex, while those who were *trying* to concentrate or *forcing* themselves to concentrate—wanting to concentrate—showed bursts of high activity in the cortex.

Further evidence of increased coherence and efficiency during peak performance brain states comes from research into the neurophysiology of attention and concentration by Dr. Jean Hamilton, who measured "cortical activation" (the amount of electrical activity in the cerebral cortex) in response to various lights or tones. She found that subjects who rarely experienced the state of "flow" showed increased cortical activation in response to the stimuli. But tests on the subjects who reported being in flow frequently were surprising: When the subjects were concentrating, their cortical activation actually *decreased*. Instead of requiring more effort, concentrating actually seemed to result in decreased effort. A separate measurement of attention showed that people in this low-effort flow group were actually more accurate in a sustained attentional task.

Observes University of Chicago psychologist Mihaly Csizkszentmihalyi, the leading explorer of the flow state: "The most likely explanation for this unusual finding seems to be that the group reporting more flow was able to reduce mental activity in every information channel but the one involved in concentrating on the flashing stimuli." This in turn suggests, says Csizkszentmihalyi, that people who are in flow states, or are peak performers,

> have the ability to screen out stimulation and to focus only on what they decide is relevant for the moment. While paying attention ordinarily involves an additional burden of information processing above the usual baseline effort, for people who have learned to control consciousness focusing attention is relatively effortless, because they can shut off all mental processes but the relevant ones.

When it's working well—when we have "shut off all mental processes but the relevant ones"—it's as if the brain shifts into a higher gear and functions far more powerfully and efficiently, using less power. A car may reach peak revolutions, and its engine will roar and whine, as it tops out in first gear or spins its tires on ice, but the engine is functioning most powerfully and efficiently when the car is in high gear. When we're under stress, we sometimes get the feeling that our brains are revving so fast that there might be smoke pouring out our ears. There's simply too much effort, too much going on. It's when we shut off irrelevant mental processes and enter the state of effortless flow—as we do during sessions with mind tools—that we are most intelligent and perform at our peak.

RESEARCH INTO MIND MACHINES AND LEARNING

At Texas A & M, a controlled study compared the learning and thinking abilities of a control group (the subjects heard their lessons while relaxing in a dark room) with a group using the flotation tank (the subjects heard the same lessons as the control group, but listened while in a tank). The groups were later tested on how much they'd learned, with the learning being evaluated on three levels of increasing difficulty: (1) simple memory or rote learning, (2) the ability to apply the learning to new situations and problems, and (3) "synthesis thinking," the ability to combine the ideas learned in new and creative ways.

The results showed that the float group learned much more than the control group on every level. Most intriguingly, as the degree of difficulty and complexity of the learning tasks increased, the superiority of the float group over the control group increased sharply. The scientist who conducted the study concluded, "There's no question that the [float] group learned more, but *where* they learned is the most important point. People who floated learned at a different cognitive level. The results showed that the more difficult the concept, the bigger the difference in the performance of the two groups."

In another carefully controlled study of learning, Dr. Daniel Kirsch and Richard Madden compared the learning abilities of a group that was given a computer-learning task while being stimulated with low levels of cranial electrostimulation (CES) with a group doing the same computer-learning task without receiving CES. The CES group not only learned more than the control group, but over repeated trials, when the control group's learning levels dropped off (perhaps due to boredom or fatigue), the CES group's learning rate continued to *increase*. Other studies have shown increased learning as a result of CES, and still others have demonstrated increases in IQ (for alcoholics and subjects with brain damage and learning disorders).

Investigating the effects of motion devices (such as the Graham Potentializer and the Sams Potentializer), electroencephalogram (EEG) researcher Marvin Sams has found that such devices can optimize the Neuro-Efficiency Quotient—the speed with which neurons pass information—an EEG measure that is closely correlated with IQ. Ongoing studies using light/sound (LS) machines and light/color devices (such as the Lumatron) suggest that these devices can have powerful learning-enhancement effects. As we will see in Chapter 30 LS, CES, EEG biofeedback, and other types of brain tech can produce rapid and astonishing increases in the IQ of individuals with types of learning disorders. A variety of studies of subjects with attention deficit disorder/hyperactivity have shown IQ increases of over thirty points in many individuals using mind technology and *average* increases of over twenty points.

THE PLEASURES OF BEING SMART

All of this makes sense when you remember that the first thing most people experience when they use a mind machine is . . . pleasure. It's fun, of course, or most people would not be interested in mind tech. But it's also fun to learn something. Think back to the last time you learned something really important. If you're anything like me, when you learn something new—at that moment when the fog dissolves and suddenly you're looking at something in a whole new way—you feel great. A chill of excitement runs through you, you get a goofy grin on your face, your whole body feels a rush of pleasure.

There's a biological reason why this is so. Humans have been designed to learn. Like most animals, they have a "reward system" built into their brains. Neuroscientist Candace Pert, a former researcher at the National Institutes of Health who has gone out on her own to begin a biogenetic engineering firm, has studied this reward system. She points out:

> If you were designing a robot vehicle to walk into the future and survive . . . you'd wire it up so that the kinds of behavior that would ensure the survival of that species—sex and eating, for instance—are naturally reinforcing. Behavior is modifiable, and it is controlled by the anticipation of pain or pleasure, punishment or reward. And the anticipation of pain or pleasure has to be coded in the brain.

Sex and eating ensure the survival of the species, but so does learning. Sex and eating are rewarded with pleasure—a rush of neurochemicals, including the body's opiates, the endorphins, plus the "joy juices," the catecholamines (such as norepinephrine and dopamine). In the same way, our brains reward us for learning something new with a release of pleasurable neurochemicals.

The relationship between pleasure and learning was traced by Aryeh Routtenberg of Northwestern University, who first began mapping out what he called the "pleasure pathways" of the brain. These pathways, he found, were much more extensive than anyone had imagined, extending from deep in the brainstem, the oldest part of the brain, far up into the frontal lobes of the cortex, the most recent part of the brain to evolve. As he traced these pleasure circuits, Routtenberg found that, in essence, they were systems activated by the pleasure neurochemicals, such as endorphins, norepinephrine, and dopamine.

But as he mapped out these pathways, Routtenberg made an intriguing discovery—they were the same pathways that had been identified by other scientists as "learning pathways" and parts of the "learning reward system." He concluded that "the evidence clearly shows that the brain-reward pathways play an important role in learning and memory." How are learning and pleasure related? Routtenberg suggests that:

> the pathways of brain reward may function as the pathways of memory consolidation. By this I mean that when something is

learned, activity in the brain-reward pathways facilitates the formation of memory. Evidence . . . for the association of reward paths with memory formation indicates that the neural substrates of self-stimulation play a vital role in the guidance of behavior."

That is, we like to learn for the same reason we like to have sex: because it feels good. And evolution rewards us for both activities in the same way: with pleasure.

There exists a substantial body of evidence that mind technology does indeed stimulate the release of pleasure neurochemicals. Researchers Thomas Fine and John Turner at the Medical College of Ohio found that flotation increases levels of endorphins. In another study Dr. Avram Goldstein tested people who were getting "musical thrills" and found that their pleasure response was a result of higher levels of endorphins. Dr. Norman Shealy and Dr. Roger K. Cady have tested levels of neurochemicals in the blood and cerebrospinal fluid of people using CES devices and performed another study of subjects using LS. They found that both CES and LS devices sharply increased levels of endorphins, norepinephrine, and dopamine. In a more recent study, Shealy found that a light-color device significantly boosted levels of such hormones as growth hormone and oxytocin (associated with feelings of affection and love) in addition to endorphins and other biochemicals.

There's a clear association between learning and pleasure. It seems to work in a sort of bidirectional feedback loop. When we learn something, our brain rewards us for it by making us feel good. Since it feels so good to learn something, our brain seeks to learn new things.

The relationship between brain technology and learning also seems to be a two-way street. Mind tools stimulate our brains in such a way that we feel good—just as if we had already learned something and were being rewarded for it. But they also make us want to learn more. In a sense it is like priming the pump—our brains have now gotten a taste of the pleasures associated with learning, the learning-reward circuits have been opened, and now our brains want to keep them open. It seems that mind tools, by stimulating our learning-reward pathways, put us in an ideal state to learn more.

Granted the evidence that mind technology can serve as excellent accelerated learning tools, how can it be used most effectively for specific learning tasks?

ACTION SECTION—IN-SESSION LEARNING

SUPERLEARNING.

The most obvious method of mind technology accelerated learning is presenting the material to be learned while using the mind machine. The research of Bulgarian psychiatrist and educator Georgi Lozanov (popularized as *Superlearning* in the book by Schroeder and Ostrander) suggests that we can tap into the brain's extraordinary powers of learning and memory by presenting the material to be learned while the learner is in an optimal learning state. The essential elements of this optimal learning state include relaxation and alpha and/or theta brain-wave activity.

Relaxation. The Lozanov and similar accelerated learning techniques attempt to induce relaxation in the learner by using rhythmic breathing and playing slow, stately music (such as Baroque largos) intended to produce relaxation and slow brain-wave activity. Interestingly, researchers studying the Lozanov technique have found that not only is deep relaxation essential to the process, but *the deeper the relaxation, the more the student is able to learn.*

The various Superlearning techniques use music, breathing, and relaxation to shift the brain from the beta brain waves of ordinary waking consciousness to the slower alpha and theta brain waves, characterized by a heightened receptivity to new information and, as suggested by the Texas A&M study just mentioned, a heightened ability to synthesize ideas, think creatively, and master difficult concepts.

The Lozanov and other similar Superlearning techniques have proven to be extremely effective in boosting learning abilities. However, a wealth of research into the effects of brain tools suggests that they can be the most effective Superlearning tools yet developed. Evidence proves that brain-tech learning sessions can produce far more learning than any of the traditional accelerated learning techniques. It makes sense that this should be so, since the mind machines are clearly much more effective in producing the relaxation and alpha and theta brain waves that are essential to the accelerated learning process.

Relaxation. As we have seen, mind tools can assist users in rapidly attaining far deeper states of relaxation than they could reach otherwise, even though the people may have extensive training and practice in relaxation techniques.

Also, most brain tools are designed with the specific purpose of slowing brain-wave activity into the alpha and theta ranges through such techniques as entrainment, restricted environmental stimulation, or rhythmic movement of the body.

STEPS TO IN-SESSION LEARNING

RELAX TO STATE ZERO

Here's an accelerated learning program to make the most of your mind tool. First, having found a quiet spot where you will be undisturbed, use your mind tool to enter state zero, or a state of deep relaxation.

RESCRIPT OR RELEASE LEARNING BLOCKS

Next see if you are experiencing any negative emotions or scripts that might dampen the innate capacity of your mind to learn. If you are, release, rescript, or replace them with positive suggestions. Some emotional blocks emerge from negative scripts, usually learned in childhood. These include scripts or attitudes such as: "You'll never learn," "You're just a dumb blonde," "You just don't have a head for math." While they're implanted in childhood, as adults we keep these scripts active and powerful with continuing self-suggestion and self-talk, in statements to ourselves and others such as "I'm so stupid," or "I've got no musical ability at all," or "I can never remember names" and so on.

To eliminate or defuse these learning blocks, trace negative scripts back to their roots and replace them with positive scripts. Or counteract them with positive suggestions while in a hypnotic state, and continue with affirmative suggestions about your capacity for learning that you can repeat to yourself as you go about your daily life. Perhaps the most effective way to replace unwanted scripts with desired behaviors is by doing a swish. Find the image of your unwanted state (something that pictures your lack of confidence in your learning abilities, your doubts about your intelligence) and a second image of yourself as you would like to be (able to learn quickly and easily), and do your swish pattern.

Another powerful way of removing these blocks is to use the Release Technique: Find out what emotion underlies the blocks, and release that emotion; determine if your learning blocks are based on wanting approval, wanting control, or wanting security, and release those wants.

Once you have practiced this mind-tech Higher Learning program several times, you will find yourself going through this step quickly, automatically releasing any emotions or wants that might produce learning blocks, clearing away negative scripts with positive suggestions, and then moving into the learning experience.

LEARNING STATE ANCHOR

The next step is to activate your learning state anchor. If you haven't yet anchored a learning state, go back to the exercise "Anchoring a Peak State" at the end of Chapter 15; remember and reexperience a joyful, high energy, pleasurable, vivid, powerful learning state; and anchor that state with a hand signal, a word, an image, or all of these together. Now you are ready to install this learning state to enhance your learning of something new.

COMPLEMENTARY ANCHORS

Once you've triggered your learning state, you may want to activate other complementary states you've anchored. These might include your deep relaxation state and your concentration, alertness, and pleasure states.

PRESENT LEARNING MATERIALS

Once you have become profoundly relaxed, begin presenting the material to be learned. In most cases you will do this via audiocassette. Virtually all mind technology can be used in combination with audiocassettes. Some tools, such as CES devices, binaural-beat frequencies, flotation tanks, and certain acoustic field systems, can be used with videocassettes as well. And some can be used while reading, sitting at your computer or desk, walking, or jogging. If you're working with a friend, ask him or her to turn on the cassette player after you give a finger signal, or after five or ten minutes, when you've had sufficient time to become relaxed, access state zero, and release any wants or blocks. If you're working by yourself, you might want to put the material to be learned on a cassette that begins with five to ten minutes of relaxing music and/or binaural beats—sufficient time to put yourself into your optimal learning state—and then moves on to the material to be learned. Or simply keep the cassette player by your hand. Once you have reached your optimal learning state you can learn, with some practice, to press the ON button of your cassette player without pulling yourself out of state.

EMERGE FROM STATE

There's evidence that you can learn more, and maintain a higher level of learning, by limiting your learning sessions to about an hour or less. After that length of time the changes in your daily rest-activity cycle and your alternating hemispheric dominance cycle will probably make you feel like taking a break. (See Chapter 25 for information about your daily rest-activity cycle.) Several shorter learning sessions at optimal points on your rest-activity cycle will produce more learning than a single learning session of several hours.

As your learning session ends, suggest to yourself that what you have learned is going directly into your long-term memory and that you will have total recall of the material. Suggest that when you give yourself a signal—such as counting to five, or opening your eyes—you will emerge from your learning state filled with energy, confidence, and joy.

PICK THE RIGHT TIME

Remember the importance of your daily rhythms. See Chapter 25 for information about your basic rest and activity cycle. To learn information that requires your active participation or attention, the best times are the thirty to forty-five minutes after you have experienced a level of peak energy. This period—while you're on the downslope of your basic rest-activity cycle but before you hit the drowsy twenty-minute period of low energy—is a time you can relax easily yet remain attentive enough to absorb the information well. The drowsy dreamlike energy trough that follows then permits the information you have absorbed to consolidate and "set" in long-term memory. Another good spot for active learning is the thirty minutes or so after you emerge from your low energy trough. To learn anything that has to do with changing attitudes and beliefs, and to learn anything that you want to bypass your conscious mind and get directly into your unconscious, the ideal time is during the twenty-minute trough, with its natural increase in theta activity.

Many people find that they learn more rapidly and effectively when they receive the material in different states, ranging from relaxed alertness to drowsy twilight states. The best technique is to begin presenting the material to be learned while on the downslope of your basic rest-activity cycle, continue presenting the material throughout the twenty-minute trough period, and continue on into the upswing.

ALPHA OR THETA?

Since many mind tools, such as LS and binaural-beat tapes, permit the user to select a target brain-wave frequency, the question arises as to what is the best state, or the "appropriate depth," for learning: the relaxed, receptive alpha state, or the hypersuggestible, drowsy, dreamlike twilight or theta state.

Evidence suggests that alpha is ideal for learning new information, data, facts, material that you want to be fully aware of and have readily available in waking consciousness. On the other hand, theta is the ideal frequency range for the uncritical acceptance of external suggestions, for bypassing defense mechanisms and resistance and presenting important self-change messages to the deeper parts of the mind. That is, to present messages having to do with attitude or behavior change to the unconscious mind, without the critical screening present in waking consciousness, it is best to get into the theta range. As Dr. Budzynski points out, "the material is being stored in the brain much the same as verbal information assimilated during anesthetic surgery, i.e., it cannot be recalled, but does influence behavior."

Thus a suggestion for those who have LS and other variable frequency devices and want to find the best program for peak learning: If the material to be learned is informational, a useful program might be to begin by entraining brain waves from a waking EEG (anywhere from 14 to 18 Hz—experiment to find what "feels" right), ramping down slowly to a low alpha frequency (from 8 to 10 Hz, again find out what feels right), remaining at this frequency for the duration of the learning tape, and then ramping back up to a final relaxed but alert frequency (from 10 to 14 Hz).

Those wishing to learn material having to do with attitude or behavior change would begin by entraining brain waves in beta, ramping down slowly to theta (around 4 to 6 Hz seems most effective), remaining at theta for the duration of the learning session, and then ramping back up to 10 to 14 Hz. For both types of learning, the material seems to be better assimilated if the user spends several minutes after the learning material has been presented remaining in a relaxed alpha or theta state before ramping back up to beta, ending the session, and returning to ordinary consciousness.

INCREASING ALERTNESS

If you are having problems concentrating, or are experiencing some of the other symptoms of underarousal (chronic fatigue, forgetfulness, and so on), you may have too much slow (delta and theta) brain-wave activity and not enough of the 15 to 20 Hz beta required for alert attention. In that case, you may want to use your variable frequency device to ramp you up to faster frequencies: Start by ramping up to 15 Hz, and if it doesn't produce unwanted side effects (muscle tension, irritability, a feeling of being "hyper"), keep increasing each session until you reach 18 to 20 Hz. (For more detailed information, see Chapter 30.)

CES devices, of course, permit you to use a wider range of learning modalities, including reading, writing, typing, using a computer, and so on. Evidence from several studies and anecdotal reports by many CES users suggest that when you're using the machine, your memory and concentration are at a peak. Some people speculate that the electrical stimulation of the brain "turns up the volume" on the reticular activating system (the brain's alertness and attention control system) and stimulates the hippocampus (a key to the formation of memories).

HIGH-FREQUENCY BRAINWAVES

A body of research linking high beta brain waves and cognition is emerging. Dr. Charles Gray of the Salk Institute and Dr. Wolf Singer of the Max Planck Institute in Germany have found that certain types of cognition, including the "binding" of information—networks of neurons at widely separated sites in the brain firing together with each other in response to a particular stimulus—take place when networks of neurons fire in synchrony at frequencies of 40 Hz and higher. That is, when the brain "binds" together a variety of stimuli to come up with a concept or perception, the binding is a product of synchronous firings of widely separated groups of neurons. Some theorists, such as Sir Francis Crick, believe the synchronous firing at 40 Hz and above may be a key to consciousness itself.

Some types of brain tech are now using high frequency stimulation of 40 Hz and above in an attempt to facilitate this elementary cognition and process of consciousness. You may want to experiment with this yourself.

ACTION SECTION—PRE-SESSION LEARNING

Evidence suggests that certain types of learning are best accomplished *before* the mind-machine session. I described one example of this in *Megabrain.* One floater, a flower farmer from Long Island who was trying to learn Dutch (for his flower-buying trips to the Netherlands), told me that he had gone for a float immediately after his Dutch lesson. Although he didn't have time to review the lesson or to study, when he went in for his next lesson, he had virtually total recall of the last lesson, and his instructor remarked that he must have studied very hard! He felt that somehow the float had subconsciously solidified the information in his brain. Was that possible?

THE REMINISCENCE EFFECT

Shortly thereafter I read a study of sensory-restriction research in which researchers read a lengthy passage from Tolstoy's *War and Peace* to two groups of subjects. They didn't tell the subjects to remember this passage or even say why they were reading it. Then the control group stayed in an open room while the experimental group went into a sensory-restriction chamber. After twenty-four hours the groups were retested. The researchers found that while there was a steep drop in retention of the Tolstoy passage for the control group, there was *none* for the experimental subjects. In fact, the sensory-deprivation group remembered *more* after twenty-four hours than at first! In interviewing the subjects, the researchers found that none of them had expected a retest on that material, and only one reported that he had even thought about the passage during the interim. The researchers dubbed this the "reminiscence effect." Somehow, simply being in a state of sensory restriction caused an increase in memory for something that happened *before* the sensory restriction.

How can this be explained? Scientists now agree that there are at least two different types of memory, generally known as short-term memory (STM) and long-term memory (LTM). STM deals with information we need to hold in our minds temporarily, such as a phone number, but which can then be quickly forgotten. On the other hand, another type of information can be held in consciousness just as fleetingly as, say, a telephone number, but can become so permanent that it can be recalled with absolute clarity a lifetime later. An example is the memory of some brief event observed momentarily by a child but remembered clearly ninety years later. This is information that has passed into LTM.

Studies using drugs that inhibit protein synthesis in the brain have proved that STM consists of short-acting electrochemical changes; for LTM, however, protein synthesis in the brain (actual physical growth of axons or dendrites, increase in number of glia, increase in number and richness of dendritic connections) is necessary. When drugs that inhibit protein synthesis are given soon after subjects learn something, the information is forgotten—that is, it never makes it into LTM. However, when the drugs that inhibit protein synthesis are given more than an hour (in some studies two hours) after the learning, the information is *not* forgotten, which means it has already become a part of LTM. In other words, *information passes into LTM— protein synthesis takes place in the brain—during the hour or two after the information is received.* Intriguingly, there is some evidence that mind tools may boost protein synthesis in the brain, perhaps by increasing blood flow and oxygenation in the brain and by stimulating dendritic growth and the forging of new neural pathways.

Other studies by psychologists have demonstrated that interposing other events or information has a similar sort of disrupting effect on learning. That is, when subjects are given something to learn, and then, within an hour (before protein synthesis has taken place in the brain and the information has passed into LTM) something else happens—a vivid event, other types of information to be learned—the original material is not remembered as well.

To return to the "reminiscence effect": We can surmise that it results from the fact that after being given the information, the sensory-restriction group was placed in an environment that cut them off from new sensory input, from things that would compete with the information for long-term memory. Thus there was enough time for protein synthesis to take place, enough time for the information or learning to "solidify" or become a part of LTM without any external competing distractions or disruptions.

There is evidence that other mind machines, such as LS and acoustic field systems, have a similar effect by stimulating the brain with flashing lights that interrupt normal external awareness and external sensory input that might disrupt LTP.

STEPS TO PRE-SESSION LEARNING

PRESENTATION OF MATERIAL TO BE LEARNED

Clearly brain technology users can put both the reminiscence effect and the elimination-of-competing-stimuli effect to good use as a part of a high-tech accelerated learning program. The information to be learned (put into their long-term memory) should be presented or studied prior to the mind-machine session. Or for long sessions, such as multihour floats, the material also can be presented via video- or audiotapes during the early part of the session.

SESSION

The session should last at least an hour. This allows time for the necessary protein synthesis to occur in the brain to permit the information to become consolidated and committed to long-term memory. Except for unobtrusive music or environmental sounds, there should be as little external stimulation as possible outside of the device itself, to avoid competing with the material that is being learned. Devices with variable or programmable frequencies should be ramped down into theta or delta.

PICK THE RIGHT TIME

Remember the importance of your body's basic rhythms. (See Chapter 25.) An ideal period for studying or presenting the material to be learned is when you are at your energy peak or moving past your peak. After a learning period ranging from a few minutes to forty-five minutes, you will feel when your energies and attention are flagging. That's the time to begin your session, which should last through your trough period, and permit you to emerge feeling refreshed and alert, with the material now a permanent part of your memory. Upon emerging, you may find it helpful to take a brief period to review the materials you learned prior to the session.

WHAT TO LEARN

This presession learning method is ideal for certain types of learning, specifically rote-learning types of information: vocabulary words and tenses, facts, data, details—the kind of material you want to feed into your own data banks.

On the other hand, this is probably not the best time for complex or synthetic types of learning. That kind of subtle learning dependent on synthesizing ideas and information from many different sources probably does not get directly translated to LTM very effectively, since it's largely dependent on creating new information from information that already exists in LTM.

Mind technology can be a revolutionary instructional tool. Students of all fields of study are using it to rapidly absorb large amounts of information and gain insight into difficult concepts. But where mind tools can be of greatest value, I suspect, is on the cutting edge of knowledge—in solving problems, in creating new wisdom and understanding. If the learning-enhancement effect of mind technology increases as the difficulty and complexity of the material being learned increases (as the Texas A & M float tank study suggests), then scholars, original thinkers, creators, finest minds dealing with the newest and most difficult information and concepts will profit most.

ACTION SECTION—POST-SESSION LEARNING

Most mind-technology users notice a feeling of mental clarity and sensory acuity that lasts many hours after a session. This feeling can be explained by the continuing elevation of certain neurochemicals associated with heightened consciousness and with the continuing presence of slower or more coherent brain-wave activity.

As mentioned earlier, there is evidence, from tests of blood and cerebrospinal fluid, that such mind tools as LS and CES devices produce elevations in such neurochemicals as beta-endorphin, norepinephrine, and dopamine, all of which have been linked by neuroscientists to feelings of heightened mental clarity and to the formation of memories. In addition, research indicates that the slow brain-wave activity induced by the mind tools can be detected many hours, even days, after a session. One study of floaters, for example, found that a one-hour float raised theta activity sharply. But surprisingly, when the researchers did follow-up EEG tests of both the float group and a control group, they found that they could still detect higher levels of theta activity in the brains of the floaters *three weeks* after their float session.

RELAX FIRST, LEARN LATER

There's no doubt that most brain-technology users experience an increase in mental and physical acuity and a feeling of euphoria for several hours after a session. Research verifies the accuracy of that feeling: After a session users have quicker reactions, keener eyesight and hearing. The session seems to permit many of the senses to take a short vacation, so that when people emerge they are "deautomatized," in the words of psychologist Arthur Deikman, with the doors of perception cleansed and open wide.

That makes this postsession period an ideal time for enhanced, high-efficiency, high-quality learning. The brain is still extremely receptive to external information and still in a free-floating state that is conducive to imaginative and creative thinking. In the hours after a session, many people have found that they discover solutions to problems or are seized with new ideas; this is a time when reading, studying, listening to music, and so on are particularly rewarding and productive.

Remember also the Texas A & M study mentioned earlier demonstrating that users of the flotation tank not only learned more than a control group, but as the difficulty of the concepts to be learned increased, their superiority over the control group increased. And it was in the highest, most difficult type of learning—"synthesis" thinking or creativity—that the float group was most superior to the control group.

Since the period after a session still partakes of many of the elements of the session itself—relaxation, mild euphoria, heightened clarity, slow brain-wave activity, elevated mind-enhancing neuro-chemicals—it makes sense that this is an ideal time for the more diffi-cult type of learning that involves opening up to new ideas and trying to understand difficult or subtle concepts. This is the time, for exam-ple, to open up that philosophy text, or to get your mind around the ideas in that book about the new physics, or to synthesize some of the concepts in that sprawling world history or comparative religions book. This is the time when the exciting Eureka events and Aha! experiences can take place.

STEPS TO POST-SESSION LEARNING

RELAXATION

During your session, move from state zero down into profound rest and relaxation. If you use a variable frequency device, ramp down into the theta or delta range.

USE ANCHORS

Activate appropriate anchors that will enhance this experience, such as installing your healing state, deep rest, recharge, healing. The power of this state, your anchors, and accompanying suggestions will be in-creased if you use your personal hypnotic signal to put yourself into a hypnotic trance.

RELEASE, RESCRIPT, SWISH, SUGGEST

During the session release any mental blocks to learning, rewrite any negative scripts, and offer yourself positive suggestions about your abilities to concentrate, your capacity for absorbing and understand-ing new information and ideas, and your memory. Do a swish on any unwanted states.

LET GO

Spending even five minutes in this ultra-relaxed state will increase your learning ability when you emerge. However, a longer session, ranging from a half hour to an hour, will leave you refreshed, rested, and mentally sharp.

LEARNING STATE

When you feel like emerging from your session, activate your learning state anchor, and feel the excitement and pleasure of learning. Make yourself so eager to begin learning that you can hardly wait to emerge from this session and get to work.

RAMP UP INTO BETA

If you are using variable frequency brain technology, bring yourself out of the session by ramping back up into the beta range. Leave yourself at beta at about 18 or 20 Hz for a few minutes to entrain brain-wave activity at a frequency conducive to alertness and high energy. Many users report that they feel extremely focused and charged when they emerge after a few minutes at 40 Hz.

PRESENT LEARNING MATERIALS

Now that you feel relaxed, refreshed, calm, alert, and brilliant, approach the information you want to learn. This is the time to attack difficult materials, new ideas and concepts that require mental flexibility, openness, and synthetic thinking.

PICK THE RIGHT TIME

Since you want to emerge from this session rested, alert, and lucid, you may benefit by timing your session to coincide with the trough period of your body's rest-activity cycle. This will permit you to emerge as your energy level is swinging upward toward its peak. The average person whose waking day ranges from about 7 A.M. to 11 P.M. might time this prelearning brain-tech session to take place during the mid-morning slump/coffee break (usually around 10:30 A.M.), the after-lunch daze (about 1:30 P.M.), the midafternoon siesta (about 3:30 P.M.), or the after-work recovery period (about 5:30 to 7 P.M.).

SUGGESTED READING

A fine overview of accelerated learning techniques is *Superlearning* by Sheila Ostrander and Lynn Schroeder (New York: Delacorte, 1979) and their more recent *Super-Memory: The Revolution* (New York: Caroll & Graf, 1991), which includes information about the use of brain machines for enhanced mental functioning.

TWENTY
BECOMING THE ULTIMATE ATHLETE

For the past century high-performance sport has been a vast, loosely coordinated experiment upon the human organism. The first unstated aim of this great project has been to investigate how the human mind and body react to stress. Its second aim has been to adapt the athlete's mind and body to greater and greater degrees of stress. Athletic training, after all, is the pursuit of stress in order to prepare the athlete for the even greater ordeals of competition.

—John Hoberman,
*Mortal Engines: The Science of Performance and the
Dehumanization of Sport*

Legendary bodybuilder Frank Zane, three-time Mr. Olympia—the most prestigious bodybuilding title—intersperses his daily iron-pumping sessions with sessions on cranial electro-stimulation (CES), light/sound (LS), and binaural-beat machines. "I just turned fifty," he told me recently, "and yet I'm in the best shape of my life. Mind machines help me recover more quickly, rest more deeply, and, I believe, stimulate growth hormone."

In one of my Megabrain Workshops, a middle-age doctor had a session on a motion system that slowly tilted his body in all directions. "I feel really limber and energized," he told me when he got off, moving his body with a palpable sense of pleasure. Suddenly he crouched and then leaped up and did a back flip. He gasped with delight and said, "Wow! That's the first time I've been able to do that since college!"

I first stumbled on the powerful effect brain technology can have on athletic performance when, one day after a long mind-tech session, my euphoric meanderings through Greenwich Village led me to the old playground, where Angelo, local handball legend, was cleaning house. I hadn't come close to beating Angelo for ten years, but, feeling energetic and strangely loose, I challenged him. From the first serve it was like some other force was moving my body. I didn't hit the ball so much as simply alter its direction, and I watched my perfect shots with as much astonishment as Angelo. I was relaxed even in the midst of the fastest flurry of shots, and as I put away the final kill the voice in my head said, *Son, that's about as close to perfection as you'll ever get.*

In sports, it's clear when you're performing at your peak. You're out there, in the zone, grooved, magic, flowing, moving effortlessly through a slow-motion world. Most of us would like to be there all the time, but for most of us it's rare and memorable. That's why athletes are always experimenting with new tools or techniques. Like scouts far in advance of the rest of society, they're on the lookout for new approaches that will give them an edge: help them jump higher, run faster, lift more; help them get into those peak performance realms more frequently, more reliably.

Athletes were among the first scouting out practical uses of self-hypnosis, autogenic training, visualization, Progressive Relaxation, and positive suggestion. Long before the technologies were accepted by the medical establishment, athletes were using whirlpool baths, electrostimulation, ultrasound, soft lasers, infrared, biofeedback, computerized training devices, videotape analysis, and much more. Now increasing numbers of athletes are using mind technology to help them reach and maintain peak fitness, to help them master the "inner game," to boost them into peak performance states, and to help trigger the release of the essential peak fitness biochemical, growth hormone.

SPORTS AND STRESS

As sports psychologist John Hoberman asserts in the epigraph to this chapter, sports training in recent years has become not so much an escape from stress as a confrontation with it. So it's important to remember that brain technology is most widely known, and has its greatest clinical use, as a "stress reduction device." Increasing numbers of athletes are finding that by producing unmatched states of deep relaxation, mind tools can help them overcome the stress of training, thrive under the stress of competition, and learn to operate at peak performance levels under greater and greater degrees of stress.

Many athletes I've spoken with have noticed dramatic improvements in their fitness and performance as a result of their use of mind technology. As the previous anecdotes suggest, the improvements take place on a number of levels. I will briefly describe a few of the areas where the use of mind technology has produced striking and in many cases unprecedented benefits.

MUSCULAR RELAXATION

Peak athletic performance flows from relaxation; our descriptions of peak play emphasize looseness, fluidity, effortlessness, maintaining cool. By comparison, the athlete who's making errors is a study in muscular tension—jerky and struggling, making the simplest plays look difficult. A growing body of research using electromyographs (EMG), which measure muscular tension, has proven that brain tools can produce physical relaxation far deeper than levels produced by traditional relaxation techniques. Loose muscles lead to improved performance, greater stamina, speed, strength, and coordination. According to bodybuilder Zane, his mind machines provide him with "The deepest form of relaxation that I've experienced." What's most important, he says, is that "it's there when I need it. Sometimes after a high-intensity workout I wake up in the middle of the night. I just put on my light/sound machine, and it eases me right back to sleep. And it feels like the sleep I get with the mind machines is more restful somehow than ordinary sleep. Somehow, the machine helps counteract the physical stresses of the high-intensity workout."

DECREASE IN INJURIES

More relaxed muscles mean not only better play and training, but safer play and training. According to sports doctors, most sports injuries are not contact injuries but are the result of "inappropriate muscular tension" and could have been prevented by proper relaxation. The best defense against injury is looseness. Many athletes start their workouts with stretching, but stretching provides only relative relaxation. Many runners, for example, often stretch conscientiously, yet they still have piano-wire-tight hamstrings, calves, and lower backs. In fact, many authorities believe that most people have *never* experienced complete relaxation, so they have no conception of what it feels like and no idea of how to make their bodies reach that state. Brain tech can ease users into states of relaxation so profound that they last for days.

MIND-BODY RELAXATION

Muscular tension is just one component of the mind-body reaction called the fight-or-flight response. Triggered by stress, pressure, or emotions generated in the heat of competition, this whole-system response cranks up blood pressure, heart rate, oxygen consumption, and levels of such stress biochemicals as adrenaline and cortisol. It also disrupts normal brain activity, scrambling brain waves into bursts of random static. This automatic response is great for running like hell from saber-toothed tigers or tearing out someone's liver in a mindless frenzy, but it's not great for the kind of mental clarity and fluid mind-body coordination required in most sports.

But when the relaxation response is triggered, it quickly counters the deleterious effects of stress. The most effective tools for helping trigger a powerful relaxation response are the mind tools. Scientific studies, and an enormous and growing amount of anecdotal reports, indicate that a mind-tech session, by triggering a strong relaxation response, can lower heart and pulse rate and blood pressure, decrease muscle tension and oxygen consumption, increase visual acuity and manual dexterity, decrease levels of the stress hormone cortisol and of lactic acid in the blood and muscles, and increase intellectual functions such as learning and problem solving, among other effects.

Blood tests and cerebrospinal fluid tests also indicate that some brain devices can sharply decrease levels of stress neurochemicals such as cortisol and produce elevated or enhanced levels of various neuro-chemicals, including serotonin and beta-endorphin, that are experienced as both physically relaxing and mentally calming. These effects are cumulative and can last long after your session.

RECOVERY

High-intensity training and peak output in competition pushes the body to its limits. Muscle tissue is ripped and torn, and filled with lactic acid, which causes fatigue and pain. The system is flooded with fight-or-flight biochemicals such as adrenocorticotropic hormone (ACTH), cortisol, and adrenaline, which can cause irritability, depression, and anxiety. After a hard workout or competition, these substances must be cleared away and damaged muscle tissues rebuilt, a process that can take days or even weeks.

Intense workouts demand intense rest. Maximum efforts require maximum rest. The new mind machines, by providing uniquely deep, total rest and relaxation, are the perfect technological answer to the increased physical demands of high-intensity training created by high-tech training devices. These high-tech mind tools speed up the recovery and rebuilding process enormously. The deep whole-body relaxation they produce causes blood vessels to relax and dilate, which speeds up the flow of healing, tissue-building nutrients to all cells as well as the clearing away of lactic acid and other wastes. Some marathon runners, for example, have found that a single brain-machine session can speed up their postrace recovery by several days. Bodybuilders and other athletes engaged in high-intensity training intersperse hard-workout days with mind-machine sessions, to allow for quicker recovery, more efficient protein synthesis, and therefore more rapid muscle growth.

THE CORTISOL-TESTOSTERONE CONNECTION

Peak effort is stressful. Too much stress and not enough rest leads to a condition of chronic tiredness, irritability, and depressed immune functioning known as *overtraining,* in which muscle growth stops and muscles actually begin to weaken.

In the past, overtraining was rare. Compared to the workouts of today's Danskin-clad Yuppies in their step-aerobics classes, the training regimens of even top athletes of one hundred, fifty, or twenty years ago seem absurdly modest. In every health club you can see fierce seekers of instant muscle growth pump iron with a full-tilt, over-the-edge, no-pain-no-gain intensity that is scary even to look at. The result is an epidemic of overtraining.

A key indicator of overtraining is the stress hormone cortisol. When you are overtraining, your levels of cortisol rise and remain elevated. The symptoms of elevated cortisol levels are identical to those of overtraining: depressed immune function, diminished sex drive, moodiness, chronic tiredness. Scientists have also found that elevated levels of cortisol accelerate the process of protein breakdown: That is, instead of building muscles, *cortisol actually tears them down.* That's why athletes who are overtraining find it hard to improve their strength or performance.

One key effect of cortisol is that it inhibits testosterone production. Testosterone is absolutely essential to athletic training and performance, since it promotes muscle, bone, and blood-cell growth. Optimal levels of testosterone are also associated with feelings of well-being and confidence—important for peak athletic performance. Exercise increases testosterone and thus helps increase physical strength and fitness. Overtraining, on the other hand, increases cortisol levels and thus suppresses testosterone.

So it's crucially important to know that mind machines can reduce cortisol and increase testosterone levels both directly and indirectly. Studies of CES devices, for example, have shown that after only a few minutes of use, cortisol levels decline substantially. Users of flotation tanks show dramatic drops in cortisol levels. LS produces rapid drops in cortisol. One recent study of photic stimulation and color therapy (using the Lumatron) has shown rapid increases in a variety of neurochemicals and hormones, including luteinizing hormone (LH). Significantly, LH stimulates the release of testosterone.

Thus, by decreasing cortisol and increasing testosterone, mind technology can help increase your ability to exercise at your peak without overtraining.

INCREASED TOLERANCE FOR STRESS

All well and good, you say, it's nice to be able to use my mind technology when I get a chance to relax, but how can I take a find a quiet spot, take a passive attitude, and divert my attention from externally oriented thoughts when I'm in the heat of competition or training?

Fortunately, the beneficial effects of the relaxation response are cumulative—that is, as you use mind tech regularly, day by day, you will not only become more relaxed more quickly, but you will tend to stay at that more relaxed level throughout your daily activities. The effects are not just cumulative; they can be extremely long-lasting. In some tests certain salutary effects of mind machine–induced deep relaxation lingered for weeks.

What this means for athletes is that you will not only be relaxed—which means looser muscles and fewer tension-related injuries—but you will carry this deeper state of day-to-day relaxation with you into training and competition. In other words, brain technology not only keeps you relaxed, it actually *increases your tolerance for stress*, or makes you more resistant to the effects of stress, by readjusting the level at which the body begins to pour out fight-or-flight biochemicals. According to researchers Thomas Fine and John Turner of the Medical College of Ohio, a deeply relaxing session "could alter the set points in the endocrine homeostatic mechanism so that the individual would be experiencing a lower adrenal activation rate." So a pressure situation that might ordinarily have put your choke meter up to level ten may, after a mind-machine session, be perceived as only a mildly arousing level three or four. For athletes, this means competitive pressure that might once have caused choking will be easier to tolerate.

THE RELAXATION ANCHOR

Also, increasing numbers of athletes have found that by using mind tools to get into deep relaxation states, they can learn to reexperience quickly and reliably that deep relaxation even in high-pressure situations. They do this by first practicing using their mind tools to get into deep relaxation states and then using some of the self-suggestion and self-programming techniques discussed earlier (such as anchoring the deep relaxation state with a verbal or finger signal). Then, in the game or training situation, they can reactivate that sense of relaxation and confidence by triggering their anchor. At that instant, they feel their bodies releasing tension, letting go, becoming loose, limber, supple, ready to function at peak capacity.

PAIN REDUCTION

Bob Said is a racecar driver—a Grand Prix champion in the 1950s, he set a speed record at Daytona Beach. For over twenty years he focused on driving a four-man bobsled down an icy course, and has been on two Olympic teams and captained five U.S. World Cup teams. In 1984, at the age of fifty, he was still driving hard, preparing his team, his sled, and himself for the Olympic trials. Each morning he would rise before dawn and climb into his flotation tank. Originally he began using it to help his visualization. But he soon found it was an extraordinary tool for pain reduction. He told me that each rattling bobsled run was like "falling down a long flight of stairs" and the stress of five or six practice runs a day was "the equivalent of running a marathon." Even so, at fifty years old, he told me, "I come jumping out of that tank at seven thirty every morning feeling *just great*. I mean, loose and ready for it!" Even a severe injury in a sled crash didn't stop his training. "Floating just blotted out a lot of aches and pains," he said.

Mind tools have been proven to eliminate or significantly decrease pain. One reason for this is the stress reduction—when you're relaxed, pain is not only actually reduced, but also it *seems* less painful and stressful. In addition, a variety of studies have proven that brain tools sharply increase the levels of the body's own opiates, the endorphins. One recent study of CES, for example, documented a 90 percent increase in beta-endorphins within minutes of beginning use. Another study of LS devices found a similar rise in endorphins. These natural painkillers, thought to be the cause of the "runner's high," also create pleasure and could be the source of the euphoria frequently noted by mind-tool users. Some sports, such as running and swimming, require competitors to tolerate and move through increasing levels of pain. A brain-tech session before competition in such sports could enable us to go farther before experiencing pain and increase our capacity for bearing pain when it does come. A session after a high-intensity performance could help eliminate or reduce any aches and pains, while boosting the body's natural recovery and repair systems.

BODY AWARENESS

Most mind-tool users find that, during a session, their attention turns away from external events and stimuli. As attention turns inward, it tends to focus first on the physical body. Many athletes have found that mind tools improve their fitness and performance by sharpening their sensitivity to their own body. My friend Herbie, a marathon runner, explained how his use of a float tank helped him avoid injuries by making him aware of points of stress or imbalance *before* they became actual injuries. "While I was floating," he said, "there might be a feeling of heat or tightness in the back of my leg, and I'd know my hamstring was getting ready to act up again, so I'd be extra careful to keep it super loose." Brain-tech–trained athletes have noted this predictive-preventive effect frequently; they spend a part of most sessions simply paying attention to their body, becoming aware of tension, rigidity, misalignments, and points of weakness or imbalance. They can then work to heal and correct any problems by using visualizations and suggestions. Moshe Feldenkrais, perhaps the single most influential body therapist of the century, explains a key to the increase in body sensitivity experienced by mind technology users in this way:

> All sensations in which muscular activity is involved are largely dependent on the smallest amount of tonus persistent in the musculature. When the tonus is the smallest possible, you sense the finest increase in effort. Easy and smooth action is obtained when the aim is achieved by the smallest amount of exertion, which, in turn, is obtained with the minimum tonus present. . . . People with a fine kinaesthetic sense tend to a low tonic contraction, and are not satisfied until they find the way of doing which involves the smallest amount of exertion. . . .

What this means is that *tight muscles don't feel,* or at least don't feel as well as loose muscles. It also explains why what Feldenkrais calls "easy and smooth action" is produced by loose and not tight muscles.

THE CURARE EFFECT

Feldenkrais's comment also provides insight into how the deep relaxation provided by mind tools can increase our control over the autonomic nervous system, including our body's self-healing mechanisms: Our sensitivity to and awareness of the body's subtle processes is enhanced when extraneous muscle tension, "background muscle noise," has been turned down low. This is, in essence, "the curare effect." The effect was discovered in biofeedback experiments of rats whose muscles had been totally relaxed to the point of immobility with the drug curare. These rats learned to control autonomic functions far faster and better than did nonrelaxed rats. Researcher Leo DiCara pointed out that the curare effect works because the drug "helps to eliminate variability in the stimulus and to shift the animal's attention from distracting skeletal activity to the relevant visceral activity. It may be possible to facilitate visceral learning in humans by training people . . . to breathe regularly, to relax, and to concentrate in an attempt to mimic the conditions produced by curarization." To a greater or lesser degree, from float tanks to binaural-beat tapes, mind tools clearly "facilitate visceral learning" by means of the curare effect.

INCREASED MUSCLE GROWTH AND GROWTH HORMONE RELEASE

The key to muscle growth is growth hormone (GH). In response to high-intensity or peak effort exercise, the pituitary gland releases GH. The body rushes blood to the muscle tissue that has been stressed, flooding it with GH and nutrients. Thus, in the period that follows high-intensity exercise, the body rebuilds the overworked muscle tissue, so that the new muscle tissue is larger and stronger than before.

As teenagers, we produce large quantities of GH—virtually any kind of exercise or physical activity, in addition to deep sleep, will cause our brain to release a pulse of GH. This explains not only our ability to grow and put on lots of muscle fast, but also our capacity to eat unlimited quantities of burgers and chocolate shakes and never gain an ounce of fat.

Exercise-induced GH release continues into our twenties. Once we're past thirty, however, most of us can no longer trigger any significant GH release with exercise. That's why it's so hard to put on lean body mass (muscle tissue) after we're out of our twenties. Most adult GH release takes place in a brief spurt when we're in deep sleep. Apparently, either the profound relaxation or the slow delta brain waves of sleep send a signal to the pituitary to release a pulse of GH.

As GH flows through our body, it performs a number of valuable functions: It builds and repairs muscles, burns away fat, and stimulates the immune system. GH is so essential to the body's powers of growth, repair, and regeneration that it is no exaggeration to call it our natural rejuvenation biochemical. Sadly, like youthful vitality, our levels of GH naturally decline with age.

Many people are so eager to increase their levels of GH that they will stimulate it artificially by taking dangerous (and illegal) steroids. And for good reason: GH seems to be the key to the fountain of youth. One recent sensational study has suggested that if we could restore our body's ability to secrete GH, we could reverse many if not most of the effects of aging.

RESTORING THE FOUNTAIN OF YOUTH

The sensational study linking GH to rejuvenation got splashed all over front pages when it was published in the *New England Journal of Medicine*. No wonder—it had all the elements of a science fiction saga. The researchers selected elderly frail men between sixty-one and eighty-one years of age and gave them GH injections to bring their GH levels up to those of healthy young adults, where they stayed for six months. The old men rapidly put on muscles and increased their lean body mass by 8.8 percent, decreased their adipose (fat) tissue mass by 14.4 percent, increased skin thickness by 7.1 percent, and actually increased the average density of their lumbar vertebrae. Each of these four measures indicate clear *reverses* in the normal aging process.

The study concluded that "Diminished secretion of growth hormone is responsible in part for the decrease of lean body mass, the expansion of adipose-tissue mass, and the thinning of the skin that occur in old age." In their breathtaking conclusion, the researchers asserted that "The effects of six months of human growth hormone on lean body mass and adipose-tissue mass were equivalent in magnitude to the changes incurred during 10 to 20 years of aging."

The before-and-after photos were astonishing—men who were sickly, stooped, and fragile before now stood erect, filled with vigor, skin taut, faces glowing. It was as if they had grown twenty years younger overnight. Then, after the study was completed and the GH injections stopped, the men's GH levels plummeted again. Inexorably they lost their briefly regained youth and reaged by twenty years, returning to their former frail state, saddened and a bit confused by the experience.

The story is poignant and thought-provoking, and illustrates the crucial importance of GH—not just to athletic fitness and training but to health and longevity. As I mentioned, people now go to great lengths to stimulate GH release. Since it is available by prescription only for the treatment of dwarfism or retarded growth in children, black market synthetic GH is now being sold to wealthy buyers who are willing to pay $25,000 to $50,000 a year for a steady supply.

MIND TECH AND GH RELEASE

Intriguingly, there is evidence that at least some types of mind technology stimulate GH release. In a recent study, Dr. C. Norman Shealy measured the levels of a variety of neurochemicals and hormones before and ten minutes after subjects were exposed for twenty minutes to a mind machine that flickered violet, green, or red lights in their eyes at a rate of 7.8 flashes per second and in one case 31.2 flashes per second (4 times 7.8) of red. Among the results he noted: "significant increases of more than 25 percent" in GH in response to the 7.8 flickers of each color. He also noted that the changes were "significantly more substantial" in response to the 31.2 Hz flickers of red.

Shealy also noted significant increases of more than 25 percent in levels of luteinizing hormone. LH stimulates the secretion of testosterone, which promotes muscle growth and increases sexual drive.

The study is intriguing, because it raises several questions. First, each color—violet, green, red—triggered GH in certain individuals. Does that mean that any colors would trigger GH? GH was triggered at 7.8 Hz—the Schumann Frequency, the resonant frequency of the earth's ionosphere cavity. As I wrote in *Megabrain:*

This has been found to be one of those "window" frequencies that appear to have a wide range of beneficial effects on human beings, ranging from reports of enhanced healing to accelerated learning. When a biological system vibrates at this frequency, it can be said to be in a state of resonance or entunement with the planet's own magnetic frequency . . . the "natural" electromagnetic matrix for all life on this planet, the frequency in which all life forms evolved, and, until recent decades, the dominant electromagnetic frequency in which all life took place.

Do Shealy's findings mean that 7.8 Hz is in some way a "window" frequency for GH release? Does that mean that any LS device that is set to 7.8 Hz will also trigger GH?

One individual Shealy tested received red lights on different occasions at both 7.8 and 31.2 Hz, and secreted greater amounts of GH in response to the higher frequency. Does that mean that the higher, and probably more arousing, frequency would trigger GH in other individuals? In adults, GH release is triggered by a number of highly stressful and/or arousing occurrences, including trauma, the extreme heat of a sauna, hypoglycemia (low blood sugar), fasting, ingestion of niacin, and certain dopamine-stimulating drugs. Do Shealy's findings suggest that the colors, or the flickers, or the specific frequencies trigger GH through similar sort of arousal mechanisms? These and other questions must remain unanswered for the time being.

MIND TECH, DEEP RELAXATION, AND GH RELEASE

For most adults, our greatest GH release takes place in deep sleep, about an hour and half after we first fall asleep, when our dominant brain-wave frequency is very slow, regular delta. Intriguingly, there is evidence that certain mind tools (ranging from biofeedback electroencephalograms [EEGs], to LS systems, to floating, to binaural beats, to certain CES devices) can induce this delta sleep state and trigger GH release.

The first suggestion that mind technology might induce GH release came from Michael Hercules, an aerospace engineer, who had designed a variable-frequency CES device he called Pulstar. In 1987 and 1988 he consulted with me on an informal study with a group of individuals who were suffering from a variety of chronic illnesses, ranging from AIDS, to multiple sclerosis, to chronic fatigue immune deficiency syndrome (then known as Epstein Barr virus). All subjects used a Pulstar and spent at least an hour each day stimulating their brains at a delta frequency of about 1.05 Hz.

The subjects noted that this delta stimulus made them extremely drowsy. But they also noted some interesting side effects. One man with male-pattern baldness found that not only was his hair growing back, the new hair was the same color red his hair had been when he was young. Others also reported increased growth of hair, nails, improved complexions, and rapid healing of wounds. Some noted increased immune system strength, such as increased T cells, key components in the immune system. Some recovered completely from their ailments. Could it be, Michael asked me in a series of breathless late-night phone calls, that by entraining brain waves at this slow delta frequency and bathing the brain with an electrical current pulsed at the same frequency, the Pulstar was hitting a "window" frequency that tripped the pituitary's growth hormone switch, stimulating the immune system and helping the body to repair itself? Michael was preparing to conduct a more rigorous study into possible links between EEGs, electrical stimulation, and GH release when he died unexpectedly of a long-standing heart ailment.

However, there is evidence that other types of mind technology—including LS, float tanks, acoustic field systems, pulsed electromagnetic field devices, and others—can also alter brain-wave activity into the delta range and help thrust users into profoundly relaxed hypometabolic states. And there are suggestions that these deep delta states seem to produce effects very much like you might expect GH to produce, including extraordinary healing, boosted immune function (such as increases in immunoglobulin A), and—most relevant to this chapter—increased strength and muscle growth.

ACTION SECTION—TRAINING TIPS AND TECHNIQUES

RELAX

The harder you exercise, the more you need to relax. If you work out frequently, you should use brain tools every day for at least a twenty-minute relaxation session, getting yourself down into deep alpha, theta, or even delta, so that your whole body has a chance to let go, release tension, and reach a state of total rest. Some people like to have their session right before their workout, so they can make use of some of the "inner game" techniques we'll explore in the next chapter. Remember, if you use brain tech actively—for visualization or self-suggestion—you should also give yourself a session in which you simply let go, do nothing, and let your body rest and recover.

RELEASE

Become aware of your emotions, particularly any emotions that might affect your training or competition. Are you anxious about the upcoming game? Do you have fears about your own abilities? Are you letting your anger at someone or something carry over into your training and disrupt your concentration? What are your wants? Do you want to control so much that you're pushing yourself into overtraining? Is wanting someone's approval causing you to behave unwisely? Once you feel your emotions and your wants, release them.

MINDFULNESS BODY SCAN

One of the most valuable ways you can use brain tech in training is to increase your awareness of your body. To use it in this way, use your brain tool and relaxation techniques to get down to state zero. Then simply be there, in a state of relaxed attentiveness. Let your being unfold without prejudgment. Be open to whatever sensation or perception that arises. If it is a thought, be aware of it, then let it go and return to your state of relaxed attentiveness. Let yourself experience whatever is going on in your body. Soon you will begin to notice your attention moves to a specific part or parts of your body. You may notice discomfort in your lower back, or tension in your neck, or a deep ache in your foot. Let yourself become aware of your body. Along with your awareness of tensions, torsions, aches, and pain, you may find thoughts arising—thoughts that are associated with the specific ache or tension. Pay attention to these thoughts—they may have something important to tell you—and then let them go, return your awareness to your whole body, and continue. Soon you should have a sense of your entire body and an idea of how you need to treat it.

BREATHING

Having completed a body scan, you might want then to use one of the breathing techniques described in Chapter 14 and visualize each breath as a white light that flows to specific body parts or systems. As you inhale, the energizing light flows directly to the source of your tightness, or the place you want to strengthen, where it creates a glowing ball of light. With each inhalation, the ball of light grows in intensity; with each exhalation, you visualize yourself exhaling pain, toxins, fatigue. In a very short time you'll find that your body feels different.

HYPNOSIS AND SUGGESTION

After completing your releasing and body scan, you may want to do a self-hypnosis induction. Having reached a state of hypersuggestibility, you may suggest to yourself that your pain or tension is gone, or that the area that needs to be strengthened is growing stronger. Such suggestions can be strengthened by using different sensory modalities—for example, visualizing your bruise or tense muscle as a tight knot and then seeing it loosen, expand, and dissolve, like a Chinese paper flower in water; or experiencing your pain as being red hot and then replacing it with ice and feeling it become cool; and so on.

HIGH-INTENSITY RECOVERY

High-intensity workouts increase your need for deep rest and recovery. End hard workout days with an extended deep relaxation session—at least forty-five minutes to an hour of deep theta or delta "do nothing" relaxation. This will speed your recovery, by accelerating the clearing of lactic acid and other toxins and increasing the flow of proteins and other anabolic nutrients to your cells. It will also speed up your body's recovery by stimulating the release of calming, counterstress neurochemicals such as serotonin and beta-endorphins. Your mind-tech session may also trigger the release of GH. Alternate hard workout days with days of rest, including another extended brain-tech session. During this off-day session you might want to include some visualizations, suggestions, and other sorts of mental training.

TWENTY-ONE
THE MENTAL EDGE:
PEAK PERFORMANCE AND THE INNER GAME

At the level of the Olympics nowadays, there's not a whole lot of difference among the athletes in terms of physical talent and training. Ultimately, it's going to come down to what's between their ears.

—Shane Murphy, sports psychologist, director of sports science of the U.S. Olympic team

"There are many physically capable athletes in Alpine Speed Skiing," says C.J. Mueller, World Cup champion speed skier and the first person to ski over 130 miles per hour. Mueller was unable to cross the 200-kilometer-per-hour (km/h) barrier until he began training with brain technology. Within a few months, he finally broke that barrier and won first place for the first time in international competition. Within the next year he won several international competitions and blasted past the 210 km/h (130 mph) barrier. Soon he was battling it out for the World Cup speed skiing title. "Mental capability is what allows some to outperform the others," he says. "The slightest mental lapse can slow a speed skier so much that even with the best equipment, a top-ten finish is not possible." He calls his mind-tech device "one of my most valuable pieces of equipment" and claims "it has enabled me to become more relaxed at the start and more focused during each run."

The levels of performance have increased dramatically in all sports in the last two decades. What once might have been a world record might now be only a fair amateur performance. Yesterday's superhuman feat is today's average world-class play. Of course, much of this performance increase can be attributed to physical improvements: Breakthroughs in nutrition, sports physiology, and training equipment have produced athletes far stronger and better trained than in the past. But a substantial part of the advances, as Shane Murphy's statement suggests, comes not from physical but *mental* improvements.

Virtually every aspect of our lives has gone through the same intensification we see most clearly in sports: The pace has gotten faster, the competition tougher, the stress greater. Today the level of performance demanded just to stay in competition is what would have been called superhuman just a few decades ago. So it makes sense that the same "mental edge" techniques that are helping athletes improve their performances can help the rest of us enhance our performance in the arena of daily life. The same "inner game" techniques that help a high jumper clear the bar can help a business executive make a crucial presentation in the boardroom; a surgeon prepare for a difficult operation; a lawyer, pianist, teacher, or student perform at his or her peak in high-pressure situations. So, while the peak performance techniques discussed in this chapter will be couched in the language of sports and addressed to athletes, they can be applied in all areas of life.

SEEING IS BELIEVING

As he careens down the bobsled chute, the driver's eyes jitter, his fingers twitch, he anticipates that hairpin turn coming up and steers the sled into the right groove to take it low. . . . As he zips over the bobsled course, Bob Said is naked, floating in the total darkness and silence of a float tank. Said told me how he trained for the Olympic bobsled trials by visualizing every foot of the run as he floats. "In the sled," he says, "you know where you want to be in each corner, but often you find yourself someplace else. So you try to visualize all the different ways you can get into each corner, so that when you get into the corner, you're already programmed for coming out." By the time he emerges from the tank, ready for the actual run, Said claims, he has assimilated the real experience and "muscle memory" of hundreds of runs. This muscle memory frees him from the need to think in situations where thinking is simply too slow. "If you have to *think* a reaction in the sled," Said told me, "even if you have the world's fastest reactions, you're too slow. I'm definitely sharper from floating, but it's not a sharpening of abilities so much as it's allowing one's abilities to function the way they're supposed to, by getting rid of the chatter."

We've already taken a look at how visualization works and explored several visualization techniques. Sports psychologists are finding that visualization can have extraordinary performance-boosting effects. Psychologist Richard Suinn has done extensive work with mental imagery, including coaching various collegiate and Olympic skiing teams. In one early experiment he asked half the members of a ski team to become deeply relaxed, visualize themselves skiing the run, seeing and feeling it in every detail, using all sensory modalities. If they made an error, they were told to go back and correct it mentally. The other group practiced normally, without relaxed visualization. But the experiment was never completed: The visualization group showed such improvement that they were the only ones selected by the coach for competition. The nonvisualizers demanded to be permitted to visualize. According to Suinn, "What visualization does is program the muscles. Every time you do it, you're setting up a kind of computer program. When you get to the competition, all you have to do is press the start button and your body takes over—you're along for the ride."

As Suinn and other experts on visualization techniques point out, real visualization is not just "imagining" something in your mind. The key to successful visualization is control of the image and its clarity and vividness, which means vividly experiencing as many sensory modalities as possible. And, as Suinn has discovered, this kind of controlled and vivid mental imagery (which he calls "visuo-motor behavior rehearsal," or VMBR) is possible for many people only when they're in a state of deep relaxation. "I have been extremely impressed by the quality of imagery that is possible after deep muscular relaxation," says Suinn. "This imagery is more than visual. It is also tactile, auditory, emotional and muscular. . . . The imagery of visuo-motor behavior rehearsal is more than sheer imagination. It is a well-controlled copy of experience, a sort of body-thinking similar to the powerful illusion of certain dreams at night."

THE COUCH POTATO WORKOUT

We've all experienced how mental imagery can improve performance. Many of us have had the experience of spending hours vegging out in front of a tennis or golf tournament, and then going out onto the court or course and suddenly playing over our heads, in the zone. Unknowingly, as we have stretched out, relaxed, glued to the tube, we have opened ourselves up to and absorbed the images of the pros executing the strokes with mastery, and they have become imprinted in our memory or our nervous system *as a whole*. As a result, our own play has improved, through what psychologists have called "muscle memory programming" or "neuromuscular programming," in which we unconsciously "practice" playing perfectly through undetectable micromovements of appropriate muscles in response to the image of the pros we are watching on TV. That is, we have absorbed the athletic performance techniques not with the analytical verbal, rule-oriented left hemisphere; and not simply with the more visual, gestalt-oriented right hemisphere; but with the deeply unconscious, primitive whole-body awareness of the limbic brain.

The biological basis of "muscle memory" has recently been demonstrated by neurologist Scott Grafton of the University of Southern California, who used advanced brain-mapping equipment to find that "the brain learns a new skill by fine-tuning the specific neural circuits that are involved in making the motion." When people are learning a new physical skill, there is simultaneous activity in different areas of the brain. "They are literally scatterbrained," says Grafton. But as they become more proficient, the skill becomes "grooved," as brain activity becomes focused on the neural circuits directly involved with the physical activity.

There is increasing evidence that mental imagery can produce this muscle programming. Psychologist Peter Fox of the University of Texas at San Antonio performed brain maps of people who were performing physical activities and of those who were only imagining performing the activities. The actual performance was linked to the interaction of several specific areas of the brain. However, simply *imagining* the movement also activated the identical areas of the brain, with the exception of the motor cortex, which is like the clutch that actually activates the movements of the individual muscles involved in the performance. Thus mental imagery of a performance produces a neural rehearsal or workout that is virtually identical to the real thing.

OPEN WIDE FOR CHUNKING

Another way of explaining: Everyone probably has tried to explain some simple act to someone who just doesn't seem to get it—the more we try to put it into words, the more incomprehensible this seemingly simple act becomes. Then we stop trying to explain and simply *show* the person how it's done. Ahhhhh! Peak athletic performance is based on enormously complex combinations of actions. To be conscious of trying to do each action leads to paralysis. But seeing it done perfectly, and being able to see it done perfectly in your mind, turns it from something dauntingly complex into something easy. "The conscious brain can process only about seven bits of information at one time," says Dr. Roderick Borrie, a therapist with much experience in training athletes using one type of brain tool, the float tank.

> Complex athletic movements are made of far more than seven bits of information at a time. Visualization puts all those bits in one chunk, like putting together a bunch of random letters, which would be impossible to remember, so they form a word, which can be very easily remembered. While floating you put many actions together into a total image, so when the time comes to perform, the entire action is "remembered" as a single image.

Suinn's VMBR technique is a simple combination of deep relaxation with imagery. Interestingly, he has found that the most difficult part of the technique to teach is not the vivid visualization but relaxation. He has found that athletes, like most other people, don't really know what true relaxation feels like. So he spends a considerable part of his time teaching the athletes to relax. Clearly this is where brain tech, with its capacity to rapidly produce states of profound relaxation, can accelerate the process enormously.

MIND MACHINES AND VISUALIZATION

There can be no doubt that mind technology dramatically amplifies and intensifies mental imagery. Mental imagery experts have found that there's a direct correlation between relaxation and visualization: The deeper the relaxation, the more vivid and controllable are the mental images. Mind tools, as we have noted earlier, not only produce deep relaxation states, they are known to stimulate and facilitate vibrant, distinct mental images.

CHANGING BRAIN WAVES

Brain tools stimulate distinct mental images because they can promote strong theta brain-wave activity, producing the "twilight state" that is associated with the production of powerful mental imagery. Another reason for the visualization boost produced is that, in general, mind tools can shift hemispheric dominance quickly, enhancing the activity of the right hemisphere, which is associated with mental imagery.

In one recent study, sports scientist Debra Crews at the University of North Carolina-Greensboro studied the electroencephalograms (EEGs) of thirty-four skilled golfers while they attempted twelve-foot putts. She found that the better performers showed decreases in left-hemisphere activity—associated with analytical processes—and increases in right-hemisphere activity—linked to visual-spatial processing—just before the putt. The worst performers had the highest left-hemisphere activity, using analytical and biomechanical cues to guide themselves—keep the club head straight, don't move your body, and so on.

The study had the golfers test three different training techniques: visualization, relaxation, and biofeedback EEG training in which they learned to produce the proper shifts in brain-wave activity associated with peak performance (that is, shifting from the analytical left hemisphere to the spatially oriented right). The results were clear: Both visualization and brain-tech training improved performance, while the relaxation sessions alone resulted in worse performance. Dr. Crews concluded, "You want the body relaxed, but the mind focused."

An EEG study of skilled marksmen done by psychologist Brad Hatfield at the University of Maryland found that just before an expert shooter pulls the trigger, the left side of the brain goes through a sudden release and shifts into producing high-amplitude alpha waves. This is another indication that the analytical left hemisphere enters a state of relaxation, relinquishing control, and permitting the visual and spatially oriented right hemisphere to swing into action.

Psychologist Dan Landers of Arizona State University monitored the EEGs of novices going through a fifteen-week training course in archery. He noted that their improvements in skills were directly correlated to changes in EEG patterns: As they improved, they increasingly produced the same burst of left-hemisphere alpha prior to a shot that researchers have found in elite archers.

Next Landers designed a study to see if the archers could improve their skills by learning to control brain waves. Subjects received EEG biofeedback and learned to produce the appropriate burst of alpha in their left hemisphere. When compared to a control group going through normal archery practice and training, the brain-wave training group improved dramatically, putting their arrows an average of an inch closer to the bull's-eye than the control group.

Dr. Hatfield speculates that this relaxation of the analytical processes, combined with the freeing up of the spatially oriented right hemisphere, can help produce the trancelike "flow" state most conducive to peak performance.

We have already explored in Chapter 5 the numerous EEG biofeedback devices now available and the wealth of research proving their effectiveness in learning to produce alpha waves and states of whole-brain integration. Clearly EEG training using mind technology can help us quickly learn the optimal brain-wave states for relaxed focus and peak performance. In addition, the evidence continues to accumulate that other types of brain technology, including light/sound (LS), ganzfeld, acoustic field generators, flotation, motion systems, and more, can help shift brain-wave activity into desired frequencies and induce the relaxed whole-brain states that seem most conducive to peak performance.

For example, recent studies have focused on the effects of flotation on athletic performance. They found that using visual imagery in a flotation tank significantly improves performance in gymnastics, tennis, basketball, and other sports.

ACTION SECTION—INNER GAME
TRAINING TECHNIQUES

RELAX, RELEASE, RESCRIPT

The first step, of course, is finding a comfortable place to use your brain-technology relaxation techniques and get to state zero. Once in a state of profound whole-body relaxation, you may want to feel what your emotions are concerning your projected workout or competition. Focus for a moment—let yourself experience what is on your mind. Are you nervous? Angry? As described in the section on the Release Technique in Chapter 17, you may find it helpful to release those emotions. Behind the emotions you may find a want—do you feel a wanting approval? Wanting control? Wanting security? Remember, wanting implies not having, so letting go of wants can help improve performance and attaining goals.

SELF-TALK

Perhaps in your focusing and releasing you find that you, your athletic training, or your competitive capabilities are being limited or inhibited by some negative self-talk, such as "I can never do that," or "I could never win against this kind of competition." Obviously you want to replace negative self-talk with positive affirmations. But just as you can't paint over rusty spots, you can't just whitewash negative thoughts.

Become aware of the nature of these thoughts—where did they come from? How long have you been saying them? Do you remember when they got put into your head? Do you find yourself remembering some childhood experience in which someone else discouraged you? Some rescripting may help you. As your mind goes back to that football game when you just barely missed that pass in the end zone, replace that image with an image of yourself making the catch and becoming a hero, or with the image of a kind coach, or loving parent, hugging you and telling you that even the best receiver couldn't have caught that ball, reminding you of all the times when you played with real skill and mastery. . . .

Now be sure you've replaced your negative self-talk with positive messages. These include general positive statements that you will use not only now in your deep relaxation state zero, but at any time—for example, "I'm a winner," "I respect and appreciate myself," "I enjoy great physical gifts and health," "I am in control of my mind and body now," "I feel my body glowing with strength and energy," and so on.

You also will want to include more personal positive messages directed toward your specific goals and skills. You can affirm them now in your relaxed state zero, but you also should repeat them in specific situations when needed and throughout your day—for example, "If I keep my head down and follow through, my kick will be perfect," "I keep my eye on the ball," "I listen closely to my body and respond to its needs," and so on.

SUGGESTION THROUGH IMAGERY

Once you're relaxed, have let go of wants and emotions, have conducted any rescripting you feel would be helpful, and have offered yourself appropriate positive self-statements and affirmations, you may want to begin your positive mental imagery. As we've seen, positive visualizations—shooting free throws, hitting the bull's-eye with darts—act as positive suggestions and enhance performance. We know that brain tools are a perfect adjunct to self-hypnosis and suggestion. Sports performance training offers an ideal opportunity to use positive suggestion: Your goals can be very specific (you want to shoot more accurately, have more confidence in your serve, improve your backhand, have more speed, and so on), so you can offer yourself specific positive suggestions and affirmations. These can be verbal, visual, or—ideally—a combination of multiple sensory modalities.

The use of mental workouts is known by many names—cognitive restructuring, goal setting, positive thinking, mental practice, visuomotor behavior rehearsal, psychocybernetics, visualization, muscle-memory programming. Brief descriptions follow of some of the variations that seem to work most effectively with mind tools. Each athlete must discover what technique works best—try the ones that interest you, see what works, and always be willing to change or improvise whenever you feel the impulse.

In general, except when you specifically want to let go of all thoughts and words and be in a state of total openness, mental images can be enhanced by combining them with repeated, simple, positive suggestions using the principles for creating suggestions outlined earlier, such as: "I keep my head down and my eye on the ball," or "I am running easily, effortlessly, powerfully."

Also, it's a good general guideline to *focus on what you can control*. You can't influence the weather, the performance of your competitor(s), the decisions of the judges or referees. You can control your own performance. Thus you should focus on doing your best, whatever else may happen.

POSITIVE PROGRAMMING—SUCCESS REHEARSAL

Experience as fully as possible, using all sensory modalities, the end result you are seeking, whether it is the successful execution of a shot, peak performance in pressure situations, yourself crossing the finish line at a personal record, or your victory in the tournament. In the words of positive self-programming innovator Maxwell Maltz, in *Psychocybernetics:*

> Call up, capture, evoke the *feeling of success.* When you feel successful and self-confident, you will act successfully.... Define your goal or end result. Picture it to yourself clearly and vividly. Then simply capture the *feeling* you would experience if the desirable goal were already an accomplished fact. . . . Then your internal machinery is geared for success: to guide you in making the correct muscular motions and adjustments; to supply you with creative ideas, and to do whatever else is necessary in order to make the goal an accomplished fact.

This success feeling is enormously helpful in removing negative beliefs, scripts, or programs that unconsciously may be hindering our performance by leading us to imagine or expect a negative outcome. By planting this image of success, the mind—and through the mind the body—is redirected away from the negative scripts toward positive outcomes.

If you are focusing on a major project or long-term goal, this success programming will be enormously helpful, by providing a sort of inner radar that will keep you on track toward your goal. However, you will also find it helpful to divide the major project into several steps or short-term goals. That way, each time you succeed in reaching one of the short-term goals, you will experience that glow of success, and the positive feedback will help propel you on toward the next step.

MULTISENSORY PERFORMANCE REHEARSAL

As you relax, go through your performance step by step. See yourself executing each move perfectly. If you make a mistake, go back and do it correctly. Practice over and over again. See it, feel it, hear it, taste it, smell it. The more clearly you present the image of peak performance to yourself, the more your body incorporates and "grooves" that performance. Remember, this mental practice is no pale substitute for the "real thing." In everything from shooting baskets and darts to kicking field goals, mental practice has been proven just as effective as actual physical practice. If you make it vivid enough, it *is* the "real thing."

THE MIND MOVIE

Here's your opportunity to be a star, by taking your performance rehearsal and turning it into a big-budget Hollywood feature. You are the producer, director, scriptwriter, and star of your own mental movie. Use all the potentials of moviemaking. First, be sure you have the story straight. Whatever sport or move you want to improve, see yourself doing it perfectly from beginning to end. Run that through a few times. Film it from a distance, so you can see the whole field of play. Film from many angles. Take a close-up of your hands, your face, your feet. Hear the click of the ball hitting the sweet spot. Do a slow-motion shot of your swing, your feet, the ball hitting the bat. Reward your perfect plays with an instant replay. Reward your successes by cutting to the cheering audience—they're going wild! If you happen to fall down or make an error, get up, rewind the film (or run it backward), do it again, and get it right. And again, and again.

Give yourself motivation—your true love is waiting at the finish line to embrace you and take your clothes off. See your name in the headlines of the sports page. Watch yourself deliver an acceptance speech for a coveted sports award. Experience what it feels like to drive the ball right down that rival's throat, or run past her as if she's standing still. Find out what sort of mind movie works best for you— romantic slow-motion shots in the style of *Chariots of Fire*, TV announcers describing instant replays of your perfect form in the Olympics, gritty *cinema verité* shots of you stomping rump at the grade school playground. . . .

Vary Submodalities. Remember, don't just see your mental images— experience them using all your senses. Once you've brought your senses into action, try manipulating and combining submodalities. For example, take the visual scene you're seeing and make the colors more intense, make the image brighter, sharper, bigger, even bigger, so huge it fills your whole mental screen. Take your rival and make him get smaller, shrink that image, make it move far away into the distance. . . . Make the sounds get louder. . . . Remember the sound of your lover's voice; now multiply it by ten thousand, speed it up, make it louder, hear it coming from all around you. . . . Think about a great victory you experienced in the past, or some success you are very proud of. Where is that memory located? Does it feel as if it's behind you? Where is it exactly? Now take this new image of yourself performing your sport perfectly, and put it in that spot in your head where you stored that other memory of success.

Change Points of View. Make sure you see yourself from all points of view. Picture yourself performing perfectly while you're *associated* with it, fully experiencing it from inside your own body, feeling the flow of your muscles, the movement of your arms, the movement of your feet. Now switch to a *dissociated* state—observe yourself in action objectively, from a detached, distant point of view, like a movie. Do an instant replay and make your perfect swing over and over.

Swish. Use the swish technique to take an undesired or unpleasant scene and make it shrink, dim out, and disappear while a pleasant or desired scene grows bigger, brighter, expanding to fill your entire mental space, linked with excitement, pleasure, thrills. . . .

Just how powerful these mental movies can be is attested to by javelin-thrower David Schmeltzer of the New York Pioneer Track Club, who used visualization in a float tank to "watch" himself throwing perfectly. Shortly after he began using mind technology, he surpassed his personal record by several feet. He recalls that "when I released the javelin on that day, it was like déjà-vu. At the point of release, I said, 'I know this throw, I've thrown this throw before!' "

MODELING

Think of someone whose talents at your sport you respect—a master, who makes every play look effortless. Now imagine that you *are* that person. You see yourself standing, walking, running, swinging the bat, wearing your clothes, tying your shoe, blowing your nose the way that person does. You are that person. Now imagine that person going through the training routine you have to go through. Imagine yourself as that person doing your training routine—every repetition perfect, every swing superb, effortless, flowing. . . . Now imagine yourself as that person in the competition you will be facing. How will you, as your hero/master, perform? Do it. See what happens.

ROLE SWAPPING

Every now and then seeing yourself doing things in a very different way from usual helps blast you out of ruts and habits. For example, if you are a slow, plodding runner, use a mental imagery session to imagine yourself running like a sprinter, flying like the wind—experience the joy of speed, break out of your slow-foot patterns.

If you are a highly aggressive player, do a session in which you're incredibly laid back, cool, relaxed. Nothing bothers you, you just ease on down the road. . . . See if there are any satisfactions to this style of play that you weren't aware of. Maybe there's something to this style that could help you in your own aggressive play . . . see how this affects your future play.

MENTAL WORKOUT

While deeply relaxed on your mind technology, experience yourself going through a training session. If it's a weight workout, see yourself selecting the pounds, putting the plates on the bar. Feel with all your senses yourself lifting the weight, strongly, in perfect form, completing each rep, each set. Experience yourself going through each set at an accelerated rate of speed and with enormous strength and endurance; experience yourself working up to and surpassing your normal capacity, without fatigue, keeping correct form. Feel your muscles pump. I've been told by bodybuilders and other athletes that since there's no need to wait or rest between sets, they can run through an entire hour's workout in just a few minutes of mental imagery, and the muscle-growth effect of the visualized workout seems to be as strong as the actual workout! This makes sense in light of the evidence that imagined actions cause genuine micromuscular contractions and also mobilize other systems of the body to act "as if" the visualized action were really taking place. Research by sports physiologists suggests that visualized workouts can in fact increase strength and agility.

THE INCREDIBLE JOURNEY

In the movie *The Incredible Journey*, miniature astronauts take a journey through a human body, in which blood cells have become the size of trucks, blood vessels like the Lincoln Tunnel. With mental imagery you can vividly, graphically experience your body growing stronger in response to your training program. See the energy like white light sweeping through your body. Experience the rushing flood of blood carrying nutrients, oxygen, and growth hormone into your muscle cells. As you do your biceps curl, put yourself deep inside the muscle fibers of your biceps, feel them contract as tightly as possible, and then release; feel the pump as the muscle fibers fill with blood . . . feel the fibers being renewed, healed, growing bigger and stronger.

ANCHORING POWER STATES

We've discussed earlier how to anchor a peak or power state. Essentially this involves using your mind tool to become deeply relaxed and get into your state zero. Then recall, visualize, and actually reexperience as fully as possible the state you wish to anchor.

Once you are fully experiencing that desired success state, feeling really pumped and charged, create an anchor, such as a finger signal or a mental image or a signal word. Suggest to yourself that whenever you want to reactivate this power state, all you have to do is use the signal, placing your fingers together, saying your cue word, or visualizing the special image, and you will be injected immediately into a whole-body/mind experiencing of that state. To experience the state you want to anchor, you may want to call on your memories of your own past positive experiences, but using some of the mind movie and modeling techniques just described will also be helpful—see the athlete whose performance you want to emulate performing perfectly, put yourself into that experience as fully as possible, and anchor it.

Some of the power states that are particularly useful for sports training and competition include the following.

Power. Experience a sudden jolt of physical strength and energy flooding through you. This is good to use during the final stretch of a distance run or to push yourself through those last reps of a weight-lifting set.

Flow. Feel yourself flowing effortlessly, all your motions smooth, fluid, and perfectly coordinated. It's useful to activate this anchor in the midst of competition when you feel yourself becoming too conscious of your performance.

Focus. Experience yourself becoming totally focused on your activity, completely ignoring or blotting out any external or internal distractions. Trigger this anchor as you stand at the plate waiting for the pitch, for example, or aiming at the target, or when you want to ignore conversations (or cheers or boos) going on around you. This kind of total attention to the task at hand, with internal conscious thoughts almost totally blanked out, is the trancelike state that athletes call being "in the zone."

Relax. This command is useful in high-pressure situations when you feel your performance is deteriorating because of muscle tension.

Let Go. Using your experience with the Release Technique, you can anchor a feeling of release to be used during training or competition when you find that you're experiencing emotions or wants that disrupt your performance. For example, your anger at an opponent can destroy the fluidity of your serve or cause you to play recklessly. Or your wanting approval of the fans who are watching may distract you from the total focus you need. Activate your release anchor, and let go of those emotions or those damaging wants.

Remember, the more intense or heightened your mental state, and the more fully you are experiencing the state you want to be anchored, the more powerful and long-lasting the anchor will be. That makes brain technology the ideal tool for creating powerful and long-lasting anchors—probably the most effective and rapid way that has been discovered yet. Also remember, repetition of the anchoring experience helps increase its power.

EXTERNAL ANCHORS

Once you've strongly anchored the desired behaviors and brain states, activate and rehearse them frequently. One of the best ways for doing this is with an external signal generator, such as the MotivAider. One tennis pro, for example, used deep relaxation techniques to visualize herself getting back earlier for her backhand stroke. Then she set her

MotivAider at three-minute intervals on the court, and each time it vibrated she would say to herself "early preparation." Off the court she set it at forty-five-minute intervals, and each vibration would trigger a visualization of her serving, handling a service return or passing shot, or playing at the baseline. "I'd really emphasize feeling the ball and feeling my movement visually," she said. Her game improved so much it propelled her into that year's Wimbledon quarter finals.

SUGGESTED READING

A superb exploration of peak performance in general is *Flow: The Psychology of Optimal Experience* by Mihaly Csikszentmihalyi (New York: Harper & Row, 1990). *Golf in the Kingdom* by Michael Murphy (New York: Dell, 1972), purports to be about golf, but is really a keen description of the mental aspects of all sports. *The Joy of Running,* by Thaddeus Kostrubala (Philadelphia: Lippincott, 1976), describes particularly the mental and spiritual aspects of running in ways that can be applied to all sports. *Peak Performance: Mental Training Techniques of the World's Greatest Athletes,* by Charles Garfield and Hal Bennett (Los Angeles: Tarcher, 1984), is a down-to-earth compendium of peak performance techniques. *The Psychic Side of Sports,* by Michael Murphy and Rhea White (London: Addison-Wesley, 1978), describes some of the extraordinary mental states athletes experience when performing at their peak. Also recommended: *The Ultimate Athlete* by George Leonard (New York: Viking, 1975), *The Warrior Athlete: Body Mind and Spirit* by Dan Millman (Walpole: Stillpoint, 1985), and Timothy Gallwey's *The Inner Game of Tennis,* (New York: Random House, 1974).

TWENTY-TWO
BRAIN-POWERED SEX

The ancient tradition that the world will be consumed in fire at the end of six thousand years is true . . . the whole creation will be consumed and appear infinite and holy, whereas it now appears finite and corrupt.

·

This will come to pass by an improvement of sensual enjoyment.

—William Blake,
The Marriage of Heaven and Hell

I first got an inkling of the enormous impact mind technology could have on sex during an early Megabrain Workshop, when a married couple in their fifties sat down and put on the goggles and headphones of a light/sound (LS) device. I operated the controls and buzzed them through various frequencies and light patterns as they talked with each other about what they were seeing. "Ohhh, do you see that blue spider web?" she asked her husband, and he responded, "Yes, now look, it's getting green, like a green pasture." Pretty soon, as they went deeper and deeper into alpha and then theta, it became clear they were sharing the same experience, a sort of mutual hypnotic trance. They both walked into a deep cave—they turned and looked at each other—and in the cave there was a lovely spring surrounded by cushions and dazzling jewels. Their descriptions tapered off to just a word now and then interspersed by long minutes of silence. They were both breathing deeply, very relaxed, smiling in easy pleasure. "Oh, John," the woman said. "Ummmmm, yes," he responded. It was clear something was going on that they were both involved in. I let them stay there for a long time before speeding up the frequency and bringing them back to normal consciousness. As they removed the goggles they looked at each other with amusement and joy, and then burst into laughter. They hugged each other and wandered off to sit down and talk in a corner of the room. They later explained to me that they had both experienced the same thing—an extraordinarily sensual and energetic sexual encounter. "It's the best sex we've had in years," the husband told me.

This is not to suggest that techno-sex is only in your mind. It does emphasize, however, how important our mental images and internal experiences are to sexual pleasure, and how a sharing of images and internal experiences can enhance and intensify sex.

LINKED BRAIN WAVES AND "SILENT COMMUNICATION"

Neurons, as we know, are powered by electricity. Large numbers of neurons firing together can create electrical fields and signals that we detect with the electroencephalograph (EEG) and other devices. Scientists have long suspected that neurons and groups of neurons generate some sort of "neuronal fields" that can extend far beyond the brain and, theoretically, interact with other neuronal fields. This might explain how it is we can sometimes feel "in sync" or "tuned in" to someone we have just met, or have the immediate sensation that "we're on the same wavelength."

A series of experiments at the University of Mexico, reported in the *International Journal of Neuroscience,* has proven that some sort of neuronal communication does take place. The experimenters first grouped subjects into pairs. The brain-wave activity of each subject was continuously monitored with an EEG. Initially, the brain waves of the pair showed no correlation. Then each pair was told to close their eyes and "feel each other's presence," or try to "communicate by becoming aware of the other's presence and to signal [the experimenter] when you feel this has occurred."

The EEGs showed that when the subjects reported communicating, "the interhemispheric correlation patterns of each subject are very alike." What the EEG patterns show, in fact, is an astonishing degree of synchrony—patterns of peaks and valleys that were totally unrelated suddenly fall into exact synchrony, the peaks and valleys of each subject's brain waves virtually identical with those of the other member of the pair.

SYNCHRONY RULES

"The subject with the highest concordance [synchrony between right and left hemisphere] was the one who most influenced the sessions," said researchers Jacobo Grinberg-Zylberbaum and Julieta Ramos. That is, the EEG of the individual with less synchrony between hemispheres tended to fall into synchrony with the brain waves of the person with most synchrony. The sessions all took place in a Faraday cage (a lead-screened room that shuts out most electromagnetic activity from outside), so the EEG synchrony was clearly a result of some sort of "silent communication" between the partners.

There was no talking or touching during these sessions, yet after them the partners reported a feeling of having "blended." Some subjects experienced physical sensations or strong mental images of their partners. This silent communication is not linked to being acquainted previously, since in most cases the pairs had not met or did not know each other before they were paired. One subject's EEG fell quickly into synchrony with each of three separate partners with whom he was paired. *Que simpatico!* After the sessions, when the pairs stopped trying to communicate, their brain waves showed no synchrony.

This evidence of EEG synchrony between people who want to communicate with others provides us with at least one explanation for the silent, totally mental sexual experience shared by the couple using the light and sound device. We can surmise that since they were both receiving LS stimulation at the same frequency, their EEG patterns fell into synchrony and they experienced "silent empathic communication."

SEX AND SYNCHRONY

Given this evidence (and all our personal intuitions and experiences) that two people can join together in a nonphysical as well as physical way, the next step is to use the "silent sync" effect to enhance communication and empathy with your sex partner. Since it seems that the silent communication and "blending" is linked to synchronous brain-wave activity, it makes sense to use brain machines that directly alter and synchronize brain-wave activity. The most obvious devices are the LS systems. There is some evidence that they can increase synchrony. They are also ideal for a shared experience, since most LS devices can power two sets of goggles and headphones. Even devices with only one jack for goggles can be turned into two-user systems by purchasing an inexpensive "splitter" that plugs into the jack and provides two outlets. By purchasing a second pair of goggles, you're all set for a shared session.

You can use a shared session to increase your mutual pleasure in a variety of ways. The first is simply to relax, let the LS take you into a deeply relaxed state, and, as in the University of Mexico experiment, first try to "feel each other's presence" and then "communicate by becoming aware of the other's presence." What you feel, and what you communicate, will be a product of your own openness and willingness to share your experience. Many users have found that this "empathic communication" by itself thrusts their relationship to a higher and more rewarding level. The silent communication can move beyond simple empathy to more overtly sexual communication. Again, the intensity of this communication is linked to your own capacity to be open to emotions, to share your feelings with your partner, and to be fully receptive to what your partner is communicating. The sky's the limit.

In many cases, silent communication leads directly to physical sexual experiences. When you're in the same brain state as your lover, the shared experience of physical sex can be amplified dramatically. The central message of a million sex therapy books has always been "pay attention to your partner." By this sharing of brain states, you can share the sexual experiences of your lover in a direct, empathic way. The subjects in the EEG experiments at the University of Mexico reported "blending" with each other without any touching or speaking at all. Imagine the kind of blending that you can experience when your EEG synchrony extends to your physical body. Try it out. Followers of Tantric yoga believe that the universe was created when the Hindu gods Shiva and Shakti united sexually and spiritually. In a Tantric scripture, Shiva says to Shakti,

> You, O Shakti, you are my true self;
> There is no difference between you and me.

OTHER DEVICES

LS functions in part by directly altering brain-wave activity, and thus I have focused on using it to take advantage of the silent communication fostered by brain-wave synchrony. But other mind tools also induce brain-wave synchrony, including EEG biofeedback systems, ganzfelds, motion systems, binaural-beat cassettes and compact discs, the float tank, and acoustic field generators. I suggest you and your partner explore the sexual effects of all of these mind tools.

At least one type of EEG system is now available that gives feedback only when both users are generating the same type of brain-wave activity. The Interactive Brainwave Visual Analyzer and other EEGs can monitor two users simultaneously. Another EEG, the Biofeedback Brainwave Synchronizer, can be modified so that up to five people can be hooked up to it at once, and it will provide light and sound biofeedback only when each subject produces synchronous brain waves. I have used this system in my Megabrain Workshops. Whenever I hooked up five people at once and let them learn to generate synchronous brain waves, invariably the people—who may have been complete strangers—felt that they had experienced some ineffable but profound sense of sharing with the others. And I can attest from experience that two people floating side by side in a float tank can lead to an astonishing level of silent communication.

GET THE JUICES FLOWING

There is intriguing evidence that mind technology can literally turn up your juices by stimulating increased levels of sex hormones. As described earlier, Dr. C. Norman Shealy measured levels of sex hormones in subjects just before and then ten minutes after a twenty-minute session on a light-color stimulation device. The subjects were exposed to flickering violet, green, or red lights at 7.8 Hz. Shealy noted "significant increases of 25% or more" in some (not all) of the subjects of luteinizing hormone (LH), oxytocin, progesterone, prolactin, and growth hormone as well as significant increases in serotonin and beta-endorphin. LH has shown evidence of increasing sexual drive and sexual arousal. Oxytocin is now widely known as the "love hormone," since it is the hormone secreted by mothers giving birth, during nursing and during sex, that seems to increase affection and bonding (men also release oxytocin during sex, though in somewhat lower amounts). Beta-endorphin is also secreted when people feel loved and secure, while reduced levels of endorphins are found in infants suffering separation anxiety.

Other studies by Shealy and associates suggest that not only light and color stimulation, but also cranial electrostimulation (CES) can boost secretion of a number of these sex hormones. In addition, there is evidence that LS, CES, flotation, and other types of mind technology sharply boost levels of endorphins.

TIGHT MUSCLES DON'T FEEL

I mentioned earlier that muscle tension decreases the sensitivity of those muscles. According to a body of evidence, people with high levels of tension are less sensitive to physical sensations. This may be in part because of the "body armor" they wear to protect themselves. It's hard to feel a gentle touch or a loving kiss through thick armor.

Brain tools, of course, by quickly inducing a state of deep relaxation, lead to increased sensory acuity. A sensual touch that might have been completely ignored when you were in a tense state can flood you with ecstasy when you're deeply relaxed. For this reason, many users of brain tools have found that one of the unexpected side effects of frequent use has been a huge increase in sexual pleasure. The simple physical relaxation produced by the session increases their sensory acuity and opens them up to unexpected levels of sexual pleasure.

Many chiropractors, physical therapists, bodyworkers, and massage therapists make use of this relaxation effect of mind tools to enhance the effects of their work. New York bodyworker Ronald Brecher, for example, has his clients use a LS machine while he is working on them and then plops them into a float tank. When clients use the LS machine, says Brecher, "that person quickly becomes very relaxed, so I can begin at a much deeper level. That means the session can have more profound and lasting effects."

The sensual pleasure of a massage is profoundly increased by combining it with mind tools. So imagine the new levels of bliss you can reach when one partner is deep in a brain-tech session, hypersensitive, totally focused on the body, and the other partner moves from gentle massage to stimulation of erogenous areas. "When you're using a mind machine," one user remarked to me, "the whole body becomes an erogenous zone."

BEFORE DURING AFTER

In effect, by increasing relaxation and sensory acuity, mind tools act as aphrodisiacs. In the words of sex researcher Rudolf Von Urban, "when lovers relax deeply together, a resonance effect begins to take place between their energy fields that brings profound healing to both." When this happens, says Von Urban, the lovers "can enjoy a long-lasting, whole-body orgasm." A mind-machine session before sex can increase pleasure and satisfaction in a variety of ways. A shared session in the afterglow of sex can intensify the empathy and bonding of the experience. According to Ernest Lawrence Rossi, a leading authority on body rhythms, "This bonding and comfort period, which lasts ten to twenty minutes, is obviously synonymous with the Ultradian Healing Response." A session *during* sex can create a whole new experience. Having sex while on LS machines, which can inject people into a tumbling kaleidoscopic stream of vivid images, is similar to the sensory overload experience produced by some psychedelics; or it can lead to a shared "fantasy" in which both partners experience the same mental imagery.

YOU MAKE ME TINGLE ALL OVER BABY

We've probably all had the sensation during a powerful sexual experience that some sort of electrical charge is passing between us and our partner. Certain types of CES devices intensify that feeling by passing an actual electrical charge through partners. Most CES devices are bipolar or biphasic, which means the electrical current flowing between the two electrodes changes polarity frequently. That is, the current will flow from electrode X to electrode Y, and then from electrode Y to electrode X. Some sensualists have discovered that if one partner wears one electrode (pressed against the head with a headband, for example), and the other partner wears the other electrode (strapped around the ankle, for example), when their bare skin touches, the electrical circuit is completed and the current flows back and forth between them, producing a pleasurable sensation of being electrically charged, with tingling energy flow between them. Monopolar or monophasic CES devices produce similar effects, though the flow of the current is in one direction only, from positive to negative electrode.

When large surfaces of the bodies are placed together, the electrical flow is widely dispersed, and mild or imperceptible. When smaller surfaces, such as tongue or sexual organs, are placed together, the flow is focused through that surface. Depending on the intensity of the current, this can produce a powerful tingling sensation or even the feeling that sparks are leaping back and forth between tongues, genitals, and so on. There is something to be said for the feeling of an electrical current flowing into and out of a sensitive part of your anatomy. Placing electrodes on different parts of the body produces varying effects.

Since CES, LS, floating, and other types of mind tech have been shown to produce sharp rises in neurochemicals associated with pleasure, they can increase sexual energy and sexual pleasure neurochemically, in addition to the tingling pleasure of the electrical charge and the increases in sensory acuity produced by relaxation.

SHARED VISUALIZATION

Since the evidence about shared brain-wave activity suggests that brain tools can enhance united or linked brain states between partners, and since brain tools can intensify our powers of visualization, these devices can produce especially profound experiences of shared visualization. Recall the couple I described who found themselves sharing the same dreamlike fantasy while they were using a LS device. The ways mind technology can be used to produce states of mental fusion or shared fantasy experiences are limited only by the imagination of the users. Here's one suggestion.

Both partners use their mind tools to relax together—perhaps while holding hands or embracing—and to reach state zero. There they should attempt to reach out mentally and sense the other's presence. This can be facilitated by prearranged signals—for example, a gentle hand squeeze can indicate that one is ready to proceed with the shared visualization. The visualization can be totally spontaneous, with the partners simply following whatever mental imagery appears, or it can emerge from a prearranged scenario. For example, the partners could agree before their session that when they meet mentally, they would be in a favorite romantic setting—a deserted tropical island, a sunny clearing in the forest. Then, while in the session, they can simply permit their shared visualization to proceed spontaneously and enjoy whatever fantasy emerges.

Later, after the session, while still in a state of relaxation and enhanced sensory acuity, the partners can share with each other the content of their visualization—in words, actions, or both. Often the partners will find that their visualizations were quite similar. Partners whose visualized experiences led from the common starting point into dramatically different directions can share the delight of describing to and exploring with each other their differing fantasy experiences.

SUGGESTED READING

Fascinating books about nonwestern techniques for enhancing sexual energies and pleasure are: *Taoist Secrets of Love: Cultivating Male Sexual Energy* by Mantak Chia (New York: Aurora Press, 1984), *Healing Love Through the Tao: Cultivating Female Sexual Energy* by Mantak Chia and Maneewan Chia (Huntington, N.Y.: Healing Tao Books, 1986) can enhance sexual communication between men and women by increasing their awareness of innate biological differences in sexual responses and desires. *Sex and the Brain,* by Jo Durden-Smith and Diane DeSimone (New York: Warner Books, 1983), and *Introduction to Tantra* by Yeshe Thulsten (Boston: Wisdom, 1989). My own book, *The Anatomy of Sex and Power: An Investigation of Mind-Body Politics* (New York: Morrow, 1990) takes a deeper look at the biopolitics of sex.

TWENTY-THREE
CREATIVITY

It is a highly significant, though generally neglected, fact that those creations of the human mind which have borne preeminently the stamp of originality and greatness, have not come from within the region of consciousness. They have come from beyond consciousness, knocking at its door for admittance: They have flowed into it, sometimes slowly as if by seepage, but often with a burst of overwhelming power.

—G.N.M. Tyrell, *The Personality of Man*

•

While the picture we have here of human consciousness boxed up inside the skull might appear to be true where everyday states of consciousness are concerned, it ceases to explain what happens when we enter nonordinary consciousness states such as trance states. ... The amazingly broad spectrum of experiences that become available under these circumstances clearly suggests that the human psyche has the potential for transcending what we ordinarily consider the limitations of space and time. Modern consciousness research reveals that our psyches have no real and absolute boundaries; on the contrary, we are part of an infinite field of consciousness that encompasses all there is—beyond space-time and into realities we have yet to explore.

—Stanislav Grof, M.D., *The Holotropic Brain*

What is creativity? Someone who is involved in marketing recently told me "Creativity is hot, it's in. Everybody wants to be more creative." He told me books and tapes on ways of increasing creativity were selling in larger numbers than ever before, that numerous "creativity consultants" were in great demand by corporations to conduct seminars on "increasing corporate creativity."

As I looked through some of the books on creativity, I got the uneasy feeling that for many people creativity is a "subject" to be learned, like a foreign language—take this course and your creativity grade will go up from a C to a B plus. Others seem to approach it as a skill that simply takes practice, like learning to ski. Others see it as a craft or art, requiring work and dedication, but paying off in the long run with mastery, like tai chi, backstrap weaving, or golf. Still others, who have attained wealth, see creativity as another acquisition, like a Maserati or a Van Gogh—people value creativity, it has a certain rakish charm, so why not hire a creativity consultant and acquire some oneself? I get the feeling that creativity is approached as just another psychological process—release inhibitions, let whatever's in your subconscious pop out, express it, and voilà, creativity.

Absent from all these approaches is the sense of profound mystery, unpredictability, and what philosopher G.N.M. Tyrell calls the "burst of overwhelming power" from some source beyond the individual, beyond consciousness, that is a key to true creativity. Nowhere to be found is the sense that creativity is not something pleasant and sociable, but an experience of something beyond the boundaries of normal consciousness. "Creativity can be learned by anyone," say some of today's creativity consultants, "it's just a matter of opening up to your unconscious." But the true creative geniuses have a different story to tell.

Percy Bysshe Shelley believed that "Poetry is not like reasoning, a power to be exerted according to the determination of the will. A man cannot say: 'I will write poetry.' The greatest poet even cannot say it. It is not as though this material came passively floating towards them."

"Straightaway the ideas flow in upon me, directly from God," Brahms explained to a biographer, "and not only do I see distinct themes in my mind's eye, but they are clothed in the right forms, harmonies, and orchestration." George Eliot asserted that in her best writings some spirit took possession of her, making her "merely the instrument through which this spirit, as it were, was acting."

Said William Blake of his writing of *Milton*, "I have written this poem from immediate dictation . . . without premeditation, and even against my will." Puccini used similar terms to describe the creative inspiration for his opera *Madam Butterfly:* "The music of this opera was dictated to me by God; I was merely instrumental in putting it on paper and communicating it to the public."

As Shelley accurately observed, "One after another the greatest writers, poets, and artists confirm the fact that their work comes to them from beyond the threshold of consciousness."

ORDER OUT OF CHAOS

Why is it that true creativity seems to appear from beyond the threshold of consciousness, as if the creative genius is suddenly "tuned in" to some inconceivable other-dimensional broadcasting system unheard by ordinary people? I believe it is because in the act of creation, our mind physically reorganizes itself in a new way that it is impossible to predict beforehand.

Our brain/mind is what physicists call an open system—a structure through which is flowing or passing a constant stream of matter and energy, such as blood, oxygen, nutrients, thoughts, and information. This influx of energy and matter causes the brain to vibrate or fluctuate. Ordinarily, in normal states of consciousness, our brain is able to absorb these fluctuations and still maintain its structure or internal organization (that is, our ego; reality continues to "make sense").

However, as more and more energy flows through the system (as the creative thinker absorbs more and more information, has more and more thoughts, feels more and more emotion), the fluctuations increase, until they are too turbulent to be absorbed by the system. The structure becomes increasingly unstable until it reaches a critical point, like a complex machine thrashing around on the verge of flying apart. Finally, the turbulence grows so great that the system can no longer maintain its organization or structure. At this point, it has the potential to move in an almost infinite number of unpredictable directions.

ESCAPE TO A HIGHER ORDER

Now, even a small fluctuation can be sufficient to push the system "over the edge." When that happens, the entire system seems to shudder and fall into chaos. Things stop making "sense." In some cases the system may be destroyed. Or it may survive by emerging from this chaos into a new structure, a new pattern, a new organization that is characterized by a higher level of coherence—a structure that can pass more energy through it without turbulence. Things now make sense again, but in a whole new way we could never have imagined. The system has taken a leap into the unknown and "escaped into a higher order."

It has had a "creative" insight. This happens not just for artists or "creative" people but for everyone who experiences personal growth: It's not an accident that major upsets, personal crises, an experience of chaos, and a disintegrating ego can lead to the most growth. One of the most memorable prototypes of this progression is Dante's *Divina commedia,* in which the reader must first pass through the gates of Hell before finding answers to the perplexities of life.

Since this breakthrough to a higher order and higher coherence can happen only when the existing structure—the "conscious" mind, or our normal state of consciousness—breaks down (into what the artist or creative thinker often experiences as a tumult of ideas, teeming images, confusion, uncertainty, disorder), then the reorganization at a higher level must by definition appear out of chaos or disorder, must appear to "emerge" from "beyond" consciousness. Research has proven that the reorganization that takes place after collapse is not related in any causal or linear way with the structure that existed before. There's no way it could have been predicted from prior conditions. In that sense, it's a true quantum leap, a death that leads to a rebirth.

This, of course, explains why traditionally artists and other creative thinkers have been thought to be a little nuts. In fact, a number of recent psychological studies have concluded that there is a very strong connection between creativity and mental turmoil or "disorder." Seen from another angle, this finding means that these creative people are not afraid to open themselves up to new ideas and experiences, not afraid to let go of their ego and their sense of "what makes sense," and plunge into the unknown. Creative people have faith: They stake their lives on the belief that as they plunge ahead into the unknown, they will emerge with a higher sense, a new vision.

There is evidence that artists who work in this way, through a process of constant discovery and movement into the unknown, are more successful and creative. Mihalyi Csikszentmihalyi conducted a long-term study of artists beginning in 1964. Almost twenty years later he found that those artists who worked by a process of discovery and movement into the unknown were far more successful—by the standards of the artistic community—than their peers who worked out their finished painting in their minds beforehand.

This theory also offers an explanation for the mind-altering powers of the mind machines. They all employ various types of energy that flow through the brain all the time—light, color, sound, motion, electricity. But the mind machines use state-of-the-art technology to amplify and intensify these forms of energy to a degree that is rarely, if ever, encountered in ordinary life. They send a stream of energy through the brain that is so powerful it sets up fluctuations and turbulence that cause the brain to alter in some way.

In an absolutely literal and physical way, it's clear that mind technology can alter the electrical activity, the neurochemical activity, and the very structure of the brain, by stimulating neural growth. High-amplitude brain waves, such as powerful synchronous theta activity, produce actual fluctuations in the brain that can tear apart old neural pathways and create new networks. Transformative experiences, it is now becoming clear, literally produce a "rewiring" of the brain by forging new neural connections.

WAYS OF HANGING ON

Some people will be reluctant to go through the fluctuations and de-stabilization necessary to escape to a higher order, preferring to retain their usual rigid reality, determined to hang on to their present structure no matter what the cost in terms of lost potentials. It's a natural tendency to resist the unknown and to want to protect the established structure (your ego). But it's a destructive tendency in the long run, because it cuts us off from growth. Pioneering human potential psychologist Abraham Maslow observed:

> Not only do we hang on to our psychopathology, but also we tend to evade personal growth because this, too, can bring another kind of fear, of awe, of feelings of weakness and inadequacy. And so we find another kind of resistance, a denying of our best side, of our talents, of our finest impulses, of our highest potentialities, of our creativeness.

People tend to resist in three ways: dispersal, blocking, and distraction.

In *dispersal*, people attempt to disperse the fluctuations caused by the increased energy flowing through their system, through expression via energy-consuming activities such as talking, screaming, anger, crying, compulsive sex, exercise, and the like.

In *blocking*, people resist, suppress, or block the energy that's flowing through their system by withdrawal, depression, sickness, loss of appetite, extreme fatigue.

People also *distract* themselves from the fluctuations and sense of impending disorder and chaos through drugs and alcohol, compulsive eating, sex, shopping, gambling, reading, watching TV, and the like.

Here's a valuable exercise: Recall some examples from your own life of some of these behaviors. Could they have been attempts to resist creativity and growth?

THE JOYS OF LETTING GO

Having a creative insight, leaving behind old ideas, and seeing the world in a new way should not be considered a frightening or even daunting prospect, any more than we are frightened to meet new people or travel to foreign lands. As I wrote in *Megabrain*:

> what we're talking about, after all, is simply a process of increasing brain coherence. It's a process that most people experience as one of the most pleasurable in life. It happens when making love, watching our child sleep, absorbing a work of art or being moved by music,

perceiving beauty, feeling the birth of a new idea, and at all moments of self-realization, fulfillment, achievement, illumination, peace and joy—the process of our brain's components rearranging themselves to accommodate themselves to reality in a new way. It's an occurrence psychologist Abraham Maslow devoted his career to exploring, and which he called having "peak experiences."

One characteristic of peak experiences is that they feel good—so good that most of us would willingly have them as frequently as possible. One of the most powerful human drives is toward peak experiences. Much of the energy and time we expend in our lives—in seeking or using sex, drugs, money, prestige, power, wisdom—is devoted to confused or misdirected attempts to have these peak experiences. How nice if we could have them at will.

As Csikszentmihalyi observes, "Enjoyment seems to be the mechanism that natural selection has provided to ensure that we will evolve and become more complex." I have argued earlier that evolution has ensured that we will learn by rewarding our learning experiences with pleasure neurochemicals. We are similarly, but more powerfully and often more ecstatically, rewarded for our creative insights, our breakthroughs to higher orders, for, in Csikszentmihalyi's words, doing things "that push us beyond the present and into the future."

ACTION SECTION—USING MIND TECHNOLOGY TO OPEN UP TO CREATIVITY

How can we use brain tech to increase our own creative powers? The description of creativity as a sudden mental reorganization at a higher level can be broken down into several components, including preparation, letting go, breakthrough or illumination, and integration. Mind tools can play a key role in each of these steps or components.

PREPARATION

Creative breakthroughs in quantum physics generally take place in the brains of people who know something about quantum physics. Musical creativity usually expresses itself through people who have listened to much music. New insights into computer design do not occur to people who have never used a computer.

Numerous tales of creative breakthroughs make it clear that the moments of illumination and sudden insight usually emerge only after the individual has devoted enormous mental and emotional energy to accumulating information and insight about the problem or field. Some students of the creative process have called this the "input mode," the time when you assign your unconscious mind a problem and give it as much information as you can to help in solving that problem. But it is not simply a matter of inputting information and expecting your unconscious computer to spit out the correct "creative" answer.

This preparation period is most effective when it is accompanied by an investment of emotional energy, such as a desire for a solution to a problem, or an intense longing for insight. In the words of composer Richard Strauss, "I can tell you from my own experience that an ardent desire and fixed purpose combined with intense inner resolve brings results. Determined concentrated thought is a tremendous force. . . . I am convinced that this is a law, and it holds good in any line of endeavor."

What Strauss is describing is an increased flow of energy—in the form of information and emotional arousal—through the structure of the brain. This increased energy flow causes the brain to fluctuate, to vibrate, to become destabilized and ready to move in new directions. Thus the emotional charge associated with this period not only contributes to the fluctuations, it is also a result of the increasing fluctuations. As this charge builds up, one temptation is to escape or resist through some of the expressing/suppressing/distracting behaviors described earlier.

Using Mind Tools for Preparation. Since much of preparation consists of study, accumulating information, and immersing yourself in the subject or problem, mind tools can serve as perfect "information input" devices. To prepare yourself to attack a problem or find a creative solution, immerse yourself in the information using the accelerated learning techniques described in Chapter 19. Get yourself into your receptive state, and bombard yourself with every sort of information you can. Your mind tool can be useful during this period in helping you to visualize various possible solutions to the problem.

Equally important to information input during this preparation period, as we have noted, is intense emotional concentration. This emotional arousal can be accomplished through anchoring and activating the anchor for highly charged emotional states. For example, you may remember a period of ferment and agitation you experienced prior to an earlier creative or emotional breakthrough. Using the techniques described in Chapter 15 for anchoring peak states, reexperience that intensely emotional state and link it with the problem with which you now are dealing.

We've mentioned the tendency to flee the feelings of uncertainty that accompany this period. Mind tools can be enormously effective in helping you reach a breakthrough simply by keeping you relaxed enough to move ahead toward a solution rather than escaping into self-destructive or creativity-sabotaging behaviors. As you feel your emotional arousal increase, instead of escaping, use brain tech to get into a calm, centered state. By keeping on target, you permit your mind to work more rapidly toward a solution.

LETTING GO

Students of creativity have called the letting-go phase "receptivity," the "incubation period," or, in comparison with the input mode, the "processing mode." During the preparation period the mind has taken in so much information, generated so much emotional concentration, that the energy flowing through the system has become too great to suppress, resist, or escape. The mind has reached its "bifurcation point." Now the old organization, the old structure, the old sense of reality is ready to break down and move in an infinite number of directions.

Using Mind Tools for Letting Go. First, a key to letting go is relaxing. Obviously, using mind tech to put you into a state of centered calmness can help you release control and let your mind rearrange itself freely, as it moves toward a higher order.

Also, it's interesting to note that for many creative people, this letting-go or incubation period is one during which potentially distracting or extraneous information from the external world is cut off, sensory input is shut down, and they turn inward. This period may take the form of gazing spellbound into the fire, a long walk through the woods or on the beach. If it's impossible to escape the distractions of ordinary life, the creative person simply turns inward and ignores them. Thus the tales of the "absent-minded professor," so deeply immersed in the processing mode, so cut off from the extraneous matters of normal reality that he wears unmatched socks or forgets to eat.

Mind technology, then, can provide an ideal means of shutting down external stimulation to permit you to let go and immerse yourself in whatever is happening in or emerging from the inner reality. Some of the tools, such as float tanks, ganzfelds, and LS devices, act directly on the nervous system to turn its awareness inward by either cutting down on external stimuli or providing a monotonous or unvarying external stimulus. In this sense, mind tech simply provides a high-tech alternative to fire-gazing or long walks.

This letting-go or incubation period is connected with increased theta brain waves, which produce the "twilight state" associated with vivid mental imagery, recall of childhood memories, the arising of spontaneous and unpredictable thoughts and ideas. As discussed earlier, most adults produce large amounts of theta only when they're falling asleep or emerging from sleep. Theta waves also predominate when we're drowsing before the fire, nodding out after a heavy meal, lost in reverie, and so on.

One reason high-amplitude theta activity seems to be a precursor to creative insights is that while theta can be experienced subjectively as deep relaxation or reverie, in the brain it literally means increased fluctuations. The low-amplitude random firings of beta activity have given way to the slower, more powerful alpha activity, and then alpha has itself given way to the even more powerful theta brain waves. In all probability, the amplitude of the theta waves is increased even more by the fact that this theta activity seems to become synchronous—that is, neurons in large areas of the brain are all firing *in phase*.

Let's compare this with a large number of people walking across a shaky bridge. If each person walks at his own rhythm, the resulting sound of the footsteps will be high in frequency but low in amplitude—and the fluctuations of the bridge itself will be low. But if everyone begins marching in step, the resulting sound will be a lower frequency but a much higher amplitude, and the fluctuations will increase enormously. In fact, if there are enough people marching in step, the fluctuations will become so great the bridge (which, as a closed system, cannot dissipate the entropy created by the marching feet) will collapse.

The increasing amplitude and synchrony of the theta brain waves increase the fluctuations in the brain. People who resist this process will try to "hold on" in one way or another. People who are open to change, however, who have experienced the benefits of creativity, new ideas, and a new vision of reality, will recognize the increasing fluctuations for what they are and willingly let go. Since the brain, unlike the bridge, is an open system, it does not need to collapse but can evolve by reorganizing itself at a higher level, by forging new neural connections and networks.

As noted earlier, EEG biofeedback researchers found that when individuals were trained to go into a theta state daily, they experienced an enormous increase in creative ideas. Clear evidence shows that brain tools can quickly and reliably help users enter this powerful theta state that is so essential to the creative process.

ILLUMINATION

When it finally takes place, the creative insight generally comes by surprise, emerging in an all-at-once fashion, as mathematician Johann Friedrich Karl Gauss described his sudden solution to a long-standing mathematical problem: "Finally, two days ago, I succeeded, not on account of my painful efforts, but by the grace of God. Like a sudden flash of lightning, the riddle happened to be solved. I myself cannot say what was the conducting thread which connected what I previously knew with what made my success possible."

Here, overwhelmed by the fluctuations, the old structure has given way and suddenly reorganized in a new way: Reality has become new. Research into dissipative structures and chaos have proven that the new order that emerges from the chaos is by definition unpredictable—when the fluctuations become so great that a structure collapses, it can be destroyed or reorganize in an infinite number of new ways that cannot be predicted. In that sense, the creative breakthrough is truly a death that leads to a rebirth.

Interestingly, this breakthrough is usually described in visual terms: insight, lightning bolt, illumination, a vision, the light bulb in the brain. Not only do we suddenly know, we "see" things all at once—in a flash. Creativity itself is often equated to "imagination," a word that clearly illustrates the centrality of the act of mental imaging.

Creativity is inseparable from imagination. Imagination is one with mental imagery and visualization. Mental imagery and visualization are profoundly enhanced in the theta state. Mind machines directly induce theta and significantly increase visualization abilities. In this sense, at least, these new brain tools may in truth be called Imagination Machines, Creativity Engines.

Using Mind Tools for Illumination. These Creativity Engines offer unique ways to accelerate toward the desired breakthrough or illumination. One way to do this is actually to increase the amount of energy flowing through the brain by increasing the length of your sessions. This happens naturally as you progress through the receptive or letting-go phase by producing progressively more and more slow, synchronous, and high-amplitude brain waves. In doing this, you inexorably increase fluctuations in the brain and move ever closer to the breakthrough.

Increasing Unpredictability. To this can be added another technique: increasing the amount of fluctuation in your system by intentionally altering in unpredictable ways the type of stimulation you are receiving. Thus, for example, clinical users of LS systems linked to EEG feedback have found that they can create rapid breakthroughs not just by entraining brain-wave activity down into the theta or delta ranges, but by alternately speeding up and slowing down brain waves. One successful clinical system alternates one minute of upward entrainment with one minute of downward entrainment. Varying the upward and downward periods randomly alters this pattern and makes it even more unpredictable.

If you use an LS systems without EEG equipment, you can approximate the effects. Simply find a comfortable frequency in which you feel the LS stimulation seems to "lock onto" your own brain-wave activity (usually in the 12 to 16 Hz range). Then gently draw your brain waves down for a period of time by slowing down the LS stimulus, trying to keep your brain waves locked onto it, then speed up your brain waves again by speeding up the LS stimulus. Alternate this at random intervals. (How do you know when you're "locked on" to the LS frequency? All I can say is that you can feel a real sense of "linkage" or "connection" between your brain and the light stimulus, so that as the stimulus changes frequency, you can feel yourself responding to it with your own changes of brain-wave activity. Similarly, you can feel when your brain waves "break loose" from the stimulus as a sudden loss of connection or linkage with it.) This free-ranging up-and-down movement produces a sort of energizing whole body-mind dive-bomber or roller-coaster effect that many people find euphoric. In essence, it's setting up an ever larger fluctuation in your brain rhythm within the already existing fluctuations of your high-amplitude theta brain-wave activity.

These fluctuations can be increased with LS systems with rapid switches of light patterns (for example, switching between all lights flashing simultaneously to right eye alternating with left eye), combined with rapid switches in sound patterns. Some LS systems can be programmed to go through thousands of changes in a session. Another powerful technique is to have someone manually control the session to forcefully drive you through unpredictable changes.

Inexperienced users should approach these techniques with caution as they can induce vertigo, nausea, and even anxiety.

Another way of increasing fluctuation is by using different types of mind tools. For example, you might alternate between deep theta or delta sessions on an LS device, sessions in a float tank, CES, the use of a variety of audio programs, back to LS with upward and downward roller-coaster movements, and so on. These fluctuations can be maximized by linking them with your larger mind-body rhythmic fluctuations. (Try blasting yourself, for example, with energizing sessions during deep trough periods, or relaxing sessions at high energy peaks, and vice versa.) All of these fluctuation increases can be integrated with increasing periods of deeply relaxed, high-amplitude theta, during which you consciously let go, release, open, and entrust yourself to what is to emerge.

INTEGRATION

As we all know, there is a great difference between true creative insights and ideas that seemed like creative insights at the time but turn out to be crazy schemes, wild visions, and wishful dreams. Creative insights need to be tested, verified, and integrated into your life. One way is to see how they work over time. Another more personal way to test your creative breakthrough is to see if it produces dramatic reductions in stress, if you can now handle with ease events or life circumstances that once caused you stress. This is what we would expect from a dissipative structure reorganizing at a higher level: Energy that once caused huge fluctuations while flowing through the old system should now pass through the new, more highly evolved system easily.

USING MIND TOOLS FOR INTEGRATION

Once you've experienced a creative breakthrough, the next step is to put it into practice. That means, for many people, the actual hard work of comprehending, organizing, and implementing all the insights and information that appeared all at once in the lightning bolt of illumination. Generally, such breakthroughs in one area of life will have a domino effect on the rest of your life. Suddenly you'll be seeing changes everywhere.

During these times mind tools can prove their practical value. You have had an insight that you see needs to be integrated into your life. How can that be done? In what order? Where should you start? The first step toward answering these questions is to take a brain-tech session. Once you're relaxed, with your mind clear and free of distractions, you can go about the detailed planning work necessary to make the most of your creative insights.

ACTION SECTION—EXERCISES IN CREATIVITY

VISUALIZATION

Creativity is closely linked with imagery and visualization. And imagery seems to be the language of the unconscious mind. Go back now to Chapter 16 and practice some of the techniques detailed there, including using *active* visualization, *receptive* visualization, creating visual scenarios and observing what happens, and asking questions of your unconscious and receiving an answer in the form of mental imagery. When used in combination with the creativity-inducing suggestions just offered, they should help project you into intense and powerful visual experiences.

INNER DICTATION

These visualization techniques are simply ways of opening yourself up to the flow of images and information from your unconscious mind. Other ways can be equally powerful. One favorite technique is what has been variously called spontaneous writing or automatic writing. Using mind technology, you reach a state of deep relaxation and openness. Then, holding a pen in your hand, or seated at your computer or typewriter keyboard, simply let the words flow out of you. Don't pay attention to what you're writing or saying, and above all don't let that editor in your head tell you that what you're writing is ungrammatical, meaningless, or embarrassing. Simply let the words flow out, finding their own rhythm, their own style. You will be surprised at what emerges.

A variation of this that many find more easy to use during a session is simply to keep a tape recorder microphone clipped to your shirt collar. As ideas or mental images arise, state them as simply as possible without arousing yourself from the deep trance or theta state you are in. A few words will generally serve as touchstones, so that when you replay the tape later, they will enable you to remember the images fully.

Some users of mind tools have found that by learning to enter these deep states and then communicating verbally (whether in writing or speech) what they are experiencing as they experience it, they seem to open themselves up to a more or less coherent other personality hidden away within their unconscious. It may take the persona of an "inner child" speaking of events that have been long forgotten, or it may be what seems to be a relatively autonomous individual. These kinds of experiences are the source of what is widely known as channeling. Some people believe that the channeled information is actually being communicated from some other reality, or some other personality—a "voice from beyond." It may be that in these deep trance states individuals are able to gain direct access to Carl Jung's "collective unconscious." But whether the information comes from the individual's own unconscious, from the collective unconscious, or from some other dimension, it's clear that the images, insights, and information can have profound importance for the person. It's also clear that mind-tech Creativity Engines can help users quickly and reliably enter the deep trancelike states in which they can gain direct access to these otherwise hidden images and information. For many users, this constitutes the greatest value of mind tools—as facilitators of information retrieval.

SUGGESTED READING

An excellent exploration of creativity is *Higher Creativity* by Willis Harman and Howard Rheingold (Los Angeles: Tarcher 1984).

A truly astonishing book that contains exciting insights into the unique value of creativity and creative artists in our time is *We've Had 100 Years of Therapy and the World's Getting Worse* by Jungian psychiatrist James Hillman and writer Michael Ventura (San Francisco: HarperCollins, 1992).

For a more detailed exploration of the theory of the brain as a dissipative structure, see my *Megabrain* (New York: Ballantine, 1986, 1991), Chapter 4 and Chapter 5.

TWENTY-FOUR
AWAKENING AND TRANSCENDENCE:
TECHNO-SHAMANISM AND THE
DEMOCRATIZATION OF BLISS

The very beginning, the intrinsic core, the essence, the universal nucleus of every known high religion . . . has been the private, lonely, personal illumination, revelation, or ecstasy of some acutely sensitive prophet or seer.

—Abraham Maslow,
Religions, Values and Peak Experiences

By now it must be clear that many individuals have found that brain tools can offer them direct access to transpersonal and transcendent experiences. Some readers may find it strange or surprising that the technological products of materialistic modern science are being used as tools for spiritual experiences. But as Stanislav Grof, M.D., observes, our "transcendental impulse" or "spiritual craving" has been one of the most powerful forces driving human behavior—a compulsion more basic than the sex drive. And in our compulsive pursuit of such transcendental experiences, humans have always used the most advanced technology available to them, from the earliest technology of creating and manipulating fire and light, to the technology of drums and chants, onward through human history. Technology, after all, comes from the Greek words *technos* and *logos,* meaning, in essence, an organized way of using reason or the systematic application of a body of knowledge. Using technology, then, has much to do with what it means to be human.

One of the most ancient spiritual technologies is shamanism. This pragmatic system of mind-body techniques is, in the estimation of anthropologist Michael Harner, at least 30,000 to 50,000 years old, and surely emerges out of techniques developed over the course of human evolution. Out of shamanism and paralleling it have emerged other spiritual technologies, including the mind-body exercises of yoga, and a rich variety of esoteric schools, mystery cults, and technological rituals, including gnosticism, Sufism, Kaballism, tantricism, taoism, and alchemy.

POWER TO THE PEOPLE

One central impulse throughout history has been to find ways of systematizing and simplifying these spiritual technologies to make them more easily taught and to provide access to the core mystical experience to as many people as possible. As Dr. Herbert Benson observes in *The Relaxation Response,* "By the twelfth century . . . it was realized that this ecstasy could be induced in the ordinary man in a relatively short time by rhythmic exercises, involving posture, control of breath, coordinated movements, and oral repetitions."

In many ways the Western rationalist, materialist scientific tradition of the last five hundred years can be seen as an attempt to systematize and make accessible to all—that is, to *democratize*—these mystical experiences. Power to the people. The development and explosive growth of printing, for example, made it possible to pass along to an infinite number of potential readers essential information about spiritual technologies that previously had had to be handed down laboriously from teacher to student, from generation to generation. The development of modern science was to a large degree an attempt to reveal to human understanding the coherent, mystical order or organizing principle of the universe.

Modern academic and materialist science, with its emphasis on a limited definition of reality, has generally denied and repressed the transcendental impulse. As Grof notes, "Within the present century, academic psychology and psychiatry dismissed spirituality as a product of superstition, primitive magical thinking, and outright pathology." But the spiritual drive, the transcendental impulse, is so powerful that orthodox science has been unable to suppress it. Abraham Maslow has pointed out that virtually all humans report having a profound sense of "unitive consciousness" at some point in their lives. In this most secular and materialistic era, a recent survey found that over 80 percent of Americans described themselves as strongly "religious" or "spiritual."

More astonishing is the substantial number of Americans who report having what can only be called mystical experiences. In a 1989 survey, fully a third of respondents answered yes to the statement "You felt as though you were very close to a powerful spiritual force that seemed to lift you out of your self." And a full 12 percent claimed that they had experienced this transcendent feeling "often" or on numerous occasions.

TOOLS FOR TRANSCENDENCE

Says Arnold Scheibel, professor of medicine at the University of California at Los Angeles, speaking of himself and his wife, Marian Diamond, neuroanatomist at UC Berkeley, "We like to think that somehow the brain in a sense will become the religion of the future. . . ."

In many ways it makes most sense to see the Brain Revolution as a spiritual quest: a sudden blossoming of scientists driven by a compulsion to understand the mystery of the universe by understanding the workings of the "last frontier," the most complex system in the universe. They are spiritual seekers using all their sophisticated technology to uncover what happens in this mysterious human brain when it is going through the ineffable experience known as illumination or transcendence.

As we have seen, these experiences of awakening are linked to certain clear physiological changes in the brain, including alterations in its chemistry, and changes in its electrical activity.

It has been established beyond doubt that the mind tools described in this book can produce the very same dramatic alterations in brain chemistry and in patterns of brain-wave activity that are found in individuals spontaneously undergoing transcendent, metanormal, or transpersonal experiences. It makes sense to assume that by reproducing the same patterns or fluctuations in brain chemistry and electricity, the mind tools can actually induce these extraordinary experiences. A wealth of evidence, in the form of reports by thousands of individuals, shows that mind tools not only can but do produce spiritual experiences for many of their users.

I believe that mind technology can produce transcendent experiences in the same way it produces the creative breakthroughs and illuminations described in the last chapter. Just as increasing turbulence and fluctuations in the brain can lead through chaos into a higher creative order, so can they lead to a direct experience of the highest order—the experience of illumination, mystical insight, satori, oneness with God.

Seekers of these transcendent experiences will find that mind technology can provide a sort of spiritual catapult. As with creativity, spiritual breakthroughs depend on your own mental preparedness, your openness to new experiences, your willingness to let go of your existing order, your desire to experience something more, your spiritual craving. Depending on your resistance, these transcendent experiences can range from gentle awakenings to bliss and moments of serene clarity, to full-blown blinded-by-the-light, knock-down, drag-out spiritual deaths and rebirths, such as that experienced by Saul on the road to Damascus.

Those who are already engaged in a spiritual practice will find that mind technology can intensify and accelerate their own spiritual growth process. Meditators who use brain tools during their meditations often discover they get to deeper states more quickly and reliably and that they can become mentally clear and lucid more easily than without the tools.

The techniques for using mind technology to stimulate transcendent or peak experiences are identical to those for stimulating creativity, described in the last chapter. These techniques include: reaching states of profound relaxation; letting go and releasing any wanting for control or security; increasing the length and frequency of sessions; augmenting fluctuations by entering states of higher-amplitude, synchronous brain-wave activity in the delta and theta ranges; escalating fluctuations even more by increasing levels of unpredictability (by shifting between more rapid and slower frequencies, shifting types of stimulation and devices, etc.). A variety of mind-altering substances that have been used to produce transcendent experiences also seem to be potentiated or intensified in power when used in combination with mind technology.

AT THE STILL POINT

Lest spiritual seekers think I place too much emphasis on the turbulence and hubbub of creative and spiritual breakthroughs, I want to point out that all spiritual traditions and teachers have taught that authentic transcendent insights come from direct experience of God, or the divine spirit. This experience often emerges as a bursting forth, a breakthrough, a blinding light, and escape to a higher order. Then again, it often emerges out of total silence, the void, nothingness, emptiness, the still point of the turning world.

Seekers have pursued this stillness by withdrawing into caves, or deserts, or silent retreats. They have approached it through repetitions of mantras and prayers. As we have seen, mind tools represent a technological approach to these various blank-out or sensory deprivation approaches. Several hours in a flotation tank can produce as profound a stilling of the mind and senses as days of desert isolation. An effective ganzfeld can produce a blank-out experience that opens into the pure silence of the void where the presence of the divine spirit can make itself known.

And ultimately, the silence of the void is simply another face of the divine spirit that flows through life, creating the fluctuations, turbulence, and chaos that can cause us to let go of old, restraining structures and escape into higher orders. Mind tools allow users to amplify, intensify, and accelerate this movement of the divine spirit.

They *allow* it. It is not a requirement, and it is not a guarantee. A recent article about mind machines in a national magazine condemned them, claiming that "Plugging yourself into a machine is not automatically going to make you a deeper or finer person." The writer, a longtime meditator, feared that to use them would mean that he had to "write off the last 20 years of practice as a waste of time." In his opinion, mind tools did not automatically produce a state that was identical to meditation, and therefore were attempts to "cheat the Buddha."

If this was not so weird, it would be comical. Condemning mind machines because they do not automatically make you a better person is like condemning airplanes because flying in one does not automatically turn you into a saint.

There are a lot of ways to get from New York to San Francisco. You can walk. You'll meet a lot of people along the way and have lots of interesting and life-altering experiences. Or you can fly. Whether you walk for three months or fly for six hours, you reach the exact same place: San Francisco. You may arrive a different person if you walk than if you fly, but you're still at the same place. What you do there is up to you. While one person may seek enlightenment from the monks in Golden Gate Park, another may seek dope and whores in the Tenderloin.

Mind technology, like airplanes, can get you places very quickly, and very reliably. Just because many of us choose to fly doesn't mean we don't choose to hike sometimes, or condemn those who choose to hike all the time. Just because I choose to fly from San Francisco to New York doesn't mean that "I have to write off 20 years of hiking practice as a waste of time." Nothing is ever wasted. And choosing flying instead of walking in no way "cheats the Buddha." As the Buddha said, "Everything arises and passes away. . . . When you see this, you are above sorrow. This is the shining way." I believe the shining way is a path that can be hiked just as well on a 747 as on the highways of America.

HOLOTROPIC BREATHWORKS

A problem for many people who are interested in exploring the peak experience states produced by substances such as psychedelics is that these substances are illegal, long-lasting, and can have harmful side effects. For many years consciousness researchers and scientists investigating transpersonal states have searched for some sort of tool or technique with the profound transformational effects of psychedelics, but without the drawbacks.

One of the leading figures in this search has been psychiatrist Stanislav Grof. Beginning in the 1950s, Grof studied the effects of psychedelics, and was producing extraordinary results in the treatment of alcoholics, drug addicts, terminal cancer patients, and many others by using these drugs to guide them into transcendent, spiritual experiences. With the banning of psychedelics in the 1960s, Grof began exploring the effects of deep and continuous breathing and found that it could produce psychedeliclike effects, quickly and reliably.

Throughout the 1970s and 1980s Grof explored the effects of

continuous hyperventilation. Modern medicine looks on hyperventilation as something to be avoided, leading to seizures, anxiety, panic states, and even blackout. Grof, however, discovered that, when done intentionally, confidently, and calmly, continuous deep breathing moves an individual through the transient symptoms of hyperventilation into states of expanded consciousness, euphoria, illumination, and transcendent, life-transforming experiences. Based on years of experience in guiding individuals and groups through transcendent experiences by means of continuous deep breathing, Grof developed a procedure called Holotropic Breathworks (also widely known as Grof Breathing). Grof created the name from the Greek words *holos*, meaning "whole," and *trepein*, meaning "moving toward." Thus, Holotropic Breathing is breathing that "moves toward wholeness."

In Holotropic Breathworks, a "sitter" or partner is present as a caretaker and to provide human contact, as one or more individuals lie on their backs, close their eyes or cover them with sleep masks, and begin breathing deeply, accompanied by appropriate music. The breathing, while not forceful or hurried, is deep and rapid enough that the breather soon becomes light-headed. Often a sitter is not required, since the subject frequently is quickly immersed in a stream of powerful mental imagery and dreamlike experiences. At times the subject may become so immersed in the experiences that the breathing rate may slow down. At those times, the sitter can gently remind the subject, with a touch or a word, to continue the deep breathing.

Many subjects experience no dramatic physical effects and move directly into dissociative and transcendent states. Some, however, have strong physical sensations and experiences, including involuntary muscular contractions or spasms (or *tetany*), often of the hands or feet. These can develop into whole body movements, such as clenching, twisting, writhing. Subjects often find their breaths becoming moans, groans, howls, cries. At these times the sitter can gently remind the subjects to let go, release, and continue breathing. As the subjects move through experiences that may include reenacting and reexperiencing their own birth, the sitter tries to ensure that the music being played supports or intensifies the experience.

On occasion subjects reexperience painful or frightening events, such as birth traumas, and may feel they are choking or suffocating. The sitter can help them pass through these events by physically helping them to release, let go, open up, stretch their chests and throats, manipulate their larynx, shout and howl. Passing through these painful or traumatic experiences seems to have a profound healing and transformational effect. As Grof observes:

> Holotropic experiences encountered in the process of in-depth self-exploration have intrinsic healing potential. Those that are difficult and painful in nature—if completed and well-integrated—seem to

eliminate sources of disturbing emotions and tensions that would otherwise interfere with everyday life. Ecstatic and unitive feelings of belonging infuse the individual with strength, zest, and optimism, and enhance self-esteem. They cleanse the senses and open them for the perception of the extraordinary richness, beauty and mystery of existence. . . .

HOLOTROPIC MIND MACHINES

I have explored the effects of combining mind tools with Holotropic Breathworks. As might be expected, the mind tools seem to intensify and accelerate its mind-altering effects. Together, brain-stimulating technology and Holotropic Breathworks seem to provide a rapid route to extraordinary and transcendent experiences.

In many of the other applications of brain technology, we have observed that it is often helpful to focus attention on a specific problem or area to be addressed in a session, ranging from a visualization of an athletic performance to the types of suggestions you want to offer yourself. However, in holotropic brain-tech sessions no such intentionality seems necessary or even advised. What seems more important is a willingness to release all intentionality, let go of attempts to control what you will experience, and let your unconscious be your guide. The unconscious mind seems to have an uncanny knack for presenting to you exactly what you require. As Grof observes, "Non-ordinary states of consciousness tend to work like an inner radar system, seeking out the most powerful emotional charges and bringing the material associated with them into consciousness where they can be resolved."

People who are interested in exploring Holotropic Breathworks, either by itself or in combination with mind machines, should do so only with a sitter or trusted friend present. Physical symptoms such as choking or convulsions, while not typical, can occur. And in those cases an experienced sitter can keep you from hurting yourself and can play a crucial role in helping you forcibly open up your breathing. While generally you can move through whatever frightening or traumatic materials may arise, sometimes these experiences can be so overwhelming that you may become lost in a sort of holotropic "bad trip." On such occasions, a sitter can bring you back to yourself, gently encourage you, and help you push through the experience to its healing conclusion. Since mind technology intensifies the Holotropic Breathworks effects, always have a sitter present as you explore the experience.

SUGGESTED READING

The writings of Stanislav Grof, M.D., including *Adventures in Self Discovery* (New York: SUNY Press, 1985), and his recent *The Holotropic Mind,* with Hal Zina Bennett, Ph. D.; (San Francisco: Harper-Collins, 1992), are at once visionary and supremely practical.

TWENTY-FIVE
RIDING THE BIG WAVE:
ULTRADIAN RHYTHMS AND MIND MACHINES

Not knowing that one has a time structure is like not knowing that one has a heart or lungs. In every aspect of our physiology and lives, it becomes clear that we are made of the order we call time.

•

Because the clocks and calendars of social activity are designed for economic efficiency or convenience, an individual may have to learn to detect his own cycles, and become aware of scheduling to protect his health.

—Dr. Gay Gaer Luce, Report of U.S. Department of Health, Education, and Welfare

•

The night time is the right time.

—The Strangeloves

•

I like it much better in the morning.

—Genya Ravan, 1970s rock singer

Back in the early 1980s, when I began exploring the effects of the flotation tank, I was intrigued to find that my experiences in it were quite different at different times of day. For some reason there was an enormous difference in "feel" between an early-morning float and one in the late afternoon, and between an early-evening and a late-night float.

I talked with other floaters about this and found that they too had noticed how the time of day influenced the quality of their float. One lawyer loved to hop in the tank for a 6 A.M. float on days when he had court appearances—he would emerge an hour later feeling charged with an electrical power and energy. But he noticed that when he floated in the evenings he emerged feeling relaxed, drowsy, and ready to go to sleep.

An architect with multiple sclerosis usually would go in for a float around noon, and said that he would quickly sink into a state of profound rest, with no thoughts—he felt his body was healing and restoring itself, and called it his "healing time." But when he went in the late afternoon after work, his experience was quite different—as he floated his mind was busily visualizing and working on his current projects.

As I began experimenting with longer floats—staying in the tank for eight or ten hours at a stretch—I found that they had a wavelike quality. At first I might sink rapidly down into a deeply relaxed state in which I had no awareness of time, no thoughts—a deep theta or even delta state. But after a period of time, like a diver slowly rising toward the surface, I would slowly regain consciousness, my mind would become more alert, my thoughts more intentional. Gradually my body would become more active—I would feel the need to stretch, move, tense and release my muscles. And then, after rising to the surface, my consciousness would again turn downward, and I would sink into the depths, returning to the dreamlike imagery of theta or the bliss of total emptiness. I began to think of it as "riding the big wave."

As I paid attention, I found that these waves of rising and falling awareness were rhythmical—I seemed to pass through one complete cycle of rising and falling about every 90 to 120 minutes. Upon further exploration I found that different parts of the wave seemed most conducive to certain types of consciousness or work. For example, the tank was often a great place to get writing done—at times I could spin out page after page of wonderful prose, and store the words clearly in my mind, ready for access when I sat down at my typewriter. But I quickly found that the writing happened only when I was at a certain point on the wave. As I sank deeper, a different type of creative thinking would take place—I might see or "feel" the entire structure of a book at a single flash, experience spontaneous images, bizarre thoughts, unpredictable flashes of insight. And then I sank even deeper, into a place beneath consciousness—a state that was not sleep but was without content.

But when I emerged from that deep wordless and thoughtless place, I rose back up through the mysterious, unpredictable twilight theta space again, where I would often find my brain filled with sudden new ideas, mental fireworks, chains of thoughts veering off in unexpected directions—it was as if the time in deep unconsciousness had charged my brain with new energy. And as I rose higher up on the wave I would once again be at that point where I found the words running through my mind—if I wanted to, I could write whole chapters, articles, stories, songs, plays, poems. And then I would rise even higher on the wave and become too conscious to write—it would be time to stretch, scratch an itch, think about what I would cook for dinner that night, make active plans. And as the mundane thoughts passed, I would once again begin to slip downward, sinking deeper, riding the wave. . . .

As I became more aware of the wavelike nature of consciousness, I also discovered that there were certain points on the wave ideally suited for certain types of activities or nonactivities. For example, I discovered that if I offered myself suggestions while moving downward into the theta range, just before I slipped into that level of deep theta where I was no longer actively conscious, the suggestions seemed to become implanted and take root while I was in the deepest part of the wave, before I rose again into consciousness. Having taken root, they would have powerful effects. On the other hand, if I offered myself suggestions while I was moving upward on or reaching the peak of the wave, the suggestions had little effect—it was as if my mind was too busy or too conscious and analytical to take note of (or permit me to believe) them.

I made similar discoveries about learning—I seemed to learn most effectively information that I heard over underwater speakers in the tank while sinking downward on the wave and before I passed into its unconscious, deepest, part. On the other hand, I felt that I was much more capable of making effective plans, organizing my activities, while riding upward on the wave.

OBSERVATIONS OF THE CHRONOBIOLOGISTS

What I was exploring, though I didn't know it at the time, was the realm of chronobiology (the interplay between biology and time). Scientists had long observed that humans were influenced by a variety of biological rhythms. These include the long rhythms of the human genetic life span, the yearly rhythm of the passing seasons, the monthly menstrual rhythms, the sleeping and waking rhythm of night and day, and the waves or cycles that rise and fall several times each day, including sexual arousal and hunger.

These latter rhythms are called *ultradian* (pronounced ul-TRAY-dian) rhythms (from the Greek *ultra-dies*, "beyond" daily, or many times a day). And during the last few years chronobiologists and others have made some astonishing discoveries about ultradians and their influence on our bodies and minds.

One key finding that has emerged in recent years is that humans have been genetically programmed to operate on a 90- to 120-minute ultradian rest-activity cycle, known as the Basic Rest-Activity Cycle (BRAC). This cycle seems to regulate a wide array of mind and body activities.

HEMISPHERIC DOMINANCE

As I noted earlier, neuroscientist David Shannahoff-Khalsa of the Salk Institute for Biological Sciences did electroencephalogram (EEG) studies of both right- and left-brain activity simultaneously and found that hemispheric dominance shifted back and forth in a wavelike rhythm. The average time for the cycle from right to left back to right, he found, was about 120 minutes.

BODY SIDE DOMINANCE

Not only the brain hemispheres, but the actual sides of the *body* switch dominance every 90 to 120 minutes, according to Shannahoff-Khalsa and associates. By sampling neurotransmitter levels in blood taken from both arms every 7.5 minutes, the researchers found that catacholamines—dopamine, norepinephrine, epinephrine (adrenaline)— became more concentrated on one side or the other in a regular cycle that accompanies the basic rest-activity cycle.

VERBAL AND SPATIAL SKILLS

Since certain types of mental activity are linked with specific hemispheres, Shannahoff-Khalsa's identification of a rhythmic shift of hemispheric dominance suggested that human mental activity might go through similar ultradian rhythms. Other scientists tested subjects at regular intervals on verbal (left-hemisphere) and spatial (right-hemisphere) tasks. They found that when verbal ability was high, spatial ability was low, and vice versa, and this alternating pattern continued throughout the day and night in cycles of about 90 to 100 minutes.

COORDINATION AND MEMORY

Scientists studying subjects playing video games measured various skills, and found that hand-eye coordination, learning, and short-term memory all showed a pattern of peaks and valleys. The peaks in performance occurred about every 90 minutes.

PHYSICAL ACTIVITY

Scientists observed subjects who were left alone in a neutral environment—a quiet, sparsely furnished room—and found that they showed a clear basic rest-activity cycle of around 110 minutes.

MENTAL ALERTNESS

When subjects were tested on complex tasks that demanded intense concentration and alertness, their performance rose and fell in an unmistakable 90- to 120-minute cycle.

CREATIVITY

Performance on a number of tests that measure creativity shows that it tends to rise and fall in the ultradian rhythm of around 90 minutes.

SUGGESTIBILITY AND RECEPTIVITY

Hypnotherapist Milton Erickson found that people went through natural short (15- to 20-minute) periods of relaxation and heightened receptivity that he called "common everyday trances," and that these natural trances occur on a basic 90- to 120-minute cycle.

OPTIMISM AND PESSIMISM

During high-energy phases, according to psychologist Robert Thayer, people can be overoptimistic and tend to overestimate their resources and the time and energy required for a project. Similarly, during low-energy phases, they can be overpessimistic, tending to underestimate their own resources.

REST AND HEALING

The peaks in physical activity and energy every 90 to 120 minutes are mirrored by troughs or valleys, with the deepest part of the trough being a period of about 15 to 20 minutes. Evidence suggests that the body requires this short rest or recovery period, and uses it for essential healing, repair, and growth and to replenish its stores of neurochemicals. At the same time the mind shifts away from external matters into a "common everyday trance," a period of inward focus during which some sort of mental rest and reorganization takes place. Interestingly, this is a period of increased *theta* brain-wave activity. Research indicates that this all-important period of rest and mental receptivity takes place in the approximately 20-minute transition period—the trough—between the low end of one 90- to 120-minute cycle and the beginning of the next. Psychobiologist and hypnotherapist Ernest Lawrence Rossi, a leading authority on ultradian rhythms, calls this approximately 20-minute transition period or trough the *Ultradian Healing Response*.

In sum, the 90- to 120-minute basic rest-activity cycle seems to regulate an overwhelming number of our body-mind systems. According to Rossi, "research indicates that all our major mind-body systems of self-regulation—the autonomic nervous system (activity and rest), the endocrine system (hormones and messenger molecules), and the immune system (disease fighting)—have important 90- to-120-minute basic rest-activity cycles."

WHY YOU'D BETTER LEARN TO RIDE THIS CYCLE

This basic cycle, according to BRAC discoverer Nathaniel Kleitman, is a fundamental and essential characteristic of the life process itself—it "involves gastric hunger contractions and sexual excitement, processes concerned with self-preservation and preservation of the species." He says:

> When such fundamental human processes and learning and performance, digestion and bodily repair, and sex and personality all respond to the call of the 90- to-120-minute rhythms, when even our muscles, glands, circulatory system, and organs resonate to it, and our very brain and psychological state keep time to it—these rhythms, or whatever causes them, must reflect pervasive patterns of communication between our mind and body.

ULTRADIAN STRESS

The basic rest-activity cycle seems to be programmed into our genes. In fact, there is new evidence that the BRAC regulates the most basic life process, the growth and division of cells. The entire process of cell division and growth lasts about 90 to 120 minutes, with a 20-minute period required for the buildup of a biochemical that plays a key role in the process of cell division. For millions of years our ancestors lived in close harmony with the natural rhythms of life, rising with the sun, sleeping at night, and responding to the signals of the BRAC by resting and napping periodically during the day.

Modern civilization, with its artificial lights, work schedules, and unremitting stress, tends to disrupt the 90- to 120-minute BRAC. For many of us life is a process of repeatedly overriding or ignoring the signals from our bodies and minds that it's time to take a break. Many of us have completely lost touch with our basic need for periods of rest and rebalancing. The result of this chronic disruption and desynchronization of our most fundamental rhythm is that modern plague called stress.

We all know the symptoms, starting with mental and physical fatigue, manifesting itself as mood swings, forgetfulness, loss of concentration, irritability, and burnout. When ignored, these symptoms of stress can lead to more serious stress-related disorders, including high blood pressure, heart disease, stroke, suppressed immune function, depression, anxiety, insomnia, and, in all probability, various types of cancer.

What the evidence shows, then, is that our mind and body operate on a basic wavelike 90- to 120-minute cycle. This ultradian wave is a key factor in our mental performance—our ability to learn, think, create, remember—and in our physical performance—our energy, reaction speed, strength, endurance, and much more. Other capacities, such as our abilities to control stress and to heal ourselves, our sexual energies, our immune function, our sensitivity to emotions, and much more, are directly linked to this basic cycle. The message is clear: *If we are at all interested in maximizing mental and physical performance, then we must become aware of and learn to make intelligent use of our ultradian rhythms.*

By doing so, we can both capitalize on our strengths—"peak the peaks"—and make most effective use of our down times—"trough the troughs." We can also, when necessary, learn to alter our ultradian rhythms forcibly. In Rossi's words:

> By learning to heed the signs that we are entering the active phase of the ultradian performance rhythm, we can enhance our overall performance by focusing on demanding tasks while our energy and alertness are on the upswing. And by learning to heed the signs that we are entering the 20-minute rest-and-rejuvenation portion of the rhythm, we can properly restore ourselves so that we are at our performance peak when our energy and alertness rise again.

MAPPING YOUR RHYTHMS WITH MIND MACHINES

The essential first step toward making effective use of your ultradian rhythms is very simple: Pay attention to yourself. Unfortunately, our culture does not encourage us to pay attention to ourselves, to heed the signals of our mind-body rhythms. We are, in fact, actively encouraged to ignore and override our natural rhythms. Virtually every aspect of contemporary life—the drive to produce more and more at work, the proliferation of dazzling entertainments to distract our attention—calls us away from ourselves, encourages us to ignore our natural ultradian rhythms, our life wave.

Fortunately, we now have available a variety of tools that are ideally suited for helping us pay attention to those signals: mind machines.

The following techniques for becoming aware of and making optimal use of your 90- to 120-minute ultradian life wave can be accomplished without mind machines, of course, simply by paying attention to yourself. But while the act of paying attention is fairly simple in itself, it is not easy to accomplish. We have to make an effort. Amid the cacophony of modern life, it's often hard for us to hear the messages being sent to us by our mind and body. Mind technology, however, is highly effective at blocking out the environmental distractions and disruptions. Mind machines, in a sense, act as blinders and earplugs— cutting off the external signals so that we can pay closer attention to our internal signals. By helping us direct our attention inward, mind machines can act as *sensory amplifiers*, helping us become aware of and keenly sensitive to the rise and fall of our natural life wave.

STEP ONE: PAY ATTENTION TO THE SIGNALS

The initial step is to find a comfortable place to sit down or stretch out—ideally, someplace quiet where you'll be free of jangling phones and other distractions. Use your mind technology to move downward to state zero. If your device or tapes permit you to select frequencies, choose alpha. Now, as you turn your attention inward, pay attention to your internal mind-body signals and messages.

Here are some of the signals and messages you might notice:

- Fatigue
- Feelings of impatience, irritation, anger
- Muscle tension
- Mood changes
- A desire to stretch, yawn, sigh deeply
- Drowsiness
- Daydreaming or experiencing pleasant memories
- Feeling contemplative, introspective
- Feeling passive, receptive
- Having fantasies, sexual arousal, idle thoughts
- Feeling like taking a rest and letting go
- Feeling like doodling or noodling

All of these are signals that you are on the down side or in the trough of your life wave and that your mind-body would profit from a short period of rest and recovery. You can use your brain machine to help you relax, let go, and let your mind-body make the most of this healing period.

Here are some other signals you might notice:

- You feel energized, rested and strong.
- Your mind is focused, alert.

- You're eager to get to work, to accomplish specific tasks.
- You have a clear idea of what you want to do.
- You feel you can accomplish your goals effortlessly.
- You are coming up with solutions to problems and having creative ideas.
- You are eager to play or engage in physical exercise.

These, of course, are signals that you are on the up side, or at the peak of your life wave, and that it's time to get things done. You may want to use brain tools in an active mode, to focus and amplify your energies, to solve specific problems or projects, to engage in activities and creative pursuits.

MAPPING YOUR LIFE WAVE

In the initial stages of mapping your life wave, you should use brain technology to pay attention to your mind-body signals several times a day. Ideally, you can make notes in a daily or hourly calendar. A few words describing the signals you receive each brain tech session are sufficient—for example, "wiped out," "memories of sixth grade," "back pain," "psyched up for the board meeting," "bliss," "high energy," and so on.

Over a period of days or weeks, you will begin to see patterns emerging. Perhaps you'll notice that you have a lot of your best creative insights at night or in the morning; that you feel most tired in the late afternoon, or just before lunch; that your back pain peaks at certain periods and goes away at others.

Soon you should be able to point to your peaks and your troughs

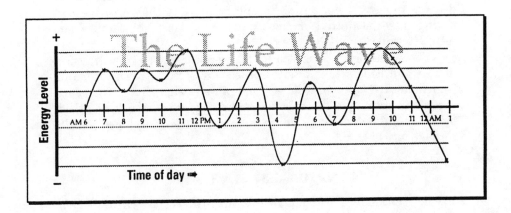

each day, and by connecting the dots you will be able to draw a line, tracing the rise and fall of your life wave throughout the course of your day. Our ultradian rhythms are flexible, of course, and can vary in response to external conditions, so your life wave map can never be exact, predicting your peaks exactly to the minute. However, your map will increase your awareness of your own rhythms, your ups and downs, your peak performance periods and the best times to take a relaxing brain-tech break.

DOWN IN THE VALLEY: THE "HEALING RESPONSE"

Once you have used brain technology to tune into your ultradian life wave, you can begin using it in ways that are specifically designed to take advantage of specific mind-body states, or points on your daily cycle. The single most important first mind-machine application for most of us is to get the most out of our body's natural rest and regeneration period, that 20-minute bottom-of-the-trough that Ernest Rossi calls the Ultradian Healing Response. By using brain tools to enhance and deepen the body's natural tendency toward relaxation and rest, we can get the most and the highest-quality rest and regeneration that is possible.

One reason this 20-minute period can be so important is that it is characterized by what Milton Erickson called the "common everyday trance." As Rossi describes it, during this common trance, "we become more introspective. Our dreams, fantasies, and reveries—the raw material of growth in everyday life as well as in psychotherapy—become unusually vivid, as the window between our conscious and unconscious opens a bit." At these times, says Rossi, we gain access to our inner selves and our inner mind. "Because the inner mind is the source of our deepest knowing," he writes, "people may be at their creative best during these meditative moments, experience insights, fantasy and intuitive leaps."

These moments, Erickson found, were the key to inner transformation and healing. In Rossi's words, "the secret of transformation from illness to health and higher levels of well-being" lies in "recognizing and facilitating a person's own mind-body resources during these brief natural windows of inner focus as they [arise] periodically throughout the day."

NATURAL THETA STATE

The descriptions of the "common everyday trance" are virtually identical to what we have described in an earlier chapter as the theta state. And, in fact, EEG evidence has now revealed that during this natural rest period, brain-wave activity tends to slow down from the beta-dominant patterns that govern our normal waking states of consciousness into a relaxed state of predominantly alpha and theta frequencies. In other words, by becoming aware of our natural life wave and troughing the trough, we can enter a natural theta state, with all its well-documented benefits.

As we have seen, theta is characterized by vivid imagery, sudden bursts of insight, and intense memories. Researchers such as Elmer and Alyce Green at the Menninger Foundation have found that going into theta regularly somehow enhances immune functioning, heightens creativity, and can facilitate profound "integrative experiences" and life-transforming moments.

Hypnotherapist Erickson seized on these moments of common everyday trance to implant life-changing suggestions in the minds of his clients—the secret to his so-called miracle cures. More recently, researchers have found that the theta state is characterized by hyper-suggestibility and hyperreceptivity. It is, they have discovered, a state in which suggestions for behavioral change can have dramatic and long-lasting effects. Again, by using brain technology to accentuate, augment, and deepen the body's natural theta state, we can learn quickly and reliably to put ourselves into hyperreceptive states. At these times, by combining mind tools with suggestions to ourselves— verbally or in the form of images or feelings—we can intensify our common everyday trance to implant powerful messages for personal growth, healing, and transformation.

By being aware that we have a natural tendency to be more pessimistic and to underestimate our own powers while in our trough, we can reassure ourselves and take a more realistic view of ourselves and our situation. Awareness of our position on the life wave helps us avoid being discouraged or disheartened, since we can remind ourselves that our current life rhythm causes us to see things a bit pessimistically.

PEAKING THE PEAKS

Once we've become aware of the rise and fall of our ultradian life wave, we'll be ready to "seize the hour" and make the most effective use of those times when we are at our peak. These are the times to undertake our most challenging tasks, to take advantage of our position atop the mountain peak to take a panoramic view of life, to use our energies and enthusiasm to communicate our ideas and visions clearly and compellingly to others. These are the times to schedule important meetings, to set personal records, to exercise, to be with friends, to make love. But it's also useful to be aware that at these times we can be unrealistically optimistic and overestimate our own powers. By being aware of this tendency as it arises at our life wave peak, we can remain optimistic, but temper our natural confidence with realism.

The most common use of brain tools is during the natural healing periods, the troughs. By using mind tools to get the most out of these periods of profound rest and regeneration, we will have more energy, more power, more intelligence, and more creativity for these peak moments: By troughing the troughs, we peak our peaks.

We can use brain technology actively in a variety of ways during our peaks to increase the power and effectiveness of these heightened moments. For example, these periods are ideal times for activating peak states and powers we have anchored in earlier mind-tech sessions.

AROUSAL AND FLOW

It has been verified repeatedly that peak performance depends on optimal levels of arousal. Too much arousal is experienced as anxiety and can cause performance anxiety, stage fright, or choking, and performance deteriorates. Too little arousal means we're simply not alert enough—too laid back or too bored—to deliver a peak performance.

One of the most valuable functions of brain machines is as tools for controlling arousal. A variety of devices permit the user to turn arousal levels either up or down (by increasing or decreasing the frequency of the light flashes or the binaural beats, for example). So once we've mapped out our life wave and are aware of our peak periods, we can make appropriate use of mind technology. If we have to give a speech or make a presentation and our arousal levels are too high or too low, we can alter our levels of arousal until we feel they are just right.

ULTRADIAN BREATHWORKS

As we noted earlier, one key ultradian cycle is the wavelike shift in hemispheric dominance. Over a period that averages 120 minutes, but that can vary from 25 to 200 minutes, dominance shifts back and forth between hemispheres. Research by David Shannahoff-Khalsa and others suggests that this dominance is mirrored by shifts in the flow of breath through the right and left nostril. In general, because the brain is "cross-wired" with the body (that is, the right hemisphere is linked to the left half of the body and the left hemisphere is linked to the right half), when the right nostril is more open (when breath flows more easily through it) the left brain hemisphere is dominant, and vice versa.

This discovery, as Shannahoff-Khalsa observed, "suggests we can exert more control over our day-to-day mental functioning. For example, certain cognitive functions, such as language skills, mathematics and other rational processes that are thought to be primarily

localized in the left hemisphere" might be boosted by "forcibly altering" our cerebral dominance. And in the same way we might "accentuate the creativity that is thought to be characteristic of right-hemisphere dominance," through similar forcible altering.

It is possible to use brain tools to learn to activate areas of the
brain or specific hemispheres selectively. Biofeedback specialists have
found that, when people are given EEG feedback from specific areas of
the brain, most can learn to activate specific areas. Some of the biofeedback EEGs described earlier can be used as training tools for
learning to activate specific hemispheres or areas of the brain.

By using brain tools to heighten our sensitivity to our rhythmic
shifts of hemispheric dominance, just as we used them to increase our
awareness of our ultradian life wave, we can learn to make optimal use
of the particular powers of each brain hemisphere.

THE INTERPLAY BETWEEN HEMISPHERES AND THE REST-ACTIVITY CYCLE

Since the rhythm of the shift of hemispheric dominance may be shorter
or longer than the rhythm of our 90- to 120-minute ultradian life wave,
we will find ourselves becoming aware of a variety of potential mind-
body states as the two separate cycles move into different relationships
between themselves. For example, many people find that reaching the
peak in their basic rest-activity life wave, with its accompanying high
physical energy, while the brain's right hemisphere is dominant, seems
to produce emotionally charged, highly creative, and productive
states. Peaking out in the rest-activity cycle while in a left-dominant
state, on the other hand, can produce a more euphoric, extroverted
state of absolute self-confidence and self-assurance.

TUNING THE DEMONS OF THE DOUBLE WHAMMY

For those who are not aware of the effects of their ultradian life wave
and the characteristics of right-hemisphere dominance, being in a
right-hemisphere-dominant state while going through the trough, or
the bottom of the wave, can produce a sort of "double whammy" that
is experienced as depression, fatigue, or unpredictable mood swings. On
the other hand, once we've become aware of the potentials of this
combination, we can use it and "tune" it with mind technology to
project ourselves into deeply introspective states in which we find
unexpected flashes of insight, or gain access to highly emotional images
and memories.

Theoretically, learning how to control hemispheric dominance
consciously can be a powerful tool for boosting our ability to deal most
effectively with the task at hand. If we're going into a conference,
taking a written test, or faced with some other task that requires

left-hemisphere capabilities, and we find that we are in a right-hemisphere-dominant phase, for example, we might want to shift quickly into left-hemisphere dominance.

THE SYNERGY OF BALANCE

However, as I mentioned earlier, perhaps the most powerful application of brain tech to hemispheric dominance is to create a state of hemispheric balance. It's been discovered that during each cycle of shifting hemispheric dominance there is a period during which dominance is equally balanced between both hemispheres. And, researchers have suggested, the brain is at its most fertile and creative at this time. Two brains are better than one. The two hemispheres are complementary and, when working together, produce *synergy*, defined by philosopher/inventor Buckminster Fuller as *"behavior of whole systems unpredicted by the separately observed behaviors of any of the system's separate parts."* Whether we are in a peak period of our ultradian life wave or going through a trough period of deep rest and recuperation, we are at our best when the two hemispheres are functioning together, synergistically.

As noted, it's also clear that the sides of the body itself shift dominance regularly. It makes sense to believe that just as brain symmetry and integration of both hemispheres seem to be linked to peak brain performance, so the integration of the right and left sides of the body are keys to peak physical performance. Says Shannahoff-Khalsa, who discovered the switch in dominance of body sides, identifying and making use of the "crossover point" may be crucial. "My chief interest," he says, "is in finding measurable changes that correlate with yogic medicine. The yogi, of course, tries to maintain a 'life force' understood to be the optimal balance of the two sides."

It's clear that a highly integrated brain, a brain in which both hemispheres are functioning in symmetry, synchrony, harmony, and unity, is a key to peak states and peak human performance. The same may be true of physical balance between the two sides of the body. But throughout history, humans have found that it's not easy intentionally to bring both hemispheres to bear simultaneously (or to reach that ideal point of physical balance when both sides of the body are working together with optimal coordination). Much of our lives we spend swinging back and forth between left-dominant and right-dominant states. This is where brain machines represent a real breakthrough: They can effectively produce more symmetrical, balanced brain-wave dominance. It's probable that they also can help the body become more integrated and balanced between right and left. And, the evidence suggests, by doing so they can assist in producing the optimal states associated with whole-brain, whole-body integration.

SUGGESTED READING

A primary source for much of the information in this chapter has been
The Twenty Minute Break, by Ernest Lawrence Rossi and David Mimmons (Los Angeles: Tarcher, 1991), which despite its "pop" title is an
excellent exploration of the influence of ultradian cycles.

PART FOUR

BRAIN-POWERED HEALING:
Therapeutic Uses of Brain Tools

All disease is memory.

—DR. RAYMOND ABREZOL

Work with people in non-ordinary states of consciousness has brought about remarkable changes in understanding and profound new insights about emotional and psychosomatic disorders that have no clearly defined organic cause. This work has shown that we all carry internal records of physical and emotional traumas, some of them biographical or perinatal in origin, others transpersonal in nature. Some people can reach perinatal and transpersonal experiences through meditation techniques, while others get results only through extensive experiential psychotherapy or psychedelic sessions. Some people whose psychological defenses are not so vigorous, may have such unconscious material surface spontaneously in the middle of their everyday activities.

—STANISLAV GROF, M.D., *Adventures in Self-Discovery*

Authentic selfhood can be defined in part as being able to hear these impulse voices within oneself. . . . No psychological health is possible unless this essential core of the person is fundamentally accepted, loved and respected.

ABRAHAM MASLOW, *Religious Values and Peak Experiences*

INTRODUCTION
TRANSFORMING THE SELF WITH
MIND TECHNOLOGY

ACCESSING THE BODY-MIND LIBRARY

Nothing is coincidence. Over the last ten years of exploring mind technology, I have come to know a number of therapists, each of whom, working independently, has developed remarkably similar views of how to use mind tech to eliminate psychological (or mind-body) problems. Each of them has come to believe that this can happen rapidly by employing the brain-altering powers of brain technology to reveal and release past traumatic experiences that have been "stored" in the mind and body.

Psychotherapist Len Ochs, Ph.D., had long experience of using electroencephalograms (EEGs) and other types of biofeedback. Then he became aware of the work of Dr. Eugene Peniston and Dr. Paul Kulkosky, who were having extraordinary success in treating drug and alcohol problems and posttraumatic stress disorder by using EEG biofeedback to get the clients into theta, where suppressed traumatic materials would emerge and the clients would undergo beneficial personality transformations.

TUNING INTO STORED TRAUMAS

While exploring the Peniston Protocol in his own practice, Ochs also learned of how EEG feedback was being linked with light/sound (LS) machines, so that the frequency of the light flashes was directly linked to the client's brain-wave activity. He began using EEG-LS stimulation, which he called EEG entrainment feedback, and found that as clients moved downward or upward into certain frequency ranges—which were different for each person—he or she would begin to experience discomfort, anxiety, or nausea. Ochs used the LS to help gently entrain the clients' brain waves into the uncomfortable frequency range. He found that as they willingly relaxed and entered that frequency range, they underwent sudden releases of traumatic material. What was even more exciting was that these sudden releases had powerful, life-transforming effects. It was as if the therapeutic effects of months or even years of traditional "talk" psychotherapy had been compressed into minutes. Ochs concluded that specific traumatic events were coded and stored in the brain according to specific frequencies, like library books stored according to call numbers.

THE BRAIN-WAVE ROLLER COASTER

In his explorations of EEG entrainment feedback, using LS to entrain brain waves, Ochs experimented with setting the computerized program alternately to speed up brain waves and then slow them down, producing a sort of roller-coaster effect. He found that when he did this, many clients experienced a rapid release of symptoms and problems. It appeared that as clients learned to move through troublesome frequencies, they released progressively more and more of the stored traumatic material. In effect, Ochs seemed to be "limbering up" the brain, increasing its flexibility, its capacity to move freely up and down through various frequency ranges.

RELEASING NEUROMUSCULAR PATTERNS

Another therapist using LS to release stored traumas is Los Angeles voice therapist Warren Barigian, who treats many entertainment stars for vocal problems. Back in the mid-1980s, he began incorporating LS into his practice. As his clients wore the goggles with flickering lights, Barigian would direct them to make physical movements and to shout or sing, while he simultaneously manipulated their larynx. He found that the clients would experience dramatic emotional releases, during which hidden material, such as past traumas, would emerge and be discharged as shouts, cries, tears, and physical movements. At this point, the clients would feel their entire vocal apparatus release, and they experienced a feeling of freedom. Not only did their singing voices improve dramatically, they often reported that they experienced remarkable transformations in all areas of their lives. It was as if the release produced by the LS experience had freed them from long-standing limitations.

Barigian, who has a background in Reichian therapy, explained to me back in 1987 that he believed traumas became "stored" in the body and mind as neuromuscular patterns or behaviors. As these behaviors were repeated, the neuromuscular patterns became habitual. "But by putting a random stimulus like the flashing light through the brain while they are doing normally habitual behavior patterns, like moving or singing," he told me, "the new stimulus is able to 'break up' those habitual neuromuscular patterns, and free the client to move and feel in entirely new ways. In the process the old patterns release the stored traumas."

COLOR-CODED TRAUMAS

At about the same time, psychiatrist Richard Frenkel, M.D., told me how he had discovered that clients would find traumatic experiences reemerging when he exposed them to specific colors while they were in a trance state. For example, a man who was severely depressed had a strong reaction to green. It turned out that he was a prison guard who had been taken hostage by inmates and held prisoner in a green room. As a result of hundreds of such experiences with clients, Frenkel came to believe that traumatic experiences, in fact *all* our experiences, are coded and stored in the brain by specific colors. The brain, according to Frenkel, is a sort of computerized color information database that stores experiences according to colors.

Frenkel developed a technique for releasing these color-coded stressful experiences. He designed a special mirror or "imagescope" that was surrounded by different colored lights, so that a client could look into the mirror and see his or her image in a selected color—green, blue, red and so on. Frenkel asked patients to focus on their image and describe feelings or memories that emerged. When they were exposed to the color associated with a traumatic experience, he found that painful memories "gushed out," often accompanied by the physical symptoms associated with the painful experience. When the experiences were released in this way, Frenkel found, they were literally eliminated. Over the years he has had extraordinary success in treating anxiety, depression, phobias, migraine, fatigue, obesity, drug and alcohol abuse, and much more.

INTO THE DISCOMFORT ZONE

I was reminded of Frenkel's work by phototherapist Jacob Liberman, who has found that specific colors can act therapeutically by triggering the release of "toxic" memories or past experiences. Liberman has developed a technique to discover what colors his patients find most disturbing or uncomfortable, noting that "the disturbing colors seemed to represent, or in some way be related to, painful experiences in patients' lives." Like Len Ochs, who uses flashing lights to move his clients' brain waves into their discomfort zone, Liberman arranges the colors for treatment from the least disturbing to the most disturbing, and then moves the patient gently into progressively more disturbing colors. As he does so, deeper and more painful issues surface and are released. He concludes:

I discovered that treating patients by way of their eyes (the windows of the soul) with colors to which they were not receptive and that were in a specific sequence would reawaken old and unresolved emotional issues that seemed to be at the core of the physical dysfunctions they were experiencing. . . . I noticed that once patients had resolved the emotionally painful issues triggered by the colors, then looking at these colors, which was originally uncomfortable, actually stimulated feelings of joy and euphoria. . . . *A major key to getting well is becoming comfortable with those aspects of our lives that were previously uncomfortable.* . . .

BODY ARMOR, MIND ARMOR

Each of these therapists, working independently, found new ways of using mind technology to release traumas that had been stored in the bodymind. Many of their findings can be explained in terms of the mind-body therapy of Wilhelm Reich, who over fifty years ago pointed out how traumatic experiences are stored away in the body as habitual muscular tensions and neuromuscular patterns he called "body armor." Though our bodies create this armor as an unconscious attempt to "protect" us from the traumatic experiences, Reich demonstrated how the armor actually cuts us off from a fulfilling experience of life—"tight muscles don't feel"—producing both physical and emotional rigidities.

ARMORING AND NONORDINARY STATES

Storing away traumas by coding them with brain-wave frequencies or specific colors, and then "protecting" ourselves from those stored traumas by rigidly keeping ourselves from reentering those regions, it seemed to me, is clearly the same process Reich called creating armor. But how does this storage actually take place? How is armor actually created? How, exactly, does an event "out there" enter the brain, where it becomes an event "in here," and then become transformed from a mental event to actual physical rigidities and tensions "stored" in different parts of our body?

Reich asserted that early imprints and scripts inhibiting the free expression of natural energies create rigidities and blockages that are anchored in the body as armor, and that these tensions are the cause of physical and mental illness. When he first expressed these ideas, they were met with great skepticism. After all, how could something that happened in the mind cause such long-lasting effects in the body? Now, as we noted in Chapter 18, we know that the traumatic events become translated into neuropeptides and other "intelligent" chemicals, which then circulate through the body making permanent changes on a cellular or genetic level in the bodymind information matrix/intelligence field. But the event itself is buried away in posttrauma amnesia—that is, it becomes unconscious, or more accurately, state dependent.

To release or undo the harmful "learning" that has become part of the body, then, we must enter a bodymind state like that in which the original learning took place. This explains why when adults enter the nonordinary state produced by mind machines they so frequently experience memories from childhood: Those memories are state-dependent memories. This also explains why people who learn to enter theta frequently are alleviated of long-standing illnesses and become more physically healthy. These early traumatic events or imprints, according to Reich, are anchored in the body in the form of muscular tightness and rigidity and respiratory blocks; these blocks in turn, through the constant tension and stress they place on the body, are manifested throughout life by physical and psychological ailments ranging from asthma, to high blood pressure, to cancer, to depression. By learning to return to the original state in which the script was laid down, adults are able to reaccess and release many of the rigidities and blockages that are the root cause of their illnesses.

TAKING OFF THE ARMOR

I have explored the idea that creativity, learning, and ultimately the life process itself depend on the brain's ability to permit energy and information to flow freely through it, setting up fluctuations that can ultimately cause it to reorganize at a higher level—an evolutionary process of growth. Just as body armor creates physical rigidities, so "mind armor" creates mental rigidities: The traumas that are armored in the mind make it more rigid—there are certain frequencies it cannot move through freely, certain colors it must protect itself against, certain thoughts it cannot permit, certain memories it cannot remember.

So armored minds lack sufficient flexibility to vibrate or fluctuate to the flow of energy and reorganize at progressively higher levels. The pain caused by past traumas, and stored as body or mind armor, is suppressed and experienced in another form as the unwitting pain of being stuck, rigid, closed down, confined to habitual neuromuscular patterns, unable to be truly creative or free. This latter type of pain is generalized, and we are often unconscious of it. But it is experienced as anxiety, depression, a lack of spirit or *élan vital*, a feeling that life is not as rewarding or exciting as it should be.

GETTING SUPPLE AND LIMBER

Another useful metaphor is physical injury. When we injure a joint or tear a muscle or ligament, movement in that joint is inhibited during the healing period. It becomes "armored" as a result of scar tissue, tight muscles resulting from immobility, and so on. The only way to restore full free movement to that joint is through releasing the armoring by stretching, movement, massage, and so on. When complete freedom of movement is returned to the injured joint, it becomes supple and limber.

People like Len Ochs, Warren Barigian, Jacob Liberman, Richard Frenkel, and others are using mind technology to exercise the brain like an injured limb—to move the brain through its stuck points, its points of armoring and rigidity. In the process they are restoring to the brain the free range of movement that it once had. With this wider, more supple and free range of movement comes psychological freedom.

These researchers have found that, in response to flickering lights or specific colors, subjects have hypersensitive responses to specific frequencies or colors—they become nauseated, anxious, uncomfortable. It is at these visual frequencies, apparently, that the traumatic material is stored. These frequencies, that is, are linked to specific states. Using the library simile, we might say that traumatic memories (in fact all memories) must be stored away in the library under several different types of codes—that is, using a filing system that allows us to access them by different "call numbers," such as colors, brain-wave frequencies, smells, sounds. By using frequencies or colors to provide subjects immediate and total access to the memory records stored away in the library, these therapists have been able to produce a sudden and dramatic releasing of the traumatic material, resulting in speedy and remarkable healings and "cures."

The work of these therapists reminded me of the speculations about the effects of LS stimulation made a decade ago by medical researcher Dr. Gene W. Brockopp. He theorized that

If we can help a person to experience different brain-wave states consciously through driving them with external stimulation, we may facilitate the individuals' ability to allow more variations in their functioning through breakup of patterns at the neural level. This may help them develop the ability to shift gears or "shuttle" and move them away from habit patterns of behavior to become more flexible and creative, and to develop more elegant strategies of functioning.

In essence, it seems that traumatic events are filed or stored away in the entire web of embodied thought, the bodymind. In the brain they become armor that restricts the free flow of brain-wave activity through the frequency ranges, just as scar tissue restricts the free flow of a joint through its full range of motion. By repeatedly moving the brain through its rigid or restricted areas, as Ochs and Barigian do with LS entrainment and as Liberman and Frenkel do with colors, we can produce "releases," "freeing" and "opening" of mental areas and capacities that dramatically enrich one's life.

CRACKING OPEN THE MIND-BODY ARMOR

In the chapters that follow, we will explore a variety of ways you can use mind technology to crack open your mind-body armor and gain access to stored memories; to release the traumatic charge, the pain, and the mind-body rigidity associated with them; and to gain greater mental freedom, flexibility, and openness to change, creativity, and pleasure. We will be working on the principle that true healing and growth depend on moving into the "discomfort zone" and on the emergence of the hidden material. As Stanislav Grof observes,

> When we start experiencing symptoms of a disorder that is emotional rather than organic in nature, it is important to realize that this is not the beginning of a "disease" but the emergence into our consciousness of material that was previously buried in the unconscious parts of our being. When this process is completed, the symptoms associated with the unconscious material are permanently resolved and they tend to disappear. Thus, the emergence of symptoms is not the onset of disease but the beginning of its resolution. Similarly, the intensity of symptoms should not be taken as a measure of the seriousness of the disease so much as an indication of the rate of the healing process. . . .

A key to the capacity of mind tools to produce rapid change and personal transformation rests in their ability to induce state change rapidly. Since the original traumatic events were stored away during nonordinary states of consciousness, they can be released most effectively by returning to those nonordinary states. There is evidence that when used properly, these mind tools can be far more effective than traditional types of therapy. As Grof points out, "There have been no conclusive studies showing that certain schools are superior to others in getting therapeutic results. It is known that 'good therapists' of different schools get good results and 'bad therapists' get poor results." But by using mind technology, we bypass the question of different "schools" of therapy or the therapist's role as "guide" or "interpreter" of the psychological material. In nonordinary states, such as those produced by mind machines, according to Grof, "the material with the strongest emotional charge is automatically selected and brought into consciousness. These non-ordinary states also provide necessary insights and mobilize our own inner healing forces with all their inherent wisdom and power. Try as we might to duplicate these natural healing processes, no school of psychology has even come close."

As Ochs remarked, "It's kind of a humbling experience to me, who has had years of schooling in learning how to 'do' therapy with clients, to find that in many cases this EEG entrainment system can produce better results in just a few minutes."

In addition to discussing ways of using brain technology to gain access to and release troublesome material, we will in the following chapters explore ways of using mind tools to help in the process of healing and personal change in a variety of ways we've already explored.

RESCRIPTING

Rescripting, described in Chapter 18, is one of the most powerful ways of using mind tools therapeutically. I urge you to reread that chapter in the context of its potential therapeutic applications, from altering addictive or unwanted behaviors, to overcoming pain, to boosting immune function.

RELAXATION AND HEALING

Many problems we experience, from physical pain, to anxiety, to depression, are a direct result of stress and physical tension. Mind technology can provide unsurpassed deep relaxation that has tremendous therapeutic and healing benefits. The body has its wisdom, and by freeing the body from external distractions and stressors, by assisting it in entering this natural state of recovery and regeneration, brain machines can be powerful tools for healing.

Many other ways in which mind tools can have powerful benefits in the therapeutic processes are described in the coming chapters. Many of them are based on qualities, effects, applications, or techniques that have already been explored.

For example, virtually every therapeutic application of mind tools will make use of their proven powers to

- Alter brain chemistry
- Alter brain-wave activity
- Induce states ideally suited for self-observation and self-healing through mindfulness, focusing, and releasing
- Increase suggestibility
- Increase mental imagery and control of visualization
- Enhance the effectiveness of rescripting and anchoring techniques

SUGGESTED READING

For a discussion of the therapeutic benefits of moving "into the discomfort zone" see Jacob Liberman's *Light: Medicine of the Future* (Santa Fe: Bear & Co. 1991). For explorations of body armor and character armor see Wilhelm Reich, *Character Analysis* (New York: Farrar, Straus & Giroux, 1972), *The Mass Psychology of Facism* (New York: Farrar, Straus & Giroux, 1945), and *The Function of the Orgasm* (New York: Farrar, Straus & Giroux, 1973).

TWENTY-SIX
FULL-SPEED RECOVERY:
ENDING ADDICTION AND SUBSTANCE ABUSE

Over the last few years neuroscientists have identified the mechanisms of the process called addiction. We now know that addiction to a substance emerges from changes in our mind-body "reward system" and results in changes in our ability to experience pleasure.

SUBSTITUTION

Some substances we can become addicted to work by taking the place in the mind-body reward system of naturally occurring neurochemicals. Morphine, heroin, and methadone, for example, take the place of the endorphins, fitting like synthetic keys into the "locks" of the receptor sites on the nerve cells that usually receive endorphins. Since there is an abundant supply of the substitute, synthetic opiates, over a period of time the brain shuts down its own production of natural opiates. And since the substitute opiates come in such unusually large quantities, the size and number of the brain's receptor sites also begin to diminish over time. Thus the brain-body becomes dependent on an external supply of synthetic opiates.

In addition, opiates have the effect of blocking the production of norepinephrine (NE, the brain's adrenaline). When the substitute opiates are cut off, and the brain's own production of opiates has been turned down, NE pours out. This flood of adrenaline is experienced as the anxiety, tremors, sweating, and other symptoms known as withdrawal.

STIMULATION

Other addictive substances, such as cocaine, seem to work in large part by stimulating the brain to produce larger quantities of its natural excitement and ecstasy neurochemicals, dopamine and NE. As the brain's supply of these neurochemicals is drained, more and more cocaine is required to squeeze out less and less pleasure-producing neurochemicals. After a certain point the brain's supply becomes depleted. The user then experiences the "crash." Since the natural chemicals for producing pleasure and excitement are depleted, the user is left feeling lifeless and depressed.

Some *behaviors* seem to be addictive for some people, acting on the brain like cocaine, producing a rush of excitement and ecstasy neurochemicals. Behaviors that seem to be addictive for some people include gambling, risk-taking, sex, romance, shopping, raging, creating emotional scenes, and much more. Much of the information contained in this chapter will be just as useful to people with these kinds of "addictions" as to those who have problems with more traditional kinds of addictive behaviors, such as smoking, drinking, and taking drugs.

WITHDRAWAL AND THE NO-FUN SYNDROME

One thing that happens when the user stops taking the drug or other addictive substance is what is known as withdrawal. This can include a flood of adrenaline, producing tremors and anxiety, and, because both the brain's production of certain neurochemicals and its sensitivity to those neurochemicals have decreased, when the external stimulation stops, a crash occurs that can be experienced as intense depression. The brain can begin to increase its production of the lacking neurochemicals, but it can take weeks or even months before production reaches optimal or normal levels. For example, methadone has been found to reduce the body's supply of endorphins so much that endorphin levels remain depressed for six to twelve months after methadone has been stopped.

This means that when the external source of pleasure is removed, the user's own natural ability to create and experience pleasure has withered away. Even those things that might normally bring pleasure—sexual experience, a sidesplitting comedy, being with friends, natural beauty—leave the user joyless, since the chemicals in the brain that would ordinarily be released and produce joy simply do not exist. Nothing is fun, because the brain has lost its ability to experience fun.

This long-lasting postwithdrawal inability to experience pleasure is known as *anhedonia*. Many experts believe that one reason addicts find it hard to keep from returning to their habit even after they've kicked the physiological withdrawal effects is that in the weeks and months that follow they find their lives devoid of pleasure. No fun.

MORE OR LESS PLEASURE FROM THE SAME PIECE OF CAKE

All indications are that each of us is born with different levels of endorphins, dopamine, norepinephrine, and so on; different levels of receptors for each neurochemical; different abilities to secrete various neurochemicals; and different sensitivities to the neurochemicals.

So, for example, some individuals with lower-than-normal levels of endorphins or endorphin receptors may make use of addictive drugs or behaviors to stimulate the release of endorphins or to replace insufficient natural opiates with externally supplied synthetic ones. The drugs or behaviors, then, may be an instinctive attempt to "self-medicate," to "tune the brain" and cause it to produce the level of pleasure that cannot be attained naturally due to endorphin deficiencies.

Similarly, others have naturally high levels of endorphins. As Yale biochemist Philip Applewhite writes, "All other things being equal, the differences among people in how happy they are may well reflect differences in how the pleasure center of the hypothalamus functions." Regarding differences in the amount of endorphins secreted in certain brain centers Applewhite says,

> Those with more endorphins released with certain activities may be happier about any given situation or event in their lives than those with fewer endorphins. That is, doing the same thing may be more pleasurable to one person than another person because for that person, more endorphin molecules are released in the brain. Happiness, then, lies not outside the body, but within. Happiness is not an illusion; it is real and has a molecular basis.

RESTORING BRAIN CHEMICALS

ELECTRICAL STIMULATION OF BRAIN CHEMICALS

Since addiction, withdrawal, and anhedonia are the result of insufficient levels of certain brain chemicals, or undeveloped pleasure centers and pleasure pathways, the most direct way of eliminating them is to restore optimal levels of the brain chemicals, to stimulate the pleasure centers and pleasure pathways. One of the most exciting breakthroughs in the treatment of addiction has been the discovery that stimulating the brain with a minuscule electrical current (cranial electrostimulation, or CES) can cause the brain quickly to pour out large quantities of the neurochemicals that have been suppressed by addictive substances.

As electrotherapy researcher Bob Beck described it to me, this was originally discovered when scientists analyzed the brains of rats that had been addicted to opiates:

> The rats that were addicted had been getting so much opiate that the little endorphin factories in the brain would shut down and say, "Look, our body's got too much of this. Quit manufacturing it." And

it would take anywhere from a week to three weeks before their rats' brains would begin manufacturing beta-endorphin again. Whereas in the brains of the control rats that had never been addicted, you would find the normal, expected levels of beta-endorphin. And then they would take a third group of addicted rats, cold turkey cut them off of the heroin, clip little electrodes to their ears, and within 20 minutes of electrical stimulation . . . the rat brain would start showing that the endorphin production had started up again. So, those rats wouldn't go through withdrawal symptoms!

This evidence quickly led to the use of CES in the treatment of humans. Among the leading researchers in this field has been Dr. Ray Smith. In the early 1970s he found that CES quickly reduced depression, anxiety, tremors, and other symptoms in alcoholics. He also found that CES could "reverse so-called irreversible brain damage" in alcoholics and produce seemingly miraculous boosts in their IQs. As he told me, "I might have been one of the first to come up with it, but certainly a lot of studies are coming up with it now—we've found that it is reversible. In fact in two years of total abstinence an alcoholic will get his memory back to where he pretty much ought to be able to be back to his original IQ, but it takes two years! Again, with CES we do it in *three weeks!*"

As Smith says, what appears to be "brain damage" could be the result of depletion of a variety of neurochemicals, including acetylcholine—which is essential for healthy brain functioning. And he points to research showing that CES can produce rapid increases not only in endorphins, but in a variety of neurochemicals, including acetylcholine, serotonin, norepinephrine, and dopamine.

THE RETURN OF FUN

In more recent research, Smith has expanded his work from treatment of alcoholics to those addicted to cocaine, heroin, and methadone, and found that CES has equally striking effects. One of the most important effects Smith has noticed is that the subjects can experience pleasure and fun once again. As he described to me the results of one of his most recent studies of the effects of CES on a group of cocaine addicts:

> The original plan was to test half the patients for three weeks and then to reverse the pattern and to give the treatment to the other half of the patient population, but we couldn't get the machines back from the patients in time to conduct the second half of the experiment! The patients knew they'd been helped, and they didn't want to give up the equipment!

Essentially, Smith claims, CES can restore the user's ability to experience pleasure by restoring the pleasure-producing neurochemicals. In many cases, he told me, "We don't have to ask the patient if there's any change . . . the patient will be the first one to tell you, 'Hey, this is some great stuff!' " Smith describes crack addicts undergoing withdrawal putting on CES and saying "I feel like I'm on crack!" and marijuana users telling him "Hey man, I feel like I'm smoking!" As Smith told me, "It'll do that within ten minutes" for certain "receptive" subjects.

Many other researchers, including Dr. Norman Shealy, have verified the rapid effects of CES on brain chemistry. In one study, for example, a single treatment with CES increased beta-endorphin levels by 90 percent within minutes. Other studies have proven that CES quickly alters levels of all the neurochemicals affected most by drug addiction.

Robert O. Becker, M.D., a longtime student of the effects of electrical stimulation on biological systems, observed the CES treatments of Dr. Meg Patterson, whose drug treatment clinic in England is centered on CES. As Becker told me, "she got very interesting results. The first of which was that the minute that you could put this [CES] on him, the patient could stop taking the drugs and would not have any withdrawal symptoms!"

PHOTICALLY STIMULATING BRAIN CHEMICALS

CES is not the only way to treat addiction, withdrawal, and anhedonia by altering brain chemicals. Recent research has proven that stimulation of the brain with a flashing light—such as is done with light/sound (LS) systems—can have effects on brain chemistry very much like those of CES. Shealy, for example, tested the effects of both CES and photic stimulation (using a simple LS system) and found that both significantly increased levels of endorphin, serotonin, norepinephrine, and dopamine.

This may explain why LS systems have been used so successfully for the treatment of drug and alcohol problems. Years ago, before Shealy's findings demonstrated the neurochemical effects of LS, biofeedback therapist Dr. Thomas Budzynski found that LS had powerful antiwithdrawal effects: "Those clients who have been abusing Valium, Xanax, or other tranquilizing prescriptions may experience fewer and less severe symptoms during gradual withdrawal if they can manage daily or at least twice weekly sessions of LS, especially at theta frequencies." Anesthesiologist Robert Cosgrove, Jr., an authority in pharmaceutics and biomedical engineering, conducted preliminary studies of LS stimulation and concluded that it was "clearly very powerful in its ability to cause deep relaxation in most subjects. Its effectiveness has been so great that we are very enthusiastic about the prospect of evaluating [LS] for its sedative properties in patients prior to, during, and immediately following surgery." Clearly, Cosgrove observed, it was having some effects on the sedating or opiate neuro-chemicals.

Work like that of Shealy, Budzynski, and Cosgrove may explain some of the antiaddictive effects of LS being noticed by clinicians and therapists. The frequent reports of exhilaration and even euphoria experienced by users of LS systems suggests that they are stimulating the release of the brain's pleasure-producing neurochemicals.

Other researchers and clinicians, such as Dr. John Ott, Dr. Jacob Liberman, and Dr. Richard Frenkel, have noted that exposure of sub-jects to full-spectrum and/or colored lights also can help in the treat-ment of addiction. Again, there is evidence that the light stimulation is restoring levels of neurochemicals that have been depressed by sub-stance abuse.

OTHER MIND TECHNOLOGY FOR STIMULATING BRAIN CHEMICALS

There is also evidence that float tanks, acoustic field generators, ganz-felds, and movement devices can stimulate the release of a variety of brain chemicals, including endorphins. Again, this may explain in part why these machines are proving successful in the treatment of various substance abuse problems. The owner of one flotation tank center told me that many of his clients were former drug addicts or alcoholics, and remarked, "They tell me that floating lets them feel good. It puts pleasure back in their lives for days and even weeks after they float. In fact, some of them felt so good they wondered at first if they could become addicted to floating."

PERSONALITY TRANSFORMATION

Interestingly, researchers have found that using CES and other types of mind technology for treatment of addiction not only relieves with-drawal symptoms, but when used over time seems to produce profound personality transformations. Ray Smith noted in his own work and in a meta-analysis he conducted of other CES research that CES seemed to produce these effects only after regular use of at least two to three weeks. As Becker told me with some astonishment:

> When I was in England, I saw a number of Meg Patterson's cases. I was impressed by one thing. They all said to me that they had a *personality alteration* as a result of using Meg Patterson's technique. That they had gone from an addictive personality to a non-addictive. That following six weeks of treatment with her device, not only were they able to be without the drugs but—even six months later—they didn't experience the craving for the drug that had inevitably fol-lowed in any of the other techniques for therapy!

Becker's observations are supported by a recent controlled study of substance abuse patients by Dr. Stephen Overcash and Dr. Alan Siebenthall. They found that the group receiving CES underwent extraordinary changes: As measured in pre- and postscores on the widely used "16 PF" psychological personality test, the experimental group showed dramatic increases in self-sufficiency (the control group did not change) and in dominance or assertiveness. (The experimental group more than doubled its scores in this area, while the control group showed little change.) And in the area of ego strength, which measures decisiveness in handling interactions with others, the experimental group nearly *tripled* its scores, becoming far more decisive, while the control group showed little change.

As for the substance abuse problem, the authors found that the experimental group "reduced their use more quickly and sustained abstinence for a longer period of time. This may have occurred because the microelectric nerve stimulation may have allowed the patients to become more relaxed and more open to the affirmations used."

The fascinating but unspoken conclusion of this study is that somehow CES can produce profound and long-lasting personality changes in areas of the personality that usually do not change much, if at all, over a subject's lifetime. Notably, these profound personality changes are in the very areas that have been linked to addictive behavior.

It's interesting to consider the possibility that this personality change may be due to the alteration in the subject's ability to experience pleasure: the level of pleasure-producing neurochemicals in the brain, and the brain's sensitivity or receptivity to those pleasurable substances. As mentioned, certain addictive personality types have lower levels of some of the pleasurable neurochemicals (a result of genetic inheritance, stressful experiences by the mother before their birth, or stressful or traumatic experiences in infancy or youth) and thus naturally lower capacities to experience pleasure. This natural experience of reduced amounts of pleasure throughout life would tend to produce certain characteristic "personality" features, including depression, anxiety, lack of ego strength and self-sufficiency. If something that seemed to produce pleasure for most people didn't seem to produce very much pleasure for you, you would not only experience less pleasure, you would be aware that something was lacking, that there was something "abnormal" about that lack.

The use of the addictive substances by some people, then, can be seen as attempts to "heal" or restore balance to their imbalanced brain chemistry and their resulting reduced ability to experience pleasure. Thus treatments such as CES that restore to them the capacity to experience pleasure naturally would tend to make them feel more "normal," increase their feelings of fellowship with other humans, increase their self-esteem—in short, would produce dramatic personality transformations such as those just noted.

Other researchers have noticed this personality transformation effect as a result of the systematic use of various types of brain technology. Significantly, the personality changes were often noted when the subjects used the brain tools regularly for at least two to three weeks.

This requirement for several weeks of use suggests that dramatic personality change can take place over time through a sort of "threshold effect." That is, daily or regular use of brain-stimulating tools can produce incremental and cumulative changes in brain activity—such as in brain waves or levels of brain chemicals—that are not noticeable or remarkable until a certain "threshold" is reached, at which point the brain seems to undergo a long-lasting or permanent change. This theory also fits in with our picture of the brain as a dissipative structure, responding to energy flowing through it by producing fluctuations, which ultimately cause the brain to reach a point where it undergoes a transformative leap or "escape to a higher order" of increased coherence and complexity. Apparently this transformative change can take place suddenly or as the result of a buildup of incremental changes over a period of time.

BEYOND THE PENISTON PROTOCOL

This "threshold effect" is one of the suggestions that emerges from the exciting findings of Dr. Eugene Peniston and Dr. Paul Kulkosky. In 1990 they published a series of reports that stunned the world of substance abuse treatment. In their research, they randomly divided a group of chronic alcoholics into two groups. One group was trained with biofeedback electroencephalograms (EEGs) to generate alpha and theta brain waves. The other group was treated using "standard medical treatment," which included abstinence, group psychotherapy, and antidepressants. Both groups were given extensive personality tests, including measures of depression.

The experimental (alpha-theta) group began with five training sessions in which they learned to relax by using fingertip temperature biofeedback. This was followed by three weeks (fifteen sessions) of daily EEG alpha-theta training.

At the end of the training period, the experimental subjects showed large increases in the amount and amplitude of alpha and theta brain waves they produced: twelvefold increases in the mean percentage of alpha waves and sevenfold increases in theta.

As they observed their subjects after the brain-wave training, Peniston and Kulkosky found that the group that learned to generate alpha and theta brain waves showed a far greater recovery rate from their alcohol problems. This improved recovery rate began simultaneously with the training. Impressively, *thirteen months* after the training, the alpha-theta group showed "sustained prevention of relapse," while the control group was, for the most part, unsuccessful in recovery. Statistically, 80 percent of the subjects using alpha-theta training showed continued abstinence at the thirteen-month follow-up, compared to only 20 percent of the control group.

PERSONALITY TRANSFORMATION: ESCAPING THE NO-FUN SYNDROME

In the most intriguing and astonishing of all of Peniston and Kulkosky's findings, the alpha-theta group showed a total transformation of personality. The researchers were surprised to find that this group's scores on the test measuring depression showed "sharp reductions," while no such changes were found in the control group.

Among other extraordinary changes, Peniston and Kulkosky found that those who had the alpha-theta training showed significant increases in warmth, abstract thinking, stability, conscientiousness, boldness, imaginativeness, and self-control, and significant decreases in behaviors labeled schizoid, avoidant, passive-aggressive, borderline, paranoid, anxiety, somatoform, dysthymia, psychotic thinking, psychotic depression, and psychotic delusion, among others. The control groups did not show these changes. Clearly some of these changes indicate that the subjects have burst through the no-fun syndrome and developed deep and vital capacities to experience pleasure.

It's intriguing and important to note that these personality transformations took place after subjects had spent three weeks of five-times-per-week sessions in which they entered deep alpha and theta states. As Peniston and Kulkosky noted, their analysis showed that increases in alpha and theta rhythms "occurred gradually across the 15 treatment sessions," indicating to them the importance of "substantially repeated sessions" for the production of "durable changes" in EEG. This mirrors the evidence gathered by CES researchers that such treatments may have cumulative or incremental effects. Subjects may require a training period of two or three weeks before they reach a "threshold" and undergo profound personality changes. These personality changes are due in large part to alterations of brain chemistry that increase the subjects' natural ability to experience pleasure.

COMBINING STATE CHANGE WITH SUGGESTIONS AND IMAGERY

Peniston and Kulkosky combined brain tech with positive visualizations and suggestions. Subjects were told to visualize scenes in which they rejected alcohol and felt good about themselves, and other positive suggestions and mental imagery. Having learned to enter the theta state, subjects were instructed to "sink down" into a theta or "reverie" state and take the visualized scenes with them. This research emphasizes how combining effective mental imagery and suggestions with receptive brain states can produce extraordinary effects.

The astonishing success rate of Peniston and Kulkosky had a galvanizing effect on the fields of EEG biofeedback and drug treatment. Very quickly a number of therapists and clinicians around the country were reporting great success in using what came to be called the "Peniston Protocol."

SHORTCUTS TO BREAKTHROUGH STATES

However, it was evident to many that new generations of mind machines could have even more profound effects. Peniston and Kulkosky had to teach their subjects to generate slow brain-wave activity using biofeedback techniques. Biofeedback requires lengthy training, discipline, and effort. Mind machines that actively alter brain waves seemed to represent a much faster way of generating the much-to-be-desired slow brain-wave states. If some of the mind machines could quickly put users into slow brain-wave states and, in the bicycle-training-wheels-effect, could teach users how to enter those states themselves, then they could be invaluable in speeding up the healing and personal transformation process.

The first step for many biofeedback therapists in using mind machines to actively alter brain-wave activity was the linking together of LS systems with EEG. Initially, therapists such as Len Ochs and many others were able to monitor brain waves with an EEG, and alter the brain waves with an LS system that was directly linked to the EEG. In this new "EEG Entrainment Feedback," as Ochs called it, "the moment-to-moment dominant or strongest EEG frequency is used as a reference against which the strobe frequency is set." Thus, if an increase in theta activity was the goal, the LS system was adjusted to "feed back" a light/sound stimulus to the subject at 95 percent of the frequency of his or her dominant brain-wave activity.

However, Ochs soon found that while increasing theta activity had powerful effects (producing "loosening of cognitive controls, drifting consciousness, dream-like imagery"), there were also therapeutic values to using EEG Entrainment to increasing beta frequencies ("greater cognitive control, better memory and attention, and greater alertness and clarity of consciousness"). Sometimes, Ochs found, such as in some cases of posttraumatic stress disorder, depression, and addiction, the best effects came when he first used EEG Entrainment to speed up brain waves into the beta range—producing improvements in memory, attention, and concentration—and only *then* entraining brain waves downward into the theta range.

Then, as described earlier, Ochs began using the EEG-linked photic stimulation to entrain brain waves *both* upward and downward, alternating between a minute of speeding up and a minute of slowing down. The results were astonishing. Subjects moved quickly into "uncomfortable" frequency ranges and underwent profound "release" experiences that left them with a feeling of joy and restored abilities to experience pleasure. As this is being written, Ochs and others continue to explore the effects of this combination EEG-LS treatment not only for substance abuse but for a wide variety of problems.

AROUSAL AND AROUSABILITY

A number of investigators have found that many individuals with alcohol and drug problems, and with other "addictive" behavior patterns such as smoking, obesity, and compulsive gambling, have extremely high levels of what is called *arousability*—they are much more sensitive to external stimulation and react more strongly to external stimuli than most people. Events that might seem ordinary to most people may seem highly stressful to people with high arousability, causing them to attempt to decrease their arousal, experienced as tension or anxiety, by engaging in anxiety-reducing or arousal-reducing behaviors, such as taking drugs or alcohol.

High levels of arousal and arousability may simply be another way of looking at an imbalance of brain chemistry: Those whose levels of pleasure chemicals are naturally high enough may find certain stimuli enjoyable and challenging, while those with low levels of pleasure chemicals would find the same stimuli threatening and stressful. What may be exciting to one person may be unbearable to another.

Researchers have found that the physical characteristics of this high arousability include high levels of rapid beta brain-wave activity and low levels of relaxing alpha and theta. Clearly, since mind tools have proven effective in increasing levels of alpha and theta and reducing beta activity, you would expect them to be effective in reducing arousability and thus many addictive behavior problems. There is evidence that this is true. For example, the late Henry Adams, Ph.D., formerly of the National Institute of Mental Health and head of the alcoholism research programs at St. Elizabeth's Hospital, Washington, D.C., found that extremely heavy drinkers treated with a single session in an isolation chamber (combined with a brief anti-alcohol message while they were in it) showed a decrease in alcohol consumption of 55 percent after two weeks. Most impressively, and reversing the usual process in which change as a result of therapy tends to diminish over time, this decrease in consumption actually grew greater, moving to 61 percent after six months. Also astonishing was the fact that even the group that experienced just one chamber session alone, with no message, showed 47 percent decreases in alcohol consumption after six months. A control group that was not treated in the isolation chamber actually showed increased consumption after six months.

Said Adams, this technique "is clinically effective, simple, easy to apply in treatment and prevention settings, and free of significant risks, hazards, and medical side effects." Although he used "dry" isolation chambers, Adams believed that flotation tanks could also prove effective. He traced the benefits to the dramatic "reduction in arousal and arousability" experienced by the subjects. Floating or the use of an isolation chamber, Adams noted, "differs from all current treatment and prevention techniques in that it quickly and consistently lowers arousal to comfortable levels, thereby accomplishing the same psychological and physiological effects which substance abusers seek from psychoactive chemicals." Most important, Adams emphasized, floating "is not a hypothetical laboratory phenomenon, but a viable, tested technology."

As noted, use of LS devices has proven effective in reducing withdrawal symptoms and in producing states of deep relaxation that reduce desires for drugs. Other techniques, including the use of binaural beats, dual-induction audio programs, and CES have proven effective in reducing arousal and arousability.

In addition, it seems clear that one of the reasons for the success of the Peniston Protocol is that simply by training subjects to increase their alpha and theta brain waves so substantially, the training is producing substantial and long-lasting decreases in arousal and arousability.

INCREASED AWARENESS OF STATES

One thing various addictions and addictive behaviors clearly do is decrease our awareness of our own psychological and physiological states. Since we aren't aware of them, we aren't motivated or able to do anything to change them. Brain technology can change that. As flotation tank researcher Peter Suedfeld of the University of British Columbia observes, "Given that attention is a limited resource, and since you can't pay attention to everything that's going on around you and inside you, you tend to ignore the latter, because for the most part what goes on inside you is less urgent." This is particularly true of people whose attention is largely devoted to satisfying or responding to their addiction. But in the float tank, or while you're involved in a mind-tool session, in Suedfeld's words,

> there are no external problems to solve, no external dangers to attend to. There are also no external positive rewards to strive for. . . . You know, *externality isn't there.* So, that information processing system is free to turn inward and start monitoring what's going on inside. And you become much more sensitive, both to psychological events and to physiological events.

While many people don't pay much attention to just how drinking, or smoking, really makes them feel, or to just how much of an effort it is to carry around twenty-five or fifty extra pounds, in the float tank, says Suedfeld (and using other mind tools, I would add) "you become much more aware of how your body feels, what your internal states are. And *you're much more motivated to do something about it.*"

ACTION SECTION—USING MIND TECHNOLOGY FOR RECOVERY

Mind technology provides tools of unprecedented power for the treatment of addiction. By providing a reliable way to reduce stress and activate pleasure pathways, mind tools can be useful in various ways and at various points in moving away from addictions.

WITHDRAWAL

During withdrawal, mind tools reduce or eliminate frightening and painful symptoms, reduce stress and anxiety related biochemicals, and stimulate the release of relaxing and pleasurable neurochemicals. As Dr. Roman Chrucky, medical director of the North Jersey Development Center, remarks, "The machine works like a tranquilizer and the effect lasts for several days."

POSTWITHDRAWAL

By stimulating pleasurable neurochemicals, mind tools alleviate the no-fun syndrome or anhedonia that often sends addicts back to their habits even after they've kicked the physiological cravings.

DEALING WITH TRIGGERS

Even long after quitting an addictive behavior, some circumstances will trigger a desire to return to that behavior: stress, anxiety, depression, an anniversary, and so on. Mind tools provide an ideal pressure valve or escape hatch: They can provide an assured alternate pleasure and avert the return to addictive patterns.

OVER THE LONG TERM

In the long run, by reducing anxiety, increasing tolerance for stress, providing alternate pleasure sources, producing increased personal satisfaction, and perhaps creating life-transforming insights and breakthroughs, mind tools can eliminate the need to resort to addictive behavior patterns.

Specifically, you can use brain tech in a systematic program that will help by (1) normalizing brain chemistry that has been disrupted by substance abuse; (2) reducing stress, or high levels of arousal/arousability, that lead to unwanted behaviors; and (3) helping change behavior patterns and attitudes through eliminating negative scripts and attitudes, and using positive suggestions, visualizations, and rescripting, during deeply relaxed or trancelike states. What follows are some suggestions for ways you can use brain tools for these purposes.

RELAX, REVIEW, RELEASE, RESCRIPT

RELAX

First, simply use the mind technology to relax. Just relaxing for fifteen or twenty minutes every day can reduce stress and produce long-lasting reductions in arousal and/or arousability. It probably can produce long-lasting changes in your levels of pleasure-producing neurochemicals as well.

A short daily mind-tech relaxation session can produce significant and long-lasting increases in alpha and theta brain waves and also produce beneficial changes in brain chemistry to stimulate production of neurochemicals that have been suppressed. If you use brain tech daily for two to three weeks, you may undergo a threshold effect, in which you go through spontaneous and long-lasting personality changes.

Also, the mind tools clearly help alleviate withdrawal symptoms. Individuals who are using drugs or alcohol and want to stop or cut down should use mind tech as required for relaxation and alleviation of anxiety and other withdrawal symptoms.

REVIEW

Once you have become relaxed, move to state zero and focus on your body. Become aware of the effect your addictive behavior has had on it. The more intense your awareness, the more powerful and long-lasting will be your motivation to do something about it. Any of the mindfulness breathing and body-scan exercises described in Chapter 14 will be extremely helpful.

Do a similar emotional inventory: What are you feeling, and how are your feelings related to your addictive behavior? Don't worry about changing anything now, just become as intensely aware as possible of how your addictive behavior is linked to your mental and emotional state. The clearer your insight into this link, the more effective will be your actions to do something about it.

RELEASE

Since the process of releasing has both the physiological effects of reducing heart rate, blood pressure, and other stress symptoms and the psychological effect of producing dramatic reductions in anxiety, the Release Technique described in Chapter 17 can be a powerful aid in withdrawal and in the days and weeks that follow. As you use your mind tool, simply become aware of physical symptoms and emotions that arise, and release them. Frequently users will find that their unwanted habits are based on "wants" that they have not been aware of. Or they discover that the habits have been developed as ways of hiding or concealing powerful wants. Becoming aware of these emotions and wants, and letting them go, can lead to rapid transformations.

RESCRIPT

Use the mind tools to find the old scripts and imprints that have been hidden away and change them using the rescripting techniques explored in Chapter 18. The swish pattern is extremely useful as a way of using a cue associated with your unwanted habit or behavior to trigger desired behavior. Your cue could be your hand reaching for a cigarette, the smell of pot or alcohol, the mental image of having a drink or taking a drug.

VISUALIZATION AND SUGGESTION

In combination with your rescripting, or by itself, you can use the visualization and suggestion techniques described in Chapters 15 and 16. The work of Peniston and others suggests that positive suggestions and mental images have the most impact when you create them beforehand and then, while in the midst of deep alpha or theta, state them or visualize them. Be sure to suggest that you will use your brain tool every day to relax.

EXERCISE

One of the best ways to overcome addictive behavior is to engage in regular strenuous physical exercise, such as running, weightlifting, aerobics, or tennis. So include imagery and suggestion for enjoying and doing physical activity regularly.

FORGIVENESS

Also, there is evidence that a key to the recovery process is forgiveness. Dr. Eldon Taylor, who has long clinical experience in using suggestions and is creator of a series of subliminal suggestion tapes, has found that no matter what problems a client is working on—including addictive behavior, weight loss, depression, anxiety, and pain—it is essential to include suggestions of forgiving others, forgiving self, and being forgiven. Include these suggestions in your mind-tech session.

SUGGESTIONS

In addition to the general positive affirmations and suggestions and the suggestions for frequent exercise and forgiveness, here are some more specific suggestions you may find effective. Find which ones work for you, and alter the wording to suit your situation and the behavior or substance you are rejecting. These are only examples—your own suggestions will have the greatest impact. Formulate them using the guidelines offered in Chapter 15.

> I am in charge of my life. I feel my feelings and release them. I trust myself. I forgive myself. I forgive others. I forgive [person]. I know I am forgiven for all past wrongs. My life is precious. I choose healthy activities. I love my body. I treat my body with love. I am gentle and loving with myself. I heal myself. I am courageous. I flow with life. I am secure and calm. I am grateful for my life. I have fun being alive. Life is fun. I am free of all past mistakes. My life is rich with joy. I am sober and happy. I am happy to be sober. I reject drugs. I am good to myself. I have risen above the need to smoke. I breathe deeply when under stress. I have total freedom from tobacco [or other substance]. I enjoy doing things that make me healthy. I enjoy running [other exercise].

VISUALIZATIONS

Use the mind movie techniques (described in Chapter 21) to vividly see yourself behaving in desired ways and fully experience yourself being rewarded for it with health and happiness. Use visual rehearsal to visualize yourself in situations that might normally trigger your unwanted behavior, and use all your sensory modalities actually to experience yourself behaving in new ways that help you avoid your old patterns and bring you happiness and success. For example, if parties are trigger situations for your smoking, drinking, drug taking, or overeating, clearly see yourself being offered a smoke, drink, drug, or piece of chocolate cake. See yourself turning it down, and feel the rush of pleasure you get for behaving in a healthy way. See yourself having fun, without a smoke or drink in your hand, without taking drugs or overeating. Again, feel the pleasure of being in control of your behavior, of feeling healthy, of feeling clear-headed. If someone is going to insist on you having a drink or eating that chocolate cake, rehearse in your mind several clear responses, and see yourself going through them. Feel your pride and pleasure in sticking to your convictions and standing firm on what you believe.

CHANGE POINT OF VIEW

Use dissociative imagery to run through your unpleasant memories of past behavior, and replace them with full-color associative images of pleasurable behavior. Be right inside yourself, fully experiencing the pleasure and satisfaction of being in control, behaving in a way you are proud of.

MOLECULAR SELF-IMPROVEMENT, OR PUMPING IONS

Mental imagery alters physiology and anatomy. (Remember those studies of how visualization of increased breast size produced rapid growth.) Clear and strongly held mental images of alterations in brain chemistry will produce those alterations. Bodybuilders develop large muscles through a systematic program of regular efforts. Similarly, the way to shape our brain chemistry, stimulating or pumping up desired chemicals and inhibiting the unwanted ones, is through a consciously applied program of self-regulation: exercising and strengthening the pleasure centers and pleasure pathways. Mind technology provides an ideal environment and tool for such a program.

Using combined visualization and suggestion, experience your brain releasing desirable neurochemicals: See and feel a flood of relaxing, calming juices or molecules being secreted deep within your brain and spreading peace and pleasure through your entire being; or experience yourself releasing exciting, stimulating, ecstasy-producing neurochemicals. These mental images can be metaphorical (a flood of golden nectar pouring through your system), or they can be literal, based on your readings and images from widely available illustrated guides to the brain. Once you experience the specific neurochemical-associated state powerfully, anchor it with a signal that you can then use any time you want to trigger the flow of these excitatory or euphoric or relaxing neurochemicals.

ANCHORING

Use anchors (described in Chapter 15) to give you the strength to move through situations that would normally trigger your unwanted behavior, and anchor desired states such as relaxation, success, happiness. Since one of the reasons you behaved in the old way was to bring yourself short-term rewards of pleasure, create a pleasure anchor—while in a deeply relaxed state, call up an experience of intense pleasure, using every sensory modality, amp it up as high as possible (bigger, brighter, stronger!), and then anchor it in place with a signal or cue. Then later, when you feel unhappy or in danger of slipping into your old habit, activate your pleasure anchor and give yourself a charge of natural euphoria.

EXTERNAL ANCHORS

Once you've strongly anchored the desired behaviors and brain states with your brain tool, activate and rehearse them frequently. One of the best ways for doing this is with an external signal generator, such as the MotivAider described earlier.

GET INTO THETA

Simply by being in theta you are opening yourself up to profoundly healing forces. As the Greens discovered, being in theta caused people to "experience a new kind of body consciousness very much related to their total well-being," a state that brought "physical healing, physical regeneration, improved relationships with other people as well as greater tolerance, understanding, and love of oneself and of one's world," and "integrative experiences leading to feelings of psychological well-being." Just using your mind tool to get into a theta state, without any suggestions or other types of programming, can produce dramatic and transforming effects.

BREAK DOWN THE ARMOR, ACCEPT THE UNKNOWN

The breakthroughs attained by the clients of Len Ochs, Warren Barigian, Jacob Liberman, Richard Frenkel, and others seem to emerge from their willingness to let the brain-tech experience take them into "uncomfortable" areas and release the traumatic material that is stored or coded there. You can do this in ways explored earlier in Chapters 23 and 24. This includes: setting up fluctuations by alternately speeding up and slowing down brain-wave activity, changing the lengths and types of your sessions, alternating among a variety of different types of brain-tech stimulation, and combining mind tools with Holotropic Breathworks. (Do this last only with a partner or sitter present.) Something new is out there, and the only way you can find out what it is is by letting go of the old structures and compulsions and entering fully into the unknown future, willingly permitting the emergence of your future self.

SUGGESTED READING

For complete information on the Peniston-Kulkosky work, see Eugene Peniston and Paul J. Kulkosky, "Alpha-Theta Brainwave Training and Beta-Endorphin Levels in Alcoholics," *Alcoholism: Clinical and Experimental Research*, 1989, Vol. 13, No. 2, pp. 271–79. For a summary of the work of Peniston and Kulkosky and more recent clinical developments and applications, see the article by William Beckwith,

"Moving Beyond Metaphors of the Mind: Addiction, Transformation and Brain Wave Patterns," in *Megabrain Report,* Vol. 1, No. 3, pp. 6–8, and my own article "At the Crossover Point," in the same issue, pp. 4–5. For Dr. Ray Smith's illuminating comments about his research using CES for the treatment of addiction, see his interview, "Supercharging the Brain," in *Megabrain Report,* Vol. 1, No. 3, pp. 12–20. A groundbreaking exploration of the use of CES for treating addictions is *Getting Off the Hook,* Margaret Patterson, M.D. (London: Harold Shaw Publishers, 1983).

TWENTY-SEVEN
YOUR HIGH-TECH WEIGHT-LOSS SYSTEM

Literally, our bodies are an outward manifestation of our minds.
—Candace Pert, Ph.D.

If you're reading this chapter—if you are concerned about your weight—you already know an enormous amount about proper nutrition and weight loss. The problem is not ignorance of what to do, but the inability actually to *do* it consistently. This chapter deals with how you can use mind technology to do it—ways you can put into practice the weight-loss and weight-maintenance principles you already know. These include the following points.

EAT HEALTHFUL FOODS

You know what this means: the lists of healthful foods are in almost every diet or nutrition book available. Emphasize complex carbohydrates. Keep fat intake low. A mix of about 60 percent calories from carbs, 20 to 25 percent from protein, and less than 20 percent from fats is recommended.

EAT SMALL FREQUENT MEALS

Instead of skipping breakfast and gorging at dinner, eat at least five times a day. When consumed in smaller quantities, food is metabolized more completely and efficiently, and does not load you down with excess calories that are stored away as fat. This pattern will help you maintain your optimal metabolic level, so that you will get the optimum amount of energy and satisfaction from moderate amounts of food with the minimum amount of hunger.

EXERCISE FREQUENTLY

Diets don't work and will reduce your metabolism and lead to loss of lean-body mass (muscle). But exercise increases metabolism, keeps it higher for many hours, and can even raise your basal metabolism level, so you continue to burn off large amounts of calories even as you rest or sleep. Exercise also triggers the release of growth hormone (which eliminates fat while building muscles and bones) and neurochemicals that produce pleasure and satisfaction (such as endorphins and serotonin) and increase your energy and vitality (dopamine, norepinephrine). The single most effective way of losing weight and keeping it off is regular exercise.

DIETS DON'T WORK

Diets don't work first because "going on" a diet by necessity implies "going off" the diet. Americans have been dieting frantically for over thirty years, yet during that same period our average weight has gone up over ten pounds.

DIETS MAKE YOU FAT

Diets increase our tendency to store fat. We are descended from and largely biologically identical to people who were hunter-gatherers for millions of years. Our biochemistry is fine-tuned to a world in which food was often scarce or unavailable. As a result, we evolved bodies that naturally accumulated fat in times of abundance as a hedge against times of famine. Diets make us fat because our body perceives their low-calorie regimes as a time of famine, thus triggering our evolutionary fat-storage mechanism. In the past women particularly needed to store fat efficiently to provide nourishment for their offspring. Thus they not only have evolved with higher levels of body fat but are more efficient at fat storage.

DIETS FEEL LIKE SCARCITY

In a very literal way, diets activate scarcity programs that are part of our genetic makeup. Physically, we know, this results in a slowing of metabolism and increased storing of fat. But too often we forget the psychological aspects of our genetic scarcity program: Deep in our unconscious mind, diets trigger primal fears for survival, since scarcity can literally lead to starvation and death. Thus being on a diet means being in a state of chronic low-level anxiety.

EATING FEELS GOOD

Natural opiates secreted in our brains serve as a natural reward system, rewarding us with pleasure for performing acts that have survival value—eating, learning, creating, having sex. Learning, creating, and sex do not make you fat.

EATING RELIEVES ANXIETY

Our first experience of endorphin euphoria is in our mother's womb: Pregnant women produce levels of endorphins at least eight times higher than normal. After birth we continue to experience the blissful effects of endorphins via food, through the high levels of endorphins transferred to us through mother's milk. A study of baby animals revealed that when separated from their mothers, they displayed high levels of anxiety, but when given the synthetic equivalent of endorphins, their anxiety ceased. Thus endorphins not only alleviate anxiety but can act as a substitute for mother love and nourishment. I mentioned earlier how diets trigger genetic scarcity programs. It can now be seen that food knocks out anxiety both by alleviating primal mother-separation anxiety and by signaling the end of scarcity.

EATING CAN BE HABIT FORMING

We all know that eating makes us "feel good." Now it is clear that when we choose to eat to relieve anxiety, we are performing a calculated act of neurochemical self-adjustment. Just as a heroin addict is adjusting his or her neurochemical balance by consuming an endorphin substitute, we use food to trigger the release of endorphins, causing our brains to pour out the neurochemical equivalent of mother love, joy, comfort, and fulfillment.

The problem is that by choosing this form of neurochemical self-adjustment—using food to stimulate a specific brain chemical—we get two unwanted side effects: We get fat and we get addicted to eating. After endorphins are released by eating, their levels quickly diminish, and, like the heroin addict, we crave another shot of opiates. But unlike heroin, or endorphins, the food we've eaten does not disappear: It becomes stored in fat cells. There are not many fat heroin junkies, but there are lots of fat endorphin junkies. Endorphins do not make us gain weight. Using food as a mood alterer can: Eating to reduce anxiety is at the root of most all compulsive/addictive eating behaviors.

MOMMY AND FOOD ARE ONE

In light of the link between anxiety and eating, recall the research of Dr. Lloyd Silverman. Silverman conducted a classic series of studies at

New York University in which he flashed various subliminal messages to subjects. He found that groups that received the subliminal message "Mommy and I are one" showed profound changes—law students scored higher on tests, subjects lost cockroach phobias, and much more. Silverman concluded that the power of the Mommy message was a "magical fulfillment of . . . wishes emanating from the earliest developmental level, particularly wishes for oral gratification and maternal warmth." Silverman went on to suggest that the desire for fusion with Mommy represented "the search for oneness," which he characterized as the most powerful impulse in life. Here is a potentially powerful suggestion for alleviating the anxiety at the root of much "oral gratification" behavior and other unwanted behaviors rooted in anxiety or "lack of oneness." In addition to producing weight loss, subliminal "Mommy and I are one" messages have proven effective in alleviation of drug addictions, alcoholism, smoking, phobias, anxiety, and many other problems.

A key feature of the theta state is what researchers Elmer and Alyce Green have called "integrative experiences," which is another way of saying experiences of unity or oneness. So one way of satisfying the search for oneness is through the theta experience.

MIND TECH AND THE APPETITE IN THE BRAIN

If much of our overeating or unwanted eating behavior is based on a desire to alleviate anxiety or stress and produce pleasurable states by activating our natural reward system, then a clear alternative arises: using mind technology to stimulate the natural reward system. We have explored this approach in the last chapter, including the evidence that mind tools produce rapid alterations in brain chemistry, including restoring the natural balance of pleasure neurochemicals depleted by substance abuse and strengthening and exercising the pleasure pathways. Reread that chapter, since many of the approaches to substance abuse in that chapter are equally valuable in changing your unwanted eating behavior.

ACTION SECTION—USING MIND TECHNOLOGY FOR WEIGHT CONTROL

Weight loss and maintenance of optimal body weight require two simultaneous and equally important approaches: eating properly (the right food, in the right quantities) and exercising (to build lean body mass, eliminate excess fat, and maintain an optimal metabolism). Thus each of the techniques that follow can and should be applied both to eating right and to developing exercise habits.

What follows are ways you can use brain tech in a systematic program to help (1) alter brain chemistry to produce pleasure and increase levels of pleasurable neurochemicals; (2) reduce stress and anxiety that trigger overeating; and (3) help change behavior patterns and attitudes through eliminating negative scripts and attitudes and using positive suggestions, visualizations, and rescripting, during deeply relaxed or trancelike states. Many of these suggestions recapitulate techniques discussed in Chapter 26.

RELAX, REVIEW, RELEASE, RESCRIPT

RELAX

Nothing else is required. Simply relaxing for fifteen or twenty minutes every day can reduce stress, anxiety, and produce long-lasting changes in your levels of pleasure-producing neurochemicals. This alone can have dramatic and long-term effects in reducing overeating problems.

A short daily brain-tech relaxation period can produce increases in alpha and theta brain waves and also produce beneficial changes in brain chemistry to stimulate production of neurochemicals that have been suppressed. If you have daily sessions for two to three weeks, you may undergo a "threshold effect" in which you go through dramatic and long-lasting personality changes.

REVIEW

As you become relaxed, become aware of your body. One way to do this is to use the mindfulness body-scan technique described in Chapter 14. This mindful body scan may provide you with information about how you can change your body and how you might be able to change your style of living or activities to change your eating habits. As you do your body scan day after day, it also will provide you with strong feedback on what is working for you and what is not working, what is changing about your body and what is not changing. The more intense your physical awareness, the more powerful will be your motivation to do something about it. Perform a similar emotional inventory.

RELEASE

Since the process of releasing has both the physiological effects of reducing heart rate, blood pressure, and other stress symptoms and the psychological effect of producing dramatic reductions in anxiety, the Release Technique described in Chapter 17 can dramatically reduce the need or desire to eat. As you use your mind tool, simply become aware of physical symptoms and emotions that arise, and release them. Frequently users will find that their overeating or eating compulsions are based on "wants" that they have not been aware of. Or they discover that the eating habits have been developed as ways of hiding or concealing powerful wants. Becoming aware of these emotions and wants, and letting them go, can lead to rapid transformations.

Similarly release any emotions stirred up by exercise, athletic training, and physical fitness. Your previous inability to maintain an exercise routine, or lack of interest in fitness, may conceal powerful fears or wants. For example, one man found he had been unable to lose weight and get fit because he was afraid that if he did he would cease to be satisfied with his overweight, out-of-shape wife, and this would cause enormous problems in his life.

RESCRIPT

Find the old scripts and imprints that have been hidden away, and change them using the rescripting techniques explored in Chapter 18. The swish pattern is extremely useful as a way of using a cue associated with overeating (opening your refrigerator door; seeing the fork in your hand rising toward your mouth) to trigger desired behavior.

VISUALIZATION AND SUGGESTION

In combination with your rescripting, or by itself, you can use the visualization and suggestion techniques described in Chapters 15 and 16. Be sure to suggest that you will use your brain tools every day to relax. Remember to include suggestions of *forgiveness* and frequent *exercise*.

SUGGESTIONS

In addition to the general positive affirmations and suggestions, here are some more specific suggestions you may find effective. Find which ones work for you, and alter the wording to suit your self. Most important, create your own.

I shed unwanted weight easily and effortlessly. It's okay to be slim. My metabolism is set at the perfect level to burn away excess fat. At all times I am burning away excess fat. I am fit and trim. My stomach muscles are strong. My waist is becoming more slender every day. I maintain my ideal weight. I enjoy small portions of food. I enjoy a healthy, balanced diet. Losing weight is easy for me. I enjoy being fit and slender. I love to work out and exercise. Exercise fills me with energy and vitality. My exercise improves my life. My exercise is shaping my body into perfect proportions.

VISUALIZATIONS

Use the mind movie techniques (see Chapter 21) to vividly see yourself behaving in desired ways and fully experience yourself being rewarded for it with health and happiness. See yourself eating properly, see yourself exercising, see yourself with a physically fit body, see yourself being sexually attractive to others.

Use visual rehearsal to visualize yourself in situations that might normally trigger your unwanted eating behavior, and use all your sensory modalities actually to experience yourself behaving in new ways that help you avoid your old patterns and bring you happiness and success. For example, if parties are trigger situations for your overeating, clearly see yourself passing by the food table to enjoy dancing or chatting with friends. Experience with all sensory modalities the pleasure you feel in having a healthy and trim body. Visualize someone offering you a piece of cake, see yourself turning it down, and feel the rush of pleasure you get for behaving in a healthy way. See yourself having fun, without a plate of food in your hand, without eating. Again, feel the pleasure of being in control of your behavior, of feeling healthy, of feeling light on your feet, of having a slender figure. If someone is going to insist that you eat her special recipe, rehearse in your mind several clear responses, and see yourself going through them. Feel your pride and pleasure in sticking to your convictions and standing firm on what you believe.

CHANGE POINT OF VIEW

Use dissociative imagery to run through your unpleasant memories of past behavior, and replace them with full-color associative images of pleasurable behavior. Be right inside yourself, fully experiencing the pleasure and satisfaction of being in control, behaving in a way you are proud of.

THE MIRROR VISUALIZATION

Visualize yourself looking into a full-length mirror. There you see your self at your ideal body weight and shape. See as clearly and in as much detail as possible. Now experience yourself flowing into and merging with that ideal image of yourself. Become fully associated with the image, experiencing it fully using all sensory modalities. Now dissociate from the image—step back and see the full-length image from a distance. Keep it clearly in your mind. Keep it with you as you emerge from your brain-tech session, and bring it out to look at in your mind's eye whenever you are exercising, or when you sit down to eat, or when you are in a situation that might trigger overeating.

RELEASE PLEASURE CHEMICALS

Using combined visualization and suggestion, experience your brain releasing desirable neurochemicals: See and feel a flood of relaxing, calming juices or molecules being secreted deep within your brain and spreading peace and pleasure through your entire being; or experience yourself releasing exciting, stimulating, ecstasy-producing neurochemicals. Once you experience the specific neurochemical-associated state powerfully, anchor it with a signal that you can then use any time you want to trigger the flow of these excitatory or euphoric or relaxing neurochemicals.

ANCHORING

Use anchors as described in Chapter 15 to give you the strength to move through situations that would normally trigger eating, and anchor desired states such as relaxation, happiness, having an attractive figure. Since one of the reasons you behaved in the old way was to bring yourself short-term rewards of pleasure, create a pleasure anchor. Whenever you feel unhappy or in danger of slipping into unwanted eating behaviors, activate your pleasure anchor and give yourself a charge of natural euphoria.

EXTERNAL ANCHORS

Once you've strongly anchored the desired behaviors and brain states during your mind-tech session, activate and rehearse them frequently. One of the best ways for doing this is with an external signal generator. Each time your external signal goes off, for example, you might have it trigger a flood of pleasurable neurochemicals, an image of yourself at your ideal weight, a sensation of your metabolism working actively to burn away excess fat, or a suggestion such as "I eat only when I'm hungry."

GET INTO THETA

Getting into theta for even a few minutes a day can produce profound benefits, and provide an alternative route to Mommy in our "search for oneness."

BREAK DOWN THE ARMOR, ACCEPT THE UNKNOWN

The most profound breakthroughs seem to emerge from a willingness to let the brain technology take you into "discomfort zones" and release the traumatic material that is stored or coded there. You can do this in ways explored earlier in Chapters 23 and 24.

SUGGESTED READING

The Search for Oneness by Lloyd Silverman, et al. (New York: International Universities Press, 1982) casts much light on many unwanted behaviors, including overeating.

TWENTY-EIGHT
FREE AT LAST:
ENDING ANXIETY, DEPRESSION, AND PHOBIAS

Anxiety and depression are the most widely experienced negative states. Researchers at the Institute for Behavior and Health, Inc., studied the cost in dollars of anxiety disorders in one year (1990), including costs of treatment and reduced or lost productivity. They reported that anxiety disorders alone (including generalized anxiety, simple phobia, panic disorder, social phobia, and obsessive-compulsive disorder) cost the United States some $46.6 billion dollars, which accounted for *one-third of the total costs of all mental disorders*. According to the National Institute of Mental Health, anxiety disorders affect at least 12 percent of U.S. adults at some point in their lives. An inexpensive and effective treatment that would alleviate or eliminate anxiety disorders clearly could have an enormous economic and social impact on our culture.

ANXIETY

We all know the external signs of anxiety: sweaty palms, tight chest, pounding heart, butterflies in the stomach, restlessness, irritability, restlessness, trembling hands, dread, feelings of being out of control or impending panic.

Some of the brain events and patterns characteristic of anxiety include: decreased alpha and theta brain waves (suggestive of decreased relaxation and calmness); increased high beta activity (suggestive of heightened arousal); rapid shifts in brain waves and absence of brain-wave synchrony (suggestive of uncoordinated and agitated thought processes); elevated levels of stressful and excitatory biochemicals, including high amounts of epinephrine (adrenaline), adrenocorticotropic hormone (ACTH), and cortisol.

Both outwardly and inwardly, then, anxiety shares many of the features of the fight-or-flight response. This evolutionary hard-wired program responds automatically to a perceived threat by activating our sympathetic nervous system. In an adrenaline rush we pour out neurochemicals that accelerate our metabolism in various ways, all of them intended to help us deal with some external threat by running like hell or ripping out its liver with our teeth.

When the external threat exists, our response is called *fear*. In its most irrational and exaggerated form, this fear can become phobia. We can respond to an external threat appropriately and then, after activating and using our fight-or-flight response, we can relax and allow our body to activate the relaxation response. During the relaxation response the effects of the fight-or-flight response are terminated and erased, and the stress-related biochemicals and their by-products are cleaned out of the system. Even people with irrational fears—phobias—can respond to them and terminate them by avoiding whatever triggers the phobia.

But in anxiety, the threat is *internally* created: We are distressed by some potential or future event. And since there's no way to fight or flee a potential or future event, we are left in a state of arousal. We are still feeling the threat, but there is no way to escape it.

TURNING OFF ANXIETY

One way to escape anxiety is simply to turn off the physiological symptoms of the fight-or-flight response, like turning off a faulty warning signal on a machine. This seems to be one of the ways in which brain technology works so effectively to alleviate anxiety: Clearly mind tools have powerful and in many cases unsurpassed effects in rapidly producing deep relaxation by switching on the relaxation response.

Try to imagine being profoundly relaxed and experiencing anxiety. It's probably hard for you to do. There's evidence that deep relaxation and fear are mutually exclusive—when you are experiencing one, you cannot truly experience the other. So, to the degree that you permit brain technology to relax you, it will eliminate anxiety.

The image of flipping a switch—switching off your fight-or-flight response and switching on your relaxation response—may seem like an oversimplification. But there is evidence that there may be a sort of "master switch" in the brain that turns on either the sympathetic or the parasympathetic system. According to cranial electrostimulation (CES) inventor and researcher Daniel Kirsch, CES produces "a direct stimulation of the autonomic nervous system" that can act "sort of like switching on the relaxation response." And CES researcher Ray Smith, describing a study of people who suffered from phobias, told me with astonishment that "What we found, essentially, was that the CES *blocked the subjects' ability to feel fear altogether!* This suggests that the old brain . . . including the hypothalamus and amygdala, governing memories and emotional expression, is the area affected by the electrostimulation." What Smith found, in other words, was that stimulation with CES essentially switched off fear, or the fight-or-flight response.

This antianxiety effect is not limited to the minutes or hours of your brain-tech session. The effects of a single brain session can produce long-lasting relaxation effects. According to Dr. Thomas Budzynski, describing his clinical use of a light/sound (LS) system, "the device has a calming effect on nervous or anxious patients. In a majority of cases the patients feel relaxed and calm during a period of three to four days after the sessions." A study of the effects of floating found measurable electroencephalogram (EEG) changes (increased theta) *as long as three weeks after a single session*. Additional evidence suggests that the relaxation effects of brain tools are cumulative and incremental; thus repeated sessions will produce more powerful and longer lasting effects.

What's more, brain tools can help you learn to activate this relaxation response very quickly, and under even the most trying conditions. I described earlier my own experience of being trapped in a blacked-out subway, and discovering that while people were panicking, I was able to make myself suddenly feel very calm and relaxed, simply by remembering what I felt like while I was in a float tank and making my body duplicate that experience. There are other far more effective techniques, such as getting into a deep relaxation state during a mind-machine session, anchoring the relaxation state with a signal, and then giving yourself the signal whenever you want to "activate" that relaxed state you have anchored.

TURNING AWAY FROM ANXIETY

One curious quality of anxiety is that, since the external threat is not present, our attention and fear become focused on the symptoms of the anxiety itself. Thus we begin to fear that because our breathing is constricted, we will stop breathing; that because our heart is thumping, we will have a heart attack; and so on. A quick way to stop anxiety is to turn our attention away from it. You may have had the experience of suffering anxiety and then being distracted by something more urgent. By the time you remember how anxious you were, your anxiety has gone. Anxiety is a response to a perceived threat; it makes sense that if we forget about or have our attention diverted from the threat, then the physiological symptoms will disappear quickly.

One classic technique for diverting attention and focusing it on something external is the movie hypnotist's swinging watch or medallion. But simply using a brain machine can be far more powerful and effective. LS systems, by instantly presenting you with a kaleidoscopic array of dazzling colors and shifting patterns, are probably the best examples of how brain tech can eliminate anxiety not simply by diverting but by capturing your attention and holding it astonished. In fact, the earliest commercial LS device was actually sold as a hypnotic induction device.

Ganzfelds, color-field devices, acoustic field generators, binaural-beat sound programs, and dual-induction spoken word programs all have antianxiety effects that are partly due to their powers of capturing or diverting attention from the user's own internal processes.

CES AND ANXIETY

Of all the mind tools, CES is currently the most widely used for treatment of anxiety. As a result of numerous rigorously conducted scientific studies, CES is recognized by the Food and Drug Administration (FDA) as effective in treating anxiety. This means doctors can prescribe CES for anxiety and medical insurance will cover the cost of the machines. One recent survey of over 150 doctors and patients showed that more than 98 percent of the patients being treated for anxiety with CES showed improvement; over 70 percent showed "marked improvement" or complete recovery. Controlled studies by researchers measuring state and trait anxiety have consistently shown that CES produces dramatic improvements in both.

One reason CES may be so effective is that, as Ray Smith discovered in his recent study of phobia, CES *"blocked the subjects' ability to feel fear altogether."* This may be, as Smith and Kirsch suggest, because CES acts directly on the control mechanism of the autonomic nervous system: It seems to simply flip a sort of toggle switch in the limbic system that switches it from the fight-or-flight to the relaxation response. Tests of the blood and cerebrospinal fluid of subjects using CES have proven that electrostimulation also has a profound and rapid effect on brain chemistry. Among effects noted has been a 90 percent increase in beta-endorphins within just minutes of starting use of CES. Researchers also have noticed rapid increases in serotonin, also associated with relaxation and calmness, and decreases in cortisol—one of the primary stress-related biochemicals. Interestingly, CES also increases levels of norepinephrine and dopamine, both associated with alertness and feelings of pleasure. This may be why so many CES users report feeling both relaxed and alert.

LIGHT AND SOUND

LS systems also have a superior track record in the treatment of anxiety. Medical practitioners are finding insurance companies more willing to pay for LS treatment as increasing evidence of its effectiveness emerges. One way the LS systems work, clearly, is by altering, organizing, and entraining brain-wave activity. Usually, treatment for anxiety consists of entraining brain waves downward for extended periods at alpha or even theta frequencies.

By slowing and organizing brain waves, LS seems to trigger a relaxation response. Researchers measuring muscle tension, skin conductivity, fingertip temperature, heart rate, blood pressure, and other indicators have noted that LS sessions produce extremely deep relaxation, deeper than that obtained by traditional relaxation techniques, such as Progressive Relaxation.

In addition to altering brain waves and producing whole-body relaxation, LS counters anxiety by increasing the release of antianxiety brain chemicals. Dr. Norman Shealy found that LS boosts beta-endorphin levels by 10 to 50 percent. In another study Shealy conducted with Dr. Roger K. Cady, LS produced an average increase of beta-endorphin levels of 25 percent and an average increase of serotonin of 21 percent. As the researchers noted, these effects are comparable to those obtained by CES.

Recent research has focused explicitly on LS as a treatment for anxiety, with excellent results. Much of this research, which we have described briefly earlier, has come from clinical psychologists Dr. Juan Abascal and Dr. Laurel Brucato, at the Miami-Dade Community College and at Mindworks, a psychotherapy and stress reduction center in Miami. They have conducted a variety of controlled studies comparing LS groups with control groups that just rest and hear relaxing music. Findings indicate that LS clearly produces significant increases in "coping resources," measured by a Coping Resources Inventory. This suggests that the LS group perceived themselves as being less stressed by events after the series of LS sessions than before.

More significantly, Abascal and Brucato found substantial evidence that the LS users not only felt less stressed, they really were: The LS groups showed clear decreases in both state and trait anxiety. State anxiety is the level of anxiety experienced right at the time the questionnaire was administered, so it might be expected that a LS session would lower this measure. But trait anxiety is the long-term disposition of individuals to experience anxiety and is generally fairly stable over time. The fact that LS reduces trait anxiety over several sessions suggests that the LS experience has a cumulative anxiety-reducing effect.

OTHER SYSTEMS

Because I have focused on CES and LS does not mean they are the most effective mind tools in alleviating anxiety. Personally, I believe the float tank is the most powerful anxiety-reduction device on the face of the earth. A wealth of research proves that floating can produce what neuroscientist, writer and explorer of inner space Dr. John Lilly has called "the deepest relaxation available on this planet." Floating alters biochemicals, increasing endorphins and reducing stress-related biochemicals such as ACTH and cortisol. It produces profound muscular relaxation. It slows down brain-wave activity into the alpha and theta ranges. One study showed increased theta activity in float subjects some three weeks after a single fifty-minute float. A statistical analysis of people suffering from anxiety who floated as part of a medical stress-reduction program revealed that floating reduced intensity of anxiety by 74 percent, frequency of anxiety by 65 percent, and symptoms of anxiety by 65 percent.

A substantial body of research also proves the antianxiety effects of the ganzfeld. This technique definitely slows brain waves and leads to states of deep whole-body relaxation.

While less research into the antianxiety effects of other types of brain tools has been performed, abundant clinical work and anecdotal material suggests that color-field devices, acoustic field generators, movement systems, binaural beats, and multivoiced audio programs do have powerful antianxiety effects.

DEPRESSION

If anxiety is the self-generated fight-or-flight response, depression seems to be the acceptance that neither fight nor flight is a possible option. Evolution has produced the fight-or-flight response as a protective mechanism. But recent evolution seems to have provided humans with a "third way" of dealing with threat, necessitated by our complex social environment, where neither fighting nor active flight is practical. This third way is described by Dr. James Henry of the Department of Physiology and Biophysics, of the University of Southern California School of Medicine: "In a social situation in which there is a hierarchy with a single dominant or an establishment group in control, this third option is of utmost importance. It involves submitting to the demands of the dominant animal or to the establishment and involves inhibiting previous patterns of behavior." This "submission," says Henry, leads to depression "associated with the loss of control. The depressed animal . . . no longer competes but accepts the unpleasantness of frustration."

Most of us have experienced the physical unpleasantness that results from submitting to a dominant animal or the establishment— you can't fight or flee when your boss is a jerk, or the judge ignores your requests for justice, or the IRS asks for an audit. Says Henry, "helplessness is a crucial determinant of depression."

But there is powerful evidence that this submission or helplessness has very specific and damaging physical effects: In depression, levels of stress-related and immune-suppressing biochemicals ACTH and cortisol skyrocket. Laboratory studies have shown that helplessness leads to a huge rise in cortisol. On the other hand, while submission, helplessness, and depression are associated with elevated ACTH and cortisol, dominance and confidence are associated with lower cortisol. Individuals with high levels of aggression and hostility have very high levels of cortisol and ACTH and, it should be no surprise, are much more susceptible to depression when under stress.

These clear links between elevated cortisol and ACTH and depression and between helplessness/acceptance/submission and depression offer us some important insights into how brain technology is proving to be such a powerful antidepressant.

First, mind tools lower both cortisol and ACTH. Studies by Thomas Fine and Dr. John Turner have proven in a variety of ways that floating quickly reduces these biochemicals and has a cumulative effect that can produce long-term reductions. Research by Dr. Norman Shealy and associates has shown that both CES and LS decrease cortisol and ACTH.

Second, mind tools directly and dramatically reduce helplessness, submission, and acceptance of frustration. LS, for example, clearly increases "coping resources." Other studies we've cited show substantial increases in feelings of control, stability, conscientiousness, boldness, imaginativeness, and self-control as a result of brain technology. Dr. Stephen Overcash and Dr. Alan Siebenthall, who used CES to treat substance abuse patients, found that their subjects' average scores doubled and even tripled in self-sufficiency, dominance, assertiveness, and ego strength. Dr. Eugene Peniston and Dr. Paul Kulkosky have noted dramatic increases in measures of ego strength and control in subjects learning to use electroencephalogram (EEG) biofeedback to produce alpha and theta.

In addition, various types of brain tools have proven effective not just in decreasing levels of depression-related biochemicals such as ACTH and cortisol, but in sharply increasing levels of biochemicals with an antidepressant effect. For example, Shealy has found that both LS and CES boost levels of serotonin (the neurotransmitter whose effects are boosted by the antidepressant Prozac), norepinephrine, and beta-endorphin. Dr. Ray Smith and others have noted that CES also increases dopamine (a highly pleasurable and excitatory brain chemical) and acetylcholine.

HAPPY BRAIN, SAD BRAIN

In Part I we looked at recent evidence showing clear links between brain asymmetry (that is, an imbalance of EEG activity between the right and left hemisphere) and depression. Stated simply, people with more activity in the right frontal cortex than in the left tend to be sadder and more negative in their outlook, and tend to have higher rates of depression or of having been previously depressed and successfully treated for it. There is even evidence that these brain-wave patterns and emotional "styles" may be hereditary or genetically influenced.

EEG studies of LS have consistently shown increased EEG symmetry. For example, Tsuyoshi Inouye and associates at the Department of Neuropsychiatry at Osaka University Medical School in Japan found that photic stimulation in the alpha range produced hemispheric synchronization. Shealy found that photic stimulation produced "cerebral synchronization" in more than 5,000 patients. There is similar persuasive evidence that binaural beats, CES, floating, motion systems, and acoustic field systems increase EEG symmetry.

UNDERAROUSAL AND THE POSSUM RESPONSE

Many people who are depressed also show signs of "underarousal" of the autonomic nervous system. As a result of some change in the limbic system, brain-wave activity is reduced and inhibited. According to Dr. Siegfried Othmer, in depressed people "the EEG shows abnormally low amplitude overall, in particular low beta activity." That is, without sufficient beta to maintain external alertness, these depressed individuals are living their lives using brains that are predominantly in alpha, theta, or delta. No wonder depressed people often feel as if they're sleepwalking through life. As Phil Nuernberger, director of biofeedback therapy at the Minneapolis Clinic of Psychiatry and Neurology, observes, such individuals exhibit what he calls the possum response: "They just sort of roll over and play dead. Their response to fear is not arousal, but inhibition. This is marked by the typical characteristics of extreme parasympathetic discharge—decreased physiological functioning, loss of skeletal tone, mental lassitude, inactivity, and eventual depression."

ELIMINATING DEPRESSION WITH MIND TOOLS

All of this suggests strongly that brain technology should be effective in treating depression. And in fact, a number of studies have verified the antidepressant effects of mind tools. For example, brain devices can clearly reverse the low-amplitude, low-beta pattern characteristic of underarousal or the possum response. Ray Smith has made careful observations of the effects of CES on brain-wave activity of depressed patients and subjects with substance abuse problems who also showed depression. He recently told me that in studies he conducted with Dr. Eric Braverman, "the EEG changes [after treatment with CES] are more alpha, more delta, more beta, more theta—a lot more *across the spectrum*." Many others have noted that a single session on a CES produces enormous increases in brain-wave amplitude across the board.

In addition, since a key component of underarousal seems to be insufficient beta activity, various types of brain-wave entrainment devices can be extremely effective by entraining brain-wave activity in the beta range. For example, most LS systems have preset "beta perker" or "energize" programs that ramp upward into 15 to 20 Hz beta. Or the device can be operated manually, moving into beta and spending the entire session there. EEG studies show clear increases in beta activity as a result of such entrainment. When used frequently, such beta entrainment seems to help boost the brain out of its depressed possum response and produce permanent changes.

Beginning with Saul Rosenthal and Norman Wulfsohn, who published a series of studies in the early 1970s, and continuing over the last twenty years, numerous researchers have consistently found significant reductions or elimination of depression in subjects using CES. Shealy, working with Saul Liss and others, found that depressed subjects had different ratios of neurochemicals such as serotonin, norepinephrine, and beta-endorphin than did nondepressed subjects, and that CES dramatically altered the ratios of these neurochemicals. They concluded that two weeks of CES lifted the depression in 60 percent of the depressed subjects. Shealy has also found LS effective in treating depression.

Peniston and Kulkosky have found that their subjects, all of whom showed high levels of depression, had eliminated depression through their EEG alpha-theta feedback training. Dr. Charles Stroebel, at the Institute for Advanced Studies in Behavioral Medicine in Hartford, Connecticut, has been extremely successful in treating the chronically depressed with a combination of EEG feedback and CES: He hooks them up to his CAP Scan EEG brainmapper and then uses CES to "normalize" their brain-wave activity. "They can actually see how their EEG normalizes," he told me, "and can feel the difference it makes." They can then use CES and practice using EEG biofeedback to learn how to produce the "normal" brain-wave patterns themselves. "I think this could be a breakthrough in the treatment of depression," says Stroebel.

PHOBIAS

Phobias are exaggerated fear reactions triggered by external objects or circumstances. Often phobias produce such panic or anxiety that sufferers will change their lives to avoid phobic triggers. Uncounted numbers of people, it now appears, have intentionally avoided promotions or lucrative jobs that would require them to give speeches, because of their fear of public speaking.

Phobic reactions seem to result from conditioning; thus they can be eliminated through various types of deconditioning techniques. The most popular of these techniques is *systematic desensitization*, which involves creating a hierarchy of fear-producing stimuli. For a snake phobia, the hierarchy might range through ten levels, from the mildly anxiety-producing (looking at a photo of a snake) to the terrifying (having a live snake wrapped around you). The subject, after becoming deeply relaxed and calm, then confronts the least scary situation, while using various techniques to remain relaxed and calm. (Remember that fear and deep relaxation seem to be mutually exclusive—when one comes, the other goes.) The subject moves through the levels of increasing scariness while remaining calm and relaxed, becoming progressively desensitized.

The float tank and REST chamber (or "dry" float tank) seem to have unprecedented success in treating phobias through this desensitization technique. It makes sense that they should, since floating produces such profoundly deep relaxation and such dramatic increases in powers of visualization. While they have not undergone such rigorous laboratory and clinical research as float tanks, other types of brain technology that have proven effective in producing deep relaxation and boosting visualization also are effective against phobias. By producing utter relaxation, these devices enable the phobic individual to overcome the tension and fear; by increasing visualization, they help the phobic person imagine the phobic situation more clearly and vividly and to imagine him- or herself overcoming the phobia and acting confidently in that situation.

Intense fear is clearly linked to a rush of neurochemicals, and CES has proven effective in blocking them. Dr. Ray Smith has conducted the most striking study of phobia. As we've already noted, he found that CES blocked fear in the chronic severe phobics who were his subjects.

Color therapists, such as Jacob Liberman, Richard Frenkel, John Downing, and others, have noted that color therapy can dramatically reduce phobias. Psychotherapist Jill Ammon-Wexler, Ph.D., for example, has produced strong evidence of the antiphobia effects of the Lumatron. She conducted a controlled study and found that "remarkable resolution of the subjects' phobic systems had occurred over the process of the twenty experimental sessions. There was also 'across the board' evidence for enhanced self-concept, and clinically-significant reductions in both anxiety and depression."

ACTION SECTION—USING MIND TECHNOLOGY TO ALLEVIATE ANXIETY, DEPRESSION, AND PHOBIAS

Brain tools can (1) produce deep and lasting relaxation to reduce stress and the feelings of loss of control or helplessness that contribute to anxiety and depression; (2) alter brain chemistry to produce feelings of well-being and increase self-confidence; and (3) help change behavior patterns and attitudes through eliminating negative scripts and attitudes and using positive suggestions, visualizations, and rescripting, during deeply relaxed or trancelike states. What follows are some suggestions for ways you can use brain tech for these purposes. Many of these suggestions recapitulate techniques discussed in the preceding chapters.

For those who are engaged in therapy, brain tools can be extremely helpful when used during a session. Hundreds of therapists around the world now use such devices as an integral part of their therapy.

Mind tools can be enormously helpful when used either before or after the therapy session. Dr. Mel Thrash, professor of psychiatry at New York University, has found the flotation tank to be helpful both before and after therapy sessions, but what he says about floating holds true for other types of brain tech as well. "Either way, before or after, has a payoff," he told me. "Hopefully, in the session you are effective enough so that you stir things up, so that going into the tank afterward would allow [the client] to sort out a lot of questions; going in before hopefully would bring up a lot from the unconscious that you could work on in the session."

RELAX, REVIEW, RELEASE, RESCRIPT

RELAX

Simply relaxing for fifteen or twenty minutes every day can reduce stress, anxiety, and produce long-lasting changes in your levels of pleasure-producing neurochemicals. If you have daily sessions for two to three weeks, you may undergo a "threshold effect" in which you go through dramatic and long-lasting personality changes.

REVIEW

As you become relaxed, become aware of your body. One way to do this is to use the mindfulness body-scan technique described in Chapter 14. As you do your body scan day after day, it also will provide you with strong feedback on the source and physical symptoms of your anxiety, depression, or phobia. The more intense your physical awareness, the more powerful will be your motivation to do something about it. Perform a similar emotional inventory.

RELEASE

Releasing (described in Chapter 17) has both the physiological effects of reducing heart rate, blood pressure, and other stress symptoms and the psychological effect of producing dramatic reductions in anxiety. As you use your mind tool, simply become aware of physical symptoms and emotions that arise, and release them. Frequently users will find that their anxiety or depression is based on "wants" that they have not been aware of. Or they discover that the problem has developed as a way of internalizing powerful wants. Becoming aware of these emotions and wants, and letting them go, can lead to rapid transformations.

RESCRIPT

Find the old scripts and imprints that have been hidden away, and change them using the rescripting techniques explored in Chapter 18.

VISUALIZATION AND SUGGESTION

In combination with your rescripting, or by itself, you can use the visualization and suggestion techniques described in Chapters 15 and 16. Be sure to suggest that you will use your mind tools every day to relax. *Exercise* has been found to be extremely effective in reducing both anxiety and depression, so you will want to include suggestions and imagery of yourself engaging in regular physical exercise. Also be sure to include suggestions of *forgiveness* for yourself and others.

SUGGESTIONS

In addition to the general positive affirmations and suggestions, here are some more specific suggestions you may find effective. Find which ones work for you, and alter the wording to suit your self. Most important, create your own.

I am in charge of my life. I trust myself. I choose healthy activities. I am strong and filled with joy. I feel secure and calm. I have courage. I am bold and daring. I am resilient and resourceful. I am forceful and strong. I like myself. I am brave. I release fears. I reject all thoughts that lead to fear. I reject fear itself. My life is full of wonderful opportunities. I have a spirit of adventure. I deserve to have fun. My inner strength gives me power. I feel centered and calm. I feel confident and in control. I can handle any situation. I am secure. Good things come to me easily and effortlessly. I trust myself. As I fly [or am in crowds, or enter the water, or encounter any specific phobic trigger] I am calm, relaxed, and joyful.

VISUALIZATIONS

Use the mind movie techniques (see Chapter 21) to vividly see yourself behaving in desired ways and fully experience yourself being rewarded for it with health and happiness. See yourself behaving with confidence in situations that have caused you anxiety. See and experience yourself charged with joy, energy, and pleasure in being alive.

Use visual rehearsal to visualize yourself in situations that might normally trigger your anxiety or phobia, and use all your sensory modalities actually to experience yourself behaving confidently and calmly.

CHANGE POINT OF VIEW

Use dissociative imagery to run through your unpleasant memories of past behavior, and replace them with full-color associative images of pleasurable behavior. Be right inside yourself, fully experiencing the pleasure and satisfaction of being in control, behaving in a way you are proud of. Observe from a distance your past behaviors, make them black and white, shrink them into the distance.

DESERT STORM VISUALIZATION

Dr. Gerald Epstein, a psychiatrist who has long clinical experience using mental imagery, suggests this powerful visualization to alleviate anxiety: See yourself hiking across a vast desert carrying a backpack. See a dark sandstorm gathering in the distance and moving toward you. See yourself taking a tent from your backpack and setting it up in the sand as the sandstorm of anxiety moves toward you. Make sure your tent is secure, all the pegs hammered into the ground, then climb inside and close the flap tightly. As the sand roars and howls outside, you sit calmly and securely inside your comfortable tent. You know that when the sandstorm has passed, your anxiety is gone. . . .

RELEASE PLEASURE CHEMICALS

Using combined visualization and suggestion, experience your brain releasing desirable neurochemicals: See and feel a flood of relaxing, calming juices or molecules being secreted deep within your brain and spreading peace and pleasure through your entire being; or experience yourself releasing exciting, stimulating, ecstasy-producing neurochemicals. Once you experience the specific neurochemical-associated state powerfully, anchor it with a signal that you can then use any time you want to trigger the flow of these excitatory or euphoric or relaxing neurochemicals.

ANCHORING

Use anchors using the techniques described in Chapter 15 to give you the strength to move through situations that would normally trigger anxiety or phobias, and anchor desired states such as relaxation, happiness, confidence.

EXTERNAL ANCHORS

Once you've strongly anchored the desired behaviors and brain states during your mind-tech session, activate and rehearse them frequently. One of the best ways for doing this is with an external signal generator. Each time your external signal goes off, for example, you might have it trigger a flood of pleasurable neurochemicals, an image of yourself acting with calm self-assurance, or a suggestion such as "I am relaxed and joyful."

GET INTO THETA

For anxiety sufferers, theta has powerful antianxiety effects, in part because it tends to produce integrative feelings. Even a short session that frees you to spend a few minutes in theta each day can dramatically reduce tension and have beneficial cumulative effects.

BETA BOOSTING

For those whose depression is linked to underarousal, one effective approach is to use LS and other techniques (such as CES and beta-frequency binaural beats, available on some binaural-beat tapes) to increase activity in the 15 to 20 Hz beta range. To do this with LS, simply ramp up to the desired frequency and remain there for the rest of the session. Begin with fifteen minutes at 15 Hz, and increase both time and frequency to find what is most comfortable and what produces the best effects. I suggest shooting for a frequency of about 18 Hz, and spending several shorter (fifteen- to thirty-minute) sessions per day rather than one long session. These beta-boosting sessions will be most effective if done in the morning and afternoon. Evening sessions could disrupt sleep. Beta-boosting tapes and CDs often are advertised as increasing concentration or enhancing cognition and alertness. One example is the "Focus" tape of my Mega Brain Zones Series.

BREAK DOWN THE ARMOR, ACCEPT THE UNKNOWN

The most profound breakthroughs seem to emerge from a willingness to let the brain technology take you into "uncomfortable" areas and release the traumatic material that is stored or coded there. You can do this in ways explored earlier in Chapters 23 and 24.

SUGGESTED READING

For Dr. Ray Smith's discussions of his findings that CES treatment blocked the ability of subjects to feel fear, see his interview, "Super-charging the Brain," in *Megabrain Report*, Vol. 1, No. 3, pp. 12–20. For the link between brain asymmetry and depression, see R.J. Davidson et al., "Approach-withdrawal and Cerebral Asymmetry: Emotional Expression and Brain Physiology," *Journal of Personality and Social Psychology*, 58 (1990) 330–341, and J.B. Henriques and R.J. Davidson, "Regional Brain Electrical Asymmetries Discriminate between Previously Depressed and Healthy Control Subjects," *Journal of Abnormal Psychology*, 99 (1990) 22–31.

For moving "beyond boredom and anxiety," see *Flow: The Psychology of Optimal Experience* by Mihaly Csikszentmihalyi (New York: Harper & Row, 1990), and his earlier *Beyond Boredom and Anxiety: The Experience of Play in Work and Games* (San Francisco and London: Jossey-Bass, 1975).

TWENTY-NINE
ENDING THE REIGN OF PAIN

In the midst of one of my Megabrain Workshops, as people were exploring the effects of a wide variety of different brain machines, I heard someone laughing loudly and saying "It's gone, it's completely gone!" I went over to a woman who had just gotten off one of the motion systems that had revolved her around and around for about fifteen minutes. She excitedly told me and her husband that a chronic back pain had completely disappeared. "I've had that pain for over ten years!" she exclaimed. "I tried everything, from drugs to surgery, and nothing worked. Now, for the first time in ten years, it's gone."

I could recount literally hundreds of stories individuals have told me about "miraculous" eliminations or reductions in pain. Aside from relaxation, pain reduction or elimination is probably the most commonly noted effect of brain technology. Here are a few samples of the studies that have been done.

FLOATING

In Phoenix, Arizona, seventeen manual laborers who had suffered disabling injuries that produced chronic pain intractable to surgery went through a series of floats. Afterward fourteen went back to work—many for the first time in years. Their pain was in remission and their recoveries were, according to their employer, "on the order of miraculous." A two-year follow-up confirms the remission of the pain.

LIGHT AND SOUND

In two separate studies patients with chronic headaches and migraines were treated with light/sound (LS) devices. In one study, out of fifty migraines, LS devices "helped" forty-nine and "stopped" thirty-six completely. In another study fourteen of fifteen patients with sustained headaches and five of six patients with chronic headaches noticed complete relief after the LS treatment.

CRANIAL ELECTROSTIMULATION (CES)

In one study of patients using CES for pain, doctors reported that over 95 percent experienced improvements, over 50 percent experienced "managed recovery," and over 20 percent experienced "complete recovery."

Health professionals and pain sufferers also have reported to me strong reductions or complete elimination of pain as a result of using the ganzfeld, motion systems, acoustic field generators, color therapy systems, both high-frequency and low-frequency (infrasonic) sound therapy, and binaural-beat audiocassettes. Various types of biofeedback systems, including electroencephalograms (EEGs), fingertip temperature meters, and skin resistance meters have proven enormously effective in alleviating pain.

Many people have used LS, CES, and binaural-beat tapes to reduce the amount of anesthetic needed for operations and to reduce postoperative pain, or to eliminate or reduce the need for Novocaine or other oral anesthetic when undergoing dental work. As mentioned earlier, anesthesiologist Robert Cosgrove found that LS devices have strong sedative effects.

THE ENDORPHIN EFFECT

In general, brain technology seems to alleviate or eliminate pain in several ways. First, it's clear that mind tools can quickly elevate levels of the body's natural painkillers, the endorphins. Studies of CES, for example, show that it can increase levels of beta-endorphin within minutes. Similar studies of the effects of LS have shown similar increases in beta-endorphins. Float tank researchers have verified that floating boosts levels of endorphins. Research also suggests that acoustic field systems are powerful endorphin releasers. There is also evidence that types of brain tech elevate levels of serotonin, which can also reduce pain, ranging from muscle pain to migraine.

ANXIETY AND PAIN

In addition to boosting levels of the natural neurochemical painkillers, brain tech also reduces levels of neurochemicals associated with stress and anxiety, including adrenocorticotropic (ACTH) and cortisol. Both stress and anxiety can increase the perceived painfulness of pain. Studies have proven that pains such as burns or shocks are perceived as significantly more painful by subjects who are experiencing high anxiety. Therefore, the proven ability of mind machines to decrease anxiety can significantly reduce the painfulness of life's everyday pain-producing stimuli, whether it is a headache, broken bone, or broken heart.

SHIFTING ATTENTION

Anyone who has forgotten about a pain while his or her attention has been focused elsewhere by an emergency or some engrossing stimulus, such as a good book or thrilling movie, knows that pain requires attention. This fact is reflected in our language in such phrases as "painfully aware." We can have chronic joy, chronic sounds, chronic boredom, and still continue to function in our normal lives. But chronic pain is different—it demands attention. The pain is perceived by the reticular activating system, the brain's attention control center, as urgent information that could be important to our survival, and it keeps directing our attention to it. As neurosurgeon George Ojemann of the University of Washington School of Medicine points out, one way to control severe pain is to "change the reticular activating system so that it turns down the sensitivity in pain pathways." One way to do this is to shift attention to some urgent external event, as we do in an emergency. Another way is to turn attention inward, by entering a dissociative state of consciousness in which we lose awareness of our body. Brain tech accomplishes this latter form of shifting of attention very effectively.

LS devices, for example, are successful in diverting attention from pain by capturing attention—the reticular activating system directs our attention to the novel visual effects produced by the flashing light stimulus. Then, when the visual effects become repetitive, the reticular activating system turns our attention away from them, just as it turns off our awareness of other repetitive stimuli, such as the ticking of a clock. At that point, awareness turns inward, we become dissociated from our bodies, and we lose consciousness of the pain entirely. Binaural beats also seem to help turn our attention inward as a result of the repetitive stimulus of the pulsing tones. Acoustic field generators similarly first capture attention and then turn it inward as a result of the repetitive stimulus.

Devices such as the ganzfeld and the float tank direct attention inward by presenting the reticular activating system with an unvarying stimulus. Presented with the featureless visual field of a ganzfeld device, the system eventually decides that no novel or useful information is coming in through the eyes and produces the blank-out effect, turning attention inward. The float tank effectively produces the blank-out effect directly, by shutting off or dramatically reducing most external stimuli, including light, sound, gravity, and tactile sensations.

RELAXATION AND PAIN

Brain tools also aid in pain reduction by promoting relaxation. Pain produces muscular tension—the body automatically tenses muscles as if to protect itself from the pain. However, the muscular tension actually increases the pain. This creates a vicious cycle: Tension increases pain, which in turn leads to more tension. By quickly producing deep relaxation, mind technology breaks that vicious cycle with a releasing cycle: Muscles release, pain is reduced; the reduction in pain permits more muscular relaxation, which reduces pain even more, and so on.

OUTSIDE OF TIME

When we have a pain, time seems to slow down. We become aware of the passing of each second. Minutes can seem like hours. On the other hand, brain technology is effective in getting us into states in which we are not aware of the passage of time. The theta state is essentially timeless—we can experience and relive vivid and detailed memories with no sense of time, and emerge from them to find that an hour has passed, or only a few seconds. During sessions brain machine users frequently enter a state in which their pain disappears or undergoes a qualitative change—it seems to become distant, less intense, or smaller. In essence, they are experiencing the pain in a dissociative state. By altering or eliminating people's sense of time, brain tech alters or eliminates pain.

VISUALIZATION AND SUGGESTION

One of the most impressive uses of hypnotic trance is for pain relief: Hypnosis is widely used to eliminate pain during surgery, childbirth, and dentistry. As we have seen, mind tools effectively turn virtually everyone into "hypnotic virtuosos," by allowing us to enter deep trance states quickly and on demand. In these trance states we can use the powers of suggestion to eliminate or alter our sense of pain.

ACTION SECTION—USING MIND TECHNOLOGY FOR PAIN

RELAX, REVIEW, RELEASE, RESCRIPT

RELAX

Simply relaxing for fifteen or twenty minutes every day can reduce pain and produce long-lasting changes in your levels of pleasure-producing neurochemicals.

REVIEW

Use the mindfulness body scan described in Chapter 14 to focus on your pain and to become aware of how it effects the rest of your body and your life. This mindful body scan may provide you with information about how you can alleviate your pain and how you might be able to change your style of living or activities to alleviate the pain. For example, people with chronic headaches might find on an attentive body scan that they have tension in their shoulders or neck and that by loosening that tension they can eliminate their headaches. Similarly, by using your brain machine session to conduct a daily body scan, you can be aware of the increases and decreases in your pain and begin to associate levels of pain with your daily activities: You might find, for example, that your lower back pain peaks the day after you spend long hours completing a report on your computer. By changing your physical posture while at the computer, you may alleviate the problem.

HAVE COMPASSION

As you pay attention to your body, have compassion for it. In the words of Thich Nhat Hanh:

> Sometimes, when we try to hammer a nail into a piece of wood, instead of pounding the nail, we pound our finger. Right away we put down the hammer and take care of our wounded finger. We do everything possible to help it, giving first aid and also compassion and concern. We may need a doctor or nurse to help, but we also need compassion and joy for the wound to heal quickly. Whenever we have some pain, it is wonderful to touch it with compassion. Even if the pain is inside—in our liver, our heart, or our lungs—we can touch it with mindfulness.

By touching with love and compassion those parts of our body that are experiencing pain, we can become aware of the pain in a new way, a way that leads to healing and peace.

RELEASE

Releasing (described in Chapter 17) can produce sharp reductions in pain. As you relax, simply become aware of the pain and any emotions that arise, and release them. In virtually every case you will find that your pain is associated with at least one powerful want: wanting the pain to go away. This is a wanting to control. Release the wanting to control your pain. You also may find that your pain is associated with wants you have not been aware of. Or you may learn that the pain has developed as ways of internalizing or suppressing powerful wants. Becoming aware of these emotions and wants, and letting them go, can lead to rapid transformations.

RESCRIPT

Use your mind tool to find the old scripts and imprints that have been hidden away, and change them using the rescripting techniques explored in Chapter 18.

VISUALIZATION AND SUGGESTION

In combination with your rescripting, or by itself, you can use the visualization and suggestion techniques described in Chapters 15 and 16. Be sure to suggest that you will use your mind machine every day to relax and release. Remember to include suggestions of forgiveness for yourself and others.

SUGGESTIONS

In addition to the general positive affirmations and suggestions, here are some more specific suggestions you may find effective. Find which ones work for you, and alter the wording to suit your self. Most important, create your own.

My muscles release and relax. The muscles in my back [other body part] are warm, loose, and relaxed. I feel a flood of warm relaxation flowing through my back [other body part]. I breathe deeply and easily. My body is always healing itself. I feel secure and calm. I am resilient and resourceful. I am brave. I am a good person. I love myself. I deserve to feel great. I feel centered and calm. I feel confident and in control. I trust myself. I let go and release easily and effortlessly. My body is always filling me with energy and vitality. I am healthy and happy. Every pressure I feel is a signal to relax, release, and let go.

VISUALIZATIONS

Use the mind movie techniques (see Chapter 21) to vividly see yourself free of pain. See and experience yourself charged with joy, energy, and pleasure in being alive. Use cartoon or special effects such as the *Incredible Journey* movie to see the pain being dissolved or released, or filled with light, or to see your brain releasing a flood of endorphins.

CHANGE POINT OF VIEW

Use dissociative imagery to see yourself experiencing pain, move it into the distance, shrink it, and replace it with full-color associative images of yourself experiencing pleasure and moving freely without pain.

Explore other visualizations, and find what works for you. Visualize yourself going into your body carrying a container of warm golden oil, coming to your pain, and pouring the warm golden oil on the pain. See the oil completely cover the pain, and see the pain shrink and dissolve into a warm, golden point. See the point disappear, and feel your pain disappear. Or see the point begin to glow with bright golden light, light that fills your entire body with warm relaxation and pleasure.

Visualize your pain as a tight knot and then seeing it loosen, expand and dissolve, like a Chinese paper flower in water. Or experience your pain as a red-hot lump, and then replace it with ice and feel it become cool.

BREATHING VISUALIZATIONS

Visualize each breath as a white light that eliminates pain—as you inhale, the pain-relieving light flows directly to the source of your pain, where it creates a glowing ball of light. See that when you exhale the light is tinged with a dark black or brown color, as you expel pain, tension, and toxins. With each inhalation, the ball of light grows in intensity; with each exhalation, you see the light flow out tinged with sooty dark pain.

Following the mindfulness technique of Thich Nhat Hanh, be mindful of breathing into the location of the pain. With each breath, repeat, "Breathing in, I am aware of my lower back [or other body part]. Breathing out, I smile to my lower back. Breathing in, I know that my back has been working hard to keep me upright. Breathing out, I vow not to harm my back by using it improperly."

RELEASE PLEASURE CHEMICALS

Using combined visualization and suggestion, experience your brain releasing desirable neurochemicals. Anchor this state with a signal that you can then use any time you want to trigger the flow of these analgesic and relaxing neurochemicals.

ANCHORING

Use anchors to activate pain-free states, images of pain elimination (warm oil, energy flowing to the area of pain, etc.), and desired states such as relaxation, pleasure, peace.

EXTERNAL ANCHORS

Once you've strongly anchored the desired behaviors and brain states with your brain machine, activate and rehearse them frequently. One of the best ways for doing this is with an external signal generator. Each time your external signal goes off, for example, you might have it trigger a flood of pleasurable neurochemicals to the area of pain, an image of yourself acting in ways that eliminate the pain (maintaining correct posture for lower back pain, for example), or a suggestion such as "My back is relaxed and warm."

THIRTY
FROM LEARNING DISABILITIES TO
LEARNING SUPERABILITIES

Several years ago I received some calls and letters from a man in the Midwest who suffered from a severe learning disorder. He asked if he could come to the coast and work with me at Megabrain headquarters, and said he'd do just about anything to get a chance to try out some of the brain machines, on the off chance something might be able to help him. Touched by his willingness to give up everything and relocate in a strange city in hopes of, as he put it, "getting smarter," I invited him to come out.

For the first few months the man I'll call Bill was a dedicated worker, a good-hearted, warm, and loving person, but it was clear he had severe problems: a low IQ; difficulties in reading, writing, and expressing himself; and such a lack of self-esteem that he was always apologizing in advance for any mistakes he might make, telling how he wasn't sure he could do a certain task, how he was afraid he might screw it up.

I recalled having read that psychologists had used biofeedback to treat learning disorders. They had found that certain learning disorders (specifically attention deficit hyperactivity disorder [ADDH]) were linked to abnormally slow brain-wave activity in specific parts of the brain, including the premotor cortex and the superior prefrontal cortex, which are used when people pay attention or keep still. So these therapists had used biofeedback electroencephalograms (EEGs) to teach their ADDH subjects to *speed up* their brain-wave activity into the beta range (over 14 Hz). The results had been impressive: average increases in IQ of 12 to 20 points or more.

Curious, I hooked Bill up to a twenty-four-electrode brain-mapping EEG that provided me with a color topographic map of his brain activity. As the maps rolled across the computer monitor, I was astonished: Virtually all of Bill's brain-wave activity was in the theta range (4 to 8 Hz), with some in the slower delta range, usually present only in deep sleep or coma, and with some in alpha. There was no activity at all in the beta range, none above about 10 Hz. Here was a clear case of learning disorder; no wonder Bill had such a hard time reading, writing, and expressing himself—he was semicomatose all the time.

I had to leave the next day for a six-week trip to Europe, but I asked Bill to try doing a one-hour session each day on one of our light/sound (LS) machines at a frequency of 15 to 20 Hz.

I had recently read a study by a cranial electrostimulation (CES) researcher in Texas, Dr. Allen Childs (executive medical director of the Healthcare Rehabilitation Center and assistant professor of pharmacology at the University of Texas, Austin). Childs had used CES to treat patients who were suffering from "attention-to-task deficit" as a result of head injury. After three weeks he had found the patients showed "striking and significant improvement in the post treatment scores" in such areas as mental speed, visuomotor functioning, impulse control, visual and auditory perception, mental control and concentration, and much more. Childs also had used CES to treat patients suffering from short-term memory disorder and amnesia as a result of traumatic head injuries, and had great success in restoring memory. So in addition to using the LS device, I asked Bill to use a CES device daily. Bill assured me that he would use both machines regularly.

When I returned, Bill was transformed. He was now reading and writing rapidly and confidently. What was more striking, he was now filled with self-assurance, and his voice had changed from a tremulous timid semiwhisper to a resonant baritone. He was now taking charge of certain aspects of the office business and making suggestions about how we could operate more efficiently. I began finding Post-It notes pasted all over the place with messages from Bill containing suggestions for new undertakings, keen observations, and witty jokes.

Sadly, Bill was suddenly called back to his home in the Midwest due to an illness in the family—the family where he had been so bitterly unhappy. I insisted he take a CES device and LS machine with him. Several months later he called, and I could hear by his voice that he was slipping back into his old and, in his words, "stupid" self. He was not using the machines—his parents didn't approve. I got a Christmas card from him some months later that was barely legible. I haven't heard from him for a long time now, and I fear I won't hear from him again. If you're out there reading this, Bill, get in touch. I miss you.

BRAIN-WAVE PAC-MAN

Bill's case was my introduction to ADDH, learning disabilities, and the possibilities of treating them with brain technology. An extraordinary amount of breakthrough work is now being done in this area. It has been found that 95 percent of the cases of ADDH or associated learning disabilities can be recognized from an analysis of the subject's EEG alone. The EEG biofeedback studies I mentioned earlier included the groundbreaking work of Joel and Judith Lubar and Michael Tansey, who used EEG biofeedback to decrease theta activity and increase beta activity in the 11 to 19 Hz ranges. They found this produced profound improvements in subjects with ADDH, hyperactivity, dyslexia, and specific learning disorders. Tansey, for example, noted an average IQ increase in his subjects of nineteen points.

Drs. Siegfried and Susan Othmer with their IQ-boosting EEG "Pac-Man" biofeedback training system
(EEG Spectrum, Inc.)

Dr. Siegfried Othmer has further refined EEG biofeedback training and made it more accessible by developing an easy-to-use system that is also enjoyable for the subject, or trainee. In his EEG Spectrum clinics in Los Angeles and San Francisco, the trainees have their brain waves monitored by an EEG that displays a Pac-Man video game. Subjects are told to make the Pac-Man move faster. When they decrease theta (4 to 7 Hz) and fast beta (22 to 40 Hz) below the threshold, while increasing the desired beta (15 to 18 Hz) above the threshold, the video game moves faster. If activity in the undesired theta or fast beta bands increases, the video game slows down or stops.

In a controlled study, Othmer has found that this beta training produces *average IQ increases of 23 percent*. In cases where the starting IQ value was less than 100, the *average IQ increase was 33 points*. Othmer has also found dramatic improvements in visual retention and auditory memory, and the subjects showed major gains in reading and arithmetic. In a one-year follow-up study, the trainees showed major improvements in self-esteem and concentration and significant improvements in such areas as handwriting, school grades, sleep, irritability, organization, hyperactivity, verbal expression, and headaches. Othmer's clinical work with several thousand trainees has supported the findings of the controlled study.

Amazingly, the improvements seem to be permanent. Says Othmer, "the training confers increasing stability in the face of cortical hyperexcitability. The training appears to enhance self-regulation of fundamental arousal mechanisms when these are deficient. . . . Putting it crudely, we have a small, elusive 'hardware error' leading to prominent and obtrusive 'software errors' in the human brain." Once the hardware is operating correctly, it tends to continue doing so.

Othmer and many of those exploring EEG biofeedback have found that other conditions also characterized by "underarousal" also respond well to beta training. These include depression, sleep disorders, seizures, chronic fatigue, headaches, mood swings, anxiety, and head injuries such as concussion. In fact, Othmer observes that all of these problems have a high correlation to some sort of head injury, including birth trauma (which is a kind of head injury). And, says Othmer, "many of the deficits resulting from head injury in the mature person look like attention deficit disorder. . . . In beta training we appear to be dealing with conditions of underarousal, either induced by trauma of some kind, or of genetic origin."

One of the most promising findings of the 1990s, this "decade of the brain," says Othmer, "is how amenable the brain is to effecting change in its own function, if only it is given appropriate cues." The brain's own potential for healing is evident in such phenomena as the placebo effect and spontaneous remission. But, Othmer believes, "What the brain is known to be capable of randomly, we may be able to elicit systematically."

LINKING LIGHT TO BRAIN WAVES

It became apparent to many researchers, as it did to me in the case of Bill, that brain-wave entrainment in beta frequencies using LS devices might be a more rapid way to achieve these sharp increases in IQ than the multiple training sessions and frequent visits to the clinic required by traditional EEG biofeedback training. As described briefly in Chapter 5, Harold Russell, Ph.D., and John Carter, Ph.D., for example, of the University of Houston, did several studies in which they used LS devices in the treatment of ADDH and other learning disorders. They found that the LS treatment produced clear and significant increases in IQ. Interestingly, they tested subjects whose verbal IQ scores were at least 15 points or more below their performance IQ (on the revised Wechsler's Intelligence Scales for Children) and found that the LS sessions produced "major gains" in verbal IQ and no change in performance IQ. In subjects whose performance IQ scores were at least 15 points below their verbal IQ scores, the LS sessions produced major gains in the performance IQ. This suggested to Russell and Carter not only that LS devices could boost mental functioning in ADDH subjects, but that they did so by boosting the performance of the area of the brain that was functioning below normal.

Russell and Carter used 20-minute LS sessions, during which 10 Hz alpha alternated with 18 Hz beta. The periods of stimulation were separated by short periods of no stimulation. The glasses they used "had a transparent lower half that allowed the children to perform other activities while receiving the stimulation. This appeared to greatly reduce the restlessness that would otherwise be engendered by asking the child to remain still and in the dark for 20 minutes." In all studies, the LS group made significant improvements in brain functioning. Groups that began with low verbal IQ scores had pronounced gains in verbal IQ, spelling, and arithmetic. Groups that began with high verbal but low performance IQ showed significant gains in nonverbal IQ, reading, spelling, and memory.

Russell and Carter concluded that systematic regular use of LS stimulation produces "measurable improvements in brain functioning in whichever is the lower functioning hemisphere." They noted that this equalization of functioning could be of particular relevance to learning disabled and ADDH subjects. They concluded that "the degree of significant improvement in functioning is related to the number of treatment sessions."

Their subjects gained an average of 5 to 7 IQ points, using far fewer sessions than those used for EEG biofeedback training. The researchers noted that the cost of LS equipment is low, and it is so simple to use that children can learn to use it themselves. The equipment used for EEG training costs from $4,000 to $20,000 or more, and the training must be done one on one with highly trained personnel. Russell and Carter estimated that the cost of LS training "would probably be less than five percent of the cost of EEG biofeedback training. . . . A drastic reduction in cost could make treatment available to large numbers of children and adults who would otherwise never receive it." Their conclusion: LS "may be an effective low cost and easily used treatment for children with LD and ADDH problems." They have designed a special LS device that presents the alternating 10 Hz and 18 Hz stimulation they found effective. It is now available for use by other clinicians.

Russell and Carter also note that "By combining EEG biofeedback with entrainment of the EEG by the [LS device], it may be possible to increase the challenge and stimulation of the brain." This may "decrease the time and training required to bring about improvement in brain functioning. Preliminary results are encouraging." A number of therapists, including Len Ochs, are using this linked EEG-photic stimulation system and obtaining remarkable results.

Russell and Carter's research also suggests that such stimulation can improve brain functioning in people suffering from other types of brain disfunction. For example, they did a long-term study of a stroke patient whose prestroke IQ was 140. Nine months after the stroke her cognitive level was "in the 70 to 80 IQ range." After frequent LS sessions over more than a year, her cognitive level was tested again and found to be "in the 140 range" once more. In addition to producing dramatic improvements in cognition, the LS sessions restored movement to the subject's paralyzed arm and leg, resulting in "greatly decreased spasticity and increased gross and fine motor control as the number of sessions increased."

Russell and Carter suggested that use of LS devices and EEG training "may stimulate either the successful establishing of new neural pathways in the brain or re-establishing of old pathways that have been disrupted."

Other educators have been using LS to improve learning and treat various learning disorders. Educator-therapists such as Rayma Ditson-Sommer, Ph.D., of Phoenix, Arizona, and Dr. Ruth Olmstead, of San Diego, have done extensive work using LS devices to alleviate stress. They have found it substantially improves IQ and other learning by allowing the subjects, in Ditson-Sommer's words, "to function at a comfortable level without apparent threat, thereby aiding the student in decreasing anxiety and stress during the learning session." Based on their success in treating ADDH, both Ditson-Sommer and Olmstead have created special programs for use with LS systems. Their programs differ from those of Carter and Russell; rather than increasing beta activity, they consist of a relaxation program to be used in conjunction with a special relaxation tape having music on it, combined with binaural beats.

ADDH sufferers clearly experience stress due to their learning difficulties. This creates a vicious cycle in which the stress of having learning problems exacerbates the learning problems, which then leads to increased stress. Olmstead and Ditson-Sommer use LS devices to induce relaxation and stress relief, and thus clear the way for subjects to make optimal use of their natural learning capacities.

COLORED LIGHTS USED FOR LEARNING DISABILITIES

Another recently completed study of the effects of photic stimulation—in this case colored light stimulation—has produced exciting results. Carol J. Rustigan, a learning disability specialist at California State University, Sacramento, compared the effects for seventeen learning disabled adults of twenty sessions of listening to relaxation tapes (control group) with twenty sessions on a Lumatron (experimental group).

The results were clear. In reading tests, the colored lights group showed a significant increase in the number of answers attempted (on both the vocabulary and comprehension test), which demonstrated substantial gains in that group's reading rate. The colored lights group also showed significant increases in the number of comprehension questions they answered correctly, implying that their comprehension skills increased concurrently with their faster reading rate. This group also showed significant increases in the auditory processing of information, including increases in auditory retention skills on the Weschler Memory Scale (logical memory). The results support the findings of Jacob Liberman and John Downing that the benefits of this type of photic stimulation therapy are not limited to visual perception. The relaxation group, on the other hand, showed no significant changes at all on any of the scales.

Rustigan observes:

It is possible that an increase in the number of light sessions . . . would have yielded even greater research results. Lumatron practitioners generally have prescribed up to 60+ colored lights sessions (with music). . . . Since many learning disabled adults have responded favorably to multisensory input, future studies designed to study the effects of colored lights combined with relaxation exercises or music could be very beneficial.

She concludes that:

The results of this research study determined that the effects of colored lights significantly benefited learning disabled adults. Documented gains in reading rate, reading comprehension, and auditory memory skills carry promising implications for learning disabled adults confronted with inhibitive visual, reading, and retention difficulties.

CES

Many researchers have found that CES is effective in enhancing cognition in general. In the study by Madden and Kirsch described earlier, CES improved learning of a psychomotor task, which included improvements in concentration and alertness. Other researchers, such as Ray Smith, have found that CES boosts IQ and additional cognitive functions in people suffering from types of reversible brain damage. Further studies have shown that CES has a calming effect on anxiety or agitation, even while increasing alertness and concentration. And CES has proven to be extremely effective in treating the minor brain damage resulting from head injuries.

Since, as Othmer points out, learning disorders seem to be linked to some sort of minor brain damage, it makes sense that CES should have great benefits in treating learning disorders. Lawrence Wilson, Ph.D., and Allen Childs, M.D., studied the effects of CES on attention-to-task deficit. Their subjects were head injury victims, but as the researchers point out, this same deficit is a key component of ADDH. After fifteen fifty-minute CES sessions spread out over three weeks, the subjects "showed striking and significant improvement" in such areas as attention to task, mental speed, visuomotor functioning, impulse control, response inhibition, visual and auditory perception, mental control and concentration, and increasing mental speed. In addition, I have received numerous and consistently positive reports of the effects of CES on memory, attention, concentration, alertness, and other relevant cognitive functions.

While there have been no full-scale studies of CES as a treatment for learning disorders, I believe the evidence suggests that it can be extremely effective. Ruth Jones of Salt Lake City has for several years had striking success in treating learning disorders at her learning institute by using a combination of LS and CES.

NOOTROPIC DRUGS AND LEARNING DISORDERS

Several studies of cognition-enhancing drugs that have recently come to my attention lead me to believe certain of these substances may have great benefits for ADDH sufferers. A German journal of psychopharmacology reported on a double-blind study in which the effects of piracetam on the EEG frequencies of boys with learning disorders was compared with the effects of a placebo. Intriguingly, "piracetam caused a decrease in the amount of delta activity and an increase in the average EEG frequency." By speeding up brain-wave activity and decreasing delta activity, the drug should increase alertness, concentration, and learning among the learning disabled.

In a recent double-blind placebo-controlled study in Pakistan, researchers compared the effects of another "smart drug," Hydergine (ergoloid mesylates), with a placebo on improving cognitive functions and behavioral symptoms associated with learning disorders in children. They found that the Hydergine group showed significant improvement in speech (acquisition of new words, comprehensibility/meaningfulness of speech), sociability, attention/concentration, comprehension, and memory. Group members also showed improvement in behavior (emotional lability and cooperativeness). We will explore the brain-boosting affects of piracetam, Hydergine, and other "smart drugs" in Chapter 33.

ACTION SECTION—USING MIND TECHNOLOGY TO OVERCOME LEARNING DISORDERS

By now it should be clear that brain tools can be enormously effective in overcoming learning disorders. Perhaps the most important discovery has been that ADDH and other learning disorders are linked to underarousal, or abnormally slow brain-wave activity (theta and delta) and insufficient beta activity in the sensorimotor rhythm range and above (13–20 Hz). Thus I have provided suggestions for using brain tech to decrease slow brain-wave activity and increase appropriate beta activity.

Learning disabilities also have a stress component—clearly those who have learning disabilities experience stress as a result of their own learning and behavioral difficulties, and stress can also increase learning disabilities. So we will explore ways of using brain tools to produce deep and lasting relaxation to reduce stress that can contribute to learning handicaps.

Learning disabilities are also linked to problems of behavior, negative self-image, and low self-esteem. Thus I suggest techniques for using brain tools to help change problematic behavior patterns and attitudes through eliminating negative scripts and attitudes, and using positive suggestions, visualizations, and rescripting during deeply relaxed or trancelike states.

As I have mentioned, there are now well over one hundred therapists in the United States who are using brain tools in the treatment of learning disorders. These include Siegfried Othmer, who focuses exclusively on EEG biofeedback to normalize brain-wave activity; Ruth Olmstead and Rayma Diteson-Sommer, who have been using LS brain-wave entrainment; and Len Ochs and Russell and Carter, who have combined EEG with LS to produce EEG feedback entrainment. Other clinicians are exploring the effects of CES in normalizing brain functioning. Since much of the work in treating learning disorders has been with children, the following sections offer suggestions for using mind tools to work with a "subject." The subject, of course, may be any reader who wants to make use of these techinques.

BETA BOOSTING

One clear goal for most types of learning disabilities is to eliminate underarousal by increasing the power and quantity of midrange (15–20 Hz) beta brain waves while decreasing the power and quantity of slow (delta and theta) and rapid (fast beta) brain waves.

EEG SYSTEMS

The EEG systems used for beta training are relatively expensive. However, as public awareness of the benefits of beta training increases, I believe that manufacturers will make available portable home EEG beta trainers. (It would be relatively simple to create a single unit that could be effective as a trainer for beta, alpha, or theta, depending on the user's desires.) Several EEG biofeedback systems currently available can be used for beta training, though they provide feedback only with increased beta and are not programmed also to discourage slow and fast beta brain waves. Among these systems are the Mind Mirror, the Brain Exerciser, the Brain Tracer, and the IBVA, discussed in Chapter 5.

LIGHT AND SOUND

LS systems are extremely effective in entraining brain waves in mid-range beta, and several inexpensive models do the job quite well. Russell and Carter's ADDH program alternates between 18 Hz beta and short periods of 10 Hz alpha. In my experience, you can produce excellent effects by programming the LS device to start at about 10 Hz and ramp up to 15 Hz over a few minutes, and then simply remaining at 15 Hz for twenty minutes.

When this is comfortable, push the target frequency upward to 18 Hz, and remain there as long as is comfortable. EEG evidence shows this quickly decreases delta and theta activity, entrains brain waves to the frequency of the flashing light stimulus, and produces the benefits found with EEG beta training. I suggest several shorter (fifteen- to thirty-minute) sessions each day rather than a single long session. Do your beta sessions in the morning or afternoon, as evening sessions can disrupt sleep.

TAPES AND COMPACT DISCS

For beta-boosting tapes and CDs that use binaural beats, high-frequency sounds, and other techniques to increase beta activity, look for those that speak of increasing concentration or alertness or enhancing cognition, such as the "Focus" tape of the Mega Brain Zones Series.

RELAX, REVIEW, RELEASE, RESCRIPT

RELAX

Although many learning disabilities are linked to underarousal, this does not mean the subjects are relaxed. While it may seem paradoxical, normalizing brain-wave activity in the 13- to 19-Hz range increases relaxation. Therefore, individuals using EEG training or LS entrainment will probably begin to experience relaxation during the sessions. CES also produces feelings of relaxation for many individuals. Encouraging the user simply to relax with brain waves in this "normal" range for fifteen or twenty minutes every day can reduce stress, anxiety, and produce long-lasting behavioral changes. If daily use is continued for two to three weeks, a "threshold effect" may occur in which the subject goes through dramatic and long-lasting personality changes. Subjects should start at the lower frequency ranges (13–15 Hz, the sensorimotor rhythm), for relaxation. If increasing frequency causes muscle tension or irritability, keep stimulating in the sensorimotor range until the subject is fully relaxed. It may take a number of sessions at 13 to 15 Hz before the frequency can be pushed up into the 15- to 18-Hz range.

REVIEW

As the user begins to become relaxed, encourage body awareness. One way to do this is to use the mindfulness body-scan technique described in Chapter 14. As the body scan is repeated day after day, the user will become more acutely aware of the physical symptoms that need to be dealt with.

RELEASE

Releasing (described in Chapter 17) has both the physiological effects of reducing heart rate, blood pressure, and other stress symptoms and the psychological effect of producing dramatic reductions in anxiety. The user should simply become aware of physical symptoms and emotions that arise, and release them.

RESCRIPT

Use the mind tool to uncover the subject's old scripts, imprints and traumas that have been hidden away, and change them using the rescripting techniques explored in Chapter 18.

VISUALIZATION AND SUGGESTION

In combination with rescripting, or by itself, encourage the subject to use the visualization and suggestion techniques described in earlier chapters. Be sure to include suggestions of forgiveness for self and others.

SUGGESTIONS

In addition to the general positive affirmations and suggestions, create more specific and personalized suggestions. Most important, encourage the subject to create his or her own. Here are some suggestions you may find helpful.

> I have an excellent mind. I am relaxed and calm. My brain works clearly and efficiently. My mind is clear and alert. My senses are keen and sharp. I use all my senses to learn. I enjoy school. I enjoy learning. I pay attention. It's okay to have fun studying. I am clever and resourceful. I know I can do anything. I am calm and confident. I am a good person. I have great courage. I overcome obstacles. I believe in myself. I like myself. I believe I have a wonderful intelligence. I am safe and secure. My life is fun. I enjoy learning and I am always learning. I breathe deeply, easily, effortlessly.

VISUALIZATIONS

Use the mind movie techniques (see Chapter 21) to encourage the subject to vividly see himself or herself learning easily and fully experience himself or herself being rewarded for it with praise and happiness.

CHANGE POINT OF VIEW

Encourage the subject to use dissociative imagery to run through unpleasant memories of past behavior, and replace them with full-color associative images of pleasurable behavior. Prompt the subject to be right inside himself or herself, fully experiencing the pleasure and satisfaction of learning, observing from a distance undesirable past behaviors, making them black and white, shrinking them into the distance.

ANCHORING

Assist the subject in using the learning anchor (see Chapter 15) to fully experience all the pleasure of learning, and activate it during learning situations.

EXTERNAL ANCHORS

Once the subject has strongly anchored the desired behaviors and brain states during the mind-tech session, encourage him or her to activate and rehearse them frequently. One of the best ways for doing this is with an external signal generator. Each time the external signal goes off, for example, the subject might have it trigger an image of himself or herself concentrating and paying attention with mental clarity, or a suggestion such as "My mind is clear and alert."

THIRTY-ONE
SUPERCHARGING YOUR IMMUNE SYSTEM

Today our immune systems are under assault. We live in a toxic environment—in recent decades over 60,000 synthetic chemicals have been added to our world. The oceans are so polluted that many of the life-forms that live in it are dying on a large scale. The air is poison. The earth is drenched with chemical fertilizers. We consume toxic chemicals in virtually every type of food or drink we purchase at the local supermarket. Synthetic poisons have permeated our homes and workplaces in the form of pesticides and chemicals in carpets, paints, furniture, cosmetics, even in the papers and books we handle. The drinking water that pours out of our taps is filled with chemicals, heavy metals, and other toxins. The widespread use of antibiotics has created powerful strains of mutant "monster" bacteria and fungi.

Rapid transportation has spread once-isolated viruses, retroviruses, and other exotic pathogens around the world. We live under artificial lights, on human-created schedules, disrupting our deep biological connections to the natural rhythms of rest and activity, night and day, and the passing seasons. We are constantly bombarded by artificial stimuli in the form of lights, sounds, radiation, and electromagnetic fields. We must deal with vast, unmanageable amounts of information in a variety of forms.

We are subjected to unprecedented amounts of stressors and live with unprecedented stress. And our immune systems are breaking down under the burden, making us susceptible to unprecedented levels of cancers, heart disease, bacterial infections, viral diseases, and allergies. Although we are undergoing an epidemic of "immune dysfunction" diseases, such as AIDS and chronic fatigue immune deficiency syndrome (CFIDS), virtually all our most common diseases are the result of damaged immune function.

COUNTERING STRESS

GLOBAL ENVIRONMENT

Since these environmental stressors damage the immune system, and the damaged immune system permits the diseases, we can attack the diseases—and in the process strengthen our immune systems—by reducing or eliminating stressors. Such efforts can and must be undertaken on a global or large-scale level, by working to reduce pollution and change the world (or our community) to reduce stressful stimuli.

PERSONAL ENVIRONMENT

We also should work to cleanse our individual environment both externally and internally. Externally we can eliminate toxins from our food, water, and home and eliminate unwanted stress from our lives. (Some stressors, of course, such as challenging tasks, novel or exciting experiences, ecstasy, and so on, are desirable.) We can cleanse our systems internally by detoxifying our bodies and taking nutrients to boost immune function.

We can also reduce stressors by using mind technology. By spending an hour in the deep peace of a float tank, or going into deep theta while using a light/sound (LS) device or listening to binaural beats, we are changing our external environment, eliminating at least temporarily many stressors, and existing for the moment in an environment that is safe, calm, and more or less free of "noise" and other external stressors.

INTERNAL ENVIRONMENT

We can also reduce stressors on an individual-internal level—by learning to identify various stressors and how they affect us as individuals and then learning to release or relax from those stressors. To a great degree this stress reduction has to do with techniques for state change. For example, being stuck in rush-hour traffic can be enormously stressful for many people. However, if they can learn to release their tension and "reframe" the experience—look on being stuck in traffic as an opportunity to relax, listen to pleasurable music, perform some sort of meditation exercise such as mindful breathing, and offer themselves beneficial suggestions and mental images—what was once stress turns into a healing experience.

On this individual-internal level mind technology also can be an enormously effective antistress tool. We have already explored how various state-change techniques can help us release stress, change from stressful to peaceful states, and behave in ways that reduce stress in our lives. These include such techniques as mindfulness, deep relaxation, self-hypnosis, suggestion, releasing, focusing, visualization, reframing, and so on.

BOOSTING IMMUNE FUNCTION

However, no matter how effectively we alter our personal environment and learn to release stress, there's no denying that the stressors are still there, still damaging our immune systems. No home water and air filters, no organic foods and mega-nutrients, and no amount of releasing or positive suggestions is going to eliminate the poisoned global environment, toxic work situations, a polluted society.

Since it's not possible to escape these toxins and their assaults on our immune system, the one logical response is to strengthen our immune systems so that we have a higher level of resistance to the stressors. We can do this by taking immune-boosting substances, such as certain vitamins, minerals, and herbs. (These are discussed in Chapter 32.) Another way to strengthen our immune systems is with our minds.

The mind can strengthen the immune system because both are linked in a continuous bidirectional feedback loop, each influencing and being influenced by the other. We've all experienced the way our immune systems influence our minds: When we have a cold or the flu, we feel down, dull, blue. We don't want to go to a party or have a conversation with our friends not just because our bodies don't feel well, but because we're not *in the mood*.

On the other hand, how often have you been forced to go to a party or go out with friends when you felt sick and found yourself having so much fun you forgot you were sick? By changing your mood, you have changed your immune system. As biofeedback researcher Elmer Green puts it, "Every change in the physiological state is accompanied by an appropriate change in the mental emotional state, conscious or unconscious, and conversely, every change in the mental emotional state, conscious or unconscious, is accompanied by an appropriate change in the physiological state."

Mind can alter immune functions in a variety of ways, not only through state change (as by changing our mood from sad to happy, pessimistic to optimistic, anxious to relaxed), but through combining state change with mental imagery, suggestion, and belief. Humans have apparently always known this. Throughout the ages all human societies have developed sophisticated techniques and systems for inducing state change and a rich and colorful array of images, suggestions, and beliefs for changing the body and strengthening the immune system.

Shamans and witch doctors have learned to enter trances and confer with gods and spirit guides. They have known how to represent and communicate with those forces in bright masks, chants, dances, and rituals that alter the sick individual's state, mood, and beliefs—and in so doing, alter that individual's immune system. Yogis, monks, and lamas have learned to enter deep meditative states in which they can visualize energy systems flowing through the body. They can use the power of the mind to alter those energy systems and thus alter the immune system. Religions, myths, fantasies, rituals, dreams, chants, dances, psalms—all have served as ways of altering and enhancing immune function and changing the human body. As humans have always known, these techniques work most effectively when the body is deeply relaxed or quiet and the mind is in an altered state—trance, dream, reverie, prayer, meditation—a state that is distinct from that of everyday waking consciousness.

Mind technology, of course, is simply a modern way of applying these ancient techniques, a way that uses our most advanced technology to produce the deep relaxation and state change that are keys to them. We have already investigated each of these at some length. In the following sections we will explore how each can be used specifically to strengthen immune function and, beyond that, to strengthen the entire body, so that we can not only eliminate sickness but gain and maintain a high level of health.

LONGEVITY AND THE WISDOM OF THE BODY

A growing flood of research suggests that maintaining our bodies at a high level of wellness can dramatically slow the aging process and increase life span. It appears that aging is a direct result of the effects of stress disrupting homeostasis, on a molecular, cellular, and systemic basis. By maintaining an optimal homeostatic balance of biochemicals, we may live longer and healthier lives.

There is also a wealth of evidence, such as that emerging from the field of psychoneuroimmunology, that the body is far more responsive to mental influence than had been imagined. In almost mystical tones hardcore materialistic scientists are talking about how mind influences matter. The implications of the research are clear, though awesome: The mind can repair almost everything that might go wrong with the body (aside from catastrophic injuries).

This means that enormously extended life spans are not inconceivable. For example, we have explored in Chapter 20 the way youthful levels of growth hormone rejuvenated aging men, making them seem twenty years younger in just a few months. We also have learned how individuals can regulate virtually any biological function that can be monitored and fed back to us by our senses. And further, we have learned that mechanical biofeedback equipment is ultimately not necessary for learning this self-regulation—simply by intensifying awareness through deep relaxation, suggestion, and visualization, we can establish voluntary control over every biological process. That includes the secretion of brain chemicals, peptides, and hormones, such as, for example, growth hormone.

Two effects of mind technology seem most important. First, by producing profound relaxation and ways of releasing stress, mind tools free up the body's self-regulating, self-healing, self-regenerating powers. When the body is given this freedom, often enough, it will restore homeostasis and return to its optimal state, which is health. Second, by providing us with exquisitely amplified awareness of internal sensations and states, mind tools can help us learn to influence and regulate those sensations and states.

ACTION SECTION—USING MIND TECHNOLOGY FOR PEAK HEALTH

Among the ways mind technology can be effective in boosting immune function is by: (1) producing deep and lasting relaxation to reduce stress and the damaging effects it can have on the body and immune system, and permit the body's homeostatic, self-regulating powers to maintain the immune system at optimal strength; (2) altering brain-body chemistry to produce optimal levels of the various components of the immune system and to produce feelings of well-being and to increase self-confidence; and (3) helping change stressful or immune-impairing behavior patterns and attitudes through eliminating negative scripts and attitudes and using positive suggestions, visualizations, and rescripting, during deeply relaxed or trancelike states. What follows are some suggestions for ways you can use mind tools for these purposes.

Some brain tools can be extremely helpful when used during a medical treatment session—for enhancing guided imagery; producing states of heightened receptivity to healing suggestions and affirmation; opening up the unconscious to permit the emergence of beliefs, traumas, or attitudes that may be harming your health or immune function. Hundreds of medical professionals and therapists around the world are using mind tools as an integral part of their treatment of various types of illness or immune disfunction.

Michael Dullnig, M.D., of Sacramento, California, for example, has used various dual-induction and binaural-beat audiotapes in conjunction with his counseling of HIV-positive patients. In a 1990 study he noted that all patients in the study showed improvement in psychological target symptoms, and some showed significant increases in T4 cell counts, important components of the immune system. William Harris, M.D., director of the Penwell Foundation, an organization for the investigation, research, and application of different modalities for the treatment of those with AIDS/HIV, has used light/sound (LS) devices with HIV-positive patients and found them extremely effective. He speculates that the devices may boost immune function by producing states of deep relaxation, by enhancing the patients' receptivity to suggestions for healing, by improving their ability to visualize and the clarity of their visualizations. Says Harris, "I think that this type of machine may actually be stimulating . . . the body to produce its own chemical substances," and that these natural substances may enhance immune function and healing.

In any case, mind tools can be enormously helpful when used in combination with your treatment. For example, if you are receiving medication, you can use your mind technology to visualize the medication going into your body, destroying viruses or other pathogens, and/ or strengthening your immune system. Simply using the mind tool to relax is a powerful way of enhancing the effects of medical treatment. The following techniques should be effective for people to use in conjunction with treatment, for people who feel that they are not as healthy as they would like to be, and for those who feel healthy enough but would like to protect themselves from the possibly damaging effects of stress and environmental toxins and attain a state of peak or optimal health and well-being.

RELAX, REVIEW, RELEASE, RESCRIPT

RELAX

The human body has an inherent "wisdom" or tendency to move toward balance, equilibrium, and stability. This optimal state, in which all parts and systems are functioning and interacting properly, is called homeostasis. Evidence suggests that our body's homeostatic or self-healing mechanisms work most effectively when we are relaxed. Stress disrupts homeostasis.

One way stress does this is by disrupting our natural chemistry. For example, when Type A men (hard-driving, with high levels of hostility) are under stress, they secrete forty times as much cortisol and three times as much adrenaline as Type B (less hostile and aggressive) men. Cortisol suppresses immune function. These chemicals also are a key to the fight-or-flight response—they rev up the body, leading to increased blood pressure, faster heart rate, and other stressful symptoms. That's why Type A men under great stress have high rates of hypertension (high blood pressure), heart attacks, suppressed immune function, and other problems.

Relaxation reduces levels of cortisol and adrenaline and allows them to return to normal. For example, in comparisons of cortisol levels in subjects relaxing in a reclining chair in a dimly lit room with subjects using a flotation tank, the floaters had drops of over 20 percent, while the control group showed no change. Repeated periods of deep relaxation using mind tools have been shown to have a threshold effect, so that after several weeks individuals undergo lasting personality transformations. Several studies suggest that Type A personalities using brain technology may not only experience reduced blood pressure and boosted immune function, but may be changed in a more essential way, becoming less hostile and more satisfied.

Research has indicated that subjects with a high level of perceived stress to certain life events experienced a greatly decreased level of immune response—they had only a third of the level of "natural killer cell activity" of those who experienced the same life events but perceived them as less stressful, for example, and they had steep reductions in salivary immunoglobulin A (IgA). IgA speeds healing, reduces the danger of infection, and controls heart rate; reduced IgA is linked with lowered resistance to disease. It has long been known that deep relaxation can boost natural killer cell activity and IgA. Now there is evidence that mind technology can accelerate this effect. In one study at the Medical College of Ohio, both "wet" and "dry" flotation produced major increases in IgA; there were no changes in a control group, which just sat quietly for twenty-five minutes.

Regular deep relaxation seems to reset our homeostatic mechanism so that we have a higher stress tolerance—what was once perceived as highly stressful is now perceived as less stressful. This improves immune function.

Also, deep relaxation makes us feel good. In part, this happens because we're released from the stresses of life. In part, it's a result of the release of the body's natural happiness molecules. Feeling good improves immune function.

Simply relaxing for a short period every day can reduce stress, strengthen immune function, and produce long-lasting reductions in levels of harmful biochemicals and increases in levels of healing biochemicals.

REVIEW

As you become relaxed and sink into state zero, become aware of your body. One way to do this is to use the mindfulness body-scan technique described in Chapter 14. Through the "curare effect," deep relaxation leads to increased sensory awareness. Since we feel our bodies more clearly and distinctly, we are able to regulate them more effectively. As biofeedback research has shown, we have the capacity to control the firing rhythm of a single motor neuron in the body, once we are made aware of that neuron and receive feedback from it. Your body scan will alert you to stressors and the effects of stress and guide you in releasing, relaxing, and directing the healing capacities of your body toward specific locations or systems. Perform a similar emotional inventory. How to you feel now?

RELEASE

Physiologically, releasing (see Chapter 17) has the effects of reducing heart rate, blood pressure, and other stress symptoms. That means it can reduce the stressors that may impair immune function. Psychologically, releasing has the effect of making you feel much better. That is, it is an effective way to change your mental state. As you use your mind tool to relax, simply become aware of physical symptoms and emotions that arise, and release them. Frequently users will find that their stress is a product of wants that they have not been aware of. Becoming aware of these emotions and wants, and letting them go, can lead to rapid transformations.

RESCRIPT

Find the old scripts and imprints that are still being acted out. Common ones include "I get colds every winter about this time," "You'll make yourself sick if you do that," "You make me sick," "That's disgusting," "I'm sick and tired of . . .," "It's not healthy to . . ." Change them using the rescripting techniques explored in Chapter 18.

VISUALIZATION AND SUGGESTION

In combination with your rescripting, or by itself, you can use visualization and suggestion techniques described in Chapters 15 and 16. Be sure to suggest that you will use your mind tool every day to relax. Remember, *exercise* has been found to be extremely effective in boosting immune function, so you will want to include suggestions and imagery of yourself engaging in regular physical exercise. Also be sure to include suggestions of *forgiveness* for yourself and others.

SUGGESTIONS

In addition to the general positive affirmations and suggestions, here are some more specific suggestions you may find effective. Find which ones work for you, and alter the wording to suit your self. Most important, create your own:

I am filled with healing power and vitality. I feel healing energy flowing into and filling every cell in my body. My body is purifying and perfecting itself. I enjoy life. I enjoy healthy activities. My body heals and mends quickly. My body is regenerating and rejuvenating itself at all times. My body recharges quickly. I am strong and filled with joy. Every day my energy grows stronger. My body is healing itself at all times. I feel secure and relaxed. My immune system functions perfectly. Every part of my immune system is operating perfectly, and in perfect balance and harmony. Every cell in my body is filled with radiant, vibrant health. I have courage. I am bold and daring. I release all tension. I am resilient and strong. I like myself. I am brave. I have a spirit of adventure. I deserve to have fun. My inner strength gives me power. I feel centered and calm. I breathe deeply, easily, and effortlessly. I always have enough energy to do all I want to do. I am supercharged with energy and vitality.

VISUALIZATIONS

Use the mind movie techniques (see Chapter 21) to vividly see your body healing itself and fully experience yourself being charged with healing energy, joy, vitality, and pleasure in being alive. Become like the microscopic explorers in the *Incredible Voyage* and go into your body. You may find it helpful to make your visualizations biologically accurate—read illustrated books and articles about healing and the immune system, and visualize natural killer cells and T lymphocytes attacking and destroying viruses. See your thymus, hypothalamus, and pituitary pouring out healing chemicals, and so on. Or you may find it more effective to use a more figurative visualization—see your white cells as ravenous white dogs eating up the viruses, tiny scrub brushes cleaning out your liver, each breath a stream of golden healing light. Explore other visualizations, and find what works for you.

CHANGE POINT OF VIEW

You might want to see your unhealthy behavior, or your current unhealthy self, or the unhealthy part of your system, in black and white, from a distance. Turn it into a snapshot. Throw it away, burn it up. Replace it with a full-color, big, bright, radiant, ecstatic image of yourself filled with vibrant healing energy. Be right inside yourself, fully experiencing the joy, vitality, and pleasure of being so healthy and strong. Do a swish pattern on whatever it is that's keeping you from being incredibly healthy, so that each time you become aware of it, it automatically triggers an experience of radiant good health.

ANCHORING

When you experience the optimal health or healing energy state fully and powerfully during your mind-tech session, anchor it with a signal that you can then use any time you want to reactivate that state. Use anchors to boost your immune function and your natural vitality during times when you are exposed to stressors.

EXTERNAL ANCHORS

Once you've strongly anchored the healing power brain states during your mind-tech session, activate them frequently. Try using some external signal generator. You might have it trigger a flood of pure white light, or healing energy, a whole-body experience of yourself vibrating with good health, or a suggestion such as "I feel healing energy flowing into every cell."

GET INTO THETA

If you're not suffering from depression or underarousal, get into theta frequently. There is evidence that simply being in this state strengthens your immune system and produces feelings of psychological well-being.

BREAK DOWN THE ARMOR, ACCEPT THE UNKNOWN

The most profound breakthroughs seem to emerge from a willingness to let the brain technology take you into "uncomfortable areas" and release the traumatic material that is stored or coded there. You can do this in ways explored earlier in Chapters 23 and 24. Mihaly Csikszentmihalyi, a University of Chicago professor, has researched the concept of *flow*, a state in which he says we experience "a unified flowing from one moment to the next," in which we feel in control of our actions, in which "there is little distinction between self and environment, between stimulus and response, between past, present and future." Flow, that is, is what is often called peak experience. Csikszentmihalyi asked groups of highly skilled individuals ranging from surgeons to professional athletes who experienced high levels of flow in their lives to rank sixteen very different activities as being more or less similar to flow. Overwhelmingly they listed the item "designing or discovering something new" as being the most similar to their flow activity. Something new is out there. Enter the flow.

SUGGESTED READING

Jeanne Achtenberg, *Imagery and Healing* (Boston: Shambhala, 1985). Ernest Lawrence Rossi, *The Psychobiology of Mind-Body Healing: New Concepts of Therapeutic Hypnosis* (New York: W. W. Norton, 1986).

PART FIVE
BRAIN POWER NUTRIENTS AND SMART PILLS

From the moment we enter life we are limited by our genetic potential, the genome. But do we realize, either individually or as a species, all of our genetic potential?

Pharmacology participates, very modestly, in one of the great efforts of humanity, that of answering Plato's question: "Who are we?" The aim is "to know oneself," but toward what end? It seems to us that the deeper sense of this Socratic imperative is to know oneself neither in a narcissistic nor timid fashion, but in order to create oneself.

Humankind will not wait passively for millions of years so that evolution can offer a better brain. Mankind must refashion itself by realizing its highest genetic potential in the direction that evolution is taking, that is to say, by increasing the integrative capacity of the forebrain. All things considered, developing a pharmacology of the brain's integrative activity has a place in this great human undertaking.

—C. GIURGEA, M.D.,
"A Nootropic Approach to the Pharmacology of the
Integrative Activity of the Brain." *Conditional Reflex*, 8, no. 2
(1973).

DISCLAIMER/WARNING

The following information is not intended to provide medical advice. It is intended to be educational and informational only. Please consult with a health professional for medical advice. Adequate studies of both long- and short-term effects of some of these substances have not been performed, and some may have adverse side effects. All humans have different biochemical natures and sensitivities, so that safe dosages of some of these substances may vary enormously from individual to individual. Also, some substances may be dangerous for individuals not in sound mental and physical health.

I strongly recommend that anyone interested in experimenting with these substances do so with caution and under the supervision of a medical professional. Children and pregnant or lactating women should not experiment with these substances under any circumstances.

THIRTY-TWO
BRAIN POWER NUTRIENTS

You have a business meeting tomorrow, which requires that you be in top form. You have several reports to go over, many facts to memorize, and above all you have to get some rest.

Your first step? A trip to the health food store. A meeting like this is much too important to take on without fine-tuning your biochemistry. You want to create the optimal neurochemical conditions for learning and creativity. So you head for the shelf of cognitive enhancement compounds and peak performance pills, and load up your basket with bottles of germanium, glutathione, ginseng, DMG, ginkgo biloba, arginine pyroglutamate, phosphatidyl choline, DMAE, and Coenzyme Q-10.

You take the appropriate doses of these mind-expanding nutrients. Within an hour you are relaxed yet alert and creative. Your brain-wave activity has altered, and an electroencephalogram (EEG) would show that it has become more regular and has increased in amplitude in certain frequencies, causing you to feel simultaneously profoundly relaxed yet in a state of intense concentration, loose and creative as well as mentally quick and alert.

A test of your brain chemistry would show much higher levels of a variety of neurochemicals known to boost intelligence, memory, and other cognitive functions. Further, brain tests would reveal that the blood circulating through your brain has increased levels of oxygen—the tiny capillaries are carrying far more oxygen to each neuron than before. At the same time, the rate of metabolism and the energy level of your brain cells has sharply increased. You are now in the optimal state to imprint new memories, to plan new and more creative strategies, to visually rehearse every detail of your upcoming meeting or exam.

By evening you have absorbed an enormous amount of information. Now you're ready to relax. An hour before bed you take a selection of natural nutrients, including melatonin, gamma aminobutyric acid (GABA), glycine, taurine, inositol, and vitamin B_6, that gently relax you, act like "natural Valium," and send you off to a deep, restorative sleep.

The next day, an hour before your meeting, you take another selection of substances that put you in a state of calm self-confidence, relaxed but energized. Your brain is alert and lucid, ready to respond to questions and problems you encounter with clarity, peak creativity and insight.

Sound futuristic? Actually, all these cognitive enhancement compounds already exist and are widely available. Some brain-boosting substances, now widely known as "smart drugs" (described in Chapter 33) are available in the United States only by prescription, or from abroad via mail order. But all of the nutrients just described, and many others that have been proven to be enormously effective at boosting intelligence and memory and preventing brain aging, are inexpensive and easily available over-the-counter at health food stores in the United States. They are completely legal and not only safe but, when used properly, enormously beneficial to your health.

Why haven't you heard more about these legal brain-boosting substances? Probably because there are powerful organizations that would like to keep you ignorant of these beneficial nutrients.

WHAT THE FDA DOESN'T WANT YOU TO KNOW

Here's a fact: Vast amounts of money are being spent for research into cognition-enhancing drugs by huge, wealthy pharmaceutical companies that are racing to develop patentable memory-enhancement drugs and to obtain the approval of the Food and Drug Administration (FDA) for their own compounds.

The reason for the race is clear: To the winner will go wealth almost beyond imagining. Financial analysts and *Fortune* magazine estimate that FDA-approved intelligence-boosting drugs could quickly produce sales of *many billions of dollars a year* in the United States alone, outselling antibiotics and tranquilizers combined. So the competition is fierce, and all efforts are directed not toward developing the best drugs but toward developing ones that are *patentable*. Drug companies have exclusive rights to market patentable drugs for many years to come and charge enormous sums for them.

But here's the catch: The FDA focuses only on drugs that "treat diseases." The organization has not shown any interest in giving its approval to drugs that "merely" improve people's memories or boost intelligence. Quite the opposite, in fact: In 1992 the FDA stated that "Any product, regardless of its composition, that is clearly associated with smart drug claims . . . is illegal and subject to seizure by the [FDA] to protect the public health." Bizarre as it may sound, any substance, no matter how safe, is *illegal* if it is associated with smart drug claims, or if its makers even so much as hint that it might be able to increase intelligence. In other words, if evidence showed that bottled water helped improve intelligence, then bottled water would, by this definition, be automatically "illegal and subject to seizure" by the FDA.

Therefore, to get FDA approval and win the rights to this potentially lucrative market, the drug companies have to find drugs that will treat some *illness*. Even if pharmaceutical companies had a substance that they could prove improved the IQ of a normal healthy person by 40 points overnight, they couldn't get FDA approval for it—they'd have to find some *therapeutic* use for it.

So the companies are directing their efforts toward developing drugs that can treat the cognitive impairment that often accompanies aging. They hope to gain FDA approval for these drugs as treatments for age-related medical problems, such as Alzheimer's disease, multiple-infarct dementia, and senility.

These companies have no reason to search for substances that boost the brain power of normal healthy individuals. If they want something that can be patented, they must gain FDA approval. And to gain FDA approval, they must go through a process that costs, on average, over $140 million and that proves the drug is effective in treating some disease.

The big pharmaceutical companies have little interest in exploring the cognition enhancement properties of substances that can't be patented—such as all the thousands of herbs, vitamins, and other substances already known—even if those substances have enormous intelligence-boosting effects. Vitamin C is a good example: It's a proven cognition-enhancement nutrient. But, of course no one can patent vitamin C, which is cheap and readily available. And so no pharmaceutical company's going to spend millions of dollars on an advertising campaign touting the brain-building powers of vitamin C, since as soon as it got its marketing campaign under way, thousands of competitors could sell vitamin C too.

Here's another example. One widely available and unpatentable substance, DHEA, Dehydroepiandrostesone, is rumored to have demonstrated in a recent study some success in, among other things, treating AIDS, as well as cognition enhancement. However, the drug company involved in the experiments is now apparently trying to conceal the study's results until it can develop some DHEA variant that is patentable. The company has obtained a court order forbidding the scientist in charge of the study even to speak with anyone about it.

So the fact that you haven't heard of a whole raft of safe and legal substances that can boost intelligence, enhance memory, and prevent brain aging doesn't mean they don't exist. They just aren't patentable and don't have million-dollar advertising campaigns behind them.

Still, ours is the information age. Today, thanks to the information revolution, much nonsecret research finds its way into our computerized information network in one form or another. And increasing amounts of past research—vast libraries of biomedical research data—are now available to anyone with a computer. As a result, researchers are able to do a quick data scan for virtually any nutrient or substance, seeking out cognition-enhancement or brain-boosting effects. There has been an explosion of information about and research into these nonpatentable brain-boosting nutrients. And the results are exciting. In the pages that follow I describe over two dozen substances—vitamins, minerals, herbs—that have been proven to have powerful brain-boosting effects.

These megabrain nutrients produce their brain-boosting effects in a variety of ways. The following list summarizes their effects.

- Antioxidants work by countering the harmful effects of damaging free radicals.
- Nootropics have a primary effect on intelligence and boost the integrative areas of the brain.
- Brain metabolism activators stimulate areas of the brain to function more effectively.
- Neuropeptide precursors are transformed in the body into neuropeptides, the messenger molecules that are essential to the operation and communication of parts of the brain and the brain-body.
- Cholinergic nutrients stimulate the activity of acetylcholine, a neurochemical essential to brain function.
- Cerebral vasodilators increase blood flow—and therefore oxygen flow—to the brain.
- Miscellaneous nutrients function in a variety of unique ways to boost brain function.

In the sections that follow we'll take a look at each of these categories of nutrients. While I discuss the nutrients separately, such as antioxidants or nootropics, for example, in most cases these nutrients serve multiple functions and could easily be classified under several different categories.

The following nutrients have been found to have brain-boosting effects. But this does not mean that by taking high doses of a single nutrient you'll benefit from these effects. *These substances work synergistically and often are ineffective without the necessary cofactors.* Thus a multivitamin and mineral supplement is important. While I describe a few key smart nutrients that I think will be effective when taken in relatively large doses, never neglect a healthful diet and a full-spectrum supplement.

ANTIOXIDANTS

Today it seems very likely that the assumption that there is a basic cause of aging is correct and that the sum of the deleterious free radical reactions going on continuously throughout the cells and tissues *is* the aging process or a major contribution to it.

—Denham Harman, M.D.,
University of Nebraska

As Dr. Harman suggests, many gerontologists and other scientists are now convinced that aging—and many of the cognitive problems linked with aging, such as declines in memory and actual damage to brain cells and shrinkage of the brain—is caused by toxic forms of oxygen called free radicals, which cut a deadly swath through our cells.

In fact, many experts now believe that in *all* situations of disease, whether it's a broken leg, a heart attack, aging, stress, or liver damage, certain common cellular events are taking place that cause bodily damage. The common cause of this cellular tissue damage is the action of free radicals. Free radical–induced tissue damage has been scientifically implicated in every known degenerative disease.

Free radicals are highly reactive forms of oxygen that are made by the billions every day as a normal part of our body's use of oxygen to form energy. As the body uses oxygen to burn food for energy—a process called oxidation—it creates these free radicals as by-products. Their destructive power is enormous.

Part of free radicals' destructive power comes from the way they work, which is by chain reaction. Essentially, free radicals are unstable molecules because they lack an electron. Therefore they constantly attack other cells to obtain the electron they need to be stable. But when they rob an electron from another cell, that cell is damaged, creating other free radicals, which, by chain reaction, can produce hundreds, thousands, or even millions of additional destructive free radicals.

FREE RADICALS AND CIRCULATORY DISEASE

When free radicals land on cholesterol in the walls of blood vessels, they can trigger hardening of the arteries and other circulatory-heart ailments. When this process takes place in the blood vessels and capillaries of the brain, the result can be a diminished flow of blood to areas of the brain. (This means less oxygen flow to the brain—and high levels of oxygen are essential to healthy brain function.) The hardening of blood vessels and capillaries in the brain can also result in major strokes and in undetectable ministrokes that cut off blood flow to areas of the brain and result in decreased intelligence, memory, and learning abilities.

DNA DAMAGE

When the free radicals land on DNA in the nucleus of individual cells, they can break down the DNA and cause mutations that lead to cancer and other diseases. By damaging DNA, they can cause it to produce flawed copies of itself, which over time can lead to the imperfections that increase with age.

CELLULAR GARBAGE

Free radicals also attack proteins, turning them into useless sludge or lumps called *lipofussin*. This "cellular garbage" accumulates throughout the body but is particularly noticeable in brain cells. In the brain, these lumps of damaged protein are probably a major cause of age-related cognitive decline.

RANCID CELLS

Free radicals also can attack the fats in the cells' delicate membranes and turn them rancid, damaging the cell membrane and destroying the cell's protective boundary. On a microscopic, cellular level, this membrane damage and rigidity produce the same effect as aged, leathery skin.

AGING

Free radical damage to the hypothalamus and pituitary result in a decline in growth hormone (GH). Free radical damage to the adrenal glands may cause them to make less of the hormone DHEA. Both GH and DHEA are associated with youth, with the body's ability to heal and regenerate itself, and both of them decline with age. Hormones such as GH and DHEA may be essential for the protein synthesis that is an essential part of memory formation and the growth of new dendrites and synapses in response to experiences and external stimuli. That is, these hormones may be essential to the ability to learn and form memories. The decline in these hormones with age is another key to many of the decreases in brain function associated with aging.

IMMUNE SYSTEM DAMAGE

Free radicals also may be the key to the shriveling of the thymus gland, a key to the immune system. In addition, they directly attack some immune cells, such as the monocytes, causing them to produce a chemical that shuts down immune response.

All the harmful effects of free radicals that I've described so far have been linked to the cumulative effects of free radicals as part of the natural oxidative process of human metabolism. The implication has been that these cumulative effects take place over years and contribute to declines in brain function associated with aging and to the aging process itself.

ENVIRONMENTAL TOXINS

However, even the most youthful readers should take warning: There are numerous other causes of free radical damage in the body that are not associated with aging. These include smoking or inhaling second-hand smoke; drinking alcohol; breathing polluted air; exposure to ultraviolet rays from the sun; eating processed food; being exposed to X rays; stress; being exposed to low levels of electromagnetic fields, such as those produced by high-power wires, computers, clock radios, hair dryers, electric shavers, and so on ad infinitum.

Thus all of us are subject to free radical damage and its effects, which can become apparent even at relatively young ages. For example, most of us know heavy smokers who have already by their late twenties developed the leathery faces characteristic of smokers—the result of decreased blood flow to the skin and associated free radical damage produced by nicotine and the other harmful substances in tobacco. This effect is particularly noticeable in female smokers, since females have thinner facial skin than males and are therefore more susceptible to skin damage and wrinkling. Again, we're all familiar with the habitual sun-bather who, as a result of the free radical damage of solar radiation, has developed wrinkled, leathery skin.

FREE RADICALS AND PREMATURE SENILITY

Skin damage is obvious to the eye. Not so obvious is that free radical damage can have profound effects on mental functioning. It's now certain that due to the enormous array in our modern world of pollutants, processed foods, computers, and other causes of free radical damage, many people who are still youthful are suffering declines in brain function equivalent to those once suffered only by aging people. That is, many young and middle-age people today are suffering from damage and deterioration of their basic intelligence and ability to think, of their powers of memory, and of their capacity to learn. Stated another way: *Millions of so-called healthy individuals today are in reality victims of premature senility.*

Maintaining our cellular balance and health against free radicals depends on a complex system of defenses. The most active and powerful components of this defense system are substances known as *antioxidants* that actually destroy free radicals. The antioxidant defense system is composed of numerous vitamins, enzymes, and other nutrients influenced by your dietary intake. That is, you can eat foods or nutrients that are antioxidants themselves or are essential components of them. These foods or nutrients include actual antioxidant nutrients and natural enzymes.

The nutrients include vitamin A (beta-carotene and other carotenoids), vitamins C and E, zinc, and selenium. They have their greatest effect by circulating in the blood outside the cells. The antioxidant enzymes, which include superoxide dismutase (SOD), glutathione peroxidase, methionine reductase, and catalase, are produced by the body both inside and outside the cells. This means the antioxidant enzymes have a wider range of powers in combatting free radicals, since much free radical production comes from inside the cells. Specific nutrients produce these antioxidant enzymes in the body. By consuming these nutrients, you can boost your body's production of these powerful antioxidant enzymes. SOD, for example, is not effective when taken orally, since it is digested in the stomach. However, its essential components include zinc, copper, and manganese, which, when taken in proper doses, can increase the body's production of SOD.

In the following pages, I describe a variety of widely available nutrients that are powerful antioxidants. Many of them have other health and cognition enhancement values as well.

It's important to keep in mind that antioxidants function together as a team. Therefore, while you should take personalized doses of individual antioxidants, such as vitamin C or E, these nutrients will have their greatest antioxidant power when taken together with a spectrum of other antioxidants.

Nutrition researchers Durk Pearson and Sandy Shaw offer a clear explanation of how antioxidants work as teams, or with "cofactors" in the body. When a free radical is attacking a fat molecule, says Pearson, "the free radical ends up being quenched by vitamin E. . . . This turns the vitamin E tocopherol into the tocopherol radical, which is less dangerous than, say, the hydroxyl radical . . . but it's still a bad guy. Then along comes an ascorbate ion [that is, vitamin C] . . . and this turns the tocopherol radical back into tocopherol. It recycles it back into vitamin E." In this process, of course, the vitamin C is turned into a free radical—the ascorbyl radical. But, as Sandy Shaw observes, "it is less dangerous than the tocopherol radical that it quenched, but it's still a radical; it needs to be gotten rid of, and in that instance, it looks as though glutathione . . . reduces the vitamin C. And so on."

So the body needs a collection of antioxidants and nutrients designed to best deal with these sorts of chain reactions. As Pearson points out, "what they do is gradually reduce the energy of these radicals down to the point where they are more and more stable and capable of doing less and less damage."

ANTIOXIDANT FORMULA

The best way to be sure you're getting a good selection of antioxidants is to buy a multiple antioxidant formula. *This should be used in addition to your regular multiple vitamin and mineral supplement.* Increase your intake of antioxidants under times of stress or exposure to free radical damage, such as when exposed to cigarette smoke, when drinking alcohol, and so on. Be certain your formula contains the following important antioxidants and antioxidant precursors or cofactors: vitamins A (beta-carotene), B_1, B_2, B_3 (niacin), B_5, B_6, inositol, vitamin C, bioflavanoids (hesperidin, rutin, pycogenol), vitamin E, choline, zinc, selenium, glutathione (or N-acetyl-l-cysteine), methionine, CoQ-10 and dimethylglycine (DMG).

In addition to your antioxidant formula, you will want to take additional quantities of certain antioxidants, to be sure you are getting sufficient quantities of nutrients, such as vitamins C and E, for which individual needs vary widely. Depending on the state of your health and the amount of stress you're experiencing, your body's requirements for vitamin C may range from as little as a gram a day to over 20 grams per day! For their specific brain-boosting effects, I recommend you take healthy quantities of vitamin C, glutathione and/or N-acetyl cysteine, CoQ-10, and germanium.

VITAMIN C

Everybody's heard about the virtues of vitamin C. It's not only an antioxidant of astonishing power, it reduces cholesterol, boosts the immune system, and much more. It plays an essential role in the formation of collagen. Collagen is a protein that constitutes the body's connective tissue. Making up about 30 percent of the body's total protein content, it is the most abundant protein in the human body and is therefore essential for cell growth and repair. Vitamin C also has a key synergistic effect on other water-soluble antioxidants.

What most people don't know is that it's also a potent cognition-enhancing substance: Vitamin C boosts brain power. In one controlled study in which healthy individuals were tested both for levels of vitamin C and IQ, those with higher levels of the vitamin averaged 5 points higher in IQ. When those with the lower levels of the vitamin were given vitamin C supplements, their IQ scores increased by over 3.5 points. The study left no doubt that *vitamin C is clearly a cognition-enhancing substance.*

A key to how important vitamin C is to brain functioning is that humans have evolved a specific system to ensure the brain receives the highest possible levels of vitamin C. This system, known as the "vitamin C pump," works in two steps: First, vitamin C is extracted from blood circulating throughout the body and increased in concentration by a factor of ten in the cerebrospinal fluid. Next, the pump extracts vitamin C from the cerebrospinal fluid and increases its concentration by a factor of ten in the brain, bathing the brain cells in concentrations of vitamin C that are *one hundred times* more concentrated than normal body fluids.

The body's requirements for vitamin C vary enormously. An average megabrain dose might be 1 to 4 grams (1,000 to 4,000 milligrams [mg]) per day. However, when you're under a lot of stress, or exposed to a lot of free radical damage (such as alcohol, smoking, illness), your requirements might skyrocket to as much as 10 or even 20 grams per day. Vitamin C is water soluble, which means that it is excreted from the body with urine, and is active in your body only for four to six hours. Therefore you have to divide your doses, taking some with each meal and before bedtime. Vitamin C is an acid—ascorbic acid—and can cause stomach irritation. I recommend you take it buffered, in such forms of calcium ascorbate and magnesium ascorbate.

ESTER C

One new type of vitamin C, called Ester C, seems to have greater bioavailability—it reaches tissues more quickly, raises tissue levels of vitamin C more rapidly, and remains in the body longer than standard vitamin C. Health practitioners are finding that their patients need 70 to 80 percent less Ester-C than regular vitamin C. In other words, only 20 to 30 percent of the normal vitamin C dose is needed when taking Ester-C.

ASCORBYL PALMITATE

In addition to the water-soluble forms, a fat-soluble form of vitamin C called ascorbyl palmitate is absorbed into the body's fat tissue and therefore remains available in the body until needed. Ascorbyl palmitate also acts as a potent antioxidant synergist with other fat-soluble antioxidants, such as vitamin E. I recommend you take at least 250 mg of ascorbyl palmitate a day.

The best way to determine your vitamin C requirements is through a process called titration. This means starting with low doses and slowly increasing until you reach the bowel tolerance point—that is, when you experience diarrhea. At that point, cut back slightly.

GLUTATHIONE AND N-ACETYL CYSTEINE

Glutathione is one of the most common substances in the body. It acts as a powerful antioxidant and detoxicant and reverses the effects of malignant cells on healthy cells.

Basically this substance is an antioxidant: It destroys or renders harmless free radicals. But there's more: It seems to help detoxify the body by eliminating heavy metals and other harmful substances. The more toxins your body takes in, the more work your liver has to do to detoxify your system. Glutathione has been proven to protect the liver against damage caused by alcohol and other toxins. Recent research also has suggested that glutathione may destroy liver cancer.

Glutathione also has an antiaging effect, which is probably related to its power to deactivate free radicals and render lipid peroxides harmless. The glutathione levels of aging cells are 20 to 34 percent lower than those of young cells. As levels of glutathione are reduced with age, toxic substances would accumulate: This may be the aging process itself. Researchers now believe regular supplementation with glutathione could suspend or delay this aging process.

In addition, glutathione is also a brain-enhancement substance. Evidence shows that it increases the flow of blood and oxygen to the brain. This, in addition to its protective effect on the brain's cells, could boost mental functioning. It also slows declines associated with age, free radicals, and toxins such as alcohol, cigarettes, radiation, and the like.

Until recently, the only way to increase your body's levels of glutathione was by taking it itself. Now you can take N-acetyl cysteine, which is a precursor to both glutathione and glutathione peroxidase, two of the body's major detoxifying agents (a precursor is a substance used by the body to create other substances). Studies have shown that N-acetyl cysteine is a much better source of glutathione than glutathione itself, because less than half of the glutathione that is taken orally gets out of the digestive system. N-acetyl cysteine has much greater bioavailability and is far more effective.

In a study published recently in the *Proceedings of the National Academy of Science,* researchers showed that both N-acetyl cysteine and glutathione had powerful antiviral effects and can block up to 90 percent of the spread of the AIDS virus. The antiviral power in the body was directly related to the quantity of the dose.

COQ-10

> CoQ-10 is an essential nutrient that supplies the biochemical "spark" that creates cellular energy. Without it, various mechanisms in the body quickly begin to fail.
>
> —Emile G. Bliznakov, M.D., President and scientific director,
> Lupus Research Institute

CoQ-10 is, in essence, energy: It stimulates energy release. It's a vital catalyst to the creation of energy on a cellular level. Within each cell are tiny energy generators (mitochondria) that produce about 95 percent of our energy needs. CoQ-10 is held within the membranes of these mitochondria where it synthesizes a substance called adenosine triphosphate (ATP), the basic energy molecule of living systems.

Studies have shown that when levels of CoQ-10 decline, as they do with age, our organs and cells cannot meet their energy requirements. CoQ-10 supplementation has shown a variety of benefits, including energy increase, improvement of heart function, prevention of gum disease, stimulation of the immune system, and life extension.

Of greatest interest to us, perhaps: CoQ-10 has extended the life span of laboratory animals up to 56 percent. That's nothing major; it just means that if you'd normally live until the age of eighty, if you took CoQ-10, you might expect to live over 120.

But the most astonishing finding: Not only did CoQ-10 increase life span, it increased antioxidant capacity. As one study states, "CoQ-10 has the capacity to . . . protect the cells against free radicals while maintaining their required oxygen levels."

There are other effects we don't have space for here, such as the research showing that CoQ-10 leads to weight loss, immune stimulation, dramatic enhancement of athletic performance, lowered blood pressure, decreased heart disease, and enhanced mental functioning.

GERMANIUM

Germanium is causing an enormous amount of excitement among researchers. Basically, it's a mineral that received little notice for decades until a Japanese researcher, Kuzihiko Ashai, noticed that it was in highest quantities in medicinal plants. In fact, germanium is a principal component in other highly reputed herbal remedies, such as garlic, ginseng, aloe, comfrey, chlorella, and barley. After Ashai synthesized a stable organic germanium compound, germanium sesquioxide, and began testing it, he found that it had extraordinary health effects. It cured his own chronic arthritis. He and other scientists have found it to be a powerful immune system stimulator, with anticancer, antitumor, and antiviral effects. Simultaneously it acts as a powerful free radical blocker.

One primary American researcher of germanium has been Stephen A. Levine, Ph.D., a biochemist, who found that the key to the mineral's many benefits was its ability to increase tissue oxygenation and to substitute partially for or supplement oxygenation in living tissues. In fact, it has been called "vitamin O," because of its powers as an oxygenating agent. According to Dr. Levine, it activates or substitutes for oxygen—combining with red blood cells.

This means oxygenation to the brain, which means enhanced brain functioning. While the brain comprises only about two percent of the body's weight, it uses some 20 to 30 percent of the body's total oxygen consumption. Lack of oxygen means decreased brain efficiency. And there's evidence that oxygen can boost brain functioning in a variety of ways.

Germanium is showing powerful effects for those suffering from chronic fatigue syndrome, AIDS, and other complex multiple-infection syndromes, as well as candidiasis, parkinsonism, cerebral sclerosis, and eye diseases. In fact, "vitamin O" may be the most important discovery in immune system stimulation in decades.

Experts caution that only the organic form of germanium, the sesquioxide compound, can act as an oxygen catalyst. Be sure you get pure, organic germanium sesquioxide.

NOOTROPICS

The word *nootropics* is a relatively new one, created when scientists discovered a new type of drug called piracetam that boosted intelligence by increasing the power of the integrative areas of the brain. It comes from the Greek words *noos* (mind) and *tropein* (turn), meaning "acting on the mind."

The development of new nootropics is one of the hottest areas in pharmaceutical research today. Since most nootropics are synthetic, are patented by pharmaceutical companies, and are not available in the United States, I have saved the major part of my discussion of these exciting smart drugs for the next chapter.

However, scientists have recently found that certain natural substances are in fact nootropics, and these are still legal and available over the counter in the United States. Two examples are ginkgo biloba and pyroglutamate.

GINKGO BILOBA

Ginkgo specifically enhances circulation to the microcapillaries. . . . This means that ginkgo may be the most effective remedy known for many of the "side effects" of aging, such as short-term memory loss [and] slow thinking and reasoning.

—Ross Pelton, R.Ph., Ph.D., *Mind Food and Smart Pills*

This stuff sounds weird. But unlike Valium or Xanax, it's a real name of a real plant, a tree that is believed to be the most ancient tree on the planet, having been growing on the earth for over 300 million years.

The ginkgo's leaves and essences have been prescribed by medical practitioners throughout human history, and probably prehistory as well. Well over a million prescriptions for ginkgo are issued *every month* by doctors in Europe for the specific purpose of stimulating brain circulation.

It has recently been tested in the most modern scientific laboratories. The results: Ginkgo dramatically increases the flow of blood and oxygen to the brain, increases the supply and utilization of glucose in the brain (glucose is the brain's main source of fuel and energy), is a super antioxidant (it prevents free radical damage to the brain and nervous system and actually helps repair damage caused by free radicals), protects the brain and other nerve tissue from damage due to insufficient blood and oxygen, sharply increases nerve transmission, and significantly improves reaction time. It also boosts the production of adenosine triphosphate (ATP, the body's energy molecule). It is, in other words, a natural nootropic (or mind-enhancing) drug that increases brain functioning, health, and alertness.

Interestingly, EEG studies show that ginkgo extract increases the brain's alpha rhythms—the brain-wave frequencies associated with health, absence of stress, relaxation, and calm alertness—while decreasing theta activity (which can be experienced as drowsiness and inability to concentrate). Users of mind technology will find that ginkgo amplifies the effectiveness of their brain machines.

Ginkgo has been proven effective in treating any problems of reduced blood flow to the brain and extremities. This is a result of its unique property of enhancing circulation to the microcapillaries—the blood vessels that are smallest and farthest from the heart—which are the first to suffer from decreased flows of blood and oxygen, and thus the first susceptible to free radical damage and aging. Since no other substance has this ability simultaneously to relax the microcapillaries and to increase blood and oxygen flow there, ginkgo may be the single most effective remedy for many of the initial effects of aging, such as short-term memory loss, slow thinking, and much more.

Elderly subjects have shown improved memory, improved memory and reasoning, alleviation of depression, and increased energy. There's even research showing improvement in patients suffering from Parkinson's and Alzheimer's diseases.

Also of interest to sound and light machine users: Ginkgo shows evidence of improving blood flow and oxygenation in the eye and can neutralize free oxygen radicals produced in the eye.

As an herb, ginkgo is available in many forms and potencies: a 100 mg tablet may be of any potency. Check the label to be sure yours is a 50-to-1 concentration (fifty pounds of leaves to create one pound of extract), with 24 percent active ingredients (ginkgoflavonglycosides).

PYROGLUTAMATE

The amino acid from which such nootropic drugs as piracetam and oxiracetam (which we will explore in the next chapter) have been developed is pyroglutamic acid (also known as pyroglutamate or PCA). It is an amino acid that is present in meat, dairy products, fruits, and vegetables. It is also present in high quantities in human blood and cerebrospinal fluid and in the brain. That is, pyroglutamate is a naturally occurring nootropic.

Research indicates it improves learning, restores and improves memory, and reduces anxiety. Its effects seem to be quite similar to piracetam, though less powerful. Since piracetam and other nootropics are not yet available in the United States and can only be obtained from abroad, many people find that it makes sense to purchase this easily obtainable amino acid. It is available through many health food stores either alone or as arginine pyroglutamate. Most people find a dose of 500 mg to 1,000 mg of arginine pyroglutamate has pleasant as well as brain-boosting effects.

BRAIN METABOLISM ACTIVATORS

Certain nutrients and herbs stimulate the brain—or often just specific areas—and cause it to function more effectively. Tests show that these substances truly can boost IQ and have other beneficial effects on mental functioning. Some substances are only available abroad or by prescription, and I will discuss them in the next chapter. Other brain metabolism activators, such as phosphatydalserine and n-acetyl-l-carnitine, are available over the counter in the United States.

N-ACETYL-L-CARNITINE (ALC)

N-acetyl-l-carnitine (ALC) is a safe substance that in laboratory studies has increased learning and memory in young, healthy woman subjects. It has also increased alertness and attention span in those with Alzheimer's and other types of senility. Other studies have shown that these patients have improved in memory, alertness, motor activities, self-sufficiency, and social life. ALC also shows signs of protecting the brain against aging, by inhibiting the buildup of lipofuscin in the brain.

ALC falls into the category of brain metabolism enhancer. It seems to help increase the transport of fats into the mitochondria, or energy-producing centers, of the cells. Scores of studies (over fifty human trials since 1990 alone) have shown powerful effects. Also, researchers have found that ALC slows the age-related decline in nerve growth factor, which is a substance that helps keep the brain young and increases acetylcholine activity. Interestingly, ALC is still so little known that the FDA has not banned it. It should be available in your health food store by the time you read this.

DIMETHYLGLYCINE (DMG)

... DMG is a metabolic enhancer ... it maximizes the amount of energy produced for each molecule of oxygen consumed, and stimulates both branches of the immune system. DMG is an ergogenic nutrient; that is, it helps produce energy or improved physical stamina.

—Richard A. Passwater, Ph.D.

Back in the late 1970s articles were written explaining the superiority of Soviet and Eastern European athletes over Western athletes: The secret was pangamic acid (sometimes called vitamin B_{15}). Much research was cited showing pangamic acid increased endurance, strength, oxygen transport from the blood to the heart, and—here comes brain enhancement—oxygen transport from the blood to the brain.

Later research disclosed that the active ingredient in pangamic acid was dimethylglycine (DMG). In recent years, research has proven that DMG can increase oxygen transport and consumption, reduce lactic acid in muscle tissue (thus decreasing fatigue), make it easier for the body to create phosphocreatine—a vitalizing substance involved in muscle contraction—and act as a potent immune system stimulant.

Also, most interesting for users of sound and light machines, DMG has been shown to increase oxygen flow to the eyeballs, and can thus guard against any possible overuse problems caused by the flashing of the bright lights.

RNA

Ribonucleic acid (RNA) is a key to learning and memory. There's a greater concentration of RNA in the brain than anywhere else in the body. It has been shown that some of the brain fuzziness and IQ loss that accompany chronic fatigue immune deficiency syndrome, for example, is a result of decreased synthesis of RNA. RNA synthesis is absolutely essential for the creation of memory; in fact, RNA may be a memory-storage molecule itself. RNA synthesis declines with illness and declines naturally with aging—which may be why aging people seem to have less capacity for storing memories. However, oral supplementation with RNA can quickly increase the brain's supply to youthful levels.

RNA is also a powerful antioxidant and may be a key to longevity. Some experiments with rats have shown that it can increase life span by about 20 percent. RNA is present in high levels in foods such as sardines, which may be why these fish have been called "brain food." You can take pure RNA in capsule form—available at your health food store—in doses from 500 mg to 2 grams a day. Do not take RNA if you have gout or if gout runs in your family.

NEUROTRANSMITTER PRECURSORS

We now know that the brain thinks, feels, and communicates with itself, and with the rest of the body, by means of messenger molecules called neurochemicals. Some, which have relatively long-lasting effects, have been called hormones, or neurohormones. Others, with quick and transient effects, are called neurotransmitters. Some, which carry complex messages, are called neuropeptides. All of these substances are created by the body out of nutrients we consume, whether through our diet or through nutritional supplements.

Scientists have broken these neurochemicals down into their various "precursors," or substances that the body requires to manufacture them. By ingesting high levels of certain precursors, we can dramatically alter the levels of these neurochemicals in our brain and body, and thereby dramatically alter our ability to think, feel, remember, and so on. Some of these neuropeptide stimulants, such as vasopressin, are available only by prescription or from abroad, and will be discussed in the next chapter. However, an enormous variety of these neurochemical precursors are now easily available domestically, including various amino acids such as GABA, arginine, glutamine, and phenylalanine.

GLUTAMINE

The amino acid glutamine is a unique substance; it is one of the few nutrients in addition to glucose that can pass easily through the blood-brain barrier and be used as fuel by the brain cells. Thus, like glucose, it's a key nutrient and source of energy and vitality for the brain. Many describe it as a "brain energizer" or "defogger." It's a key to maintaining mental ability. In several studies, glutamine has been shown to boost IQ substantially. It also works to control excess ammonia in the body. Says Dr. Richard Passwater, "A shortage of L-glutamine in the diet . . . results in brain damage due to excess ammonia." Be sure to take glutamine, which flows readily into the brain, not glutamic acid, which does not pass through the blood-brain barrier. Experts recommend starting with 250 to 500 mg a day and building up to as much as 1 to 2 grams per day.

PHENYLALANINE

Phenylalanine is an essential amino acid used by the brain to manufacture norepinephrine (NE), epinephrine (also known as adrenaline) as well as dopamine and other neurochemicals that are called neurotransmitters, because they control the basic process of impulse transmission between nerve cells. NE and dopamine are responsible for an elevated and positive mood, motivation, alertness, and ambition and are keys to the formation of memory. In studies where NE synthesis is blocked, memory formation is impaired, and subjects also experience depression, loss of attention, and fatigue.

Heightened levels of NE in parts of the brain lead to improvements in learning, memory, focusing and attention tasks, and increases in energy and vitality. Many popular drugs, such as amphetamines and cocaine, work in part by increasing levels of NE, though they are ultimately damaging because they deplete NE levels. Stress and fatigue can also deplete NE. Levels of phenylalanine in the body decrease with age, particularly after age forty-five, so as you get older, you need more just to maintain normal levels of brain cell transmissions. By taking 100 to 1,000 mg of phenylalanine, you can boost your levels of NE—and your brain's powers—quickly.

CHOLINERGIC NUTRIENTS

Perhaps the key neurochemical involved in such fundamental cognitive and thought processes as memory, focus, concentration, and the passing of messages throughout the brain and body is acetylcholine. In fact, without sufficient acetylcholine, the brain will not function. Certain foods and other nutrients have been proven to boost the levels of acetylcholine in the brain. In doing so they also boost memory, focus, concentration, and much more. Many synthetic cholinergic drugs, such as Lucidril and Deanol, are available only abroad. However, there are excellent cholinergic substances available at all health food stores, and I will explore a variety of these nutrients below.

CHOLINE

> Our tests show that giving people choline increases their memory and learning ability . . . in other words, it makes them smarter.
>
> —Dr. Christian Gillin, National Institute of Mental Health

Choline is the nutrient that is used by the brain to manufacture acetylcholine, a principal component of brain cells and the major neurochemical messenger responsible for the processing, storage, and retrieval of information. Acetylcholine *must* be in abundant supply throughout the brain; and when acetylcholine levels drop (as happens as a result of poor nutrition, alcoholism, and aging), the result is memory loss and a decline in thinking ability. According to Harvard professor Dr. Richard Wurtman, editor of the five-volume series *Nutrition and the Brain,* "Choline or lecithin that contains choline may even improve memory among otherwise normal young people with relatively poor memory functions."

Since the choline in lecithin (phosohalydalcholine) passes through the blood-brain barrier into the brain and is transformed into acetylcholine, consuming lecithin directly increases levels of acetylcholine in the brain. It has been proven in a variety of controlled studies to prevent memory loss associated with aging and actually to *improve* memory dramatically in young, healthy adults. The brain can absorb choline very quickly, and in a period of stress, choline has been proven to provide an immediate boost in brain power. Thus a dose of choline before exams or times when you want to be at peak brain capacity can have dramatic results.

There is also evidence that choline can improve mental functioning and thought transmission by actually strengthening neurons in the brain's memory centers and slowing down the age-related loss of dendrites of those neurons.

Most important for brain enhancement purposes, a variety of studies have shown that choline supplements increase mental powers. Students at the Massachusetts Institute of Technology who took choline could learn longer lists of words and could remember better. These students had such a significant improvement in intelligence that one scientist, Dr. Natraj Sitaram, a National Institute of Mental Health Clinical Center research psychiatrist said, "We're on the right track toward the development of a 'memory pill.' " In addition to all the studies showing that choline supplements increase mental powers, the anecdotal evidence is also powerful: Again and again we hear from people who take choline that they have a clear perception that they function more effectively mentally.

Choline can be found in several forms, including choline bitartrate, choline chloride, or phosphatidyl choline (PC) as well as in lecithin. (Phosphatidyl choline is the active ingredient of lecithin.) All of these forms of choline will produce memory-boosting effects.

However, PC has unique effects that separate it from the other types of choline. In addition to passing directly through the blood-brain barrier, it is a source of the substances from which every cell membrane in the human body is made. Nerve and brain cells in particular need large amounts of PC for maintenance and growth. PC also speeds the metabolism of fats, regulates cholesterol levels, and is essential to the health of the sheaths of nerve fibers. Various types of lecithin are available at your health food store. However, lecithin that contains high levels of PC is the best for brain-boosting effects. Look for lecithin that contains at least 35 percent PC. Some brands are available that contain at least 55 percent PC. *Note:* Vitamins B_1 and B_5 (pantothenic acid) are essential cofactors for PC.

DMAE

DMAE (dimethylaminoethanol) is a naturally occurring Choline precursor found most abundantly in fish such as sardines. Small amounts of DMAE occur naturally in the brain. DMAE slips easily across the blood-brain barrier (while choline itself does not) and stimulates increased levels of acetylcholine. In this way it has a general stimulating effect on mental functioning.

There's also evidence DMAE stabilizes the cell membranes of neurons. Since degradation of neuronal membranes is one key aspect of the aging process, DMAE may have antiaging effects. In children with learning disabilities, DMAE increases attention span, decreases irritability, and increases IQ. In adults, DMAE acts as a mild antidepressant, increases mental energy, boosts attention span, and enhances the ability to concentrate while writing or studying.

Positive effects have been noted with doses ranging from as low as 10 mg per day, up to as much as 300 to 1,000 mg per day for adults. As a result of its powerful effect in stimulating increased acetylcholine, excessive doses of DMAE can cause neck and shoulder tension, insomnia, or tension headaches. Many users have noted a synergistic or potentiating effect when DMAE is taken together with phosphatidylcholine. Since high-quality (55 percent phosphatidylcholine) is so costly, many people will find it more cost-effective to combine it with DMAE.

CEREBRAL VASODILATORS

We know that the brain runs on oxygen, and the brain cells are nourished not only by oxygen but by other nutrients carried to the brain through a network of tiny blood vessels known as capillaries. When these capillaries are dilated (a process known as vasodilation), more blood can flow through them. That means more blood—and more oxygen—can flow to the brain cells. The result is a boost in alertness and intelligence. A number of natural substances, including ginkgo biloba, described earlier, and niacin, have been proven to produce increased blood flow to the brain.

NIACIN

Most people know niacin as vitamin B_3. Psychiatrists back in the 1950s and 1960s found that megadoses of niacin had notable success in curing some types of schizophrenia. Later Durk Pearson and Sandy Shaw described its aphrodisiac effects: The nutrient acts as a histamine releaser, causing flushing, tingling, and skin redness in some people. For many, this heightened skin sensitivity increases sexual pleasure. Other recent research shows that niacin is as effective as prescription drugs in lowering blood cholesterol and triglycerides. It is also a potent growth hormone (GH) releaser, producing steep rises in GH about two hours after ingestion.

Our Megabrain interest in niacin, however, springs from research indicating that it can enhance memory and other mental functions dramatically. In one double-blind placebo-controlled study, for example, only 141 mg per day of niacin boosted memory in young and middle-age subjects by 10 to 40 percent.

While timed-release niacin tablets help avoid the niacin flush, I strongly advise not using them. There have been indications the continuous release of niacin may be harmful to the liver. There are no reports of liver damage following use of regular caps or tablets, which release niacin into the system quickly. I also advise you not to substitute niacinamide for niacin: Niacinamide does not cause the niacin flush, but it also does not have most of the beneficial effects of niacin. You can minimize niacin flush by taking it with meals. Also, by starting with small doses—100 mg with each meal—and increasing your dosage slowly over a week or more, you soon become able to take up to a gram or more at a time without flushing.

MISCELLANEOUS NUTRIENTS

Numerous other nutrients function in a variety of unique ways—or in ways that are not yet clearly understood—to boost brain function. These include adaptogens and herbs of various sorts.

ELEUTHERO (SIBERIAN GINSENG)

Eleuthero is what has come be called an adaptogen: an herb that increases the body's overall immune function by a wide range of actions and restores to balance all the body's systems. In addition to its benefits for immune function, a variety of studies have shown that eleuthero can increase learning, visual acuity, color perception, and hearing acuity. It also increases the efficiency of people whose jobs require attention to detail and cause nervous tension. (One study showed that proofreaders were more effective in their work after taking eleuthero.) In addition, it can improve both physical and mental capacity under unfavorable climatic conditions. It's proven effective in treating stress-related disorders and psychological imbalances such as exhaustion, irritability, insomnia, decreased work capacity, and anxiety. This herb is something quite different from regular ginseng—be sure you look for *Eleutherococcus senticosus*.

OTHER ADAPTOGENS

Other adaptogens, including reishi *(Ganoderma lucidum)*, schizandra berry *(Schizandra chinensis)*, gotu kola *(Centella asiatica)*, panaxginseng, and astragalus *(Astragalus membranaceous)* have similar properties to eleuthero in boosting immune function, balancing bodily systems, counteracting stress, and improving mental function.

MULTIVITAMIN AND MINERAL SUPPLEMENT

Having singled out all these nutrients, I want to emphasize that nutrients in the body work synergistically: Each nutrient I described will have its greatest value when taken as part of a full spectrum of nutrients. For most people, this means that the foundation of all nutritional supplements should be a good multivitamin-mineral supplement. My mother made me take one each day, and now I'm glad she did.

As an example of how important such a simple dietary supplement can be, a recent study conducted in both Canada and England of over 1,200 young people reported that a diet supplemented with vitamins and minerals for only thirteen weeks improved the subjects' IQ by as much as *21 points!*

One double-blind study, in an Oklahoma juvenile correctional facility, had astonishing effects: Not only did the IQs of those taking vitamins increase, but, according to Dr. Stephen Schoenthaler, a sociology professor at California State University Stanislaus who conducted the study, "we basically cut the violence, the antisocial behavior, hyperactivity and all types of rule violations in half." The improvements, Schoenthaler notes, "consistently cut across all the categories. We kicked the daylights out of things like hyperkinesis, hyperactivity, insubordination, fighting, truancy and assault and battery. . . . It was really quite remarkable." The changes were so dramatic, Schoenthaler says, that

> the staff decided for itself that the improvement was too important to wait for the state government to decide the long-term policy implications of the results. The improvements took place virtually overnight—within 48 hours it chopped the rate of violence in half. Rather than go back to the way it was before the study started, the institutional staff pooled their money and bought supplements for the kids instead of waiting for the state to eventually take action.

Most studies of vitamin supplementation have been done with normal schoolchildren or adults, not those in correctional institutions. In recent years, at least six solid double-blind studies have shown that taking vitamin-mineral supplements produces significant increases in IQ. While each of these studies was by necessity short term—the subjects took vitamin supplements for only a matter of weeks—the average IQ increases were significant. And, as Schoenthaler points out, one "very important" finding of all these studies was that "one out of three kids showed a massive gain of 10 or more IQ points." To put this in a real-life perspective, Schoenthaler says, "the IQ difference between an 'average' American and a doctor, lawyer, or professor is only about 11 points. The gain observed in one out of three people [taking vitamins] is the same as might be required for an average American to aspire to be a doctor, lawyer, or professor." Most astonishing, the average length of time it took the subjects to make these massive gains in IQ was three months.

Given such impressive intellectual gains after only three months, it's interesting to speculate about what cumulative increase in IQ might be gained by taking nutritional supplements over a period of ten years or more. A word to the wise: Take your vitamins.

TO B OR NOT TO B?

In addition to the nutrients just described, you will probably want to take vitamin B supplements. One reason for this is that most multiple vitamin-mineral supplements simply don't have high enough quantities of certain B vitamins. The B vitamins are essential for many reasons, but I will limit my discussion here to their effect on mental performance and stress.

Ward Dean, M.D., and John Morgenthaler of the Cognition Enhancement Research Institute have recently called attention to an important study of the influence of several B vitamins (B_1, B_6, and B_{12}) on mental performance in target shooting. In this study one group of skilled marksmen took these B vitamins three times a day, at levels 30 to 60 times greater than the U.S. Recommended Daily Allowance (RDA). The study was controlled. (Only the researchers knew whether the participants were getting a placebo or a vitamin.) Over a two-month period, the participants were scored on their accuracy. The group that got the B vitamins showed far greater accuracy than the control group, and their superiority got better and better as the weeks passed—they showed clear evidence of long-term improvement.

On two separate occasions, competitions were held between the individuals in the study. Both the group taking the B vitamins and the control group showed declines in their accuracy—a clear result of stress. However, the B-vitamin group's accuracy declined only slightly, while the control group's accuracy declined dramatically. In a second study, the subjects received even higher doses (200 to 300 times higher than the U.S. RDA), and again, the B-vitamin group showed superior accuracy and a trend toward long-term improvement. As Dean and Morgenthaler remark, this study is "the first clear evidence obtained under double-blind conditions of improved mental functioning of the central nervous system through the use of higher-than-recommended levels of vitamins."

THIRTY-THREE
THE SMART DRUG REVOLUTION
COGNITION-ENHANCEMENT DRUGS AND PEAK PERFORMANCE PILLS*

THE EVOLUTIONARY ADVANTAGES OF GETTING SMARTER

People are ready. Just as they have seen the advantages that mind machines can bring—quick stress reduction, profound relaxation, peak mental states, enhanced performance—most people are now aware of the need of enhanced brain power. In the words of Ross Pelton, R.Ph., Ph.D., writing in *Megabrain Report*, "In a world that demands the integration of ever greater masses of information from a multitude of sources, we cannot get by with a stone age brain. During the course of evolution the mammalian brain has devoted more and more of its cortex to the task of integrating and interpreting sensory information."

Pelton points out that Dr. Corneliu Giurgea, the developer of piracetam, the first intelligence-enhancing drug, "realized that the real breakthrough represented by piracetam was that it increased the functioning of the integrative areas of the cortex." In comparing a rat brain with a human brain, Pelton points out that in the rat brain the "associative or integrative" areas are minuscule, while in humans, these areas are huge, comprising over a third of the entire brain. That is, as Pelton observes, "Most of the rat brain is occupied with receiving information and giving orders to the muscles. Most of the human brain is devoted to complex analysis of incoming information."

Pelton continues:

This human capacity to plan for the future is both a blessing and a curse. Technology has freed us from having to hunt for our food and

---

*This chapter had its origins in an article I wrote with John Morgenthaler for issue 1 of *Megabrain Report*, "Cognition-Enhancement Drugs and Peak Performance Pills: Potential Brain-Food and Mind-Machine Interactions." Thus, in many ways, John is the co-author of this chapter. My thanks to John. He has since gone on to write, with Dr. Ward Dean, the best-selling book *Smart Drugs and Nutrients*, to begin publication of the *Smart Drug News*, to establish the Cognition Enhancement Research Institute (CERI), and most recently to publish *Smart Drugs II: The Next Generation*. I will provide more information about each of these projects later in this chapter.

conquered most infectious diseases. On the other hand the pollution, environmental destruction and the population explosion threaten the existence of all forms of life on the planet. To survive we must enlarge our capacity to handle and integrate information. If ecology is the integrated functioning of life systems, the brain is a similar integrated system that must be enhanced if we are to survive.... The promise of smart pills is that they will enable us to deal with the incredibly complex problems that are pressing in on us both individually and as a society.

The fascination with smart drugs is, I believe, an intuitive cultural movement. It represents a mass gut-level understanding of this need to use our brains more effectively, to process not simply *more* information, but to process it in a way that is integrative and associative—that is, not just *process* information, but make sense out of it and emerge with new understandings.

Over the last five years there has been an exponential growth in research into and use of smart pills. As this book is being written, an enormous amount of research is going on in three key areas: (1) boosting what could be called basic or "native" intelligence, or the capacity to think, (2) increasing memory and learning, and (3) slowing down or preventing entirely aging of the brain and the deterioration in cognition, memory, and learning that seems now to be an inevitable accompaniment of human aging.

As I noted in the last chapter, researchers have divided the types of smart pills now available or now under development into six different categories:

- Nootropics, such as piracetam and related drugs, which have a primary effect on intelligence and boosting the integrative areas of the brain
- Brain metabolism activators
- Neuropeptides
- Cholinergic drugs
- Cerebral vasodilators
- Miscellaneous substances

We will examine a variety of these substances in the text that follows. At the end of the chapter I include some addresses and information about how you may order some of these smart drugs for yourself from abroad, legally.

NOOTROPIC DRUGS

PIRACETAM AND THE "SMART PILL RACE"

Piracetam has been the subject of intensive research for over twenty years. While it has proven to be a powerful intelligence booster and cerebral stimulant, it also appears to be nontoxic and to produce no side effects, even in massive acute and chronic dosages. (It's so non-toxic one Food and Drug Administration [FDA] employee reportedly claimed that since even huge doses produce no toxic effects, it can't possibly have any pharmacological effects and must be physiologically inert!) It is so remarkable in its effects and safety that its discovery by Dr. Giurgea at UCB Laboratories in Belgium sent virtually every other major pharmaceutical company scrambling to develop its own cerebral stimulant.

Some of the nootropic drugs being tested now on humans include *aniracetam, etiracetam, oxiracetam, pramiracetam, propaniracetam,* and *vinpocetine.* All seem remarkably nontoxic and free of side effects. And what's most exciting, most seem to have even greater cognition-enhancement effects than piracetam.

As yet, no nootropic drug is approved by the FDA for sale in the United States. However, drug companies, keenly aware of the multibillion-dollar potential of the drugs, are pouring big bucks into research that will satisfy FDA requirements by proving how nootropics work (which still is not well understood) and by proving their effectiveness in treating medical problems such as Alzheimer's disease and multiple-infarct dementia. No wonder. UCB Laboratories reported $1 billion in worldwide sales of piracetam in 1990 alone.

Since the first nootropic, piracetam, is still the most widely used, most readily available, and widely tested, I will explore its effects first and most fully. Brief sections on several of the most promising new nootropics follow.

Piracetam has been proven to boost learning and memory in normal subjects as well as in those who suffer cognitive deficits. It is also a cognitive enhancer under conditions of hypoxia, or too little oxygen. (Members of recent expeditions to climb Mt. Everest have included piracetam as an "essential" medication to treat frostbite and altitude-induced memory lapses.) A variety of clinical studies with human subjects, including studies of young healthy volunteers, healthy middle-age subjects with some memory decline, elderly subjects, elderly subjects with senility, and alcoholics, have proven that piracetam enhances cortical vigilance; improves integration of information processing, attention span, and concentration; and can produce dramatic improvements in both direct and delayed recall of verbal learning.

It's effective in the treatment of dyslexia, stroke, alcoholism, vertigo, senile dementia, sickle-cell anemia, and many other conditions; enhances the brain's resistance to various injuries and boosts its ability to recover from injuries; protects the brain against chemicals such as barbiturates and cyanides; and is widely used throughout Europe and Latin America (where it is sold over the counter).

The subjective effect described by a lot of people is that it "wakes up your brain." In fact, piracetam selectively stimulates the anterior or frontal part of the forebrain—that part of the brain that has evolved most recently, rapidly, and remarkably in the course of our evolution from ape to human and which is the seat of our "higher functions." The inventor of piracetam, Dr. Corneliu Giurgea, believes this integrative part of the brain is the key to human evolution. "Mankind must refashion itself by realizing its highest genetic potential in the direction that evolution is taking, that is to say, by increasing the integrative capacity of the forebrain."

Piracetam works in a number of ways to increase energy within the brain. First, it steps up the production of adenosine triphosphate (ATP), the energy storage and energy-generating molecules within our cells. It also boosts cerebral metabolism by improving cerebral microcirculation (blood flow), increasing the brain's use of glucose and oxygen. It also seems to enhance protein synthesis in the brain. (Protein synthesis is an essential step in laying down long-term memories.)

SUPERCONNECTING THE BRAIN

Perhaps the most intriguing aspect of piracetam and the piracetam derivatives we'll discuss later is that they have been proven to increase the flow of information between the right and left hemispheres of the brain. As a result of experiments with human subjects, one researcher concluded that piracetam causes the hemispheres to become "*superconnected.*" Since, as we discussed in Chapter 3, there's increasing evidence that high-level brain states—brilliance, insight, creativity, flow, peak performance, being "in the zone"—are a product of the integrated and synergistic functioning of both hemispheres simultaneously, we might suspect that piracetam enhances not only simple learning and memory but high-level, creative, or synthesis thinking.

Piracetam's capacity to superconnect the hemispheres becomes even more intriguing in light of the evidence indicating that many of the most widely used mind machines and techniques for brain enhancement (such as binaural-beat frequencies and sound and light machines) function in part by facilitating integrated hemispheric functioning. When the mind machines are used in combination with piracetam, a potentiating or synergistic effect might arise, resulting in a quantum leap in brain-enhancement effects. Initial surveys from readers of *Megabrain Reports* suggest that this is the case. In fact, the combination of piracetam with mind machines seems to draw many users into an entirely higher order of experience, which many describe as "transcendent" and "ecstatic."

Precautions. Piracetam may increase the effects of certain drugs, such as amphetamines and psychotropics. Adverse effects are rare but include insomnia, psychomotor agitation, nausea, headaches, and gastrointestinal distress.

Dosage. Piracetam, also widely known as Nootropil, is supplied in 400 mg or 800 mg tablets. The usual dose is 1,200 to 4,800 mg per day in three divided doses. (Individual tolerances and preferences vary widely.) Some literature recommends that, for the first two days, a high "attack" dose should be taken. When some people first take piracetam, they do not notice any effect until they take a high dose. Thereafter, a lower dosage may be sufficient. The drug takes effect in thirty to sixty minutes.

Sources. Piracetam is not sold in the United States. It can be purchased over-the-counter in Mexico or by mail order from the sources below.

CHOLINE AND PIRACETAM

Researchers have discovered that the combination of choline (described in Chapter 32) and piracetam has a synergistic effect that produces a greater improvement in memory and learning than the sum of each when taken alone. In one study of learning, animals receiving both substances scored four times higher than the control groups and those taking choline alone, and three times higher than those taking piracetam alone. Clinical studies of humans given piracetam and choline alone and in combination have shown similar extraordinary synergistic effects. One of the researchers, Dr. Raymond Bartus of Lederle Laboratories, suggests that in many cases (such as aging) brain metabolism is too low for optimal conversion of choline to acetylcholine; adding piracetam, which is known to boost brain metabolism, could thus produce dramatic increases in acetylcholine levels in the brain.

Individuals taking piracetam may want to supplement it with choline in any case as a safeguard, since some evidence indicates that piracetam causes acetylcholine to be used up more quickly and could deplete levels of choline inside the brain cells.

ANIRACETAM

Aniracetam, a Hoffman-La Roche nootropic, appears to be about ten times more potent in improving and protecting memory than piracetam. It was, for example, highly effective on nine different tests of learning and memory, while piracetam has proven effective on six. It seems to be more effective than piracetam in treating a wider range of problems. Unfortunately, the FDA has proven highly resistant to granting Hoffman-La Roche approval for this drug. It is not yet available, but soon may become available abroad.

OXIRACETAM

Oxiracetam, developed by Ciba-Geigy, is apparently two to three times as powerful as piracetam. Intriguingly, research shows that when oxiracetam is given to pregnant rats, their offspring proved more intelligent than control groups. Similar findings have been reported for the offspring of pregnant rats kept in "enriched environments." FDA approval is being sought for this drug as a treatment for Alzheimer's disease. It is available from overseas sources. Since it is much more potent that piracetam, doses should be smaller (between 800 to 2,400 mg per day).

PRAMIRACETAM

Pramiracetam, a piracetam analog, developed by Warner-Lambert/ Parke Davis, seems to improve learning and memory by enhancing the firing of neurons in the hippocampus (a key to the formation of long-term memories). Research suggests it is about fifteen times more powerful than piracetam. FDA approval also is being sought for this drug as a treatment for Alzheimer's disease. The drug is not yet available, but soon may become available abroad.

VINPOCETINE

Vinpocetine, a nootropic developed by Ayerst Laboratories, speeds up learning, improves memory and recall, and seems to block the action of substances that disrupt memory. It works like piracetam. In one double-blind study volunteers showed extraordinary improvements in short-term memory an hour after taking 40 mg vinpocetine. Response time on the computerized memory test was 700 milliseconds for the volunteers on the placebo, but under 450 milliseconds for those who took vinpocetine! This drug, also widely known as Cavinton, is available by mail order from the sources listed at the end of the chapter.

BRAIN METABOLISM ENHANCERS

HYDERGINE

A wealth of research going back over twenty years suggests that Hydergine may be what Ross Pelton calls "the ultimate smart pill." The substance, whose generic name is ergoloid mesylates, is made from a natural, organic source: the ergot fungus of rye plants. (It was discovered at Sandoz laboratories by the visionary chemist Dr. Albert Hofmann, also known for his discovery of another ergot derivative, LSD 25.) It increases mental abilities, prevents damage to brain cells, and may even be able to reverse existing damage to brain cells.

Hydergine acts in several ways to enhance mental capabilities and to slow down or reverse the aging processes in the brain. A few of the huge number of beneficial effects scientists have attributed to Hydergine include: increased protein synthesis in the brain; reduced accumulation of lipofuscin in the brain; increased quantities of blood and oxygen delivered to the brain; improvement of memory, learning, and intelligence; beneficial improvements in brain-wave activity; increased metabolism in brain cells; normalization of blood pressure; and increased production of such neurotransmitters as dopamine and norepinephrine. Hydergine also functions as a powerful antioxidant and thus protects the brain against the damage caused by those infamous rascally free radicals.

One way that Hydergine may enhance brain functioning is by mimicking the effect of a substance called nerve growth factor (NGF). NGF is an essential component of protein synthesis in the brain, and protein synthesis, as we have noted, is a key to the formation of long-term memory. NGF promotes the growth of dendrites—the long branching fibers by which neurons receive information from other neurons. Scientists studying the physical effects of learning on the brain have found it produces dendritic growth. Hydergine seems to work by the same neurochemical pathway as NGF to produce neural growth. NGF declines with age. Thus, supporting nerve growth may be one of the ways Hydergine has its antiaging effects.

While Hydergine is widely used for the treatment of the effects of aging on the brain, scientists have also studied its effects, both short term and long term, in normal healthy humans. These studies noted significant improvements in a variety of cognitive functions, including alertness, memory, reaction time, abstract reasoning, and cognitive processing ability.

Dosage. The U.S. recommended dosage is 3 mg per day. However, the European recommended dosage is 9 mg per day taken in three divided doses. Most of the research has been done at levels of 9 to 12 mg per day or higher. There is some evidence that 3 mg per day is simply insufficient for significant cognition-enhancement effects. It may take several weeks or even months before Hydergine produces noticeable effects. Hydergine (though not its generic counterpart) is available in a liquid capsule form (Hydergine LC), as well as a liquid and a sublingual form, all of which, according to reports, reach the brain in greater quantity then the tablet form.

Sources. Hydergine is available in the United States with a doctor's prescription. It is approved by the FDA for the treatment of senile dementia and insufficient blood circulation to the brain—your doctor may not be familiar with the uses discussed. It can also be purchased over-the-counter in Mexico or by mail order from overseas. In many cases these mail order companies sell the generic form, ergoloid mesylates. The FDA has rated the generic as biologically equivalent to the Sandoz product.

Other brain metabolism enhancers include phosphatidylserine, derivatives of griseolic acid, and naftidrofuryl.

NEUROPEPTIDES

VASOPRESSIN

Vasopressin, called "the memory hormone," is a natural brain peptide, stimulated by acetylcholine and released in the pituitary. It actually helps create, imprint, and store memories, and is essential to remembering. Apparently vasopressin is involved in picking out and chunking together related bits of information from the stream of consciousness, integrating these chunks into coherent structures, and then "imprinting" these images or concepts into long-term memory by transforming electrical impulses into complex proteins that contain memories and are stored away in the brain. Vasopressin also mediates the act of remembering the stored information.

Over twenty years ago scientists discovered that vasopressin had extraordinary effects on the memory of laboratory animals—preventing chemically and electrically induced amnesia, actually reversing amnesia, and dramatically boosting the memory and intelligence of normal animals. These findings spurred much research into the cognition-enhancement effect of vasopressin on humans. Among the key findings are that small doses of the hormone can have striking success in quickly reversing traumatic amnesia (amnesia caused by injuries such as car crashes), can reverse age-related memory loss and actually restore lost memories, and can produce sharp improvements in learning and memory using measures such as abstract and verbal memory, organizational capacities, recall, attention, concentration, focus, short-term memory, optical memory, and long-term memory. It also boosts performance in such areas as reaction speed, visual discrimination, and coordination.

Vasopressin pours out during moments of trauma or extreme arousal, which may explain why those times seem to be so deeply imprinted in our brains and are remembered with such clarity. Vasopressin is also released by cocaine, LSD, amphetamines, and Ritalin (metahylphenidate). People who make frequent use of these drugs deplete their brain's vasopressin supply. The result is depression and a decline in cognitive function. In response to this depression, the frequent user takes more of the drug, thus trying to wring more vasopressin out of their depleted brain: Ultimately the well runs dry. Vasopressin, however, is not a drug but the actual brain hormone that has been depleted, so it can produce dramatic and virtually instantaneous improvements in mood and mental functioning.

Unlike stimulants, alcohol and marijuana do not deplete but

actually suppress the release of vasopressin, which could account for the loss of memory many people have noticed when drunk or stoned, or when trying to remember events that occurred while they were high. Vasopressin can reduce the harmful effects of these drugs and enhance alertness, reaction speed, and concentration.

Anecdotal evidence suggests that vasopressin can produce a state of euphoria accompanied by self-confidence, energy, assertiveness, and a sensation of extreme mental clarity. Many people believe it is ideal for situations in which lots of new information needs to be processed and remembered—such as studying for an exam, learning a language, plowing through difficult or complex works. Some people use it for more mundane purposes, such as when they have to drive late at night and want to remain alert.

Precautions. Angina pectoris sufferers should not use vasopressin, since it can trigger angina pains. Vasopressin has not been proven to be safe for use during pregnancy.

Dosage. Vasopressin usually comes in a nasal spray bottle. Most studies showing memory improvement have been done with a dose of 12 to 16 USP per day, which is one whiff in each nostril three to four times per day. Vasopressin produces a noticeable effect within seconds.

Sources. Vasopressin (known as Diapid and produced by Sandoz) is available in the United States with a doctor's prescription, but keep in mind that your doctor may not be familiar with the uses we have discussed. (It is approved by the FDA for treatment of diabetes insipidus.) It can also be purchased over the counter in Mexico or by mail order from overseas.

Currently under investigation for their brain-boosting effect are a variety of other neuropeptides, including adrenocorticotropic hormone (ACTH) analogs, thyrotropin-releasing hormone (TRH) and its analogs, cholecystokinin-8 (CCK-8) and neuropeptide Y.

CHOLINERGIC DRUGS

CENTROPHENOXINE (LUCIDRIL)

Acetylcholine, as described in the last chapter, is the neurotransmitter used by about 90 percent of the brain's cells. Centrophenoxine, more commonly known by its trade name, Lucidril, is structurally very similar to acetylcholine. Not surprisingly, it has shown powerful effects as an intelligence booster. As a central nervous system stimulant, it increases alertness, energy, and the ability to handle stress.

Centrophenoxine has been most impressive and effective as an antiaging therapy. It has been shown to produce a thirty percent increase in the life span of laboratory animals. Perhaps the most obvious sign of aging is the appearance of brown "age spots" or "liver spots" on the skin. This pigmented material is known as lipofuscin, from the Greek *lipo* (fat) and the Latin *fuscin* (dusky), and it is the result of free radical damage in the form of the progressive buildup of toxic waste by-products of cellular metabolism, or "cellular garbage." It accumulates with age not only on the skin but also in the muscle and nerve cells. The buildup of lipofuscin in brain cells is accompanied by a decline in mental functioning and can ultimately lead to the death of the affected neurons.

Centrophenoxine removes lipofuscin deposits from brain cells (as well as from skin). That is, it actually seems to *reverse* the aging process and have a rejuvenating effect on brain cells. It also reduces the rate of lipofuscin accumulation in young brain cells and rejuvenates the synaptic structure—the area where the actual transfer of information takes place between nerve cells. This suggests that the clinical rejuvenation effects of centrophenoxine in humans may be produced by the actual regeneration of parts of the neuron.

Studies show that the drug is incorporated into cell membranes, helping them maintain their integrity longer. It also increases the rate of RNA synthesis and the manufacture of new proteins, both of which decline with age.

It is used widely throughout Europe for its antiaging properties, but studies of both animal and human subjects show that it produces improvements in alertness, learning, and memory as well.

Precautions. Centrophenoxine should not be used by nursing mothers. Adverse effects are rare but include hyperexcitability, insomnia, tremors, motion sickness, paradoxical drowsiness, and depression.

Dosage. Most experimenters take 1,000 to 3,000 mg per day. Centrophenoxine takes effect very quickly, producing an increase in alertness and a slight stimulating quality.

Sources. Centrophenoxine is not sold in the United States. It can be purchased over the counter in Mexico or by mail order from overseas.

CEREBRAL VASODILATORS

According to Ross Pelton, "Some cognitive decline in the elderly may be due to a decrease in the blood supply to the brain due to arteriosclerosis or 'hardening of the arteries' which results in a narrowing of the cerebral blood vessels." There is evidence, in fact, that as a result of free radical damage, many young and middle-age individuals suffer from a premature hardening of the arteries to the brain. Some of the beneficial effects of ginkgo biloba and niacin seem to come from their effects as a cerebral vasodilator. Vinpocetine, described in the nootropics section, also is a powerful vasodilator.

VINCAMINE

Vincamine, an extract of the periwinkle, increases blood flow to the brain and, as a result, increases the amount of oxygen available to the brain. Thus it has proven effective for the treatment of all disorders having to do with insufficient blood flow to the brain, including depression, hearing problems, high blood pressures, and vertigo.

Its major cognition-enhancing benefits are improved alertness, sharpened concentration, and improved memory. It also has impressive effects in protecting the brain against various types of memory impairment.

Sources. Vincamine is not available in the United States, but it can be purchased from European and Mexican sources.

MISCELLANEOUS SUBSTANCES

DHEA

Dehydroepiandrosterone (DHEA), a steroid hormone produced in the adrenal gland and related to the male hormone testosterone, is the most abundant steroid in the human bloodstream. It seems to trigger the release of growth hormone and is a powerful booster of immune function. Research has found it to have significant antiobesity, antitumor, antiaging, and anticancer (particularly anti–breast cancer) effects. DHEA production naturally drops by as much as *95 percent* as people age—the largest age-related decline of an important biochemical that has yet been documented. (The average drop is from about 30 mg per day at age twenty to less than 6 mg per day at age eighty.)

According to Dr. William Regelson of the Medical College of Virginia, DHEA is "one of the best bio-chemical biomarkers for chronologic age," and there's good reason to think that taking a DHEA supplement may extend your life and make you more youthful while you're alive. In animal studies, it's extended life spans up to 50 percent. In a twelve-year study of hundreds of aging humans, researchers found that DHEA levels were inversely correlated with mortality: The lower the levels, the higher the probability of death, from any cause.

Additionally, DHEA seems to be an important player in cognitive enhancement. It plays a key role in protecting brain cells from age-related degenerative conditions, such as Alzheimer's disease. The brain seems to require DHEA to function effectively. Not only does neuronal degeneration occur most frequently when DHEA levels are lowest, but brain tissue contains far more DHEA than is found in the bloodstream. In a recent experiment with brain cell tissue cultures, antiaging researcher Dr. Eugene Roberts has discovered that even very low concentrations of DHEA will "increase the number of neurons, their ability to establish contacts, and their differentiation." He concludes that DHEA plays "a significant role in normal function of neuronal cells" and that supplementation with it "may prevent neuronal loss and/or damage." DHEA also enhanced long-term memory in mice and raised the learning and memory of middle-age and old mice to the high levels found in young mice. Evidence suggests that it also can boost learning and memory in the human brain.

Dosage. The dosage of DHEA ranges from 50 mg to 2,000 mg per day. Some women have reported a slight increase in the hair on their faces or bodies with the use of DHEA. Little is known about this effect, so caution should be exercised by women. Since it's a steroid precursor with weak testosteronelike effects, it may have the same risks as testosterone. Some people taking large doses of DHEA have reported increases in feelings of aggressiveness.

Sources. DHEA is now sought by many people with AIDS because of its immune enhancement and antiviral effects. The drug is available by prescription in the United States. However, because of pressure by the FDA, it is now very difficult to obtain DHEA.

This extraordinary prescription drug, also known by its generic names phenytoin and diphenylhydantoin (DPH), was discovered in 1938 and has long been used for the treatment of epilepsy. But it's clear that it is much more than just a simple anticonvulsant. Literally thousands of scientific studies document its effectiveness in treating a multitude of medical problems, including Parkinson's disease, angina, headache, high blood pressure, hypoglycemia, asthma, diabetes, ulcers, alcohol and drug withdrawal, pain, cardiac arrhythmias, and much more.

More interestingly for our purposes, Dilantin has proven extremely effective in treating nervous disorders involving emotions and behavior: depression, moodiness, compulsive eating, violent behavior, chronic anger, irritability, fear, impulsiveness, hostility, insomnia, impatience, agitation, worry, anxiety, and pessimism.

And, even more interesting, the drug has proven to have remarkable cognition-enhancing effects. It can dramatically improve concentration abilities, boost long-term memory and comprehension, and produce sharp increases in IQ scores.

What's more, DPH increases the regeneration of tissue and speeds up the healing of wounds by promoting the growth of collagen (the most abundant protein in the body, which acts as connective tissue to hold our bodies together). It has even shown evidence of extending life span. (In one study of laboratory mice DPH prolonged their mean life span by 25 percent.)

The secret of DPH's wide range of beneficial effects seems to be that it functions by stabilizing and optimizing electrical activity throughout the body and brain. Among the ways it does this is by regulating the activity of the sodium, potassium, and calcium ions, which produce bioelectric activity; regulating the neurotransmitters that mediate bioelectric activity; and influencing the hormones (such as vasopressin, insulin, and cortisol) that function in response to bioelectrical impulses. Epileptic seizures are a product of electrical disruptions—a sudden "kindling" or firing of masses of neurons that spreads through the brain. DPH counteracts them by normalizing the brain's electrical activity. This implies that all of the disorders just mentioned, including mood and behavioral problems such as compulsive eating, moodiness, anxiety, and so on—are somehow linked to bioelectrical activity.

The idea that virtually all our capacities and functions, from healing to cognition, are dependent on the activity of a bioelectrical control system—a still little understood semiconducting DC *analog* communication system that links and regulates every cell in the human body, functioning independently of the more obvious and well understood *digital*, nerve-impulse operated "central" nervous system—is one being advanced by increasing numbers of scientists, in large part as a result of the groundbreaking research and thinking of Robert O. Becker. The extraordinary range of beneficial effects of DPH are perhaps a product of its capacity to normalize or optimize the functioning of this whole body bioelectrical system—the "body electric."

Precautions. Epileptics have been taking DPH for nearly fifty years with few problems. Side effects, which are fairly infrequent, can include nausea, headache, dizziness, insomnia, tremor, and a reduction in the body's absorption of vitamin D and folic acid.

Dosage. Epileptics generally take between 200 and 600 mg per day, but those using DPH for cognition-enhancement or life-extension purposes use from 100 to 300 mg a day, taken in two or three divided doses.

Sources. DPH is available in the United States with a doctor's prescription and is approved by the FDA as an anticonvulsant—your doctor may not be familiar with the uses we discuss. It can also be purchased by mail order from overseas.

SULBUTIAMINE

Sulbutiamine, also known as Arcalion, is a new compound that has been described as being like Hydergine, only more effective. It has been shown to facilitate wakefulness, improve long-term memory, decrease reaction time, reduce fatigue, decrease anxiety, and increase overall resistance to stress.

Dosage. Those who use sulbutiamine to combat fatigue generally take two 200 mg tablets per day, with breakfast or a morning meal, for twenty days. Users should not exceed three tablets per day, as this very powerful substance may cause severe headaches.

Sources. Sulbutiamine is not sold in the United States. It can be purchased by mail order from abroad.

DEPRENYL

Widely known as the "antiaging aphrodisiac," L-deprenyl works by enhancing the activity of the neurotransmitter dopamine. It protects brain cells that make dopamine and stimulates dopamine activity. Dopamine regulates such primitive emotions, drives, and functions as body movement, motivation, excitement, pleasure, and sexual desire. One of the main effects of cocaine is its stimulation of dopamine. The chemical structure of L-deprenyl is similar to that of amphetamine. It's chemically related to phenethylamine (PEA), a substance found in chocolate, also known as "the love drug," since people who are in love have high levels of PEA in their brains.

Developed in the 1960s by Josef Knoll, M.D., in Budapest, the drug has been proven to have a number of interesting effects. It is a very effective antidepressant of a type known as an MAO (monoamine oxidase) inhibitor. (Monamine oxidase type B seems to be the culprit in the destruction of nerve cells that causes Parkinson's disease and perhaps the process of aging itself.) In both laboratory animals and humans, L-deprenyl seems to increase sexual activity and libido. It also seems to be a powerful longevity drug, extending the life span of laboratory rats by over 33 percent.

The most widespread use of L-deprenyl has been in the treatment of Parkinson's disease, which is caused by a progressive decline in dopamine and dopamine-using cells in the brain. L-deprenyl can slow that decline significantly.

The aging process itself may be caused in part by the age-related decline in the dopamine-producing neurons. After the age of forty-five, levels of dopamine in the human brain seem to drop by about 13 percent per decade. When levels drop to about 30 percent of normal, the shaking and other symptoms of Parkinson's disease appear. The rate of change varies from person to person, and those who have a very slow loss of these nerve cells never develop the disease. However, evidence suggests that by taking small quantities of L-deprenyl regularly, you can offset that age-related decline of dopamine, and in doing so not only extend your life span, but enhance the quality of your life.

Most users report that L-deprenyl increases energy, mental alertness, feelings of well-being, sex drive, and assertiveness. Its stimulation of mental function seems to be general. In laboratory rats, those treated with L-deprenyl maintained their ability to learn for much longer than control rats. In humans, L-deprenyl has improved intelligence and mental functioning in subjects with Parkinson's disease as well as those with Alzheimer's disease.

Dosage. Dr. Josef Knoll recommends that everyone take one 5 mg tablet twice a week starting at age forty-five, and increase quantities with age to three 5 mg tablets a week after age sixty-five. He believes that this alone could increase human life expectancy by fifteen to twenty years.

This drug has a definite "Goldilocks effect" as far as dosage goes—you want not too little, not too much, but an amount that's "just right." Higher dosages are not necessarily more effective or more pleasant—most users find that too much can lead to feeling "spooky," fuzzy-headed, detached, nauseated, or "wired." Users over thirty or thirty-five may take one to two 5 mg tablets a week. Younger users find that smaller doses (1.25 to 2.5 mg per week) are sufficient.

HOW TO OBTAIN MEGABRAIN DRUGS BY MAIL ORDER

While some of the substances described are not available in the United States, or are available only by prescription, it is legal to obtain them by mail order. One reason some of these substances are not available in the United States is that they have not yet gone through the extraordinarily expensive and lengthy process required to obtain FDA approval. This does not mean, however, that using these substances is illegal. And some have been approved by the FDA for limited medical applications. This does not mean that it is not quite proper to use these substances for "unapproved" purposes.

In the April 1982 issue of the *FDA Drug Bulletin,* the agency included a policy statement clarifying the question of "unapproved" uses for drugs: " 'unapproved' uses may be appropriate and rational in certain circumstances, and may, in fact, reflect approaches to drug therapy that have been extensively reported in medical literature. . . . Valid new uses for drugs already on the market are often first discovered through serendipitous observations and therapeutic innovations." In sum, the FDA clearly approves of the "unapproved" uses as an important means for innovation and discovery.

Also, a July 1989 FDA ruling made it legal to import effective drugs used elsewhere but not available in the United States. The FDA allowed the importation and mail shipment of a three-month supply of drugs, for personal use, as long as they are regarded as safe in other countries. The ruling, FDA pilot guidelines chapter 971, was made as a result of heavy pressure from AIDS political action groups, which insisted AIDS sufferers were denied access to potentially life-saving substances that were widely used abroad but were still unapproved for use in the United States.

Recently, however, the FDA has made efforts to stop the importation of some shipments of smart drugs. As this is written, the FDA policy toward the importation of smart drugs is inconsistent and unpredictable. When you write to place an order, I recommend you send a signed letter, so that it can be returned with your shipment. This letter should include your name, address, and phone number, and your doctor's name, address, and phone number. Cognition Enhancement Research Institute (CERI) which publishes *The Smart Drug Newsletter*, suggests that the letter

should also state the following: 1) that the drug is for personal use only, 2) that the amount is within the personal-use guideline (3 months' supply), 3) that the drug is not approved in the United States, 4) that you were responsible for requesting the drug, 5) that the company shipping it to you did not engage in promotional activities related to the drug or you, 6) that your doctor will be supervising your use of the drug (provide a photocopy of the prescription, if you have one), and 7) that the drug is for treating a life-threatening or debilitating condition (you may or may not want to detail your medical condition. . . . The FDA regulations specify that the drug must be for a life-threatening or debilitating condition. If you are basically healthy, you might want to avoid the details of your medical reason for ordering the drug. If they insist, you can always argue that you are suffering from age-related mental decline [a debilitating illness] or from *aging* [a life-threatening illness].

A sample letter suggested by CERI is:

To whom it may concern:
This letter is to confirm that the enclosed medication has been obtained for my personal use under the FDA personal importation policy for life-threatening or debilitating illnesses. My physician, Dr. [name], will be providing medical supervision for my use of the drug. I have purchased the drug from [company] on my own initiative; no promotional activities on their part were involved in this transaction. If you have further questions, please call at your earliest opportunity. I appreciate any efforts you can make to expedite arrival of this important medical treatment.

[Your name, address, phone number]

[Your doctor's name, address, phone number]

Because of the sporadic crackdowns and seizures of shipments by the FDA, several overseas suppliers have shut down. Those listed below may no longer be correct when you read this. Write or fax first to obtain a price list and to be sure the company is still in operation.

FOREIGN SOURCES

QWILLERAN
P.O. Box 1210
Birmingham B10 9QA
ENGLAND

Vipharm (OL. Skouvara & Co.)
35, Agorakritoy Street, 104 40
Athens GREECE
Fax: 30-01-88-31-680

B. Mougios and Co.
Pittakou 23 T.K. 546 45
Thessaloniki GREECE
Phone: 031 859.680
Fax: 031 821.819

HDC
123 Westgate St.
Gloucester GLI 2PG
ENGLAND
Fax: 011-44-59-456-4429

World Health Services
P.O. Box 20, CH-2822
Courroux SWITZERLAND

Some sample prices are:

    Centrophenoxine (60 250-mg tablets): $10
    Hydergine (100 5-mg oral tablets): $39
    Phenytoin (Generic Dilantin, 100 100-mg tablets): $5
    Piracetam (30 1,200-mg tablets): $15
    Piracetam (60 400-mg tablets): $12
    Sulbutiamine (20 200-mg tablets): $9
    Vasopressin (12 ml nasal spray): $22

FURTHER INFORMATION

An excellent source for continuing information about smart drugs is the *Smart Drug News*, P.O. Box 4029, Menlo Park, CA 94026, (415) 321-2374. This newsletter, published by CERI, was started by John Morgenthaler, and he continues as a contributing editor. Ward Dean, M.D., is the medical editor. The editor is Steven Wm. Fowkes, who is a fount of wisdom and leading-edge information not only about smart drugs but about life extension, longevity, and health.

Morgenthaler and Dean were coauthors of the best selling *Smart Drugs and Nutrients* (Santa Cruz, CA: B&J Press, 1991), the most complete guide to smart drugs. With Fowkes, Morgenthaler and Dean have recently published *Smart Drugs II: The Next Generation* (San Francisco: Health Freedom Publications, 1993).

Fowkes publishes another excellent cutting-edge newsletter called *Forefront Health Investigations,* which focuses on more detailed, in-depth "health information on life extension and biological technology." Write to the MegaHealth Society, P.O. Box 60637, Palo Alto, CA 94306. Tel. (415) 949-0919.

Another fine source of information about smart drugs is *Mind Food and Smart Pills: A Sourcebook for the Vitamins, Herbs and Drugs That Can Increase Intelligence, Improve Memory and Prevent Brain Aging* by Ross and Taffy Pelton (New York: Doubleday, 1989).

Megabrain Report, P.O. Box 2744, Sausalito, CA, 94966, publishes cutting-edge articles about cognition-enhancing drugs along with features on other types of mind technology. Yearly subscriptions are $48 (for U.S. residents).

THIRTY-FOUR
USING SMART DRUGS WITH MIND MACHINES

POTENTIAL MIND-MACHINE BRAIN-FOOD INTERACTIONS

I took four 800 mg tablets of piracetam at a recent holistic health expo. After an hour, I sat down at a booth and donned the [light/sound] glasses and headset and put on a tape of space sounds. Within minutes, I was in theta state and out there in outer space, oblivious to the crowd. I found myself on an incredible cosmic amusement ride, flying in vast circles around the solar system. I imagined the sounds and dolphins and alien superintelligences. I had to hold back to keep from screaming with delight. Ideas for inventions and solutions to problems poured into my brain effortlessly. After twenty minutes the program ended and I leaped up, refreshed. I'd been exhausted but now I had boundless energy. A previously boring expo became a magical discovery experience.

—Wes Thomas

Writer Wes Thomas has provided us with a good description of one type of brain-machine cognitive-drug interaction. If these substances heighten our senses by turning up the volume control knob in our brains (making us more alert, heightening our perceptions), then the drugs will make our perceptions of the sensory stimuli and sensual experiences provided by the mind machines even more intense (and therefore more memorable).

But Thomas mentions another level of potential interaction that could be even more significant: dramatically enhanced creativity and problem-solving capacities. As we've noted, there's evidence that some of the cognition-enhancement substances influence brain activity in ways that are similar or parallel to the mind tools, or selectively stimulate specific areas of the brain that the mind tools also stimulate. Piracetam, for example, produces what has been called "superconnectivity," facilitating the flow of information between hemispheres, and there's increasing evidence such hemispheric integration can facilitate creativity, problem solving, and original thinking. Some of the mind machines also seem to enhance hemispheric connectivity—for example, some of the light/sound (LS) machines and the binaural-beat tapes and sound generators. Can the combination of piracetam and such brain tools be potentiating, and facilitate even greater hemispheric connectivity and greater creativity?

Vasopressin's intriguing ability to eliminate posttraumatic amnesia becomes even more intriguing when we consider recent research using cranial electrostimulation (CES) devices to treat posttraumatic amnesia (such as the work of Dr. Allen Childs, described earlier). The success of vasopressin (and Hydergine) in reversing memory loss associated with aging is also interesting in light of evidence that CES devices can have similar effects. Can CES be interacting with vasopressin or with those parts of the brain—the hypothalamus, pituitary, hippocampus—that are also affected by vasopressin or Hydergine? Could either of these substances enhance the effects of CES and vice versa, possibly leading to far more effective treatments for memory loss and the decline of other cognitive functions associated with aging?

Hydergine, Dilantin, and other cognition-enhancement substances alter or optimize electrical activity in the brain. There is also evidence that many of the brain machines, including LS, CES, motion systems, ganzfelds, and binaural-beat frequencies, alter the brain's electrical activity. Again, could there be potential synergistic effects, leading to more rapid and powerful alterations in bioelectrical patterns? Dilantin's ability to regulate electrical activity makes it extremely useful for treating epilepsy—could a combination of Dilantin and, say, LS at selected frequencies, be an effective way to "train" the brain to avoid epileptic seizures? If so, it would constitute a significant medical breakthrough.

RACHETING UP TO THE TRANSCENDENT

An even more interesting potential effect of mind tech-mind food combinations was presented to me in a conversation with an old friend. Producer of some of the greatest names in rock and R&B and former manager of "the greatest rock group of all time," this man had installed a float tank near his recording studio, where he would often go to "decompress" after long sessions. He found the float tank an invaluable tool for relaxation and recharging his batteries. After reading *Megabrain* he had become interested in the effects of binaural beats and had experimented with making binaural-beat tapes of his own. We often kept in touch over the phone. Then, some months after I had published an article about nootropic drugs in *Megabrain Report,* I got a call from him.

"Hey, Mike," he said, "I gotta tell you. . . . You know me, man,

I've never ever been what you'd call a 'spiritual' person. I've never had any kind of religious experience. You know, I'm not that kind of guy."

At that point, my interest was piqued. What had happened? I asked. "Well, after I read that article in *Megabrain Report*, I got some of those nootropics and began experimenting around. I was taking piracetam and Hydergine, and I felt pretty good. Then I took a dose and got into the float tank, and put on a beat frequency tape to listen to on the underwater speakers. Suddenly, wow, I found myself having this, well, *transcendent* experience. It blew my mind."

He told me that he had then experimented with going into the float tank without having taken any nootropics, and listening to the same binaural-beat tape, and "it was just a float. Normal. Relaxing, nice, but nothing extraordinary." So again he took piracetam and Hydergine, went back in the tank, and had another experience of God. "Each time," he told me, "it happens. I have to conclude that there is some synergistic combination of the drugs, the binaural beats, and the float that produced this transcendent experience."

Given our knowledge that transcendent brain states are a direct result of specific configurations of brain activity, including high levels of activity in the temporal regions of the brain and, perhaps, brain-wave synchrony among certain neural networks, it makes sense that some combination of brain technology—that of machines, such as the float tank, of sounds, such as binaural beats, and of synthetic analogs of brain chemicals—cleanses the doors of perception and injects us into a pure vision of a higher reality.

It's a matter of state change—a change from the state we're normally in to a state we rarely reach. We search for the right combination. In a sense, much of our lives is spent searching for that right combination of ingredients—drink a little of this, touch someone else's body in just the right way, turn the channel on the TV, eat just the right succulent foods to alter our brain chemistry . . . we all know it's out there. The right key to the right lock that opens the right door.

Mind technology is just an accelerated, amplified way of fitting all the different keys into all the different locks. Some of them don't work. Some of them open the wrong doors. Sometimes we find the right combination. And there we are. Brain tech has helped us get there. But where are we?

AFTERWORD
THE TECHNO-HUMAN LEAP:
TECHNOLOGY, EVOLUTION, AND SPIRITUAL
TRANSFORMATION

ROOT HOG OR DIE

I believe there's an evolutionary explanation for our culture's increasing fascination with tools for increasing mental powers. A driving force of evolution has been the process of adaptation to environmental pressures. Under the pressure of environmental changes—a climate growing colder or warmer, dryer or wetter—species either adapt or become extinct. It's a process evolutionary biologists call environmental selection and what others have called survival of the fittest.

Evolution is a ceaseless process. There is no guarantee that humans will continue to be a part of that process. Today we are under the pressure of enormous, unprecedented environmental changes. Our survival is uncertain. Over the past few million years, humans have responded to environmental pressures by developing new tools that gave them an advantage over other species—fire, flint tools, gathering bags, weapons, writing.

The unprecedented problems the world faces today demand mental solutions, new ideas. Human survival may depend on our ability to increase our mental powers and develop new strategies for overcoming our present crises. That is to say, *evolution may involve developing new mental powers*. Seen in this light, mind machines, devices that enhance our mental powers, may be seen as evolutionary instruments—tools for human survival.

WAKING FROM THE DREAM

One way mind technology may serve as evolutionary tools is by simply increasing our intelligence—making us smarter, able to create even better tools and devise better strategies for survival in this world, in this solar system, in this galaxy, in this universe. But they may serve as tools of evolution in another way—by providing us access to extraordinary states of consciousness that are themselves gateways into a wholly different sort of reality, one in which questions of evolution and survival take on entirely new meanings.

As the scientists investigating consciousness have discovered, the ordinary concept we have of human consciousness as something contained inside the human skull simply does not apply when we move into nonordinary states of consciousness—states such as may be experienced using mind machines or reached through hypnosis, meditation, or the use of psychedelic drugs or smart pills. In such states, reported by an immense number of people over the ages, it becomes clear that human consciousness is not bound by the concepts of the realities of space and time. Stanislav Grof, M.D., observes that "Modern consciousness research reveals that our psyches have no real and absolute boundaries; on the contrary, we are part of an infinite field of consciousness that encompasses all there is—beyond space-time and into realities we have yet to explore."

Exploration of heightened states of consciousness using mind technology confirms for many that our consensus "reality" is only one aspect of existence. For most people, the experience of this reality "beyond space-time" is one of transcendence.

THE MYSTICAL REVELATIONS OF MICHAEL JACKSON

The human spiritual craving or transcendental impulse, says Grof, is "the most vital and powerful force in human beings." But it is a force that has been systematically repressed and denied by Western culture, derided as superstition, wishful thinking, and even pathological delusion. When such a powerful human force is repressed, it emerges in other forms. When people cannot transcend their individual identities and feel themselves a part of a larger, timeless whole, they will abandon their individual identities in other ways and seek to feel part of a larger entity. It doesn't take a genius to look around and see a civilization in which vast numbers of people willingly abandon their individual identities to lose themselves in television fantasies; in which mass entertainment substitutes for transpersonal experience; in which drugs, violence, soap opera, Michael Jackson, Oprah, and the Super Bowl are the main socially approved paths to nonordinary states of consciousness.

Denied direct, transcendent experience "beyond space-time," we attempt to transcend (or escape) material reality by making our world itself something beyond space-time—a dream. As writer Michael Ventura observes:

We in the late 20th century live in the time-space of the dream. The dream's instantaneous changes, its unpredictable metamorphoses, random violence, archetypal sex; its constant cascade of supercharged imagery; its threatening sense of multiple meaning. For a quarter of a million years the dreamscape surrounded us only in our sleep, or in arts experienced by the very few, or in very carefully orchestrated religious rituals. Now, in our electronic environment, the dreamworld greets us when we open our eyes. . . . What distinguishes the 20th century is that each individual life is a daily progression through a concrete but fluctuating landscape of the psyche's projections. The surrealism, simultaneity, sexuality and instantaneous change that occur in our dreams also occur all around us. So the condition of our subconscious is now also the condition of this physical environment we've built for ourselves. . . . We reel between dream and dream—between the dreams of our sleep that speak to us alone and the dreamscape of this waking world in which we make our way through millions of dream fragments that collide around us. . . .

THE DEMOCRATIZATION OF THE ABNORMAL

Michael Murphy, author of *The Future of the Body* and cofounder of Esalen Institute, talked of a "new evolutionary domain" in which the extraordinary becomes commonplace—a democratization of the metanormal. But, denied access to the transcendent, ours has become a world in which another more sinister sort of extraordinary has become commonplace—a democratization of the *abnormal.*

The way out of the dream, of course, is to wake up. Says Grof, "Experiential self-exploration is an important tool for a spiritual and philosophical quest. It can mediate the connection with the transpersonal domain of one's own being and of existence." Many people have found that mind technology provides an effective tool for experiential self-exploration.

To some it may seem odd and paradoxical that machines—the synthetic, hard, material devices of this electronic temporal reality—may serve as gateways to the spirit, tools of transcendence. But in fact this fusion of spirituality, or the "inner quest," and science, the "external quest," is the central force of the emerging new paradigm.

THE TECHNO-HUMAN FUSION

One of the clearest examples of this emerging new paradigm is the increasing fusion of humans and machines represented by the development and evolution of "mind technology." It's clear by now that mind technology will continue to evolve, touching and ultimately transforming virtually every aspect of modern culture. I think this has now become inevitable, because mind technology embodies the central evolutionary force and historical event of the coming decade: the growing interaction and interdependence between humans and technology.

This human-machine linkage is taking many forms, some of them chilling. George Bush's war in the Persian Gulf, for example, revealed to the hundreds of millions who watched it on TV (itself one of our culture's most influential techno-human bonds) that war was no longer fought by humans armed with weapons, but by weapons armed with humans—by a human-technology fusion based on information transfer and information exchange.

But in its clear demonstration of the stunning powers of the techno-human fusion, that war also inadvertently provided a message of hope for humanity: Powers that can be used for ill can, in the right hands, be used for good. Powers that can be used to destroy a land so rapidly also can be used to turn a wasteland into a garden, to alter climates, to restore the environment, to explore space. Such wonders of human-machine information processing used to gather intelligence, direct weapons, and control armies can as easily be used to disseminate intelligence freely, promote communication, accelerate the unrestricted flow of information, provide education and medical care for billions, link us together in a global community, and promote the kind of open, cooperative scientific inquiry that can transform our lives and our universe.

As with warfare, techno-human fusion has already transformed the corporate world; entire global organizations are linked to, dependent on, and "operated by" their technological components, including immense information exchanges, databases, and processing systems. But again, as with the powers that fought the Gulf war, the enormous powers of this global human-machine system, at present guided mainly by vicious self-interest, can be used for good or ill.

There seems little doubt that if we can avoid a global cataclysm, our lives will become increasingly not just dependent on but actually fused with and inseparable from technology. For good or ill, the evolving symbiosis between humans and technology is creating our future and bringing into existence an unprecedented sort of hybrid creature, a new metahuman being who inhabits a new info-sphere reality. We are on our way to meet The Terminator—both the antihuman demon robot of the first film and the guardian angel of film II—and by the time we get there we may be surprised to find that he is us.

ACTIVE INFORMATION AND THE DANCE

This dynamic process of human-technology fusion embodies the synergetic properties of complex systems. Synergy was defined by Buckminster Fuller as "behavior of whole systems unpredicted by the separately observed behaviors of any of the system's separate parts or any subassembly of the system's parts."

Of key importance is that the evolutionary or synergetic behavior of these human-machine interactions is *unpredictable*. As I've frequently observed, information is inversely related to predictability (that is, a communication that is 100 percent predictable contains *no* information), which is why those opposed to change always oppose unpredictable events as well as the free flow of information.

This synergetic interplay among information, unpredictability, and the growing fusion between humans and technology has immense, even metaphysical implications for each of us as individuals and for the process of human evolution.

"ENFOLDMENT" AND THE DANCE OF COSMIC ONENESS

As I contemplate the growing synergetic link between humans and machines, it becomes clear that it is not only unpredictable, but also in its unpredictability and dynamism it is very much like information, an expanding, evolving network based on multidirectional informational feedback loops. This reminds me of physicist David Bohm's concept of "enfolded" or "implicate order," the key feature of which is, in his words, "that *the whole universe is in some way enfolded into everything and that each thing is enfolded in the whole.*"

Recently Bohm has proposed that this implicate order is a manifestation of what he calls active information. This active information underlies and gives form to the universe; Bohm uses the analogy of a ship on automatic pilot guided by radar waves—"The ship is not pushed and pulled mechanically by these waves," he observes, "rather, the form of the waves is sensed and a certain form of motion is given to the ship under its own power." Another analogy Bohm uses for the way a common pool of "active information" organizes the seemingly independent parts of the whole through "non-local connection" is the ballet, "in which all the dancers move together in a similarly organized way in response to the music," even though the dancers are "individuals" and may seem to be moving independently.

Bohm concludes that mind and matter, the mental and the physical, are "essentially the same process," and that active information is "a link or bridge between the two sides of reality as a whole." He emphasizes that "through enfoldment each relatively autonomous thing partakes of the whole. Through this, it partakes of all the others in gathering its information, and through the activity of this information it similarly takes part in the whole and in every part."

MIND, MATTER, INFORMATION, EVOLUTION

Perhaps this might offer us insight by analogy into the relationship between humans and technology. Like the link between mind and matter, the mental and the physical, which according to Bohm, may be "essentially the same process," the human-technology link is a product of and guided by the operation of information.

Perhaps what we are experiencing with the intensifying information exchanges and growing fusion between humans and machines is an object lesson in our personal enfoldment (as well as technology's) in the wholeness. As Bohm points out, "This wholeness is general and means that each element in the universe participates in all the others to such an extent that it is not possible to attribute what happens unambiguously to any one alone: i.e., there is a universal participation."

The idea of human-machine participation in wholeness suggests a rather startling vision. It suggests that as our human *matter* becomes linked with technological *mind* (which we still smugly call "artificial intelligence"), and as our human mind conjoins with the hard material reality of machines, our sense of a separation between mental and physical "reality" may alter. It suggests that as we learn to see that both mind and matter are essentially the same process, partaking of the implicate order, guided by "active information," our vision of our selves as relatively autonomous independent beings may alter. It suggests that perhaps, as this process is lived, we will begin to see ourselves as part of the process of "universal participation," linked beyond space and time, beyond matter and energy, to every element in the universe.

Perhaps we will see that our growing fusion with technology is not a process in which "we" are "using" technology to gain more and more control over others, or over the material reality "out there," but a process of awakening to the fact that "we" and "others" and technology, and the material reality "out there," are one. We are all dancers in the same ballet, each of us moving in apparent independence, but all guided and choreographed by the pool of active information called "the dance." And how can you tell the dancer from the dance?

HIGH-TECH CATALYST FOR SPIRITUAL TRANSFORMATION?

Of course, this vision of universal wholeness, unity, and participation is in no way dependent on our growing engagement with technology: It has been the central feature of the mystical experience for thousands of years. But likewise for thousands of years the major barrier standing between most humans and this experience of wholeness and participation in the "living spirit of the universe" has been their stubborn insistence on their essential separateness from and superiority to other existing things. Perhaps this human-technology fusion will open us up to the unitive vision by demonstrating for once and for all that we are not the lordly rulers of our domain but components of other more complex information-processing systems. What a paradox it would be, and what a refutation of the reductionist view, if our growing fusion with hard material technology, far from reducing us to something mechanical, was the catalyst for a spiritual transformation!

It's been said that the energy of human evolution has moved from genetic evolution to cultural evolution—human beings have remained genetically unchanged for millennia, while our culture has evolved convulsively at an ever-increasing rate. Yet despite our dramatic evolution we remain a flawed species, violent, frightened, unhappy, isolated from one another, destined to die alone and return to dust.

THE TECHNO-HUMAN EVOLUTIONARY LEAP

Perhaps the next great evolutionary leap will be the techno-human one. Perhaps, in learning to fuse ourselves with technology so that not only are we operating it but it is operating us, in learning to link our own biological capacities with machines so that they expand our own powers even as we enrich theirs, we may learn to leave behind our primitive sense of separateness from the universe.

In doing so we may learn to see it all—our own physical bodies and minds, the hard materials of technology, the vast universe—as configurations of active information, emerged from the implicate order, each participating in all the others and partaking of the whole, with the clear knowledge that, in the words of one mind-tech explorer, "The entire universe is everywhere alive, with everything. . . . All life is eternal. Nothing is ever lost." With such knowledge, we might begin to awaken and begin our next evolutionary step, moving at last beyond violence, fears, miseries, isolation, and death. Such an awakening might bring us, at last, to our Childhood's End.

BIBLIOGRAPHY

Abbata, D., et al. "Beta-endorphin and Electroacupuncture." *Lancet*, December 13, 1980.

Achtenberg, Jeanne. *Imagery and Healing*. Boston: Shambhala, 1985.

"An Active Voice for Glia." *Science News*, November 3, 1984.

Adam, J.E., "Nalaxone Reversal of Analgesia Produced by Brain Stimulation in the Human." *Pain* 2 (1976): 161–66.

Ader, R., ed. *Psychoneuroimmunology*. New York: Academic Press, 1981.

Adey, W. Ross. "Introduction: Effects of Electromagnetic Radiation on the Nervous System." *Annals of the New York Academy of Sciences* 247 (1975): 15–20.

Agras, W.S., M. Horne, and C.B. Taylor. "Expectations and the Blood-Pressure-Lowering Effects of Relaxation." *Psychosomatic Medicine* 44 (1982): 389–95.

Ammassari-Teule, M., et al. "Avoidance Facilitation in Adult Mice by Prenatal Administration of the Nootropic Drug Oxiracetam." *Pharmacological Research Communications* 18, no. 12 (1986): 1169–78.

Andreason, Nancy C., M.D., Ph.D. *The Broken Brain: The Biological Revolution in Psychiatry*. New York: Harper & Row, 1984.

Applewhite, Philip B. *Molecular Gods: How Molecules Determine Our Behavior*. Englewood Cliffs, NJ: Prentice-Hall, 1981.

Aranibar, A., and G. Pfurtscheller. "On and Off Effects in the Background EEG Activity During One-Second Photic Stimulation." *Electroencephalography and Clinical Neurophysiology* 44 (1978): 307–16.

Ashford, B. "To Flash or Not to Flash: The Use of Intermittent Photic Stimulation." *Australian Journal of Clinical and Experimental Hypnosis* 10 (1982): 3–11.

Assagioli, Roberto. *Psychosynthesis*. New York: Viking, 1971.

———. *The Act of Will*. New York: Viking, 1973.

Atkinson, Richard C., and Richard M. Schiffrin. "The Control of Short-Term Memory." *Scientific American*, August 1971.

Azima, H., and F.J. Cramer. "Effects of Decrease in Sensory Variability on Body Scheme." *Canadian Journal of Psychiatry* 1 (1956): 59–72.

Bailey, Ronald H., et al. *The Role of the Brain*. New York: Time-Life Books, 1975.

Baker, Deborah Ann. *Effect of REST and Hemispheric Synchronization Compared to Effects of REST and Guided-Imagery on the Enhancement of Creativity in Problem-Solving*. Faber, VA: Monroe Institute of Applied Sciences, 1985.

Bandler, Richard. *Using Your Brain for a Change*. Moab, Utah: Real People Press, 1985.

Bandler, Richard, and John Grinder. *Frogs into Princes: Neuro-Linguistic Programming*. Moab, Utah: Real People Press, 1979.

———. *ReFraming: Neuro-Linguistic Programming and the Transformation of Meaning*. Moab, Utah: Real People Press, 1982.

———. *Trance-formations: Neuro-Linguistic Programming and the Structure of Hypnosis*. Moab, Utah: Real People Press, 1981.

Banquet, J.P. "EEG and Meditation." *Journal of Electroencephalography and Clinical Neurophysiology* 33 (1972): 449–58.

———. "Spectral Analysis of EEG and Meditation." *Journal of Electroencephalography and Clinical Neurophysiology* 35 (1973): 143–51.

Barabasz, Arreed F. "Restricted Environmental Stimulation and the Enhancement of Hypnotizability: Pain, EEG Alpha, Skin Conductance and Temperature Responses." *International Journal of Clinical and Experimental Hypnosis* 2 (1982): 147–66.

Bartus, Raymond T., et al. "Profound Effects of Combining Choline and Piracetam on Memory Enhancement and Cholinergic Function in Aged Rats." *Neurobiology of Aging* 2 (1981): 105–11.

"Basic Scientific and Clinical Data of Nootropil." U.B.C. Laboratories, Pharmaceutical Division, Brussels, Belgium, 1977.

Basmajian, John V. *Muscles Alive: Their Functions Revealed by Electromyography*. Baltimore: Williams and Wilkins, 1962.

———. "Control and Training of Individual Motor Units." *Science* 141 (1963): 440–41.

Basmajian, John V., ed. *Biofeedback—Principles and Practice for Clinicians*. Baltimore: Williams and Wilkins, 1979

Bauer, William, M.D., M.S. "Neuroelectric Medicine." *Journal of Bioelectricity* nos. 2 and 3 (1983): 159–80.

Becker, R.O. *Cross-Currents: The Promise of Electromedicine, The Perils of Electropollution*. Los Angeles: Tarcher, 1990.

Becker, R.O., and Marino, A.A. *Electromagnetism and Life*. Albany: State University of New York Press, 1982.

"Becker's New Biology: Living Things in E/M Fields." *Brain/Mind Bulletin* 8, no. 11 (1983).

Beisser, A.R. "Denial and Affirmation in Illness and Health." *American Journal of Psychiatry* 136 (1979): 1026–30.

Belden, Allen, and Gregg Jacobs. "REST in a Hospital-Based Stress Management Program." Paper presented at the first International Conference on REST and Self-Regulation, Denver, CO, March 17, 1983.

Belson, Abby Avin. "New Focus on Chemistry of Joylessness." *New York Times*, March 15, 1983.

Benson, Herbert. *The Mind/Body Effect: How Behavioral Medicine Can Show You the Way to Better Health*. New York: Simon and Schuster, 1979.

———. *The Relaxation Response*. New York: Morrow, 1975.

Benson, Herbert, and R.K. Wallace. "Decreased Drug Abuse with Transcendental Meditation: A Study of 1862 Subjects." *Congressional Record*, 92nd Congress, 1st Session, June 1971.

Benson, Herbert, et al. "Historical and Clinical Considerations of the Relaxation Response." *American Scientist*, July–August 1977.

Benten, David, and Gwilym Roberts. "Effect of Vitamin and Mineral Supplementation on Intelligence of a Sample of School Children." *Lancet*, January 23, 1988.

Bentov, Itzhak. *Stalking the Wild Pendulum: On the Mechanics of Consciousness*. New York: Dutton, 1977.

Bernhardt, Dr. Roger, and David Martin. *Self-Mastery Through Self-Hypnosis*. Indianapolis: Bobbs-Merrill, 1977.

Bexton, W.H., W. Heron, and T.H. Scott. "Effects of Decreased Variation in the Sensory Environment." *Canadian Journal of Psychology* 8 (1954): 70–76.

"Bilateral 'Synch': Key to Intuition?" *Brain/Mind Bulletin* 6, no. 9 (1981).

Blackwell, B. "The Endorphins: Current Psychiatric Research." *Psychiatric Opinion,* October 1979.

Blakemore, Colin. *Mechanics of Mind.* Cambridge: Cambridge University Press, 1977.

Blakeslee, Sandra. "Clues Hint at Brain's 2 Memory Maps." *New York Times,* February 19, 1985.

Blakeslee, Thomas R. *The Right Brain.* New York: Doubleday, 1980.

Bloom, Floyd. "Neuropeptides." *Scientific American,* October 1981.

———. "The Endorphins: A Growing Family of Pharmacologically Pertinent Peptides." In *Annual Review of Pharmacology and Toxicology.* Palo Alto, CA: Annual Reviews, 1983.

Boersma, Frederic, et al. "The User of Repetitive Audiovisual Entrainment in the Management of Chronic Pain," ms., 1991.

Bologa, L., J. Sharma, and E. Roberts. "Dehydroepiandrosterone and Its Sulfated Derivative Reduce Neuronal Death and Enhance Astrocytic Differentiation in Brain Cell Cultures." *Journal of Neuroscience Research* 17 (1987): 225–234.

Borrie, Roderick A., and Peter Suedfeld. "Restricted Environmental Stimulation Therapy in a Weight Reduction Program." *Journal of Behavioral Medicine* 3 (1980): 147–61.

"The Brain." *Scientific American,* special issue, September 1979.

"Brain Electric Therapy Helpful to Cocaine Addicts." *Brain/Mind Bulletin* 98, no. 14 (1984).

"Brain 'Glue' Mimics Neuron." *Brain/Mind Bulletin* 10, no. 1 (1984).

"Brain Peptide Vasopressin Offers Clues to Depression." *Brain/Mind Bulletin* 4, no. 1 (1979).

"Brain Research Enjoying an Explosion of Interest." *L.A. Times,* January 25, 1984.

"Brain 'Self Renews' in Response to Chemical Injections, Activity." *Brain/ Mind Bulletin* 7, no. 9 (1982).

Braverman, Eric; Ray, Smith; Richard Smayda; and Kenneth Blum. "Modification of P30 Amplitude and Other Electrophysiological Parameters of Drug Abuse by Cranial Electrical Stimulation." *Current Therapeutic Research* 48, no. 4 (October 1990): 586–96

"Breathing Cycles Linked to Hemispheric Dominance." *Brain/Mind Bulletin* 8, no. 3 (1983).

Bridgewater, Gary, Clifford Sherry, and Thaddeus Marcynski. "Alpha Activity: The Influence of Unpatterned Light Input and Auditory Feedback." *Life Sciences* 16 (1975): 729–37.

Briggs, John P., and F. David Peat, Ph.D. *Looking Glass Universe: The Emerging Science of Wholeness.* New York: Simon and Schuster, 1984.

Briones, David, and Saul Rosenthal. "Changes in Urinary Free Catecholamine and 17-ketosteroids with Cerebral Electrotherapy (Electrosleep)." *Diseases of the Nervous System* 34 (1973): 57–58.

Brockopp, Gene W. "Review of Research on Multi-modal Sensory Stimulation with Clinical Implication and Research Proposals." ms., 1984.

Brody, Jane E. "Emotions Found to Influence Nearly Every Human Ailment." *New York Times,* May 25, 1983.

Budzynski, Thomas. "Biofeedback and the Twilight States of Consciousness."
In *Consciousness and Self-Regulation,* ed. G.E. Scwartz and D. Shapiro, vol
1. New York: Plenum, 1976.

———. "A Brain Lateralization Model for REST." Paper delivered at the first
International Conference on REST and Self-Regulation, Denver, CO,
March 18, 1983.

———. "Tuning in on the Twilight Zone." *Psychology Today,* August 1977.

———. *The Clinical Guide to Light and Sound.* Seattle: Synetic Systems, 1991.

Budzynski, Thomas, and K. Peffer. *Twilight State Learning: The Presentation
of Learning Material During a Biofeedback-Produced Altered State.* Proceedings of the Biofeedback Research Society. Denver, CO: Biofeedback Research Society, 1974.

Buell, S.J., and P.D. Coleman. "Dendritic Growth in the Aged Human Brain
and Failure of Growth in Senile Dementia." *Science,* November 16, 1979.

Buresova, O., and J. Bures. "Piracetam-Induced Facilitation of Interhemispheric Transfer of Visual Information in Rats." *Psychopharmacologia* (Ber-
lin) 46 (1976): 93–102.

Burr, H.S. "The Meaning of Bioelectric Potentials." *Yale Journal of Biological
Medicine* 16 (1944): 353.

———. *The Fields of Life.* New York: Ballantine, 1972.

Burroughs, William S. *The Job.* New York: Grove, 1974.

Bylinsky, Gene. *Mood Control.* New York: Scribner, 1978.

———. "Medicine's Next Marvel: The Memory Pill." *Fortune,* January 20,
1986.

Cade, C. Maxwell, and Nona Coxhead. *The Awakened Mind: Biofeedback and
the Development of Higher States of Awareness.* New York: Delacorte Press,
1979.

Calvin, William, Ph.D., and Geogre A. Ojemann, M.D. *Inside the Brain:
Mapping the Cortex, Exploring the Neuron.* New York: New American Library, 1980.

"Canadian Study Frames New Right/Left Paradigm." *Brain/Mind Bulletin* 8
(1983): 7.

Cannon, Walter B. *The Wisdom of the Body.* New York: Norton, 1932.

Capra, Fritjof. *The Turning Point: Science, Society, and the Rising Culture.*
New York: Simon and Schuster, 1983.

Carrington, Patricia, Ph.D. *Freedom in Meditation.* New York: Anchor Press/
Doubleday, 1978.

Carter, John L., and Harold Russell. "Changes in Verbal-Performance IQ
Discrepancy Scores After Left Hemisphere EEG Frequency Control Training: A Pilot Report." *American Journal of Clinical Biofeedback* 4 (1981):
66–67.

———. "A Pilot Investigation of Auditory and Visual Entrainment of Brain
Wave Activity in Learning Disabled Boys." ms., 1983.

———. "Application of Biofeedback Relaxation Procedures to Handicapped
Children: Final Report." U.S. Dept. of Education, Bureau for the Education of the Handicapped, grant no. G00800 1608, project no. 443CH00207,
1984.

———. "Use of Biofeedback Relaxation Procedures with Learning Disabled
Children." In *Stress in Childhood,* ed. H.H. Humphrey, pp. 277–300. New
York: AMS Press, 1984.

———. "Use of EMG Biofeedback Procedures with Learning Disabled Children in a Clinical and Education Setting." *Journal of Learning Disabilities* 18, no. 4 (1985): 213–16.

Ceder, G., et al. "Effects of 2-Dimethylaminoethanol (Deanol) on the Metabolism of Choline in Plasma." *Journal of Neurochemistry* 30 (1978): 1293–96.

Chase, C.H., et al. "A New Chemotherapeutic Investigation: Piracetam Effects on Dyslexia." *Annals of Dyslexia* 34 (1984): 29–48.

Cheek, D. "Short-term Hypnotherapy for Fragility Using Exploration of Early Life Attitudes." *American Journal of Clinical Hypnosis* 18 (1976): 75–82.

Ciganek, L. "The EEG Response (Evoked Potential) to Light Stimulus in Man." *Electroencephalography and Clinical Neurophysiology* 30 (1971): 423–36.

Clarke, D.L. "Vestibular Stimulation Influence on Motor Development in Infants." *Science* 196 (1977): 1228–29.

Collins, Glenn. "A New Look at Anxiety's Many Faces." *New York Times*, January 24, 1983.

———. "Chemical Connections, Pathways of Love." *New York Times*, February 14, 1983.

Cone, Clarence, and C.M. Cone. "Induction of Mitosis in Mature Neurons in Central Nervous System by Sustained Depolarization." *Science* 192 (1976): 155–58.

Connors C., et al. "Piracetam and Event-Related Potentials in Dyslexic Children." *Psychopharmacology Bulletin* 20 (1984): 667–73.

Cooper, L., and Milton Erickson. *Time Distortion in Hypnosis*. Baltimore: Williams and Wilkins, 1954.

Copeland, R.L., Jr., et al. "Behavioral and Neurochemical Effects of Hydergine in Rats." *Archives of International Pharmacodynamics* 252 (1981): 113–23.

Cousins, Norman. "Anatomy of an Illness (as Perceived by the Patient)." *New England Journal of Medicine* 295 (1976): 1458–63.

———. *The Healing Heart: Antidotes to Panic and Helplessness*. New York: Norton, 1983.

Cox, Aris, and Robert G. Heath. "Neurotone Therapy: A Preliminary Report of Its Effect on Electrical Activity of Forebrain Structures." *Disease of the Nervous System* 36 (1975): 254–47.

Csikszentmihalyi, Mihaly. *Beyond Boredom and Anxiety: The Experience of Play in Work and Games*. San Francisco: Jossey-Bass, 1975.

———. *Flow: The Psychology of Optimal Experience*. New York: Harper and Row, 1990.

Cumin, R., et al. "Effects of the Novel Compound Aniracetam (Ro-13-5057) upon Impaired Learning and Memory in Rodents." *Psychopharmacology* 78 (1982): 104–11.

Cunningham, M.D. "The Effects of Bilateral EEG Biofeedback on Verbal, Visual Spatial and Creative Skills in Learning Disabled Male Adolescents." *Journal of Learning Disabilities* 14 (1981): 208–08.

Davidson, R.J.; P. Ekman; C.D. Saron; J.A. Senulis; and W.V. Friesan. "Approach-withdrawal and Cerebral Asymmetry: Emotional Expression and Brain Physiology." *Journal of Personality and Social Psychology* 58 (1990): 330–41.

Davis, Joel. *Endorphins: New Waves in Brain Chemistry.* Garden City, New York: Dial Press, 1984.

Dean, Ward, M.D., and John Morgenthaler, *Smart Drugs and Nutrients.* Santa Cruz, CA: B&J Press, 1991.

Dean, Ward, M.D., et al. *Smart Drugs II: The Next Generation.* San Francisco: Health Freedom Publications, 1993.

Deikman, A.J. "Experimental Meditation." *Journal of Nervous and Mental Disorders* 136 (1963): 329–73.

———. "Deautomatization and the Mystic Experience." *Psychiatry* 29 (1966): 324–38.

———. "Bimodal Consciousness." *Archives of General Psychiatry* 25 (1971): 481–89.

DeNoble, Victor, et al. "Vinpocetine: Nootropic Effects on Scopolamine-Induced and Hypoxia-Induced Retrieval Deficits of a Step-Through Passive Avoidance Response in Rats." *Pharmacology, Biochemistry and Behavior* 24 (1986): 1123–28.

Desai, V.C. "EEG Biofeedback with Learning Disabled Children." Paper presented at the ninth annual meeting of the Biofeedback Society of Texas, Houston, 1983.

DeWeid, D., et al. "Vasopressin and Memory Consolidation." *Perspectives in Brain Research.* New York: Elsevier Scientific Publications, 1975.

Diamond, M.C. *Enhancing Heredity: The Impact of the Environment on the Anatomy of the Brain.* New York: The Free Press, 1988.

Diamond, M.C.; B. Linder; R. Johnson; E.L. Bennett; and M.R. Rosenzweig. "Differences in Occipital Cortical Synapses from Environmentally Enriched, Impoverished, and Standard Colony Rats." *Journal of Neuroscience Research* 1 (1981): 109–19.

DiCara, Leo. "Learning in the Autonomic Nervous System." *Scientific American,* January 1970.

DiCara, Leo, ed. *Recent Advances in Limbic and Autonomic Nervous System Research.* New York: Plenum, 1973.

Dilanni, M., et al. "The Effects of Piracetam in Children with Dyslexia." *Journal of Clinical Psychopharmacology* 5 (1985): 272–78.

Dimond, S.J., and E.Y.M. Browers. "Increase in the Power of Human Memory in Normal Man Through the Use of Drugs." *Psychopharmacology* 498 (1976): 307–9.

Donaldson, Thomas. "Therapies to Improve Memory." *Anti-Aging News,* no. 4 (1984): 13–21.

Donker, D.N.J.; L. Njio; W. Storm Van Leeuwen; and G. Wienke. "Interhemispheric Relationships of Responses to Sine Wave Modulated Light in Normal Subjects and Patients." *Electroencephalography and Clinical Neurophysiology* 44 (1978): 479–89.

Dossey, Larry, M.D. *Space, Time and Medicine.* Boulder, CO: Shambhala, 1982.

Dreyfus, Jack. *A Remarkable Medicine Has Been Overlooked.* New York: Pocket Books, 1981.

Driscoll, R. "Anxiety Reduction Using Physical Exertion and Positive Images." *Physiological Record* 26 (1976): 87–94.

Dymond, A.M., F.W. Coger, and E.A. Serafetinides. "Intracerebral Current Levels in Man During Electrosleep Therapy." *Biological Psychiatry* 10, no. 1 (1975): 101–4.

Eccles, John C. *The Understanding of the Brain.* New York: McGraw-Hill, 1977.

Eliade, Mircea. *Yoga: Immortality and Freedom.* Princeton, NJ: Princeton University Press, 1969.

Emmenegger, H., and W. Meier-Ruge "The Actions of Hydergine on the Brain." *Pharmacology* 1 (1968): 65–78.

Empson, J.A.C. "Does Electrosleep Induce Natural Sleep?" *Electroencephalography and Clinical Neurophysiology* 25, no. 6 (December 1973): 663–64.

"Endorphin Link to Pain Relief Is Confirmed." *Medical World News,* February 19, 1979.

"The Endorphins—the Body's Own Opiates." *Harvard Medical School Health Letter,* January 1983.

"Endorphins Trigger Isolation Tank Euphoria." *Brain/Mind Bulletin* 9, no. 4 (1984).

England, Ronald R. "Treatment of Migraine Headache Utilizing Cerebral Electrostimulation." Master's Thesis, North Texas State University, Denton, TX, 1976.

Evans, C., and P.H. Richardson. "Improved Recovery and Reduced Postoperative Stay After Therapeutic Suggestions During General Anaesthesic." *Lancet* 2. (1988): 491.

"Evidence Sheds New Light on Prior Right/Left Assumptions." *Brain/Mind Bulletin* 8 (1983): 7.

Exton-Smith, A.N., et al. "Clinical Experience with Ergot Alkaloids." *Aging,* vol. 23. New York: Raven Press, 1983.

Fanchamps, Albert. "Dihydroergotoxine in Senile Cerebral Insufficiency." *Aging,* vol. 23. New York: Raven Press, 1983.

Fehmi, Lester F., and George Fritz. "Open Focus: The Attentional Foundation of Health and Well-Being." *Somatics,* Spring 1980.

———. *Open Focus Handbook.* Princeton, NJ: Biofeedback Computers, 1982.

Feighner, John P., Stuart L. Brown, and J. Edward Olivier. "Electrosleep Therapy: A Controlled Double Blind Study." *Journal of Nervous and Mental Disease* 157, no. 121 (1973): 128.

Ferchmin, P.A., and V.A. Eterovic. "Four Hours of Enriched Experience Are Sufficient to Increase Cortical Weight of Rats." *Society for Neuroscience Abstracts* 6 (1974): 857.

Ferguson, Marilyn. *The Brain Revolution.* New York: Bantam, 1975.

———. *The Aquarian Conspiracy.* Los Angeles: Tarcher, 1980.

Ferrero, Enrico. "Controlled Clinical Trial of Oxiracetam in the Treatment of Chronic Cerebrovasular Insufficiency in the Elderly." *Current Therapeutic Research* 36, no. 2 (August 1984): 298–308.

Ferris, S.H., et al. "Combination of Choline/Piracetam in the Treatment of Senile Dementia." *Psychopharmacology Bulletin* 18 (1982): 94–98.

Finder, Joseph. "Dr. Bird's Brains." *Omni,* November 1983.

Fine, Thomas H., and John W. Turner, Jr. "Restricted Environmental Stimulation Therapy: A New Relaxation Model." ms. 1983

Flood, James, and Eugene Roberts. "Dehydroepiandrosterone Sulfate Improves Memory in Aging Mice." *Brain Research* 448 (1988): 178–81.

Flood, J.F.; E.L. Bennett; A.E. Orme; and M.R. Rosenthal. "Relation of Memory Formation to Controlled Amounts of Brain Protein Synthesis." *Physiology and Behavior* 15 (1975): 97–102.

Flood, J.F., G.E. Smith, and A. Cherkin. "Memory Retention: Potentiation of

Cholinergic Drug Combinations in Mice." *Neurobiology of Aging* 4 (1983): 37–43.

"Focusing: Useful Tool in Producing Insight, Creativity." *Brain/Mind Bulletin* 3, no. 17 (1978).

Foster, D.S. *EEG and Subjective Correlates of Alpha Frequency Binaural Beats Stimulation Combined with Alpha Biofeedback*. Ann Arbor, MI: University Microfilms, no. 9025506, 1990.

Foulkes, D., and G. Vogel. "Mental Activity at Sleep Onset." *Journal of Abnormal Psychology* 70 (1964): 231–43.

French, J.D. *The Reticular Formation—Physiological Psychology: Readings from Scientific American*. San Francisco: W.H. Freeman, 1975.

Friedman, E., et al. "Clinical Responses to Choline Plus Piracetam in Senile Dementia: Relation to Red-Cell Choline Levels." *New England Journal of Medicne* 304, no. 24 (1981): 1490–91.

Fukishima, Takanori. "Application of EEG Interval-Spectrum Analysis (EISA) to the Study of Photic Driving Responses: A Preliminary Report." *Archives of Psychiatry* 200 (1975): 99–105.

Gallwey, Timothy. *The Inner Game of Tennis*. New York: Random House, 1974.

"Gary Lynch: A Magical Memory Tour." *Psychology Today*, April 1984.

Gatchel, Robert J., and Kenneth P. Price, eds. *Clinical Applications of Biofeedback: Appraisal and Status*. New York: Pergamon, 1979.

Gazziniga, M.S. *The Bisected Brain*. New York: Appleton-Century-Crofts, 1974.

Gazziniga, M.S., and J.E. Le Doux. *The Integrated Mind*. New York: Plenum, 1978.

Gendlin, Eugene T., Ph.D. *Focusing*. New York: Everest House, 1978.

Gilula, Marshall F., M.D. "Protocol for 1981 Synchro-Energizer Study: Multiple Afferent Sensory Stimulation (MASS) as a Tool for Investigating Clinical Neurological Problems and Pure Noetic Research Methodology." ms., 1980.

Guili, D., et al. "Morphmetric Studies on Synapses of the Cerebellar Glomerulus: The Effect of Cetrophenoxine Treatment in Old Rats." *Mechanisms of Aging and Development* 14 (1980): 265–71.

Giurgea, C.E. "The Nootropic Approach to the Pharmacology of the Integrative Activity of the Brain." *Conditional Reflex* 8, no. 2 (1973): 108–15.

———. "A Drug for the Mind." *Chemtech* (June 1980): 360–65.

Giurgea, C.E., and M. Salama. "Nootropic Drugs." *Progress in Neuropsychopharmacology* 1 (1977): 235–47.

Glasser, William. *Positive Addiction*. New York: Harper & Row, 1978.

Gleick, James. "Exploring the Labyrinth of the Mind." *New York Times Magazine*, August 21, 1983.

Glicksohn, J. "Photic Driving and Altered States of Consciousness: An Exploratory Study." *Imagination, Cognition, and Personality* 6 (1986): 167–82.

Globus, A.; M.R. Rosenzweig; E.L. Bennett; and M.C. Diamond. "Effects of Differential Experience on Dendritic Spine Counts." *Journal of Physiological and Comparative Psychology* 82 (1973): 175–81.

Glueck, Bernard C., and C.F. Stroebel. "Biofeedback and Meditation in the Treatment of Psychiatric Illness." *Comprehensive Psychiatry* 16 (1975): 303–21.

"Glutamate May Be Key to Memory Formation." *Brain/Mind Bulletin* (1984): 1.

Gold, M.S., et al. "Anti-Withdrawal Effects of Alpha MethylDopa and Cranial Electrotherapy." Paper presented at the 12th annual meeting of the Society for Neuroscience.

Gold, Philip W., et al. "Effects of 1-Desamo-8-Arginine Vasopressing on Behavior and Cognition in Primary Affective Disorders." *Lancet*, November 10, 1979 992–94.

Goldstein, Avram. "Thrill in Response to Music and Other Stimuli." *Physiological Psychology* 8, no. 1 (1980).

Goleman, Daniel. "The Aging Mind Proves Capable of Lifelong Growth." *New York Times*, February 21, 1984.

———. *The Varieties of Meditative Experience.* New York: Dutton, 1977.

Goleman, Daniel, et al. *The Relaxed Body.* New York: Doubleday, 1986.

Gomez, Evaristo, and Adib R. Mikhail. "Treatment of Methodone Withdrawal with Cerebral Electrotherapy." Paper presented at the annual meeting of the American Psychiatric Association, Detroit, 1974.

———. "Treatment of Methodone Withdrawal with Cerebral Electrotherapy." *British Journal of Psychiatry* 134 (1979): 111–13.

Goodman, David M., Jackson Beaty, and Thomas B. Mulholland. "Detection of Cerebral Lateralization of Function Using EEG Alpha-Contingent Visual Stimulation." *Electroencephalography and Clinical Neurophysiology* 48 (1980): 418–31.

Gould, Stephen Jay. "Genes on the Brain." *New York Review of Books*, June 30, 1983.

Grady, Harvey. "Electromechanical Therapy of a Child with Down's Syndrome: A Report of a Case." *Journal of Holistic Medicine* 4, no. 2 (1982):

Graham, David. "The Effects of the Electromechanical Therapeutic Apparatus on the Electrical Activity of the Brain." ms., n.d.

Green, E.E., and Green, A.M. "On the Meaning of the Transpersonal: Some Metaphysical Perspectives." *Journal of Transpersonal Psychology* 3 (1971): 27–46.

Green, Elmer, and Alyce Green. *Beyond Biofeedback.* New York: Delacorte, 1977.

Grof, Stanislav, M.D. *Adventures in Self Discovery.* Rochester, NY: SUNY Press, 1985.

Grof, Stanislav, with Hal Zina Bennett, Ph.D. *The Holotropic Mind.* San Francisco: Harper San Francisco, 1992.

Guillemin, Roger. "Peptides in the Brain: The New Endocrinology of the Neurone." *Science* 202 (1978): 390–402.

Guillemin, Roger, and Roger Burgus. "The Hormones of the Hypothalamus." *Scientific American*, November 1972.

Haber, Ralph. "How We Remember What We See." *Scientific American*, May 1970.

Hall, Stephen S. "The Brain Branches Out." *Science 85*, June 1985.

Halpern, Steven, and Louis Sabary. *Sound Health: The Music and Sounds That Make Us Whole.* New York: Harper and Row, 1985.

Hampden-Turner, Charles. *Maps of the Mind.* New York: Macmillan, 1981.

Harding, G.F., and M. Dimitrakoudi. *The Visual Evoked Potential in Photosensitive Epilepsy.* New York: Van Nostrand Reinhold, 1986.

Harner, Michael. *The Way of the Shaman*. New York: Harper & Row, 1981.

Harth, Eric. *Windows on the Mind: Reflections on the Physical Basis of Consciousness*. New York: Morrow, 1982.

Hartmann, Thom. "The Synchro-Energizer: A Patented Device to Control Brain Waves." *Popular Computing*, November 1984.

Hatterer, Dr. Lawrence J. *The Pleasure Addicts*. Cranbury, NJ: A.S. Barnes, 1980.

Heath, Robert G. "Interview." *Omni*, April 1984.

Hebb, Donald. *Organization of Behavior: A Neuropsychological Theory*. New York: Wiley, 1961.

Henriques, J.B., and R.J. Davidson. "Regional Brain Electrical Asymmetries Discriminate Between Previously Depressed and Healthy Control Subjects." *Journal of Abnormal Psychology* 99 (1990): 22–31.

Henry, James P. "Present Concept of Stress Theory." In *Catecholamines and Stress: Recent Advances*, ed. Earl Usdin, Richard Kvetriansky, and Irwin Kopin, *Developments in Neuroscience*, vol. 8. New York: Elsevier North Holland, 1980.

" 'Higher' Brain Reorganization May Accompany Insight." *Brain/Mind Bulletin* 3, no. 6 (1978).

Hindmarch, I., et al. "The Effects of Ergot Alkaloid Derivative (Hydergine) on Aspects of Psychomotor Performance, Arousal, and Cognitive Processing Ability." *Journal of Clinical Pharmacology* (November–December 1979): 726–31.

Hochschild, R. "Effect of Diethylaminoethanol p-Chlorophenoxy-acetate on the Life Span of Male Swiss Webster Albino Mice." *Experimental Gerontology* 8 (1973): 177–83.

Hooper, Judith, and Dick Teresi. *The Three Pound Universe*. New York: Simon and Schuster, 1986.

Hoovey, Z.B., U. Heinemann, and O.D. Creautzfeldt. "Inter-hemispheric Synchrony of Alpha Waves." *Electroencephalography and Clinical Neurophysiology* 32 (1972): 337–347.

"Hormone Aids Memory Learning." *Brain/Mind Bulletin* 8, no. 7 (1983).

"Hormones Tied to Heart Ills." *New York Times*, October 24, 1982.

Hosobachi, Y.E., E. Adams, and R. Linchintz. "Pain Relief by Electrical Stimulation of the Central Gray Matter in Humans and Its Reversal by Nalaxone." *Science* 197 (1977): 183–86.

"How the Brain Works." *Newsweek*, February 7, 1983.

Hughes, J., et al. "Identification of Two Related Pentapeptides from the Brain with Potent Opiate Antagonist Activity." *Nature* 258 (1975): 577–79.

Hughes, Rohn R., et al. "An Ergot Alkaloid Preparation (Hydergine) in the Treatment of Dementia: A Critical Review of the Clinical Literature." *Journal of the American Geriatrics Society* 24 (1976): 490–97.

Hutchison, Michael. "Tanks for the Memories." *Village Voice*, July 13, 1982.

———. "Isolation Tanks: The State of the Art." *Esquire*, August 1983.

———. *The Book of Floating: Exploring the Private Sea*. New York: Morrow, 1984.

———. "The Synchro-energizer: Letting a Black Box Meditate for You." *Esquire*, February 1984.

———. "Exploring the Inner Sea." *New Age Journal*, May 1984.

———. "The Plugged-In Brain." *New Age Journal*, August 1984.

————. "Mapping the Brain for Peace of Mind." *Esquire*, November 1984.

————. *Megabrain: New Tools and Techniques for Brain Growth and Mind Expansion*, revised ed. New York: Ballantine, 1986, 1991.

————. "One Man, One Float." *Esquire*, November 1984.

————. Special Issue on Sound and Light. *MegaBrain Report* 1, no. 2 (1990)

————. "Beyond Entrainment: How to Use Mind Machines for Peak Performance." *Megabrain Report* 1 (1992): 2–12.

Iamblichus. "The Epistle of Porphry to the Egyptian Anebo." In *Iamblichus on the Mysteries of the Egyptians, Chaldeans, and Assyrians*, trans. T. Taylor. London: B. Dobell and Reeves and Turner, 1895.

Huxley, Aldous. *The Doors of Perception*. New York: Harper & Brothers, 1954.

Itil, R.M., et al. "CNS Pharmacology and Clinical Therapeutic Effects of Oxiracetam." *Clinical Neuropharmacology*, vol. 9, suppl. 3. New York: Raven Press, 1986.

Iversen, Leslie L. "The Chemistry of the Brain." *Scientific American*, September 1979.

Iwahara, Shinko; Setsuko Noguchi; Kuo Man Yang; and Oishi Hiroshi. "Frequency Specific and Non-specific Effects of Flickering Light upon Electrical Activity in Human Occiput." *Japanese Psychological Research* 16 (1974): 1–7.

Jacobson, Edmund, M.D. "Imagination of Movement Involving Skeletal Muscle." *American Journal of Physiology* 91 (1930): 567–608.

————. "Evidence of Contraction of Specific Muscles During Imagination." *American Journal of Physiology* 95 (1930): 703–12.

————. *Progressive Relaxation*, rev. ed. Chicago: University of Chicago Press, 1938.

————. *You Must Relax*, rev. ed. New York: McGraw-Hill, 1962.

Jaffe, Dennis T., Ph.D. *Healing from Within*. New York: Knopf, 1980.

Jantcsh, Erich. *The Self-Organizing Universe*. New York: Pergamon, 1980.

Jarzembski, W.B. "Electrical Stimulation and Substance Abuse Treatment." *Neurobehavioral Toxicology and Teeratology* 7, no. 2 (1985): 119–23.

Jaynes, Julian. *The Origin of Consciousness in the Breakdown of the Bicameral Mind*. Boston: Houghton Mifflin, 1976.

"Jerre Levy: Human Brain Built to Be Challenged." *Brain/Mind Bulletin* 8, no. 9 (1983).

Jevning, R. "Meditation Increased Blood Flow to Brain in UC Study." *Brain/Mind Bulletin* 4, no. 1 (1979).

John, E. Roy, and R.W. Thatcher. *Functional Neuroscience*. Hillsdale, NJ: Lawrence Erlbaum Associates, 1976.

Jonas, Gerald. *Visceral Learning*. New York: Viking, 1973.

Joudry, Patricia. *Sound Therapy for the Walkman*. Steele & Steele: 1984.

Kalil, R.E. "Synapse Formation in the Developing Brain." *Scientific American*, December 1989.

Kall, Robert. "Mind Scanner." *Omni*, February 1984.

Kammerman, M., ed. *Sensory Isolation and Personality Change*. Springfield, IL: Charles C Thomas, 1977.

Kandel, Eric R. *Cellular Basis of Behavior: An Introduction to Behavioral Neurobiology*. San Francisco: Freeman, 1976.

————. "Small Systems of Neurons." *Scientific American*, September 1979.

Kantner, R.M., et al. "Effects of Vestibular Stimulation on Nystagmus Response and Motor Performance in the Developmentally Delayed Infant." *Physical Therapy* 56 (1976): 4.

Kasamatsu, A., and T. Hirai "Science of Zazen." *Psychologia* 6 (1963): 86–91.

———. "An Electroencephalographic Study of Zen Meditation (Zazen)." *Biofeedback and Self-Control: An Aldine Reader on the Regulation of Bodily Processes and Consciousness*, ed. J. Kamiiya et al. Chicago: Atherton, 1971.

Katchalsky, A., L.E. Scriven, and R. Blumenthal, eds. "Dynamic Patterns of Brain Cell Assemblies." *Neuroscience Research Program Bulletin* 12 (1974): 1–195.

Kent, Saul. "Piracetam Increases Brain Energy." *Anti-aging News* 2, no. 10 (1981): 65–69.

———. *Your Personal Life-Extension Program.* New York: William Morrow, 1985.

"The Keys to Paradise." *Nova: Adventures in Science.* Boston: Addison-Wesley, 1982.

Kinsbourne, Marcel. "Sad Hemisphere, Happy Hemisphere." *Psychology Today*, May 1981.

Koestler, Arthur. *The Act of Creation.* New York: Macmillan, 1964.

———. *The Ghost in the Machine.* New York: Random House, 1967.

———. *The Roots of Coincidence.* New York: Random House, 1972.

Kolata, Gina. "Molecular Biology of Brain Hormones." *Science* 215 (1982): 1223–24.

Konorski, Jerzy. *Integrative Activity of the Brain: An Interdisciplinary Approach.* Chicago: University of Chicago Press, 1967.

Koob, George F., and Floyd E. Bloom. "Behavioral Effects of Neuropeptides: Endorphins and Vasopressing." *Annual Review of Psychology, 1982.* Palo Alto, CA: Annual Reviews, 1982.

Kooi, K.A. *Fundamentals of Electroencephalography.* New York: Harper & Row, 1971.

Kotter, Gary S.; Ernest O. Henschel; Walter J. Hogan; and John H. Kalbfleisch. "Inhibition of Gastric Acid Secretion in Man by the Transcranial Application of Low Intensity Pulsed Current." *Gastroenterology* 69 (1975): 359–63.

Kubie, L. "The Use of Induced Hypnagogic Reveries in the Recovery of Repressed Amnesic Data." *Bulletin—Menninger Clinic* 7 (1943): 172–82.

"Lack of Endorphins in Alcoholics Can Be Corrected." *Brain/Mind Bulletin* 9, no. 8 (1984).

Lankton, S.R., and C.H. Lankton. *The Answer Within: A Clinical Framework of Ericksonian Hypnotherapy.* New York: Bruner/Mazel, 1983.

LeCron, Leslie M. *Self-Hypnotism.* Englewood Cliffs, NJ: Prentice-Hall, 1964.

Lee, K.; F. Schottler; M. Oliver; and G. Lynch. "Brief Burst of High Frequency Stimulation Produces Two Types of Structural Change in Rat Hippocampus." *Journal of Neurophysiology* 44 (1980): 247–58.

Legros, et al. "Influence of Vasopressin on Memory and Learning." *Lancet* (1978).

Leman, K., and R. Carlson. *Unlocking the Secrets of Your Childhood Memories.* Nashville: Thomas Nelson, 1989.

Lenard, Lane. "Visions That Vanquish Cancer." *Science Digest*, April 1981.

Leonard, George. *Education and Ecstasy.* New York: Dell, 1968.

———. *The Ultimate Athlete.* New York: Viking, 1975.

———. *The Silent Pulse.* New York: E.P. Dutton, 1978.

Lester, Henry A. "The Response to Acetylcholine." *Scientific American,* February 1977.

Levine, J.B.; N.C. Gordon; R.T. Jones; and H.L. Fields. "The Narcotic Antagonist Naloxone Enhances Clinical Pain." *Nature* 272 (1978): 826–27.

Lewis, Mitch. "Sports Injuries: A Case Study." *International Electromedicine Institute Newsletter* 1, no. 2 (1984).

Liberman, Jacob, O.D., Ph.D. *Light: Medicine of the Future.* Santa Fe: Bear and Co., 1991.

Lilly, John C., M.D. *The Center of the Cyclone.* New York: Julian, 1972.

———. "Programming and Metaprogramming in the Human Biocomputer." New York: Julian, 1972.

———. *The Deep Self.* New York: Simon and Schuster, 1977.

———. *The Scientist.* New York: J.B. Lippincott, 1978.

———. "Interview." *Omni,* January 1983.

Lilly, John C., M.D., and Jay T. Schurley. "Experiments in Solitude. In Maximum Achievable Physical Isolation with Water Suspension, of Intact Healthy Persons." *Psychophysiological Aspects of Space Flight,* ed. B.E. Flaherty. New York: Columbia University Press, 1961.

Llaurado, J.G. *Biologic and Clinical Effects of Low-Frequency Magnetic and Electric Fields.* Springfield, IL: Charles C Thomas, 1974.

Lord, J.A.H., et al. "Endogenous Opioid Peptides: Multiple Agonists and Receptors." *Nature* 267 (1977): 495–99.

"Low-Level Direct Current Through Brain Affects Mood." *Brain/Mind Bulletin* 2, no. 2 (1977).

Lozanov, Georgi. *Suggestology and Outlines of Suggestopedy.* New York: Gordon and Breach, 1982.

Lubar, J. O., and J.F. Lubar. "Electroencephalographic Biofeedback of SMR and Beta for Treatment of Attention Deficit Disorders in a Clinical Setting." *Biofeedback and Self-Regulation* 9, no. 1 (1984): 1–23.

Lubar, J. F.; H.S. Shabsin; S.E. Natelson; G.S. Holder; S.F. Whitsett; W.E. Pamplin; and D.I. Krulikowski. "EEG Operant Conditioning in Intractable Epileptics." *Archives of Neurology* 38 (1981): 700–4.

Lubar, J.F. "Electroencephalographic Biofeedback and Neurological Applications." In *Biofeedback Principles and Practice for Clinicians,* ed. J.V. Basmajian, 3rd ed. Baltimore, MD: William and Wilkins, 1979.

———. "Electroencephalographic Biofeedback Methodology and the Management of Epilepsy." *Pavlovian Journal of Biological Science* 12 (1977): 147–85.

Lumsden, Charles J., and Edward O. Wilson. *Promethean Fire: Reflections on the Origin of Mind.* Cambridge, MA: Harvard University Press, 1983.

Lynch, Dudley. "Creative Flashes from the Twilight Zone." *Science Digest,* 1981.

Lynch, Gary, and Michael Baudry. "The Biochemistry of Memory: A New and Specific Hypothesis." *Science* 224 (1984): 1057–63.

MacLean, Paul D. "Contrasting Functions of Limbic and Neocortical Systems of the Brain and Their Relevance to Psycho-physiological Aspects of Medicine." *American Journal of Medicine* 25 (1958): 611–26.

———. *A Triune Concept of the Brain and Behavior.* Toronto: University of Toronto Press, 1973.

Madden, R., and D. Kirsch. "Low-Intensity Electrostimulation Improves Human Learning of a Psychomotor Task." *American Journal of Electromedicine* 2 (1987): 2–3.

Maier, W.J. "Sensory Deprivation Therapy of an Autistic Boy." *American Journal of Psychotherapy* 25 (1970): 228–45.

Mann, C.A.; J.F. Lubar; A.W. Zimmerman; A. Miller; and R.A. Muenchen. "Quantitative Analysis of EEG in Boys with Attention Deficit-Hyperactivity Disorder (ADHD): A Controlled Study with Clinical Implications." *Pediatric Neurology*, in press.

Maranto, Gina. "The Mind Within the Brain." *Discover*, May 1984.

Marcer, D., and S.M. Hopkins. "The Differential Effects of Meclofenoxate on Memory Loss in the Elderly." *Age and Aging* 6 (1977): 123–31.

"Marian Diamond: A Love Affair with the Brain." *Psychology Today*, November 1984.

Maslow, Abraham. *Motivation and Personality*. New York: Harper, 1954.

———. *Towards a Psychology of Being*. Princeton, NJ: Van Nostrand, 1962.

———. *Religions, Values, and Peak Experiences*. New York: Viking, 1970.

———. *The Farther Reaches of Human Nature*. New York: Viking, 1971.

Matteson, M.T., and J.M. Ivancevich. "Exploratory Investigation of CES as an Employee Stress Management Technique." *Journal of Health and Human Resource Administration* 9 (1986): 93–109.

Mavromatis, A. *Hypnogogia: The Unique State of Consciousness Between Wakefulness and Sleep*. Berkeley, CA: Celestial Arts, 1987.

Mayer, D.J., D.D. Price, and A. Raffil. "Antagonism of Acupuncture Analgesia in Man by the Narcotic Antagonist Naloxone." *Brain Research* 121 (1977): 360–73.

McAuliffe, Kathleen. "Brain Tuner." *Omni*, January 1983.

McCall, C., et al. "The Effect of TENS on Blood Levels of Neurotransmitters." *Association of American Dental Research*, abstract (1985).

McEwan, Bruce S. "Interactions Between Hormones and Nerve Tissue." *Scientific American*, July 1976.

McGaugh, J.L., ed. *The Chemistry of Mood, Motivation, and Memory*. New York: Plenum, 1972.

McKenna, Terence. *Food of the Gods*. New York: Bantam, 1992.

McKenzie, Richard E., Saul H. Rosenthal, and Jerry S. Driessner. "Some Psychophysiological Effects of Electrical Transcranial Stimulation (Electrosleep)." *The Nervous System and Electric Currents*, ed. N.L. Wulfsohn and A. Sances. New York: Plenum, 1976.

"Memory Enhancement Shown in New Human Studies." *Brain/Mind Bulletin* 3, no. 18 (1978).

Meredith, Dennis. "Healing with Electricity." *Science Digest*, May 1981.

Millay, J. "Brainwave Synchronization: A Study of Subtle Forms of Communication." *The Humanistic Psychology Institute Review* 3 (1981): 9–40.

Miller, E.E. *Software for the Mind: How to Program Your Mind for Optimum Health and Performance*. Berkeley, CA: Celestial Arts, 1987.

Miller, Jonathan. *States of Mind*, New York: Pantheon, 1983.

Miller, Neal. "Learning and Performance Motivated by Direct Stimulation of the Brain." In *Electrical Stimulation of the Brain*, ed. D. Sheen. Austin: University of Texas Press, 1961.

Miller, Neal, and Leo Di Cara. "Instrumental Learning of Urine Formation by

Rats; Changes in Renal Blood Flow." *American Journal of Physiology* 215 (1968): 677–83.

Millman, Dan. *The Warrior Athlete: Body Mind and Spirit.* Walpole: Stillpoint, 1985.

" 'Mind Mirror' EEG Identifies States of Awareness." *Brain/Mind Bulletin* 2, no. 20 (1977).

Mindus, P., et al. "Piracetam-Induced Improvement of Mental Performance: A Controlled Study on Normally Aging Individuals." *Acta Psychiatrica Scandinavia* 54 (1976): 150–60.

Mollgaard, Kjeld; Marian C. Diamond; Edward L. Bennett; Mark R. Rosenzweig; and Bernic Lindner. "Quantitative Synaptic Changes with Differential Experience in Rat Brain." *International Journal of Neuroscience* 2, no. 2 (1971): 157–67.

Mondodori, C., et al. "Effects of Oxiracetam on Learning and Memory in Animals: Comparison with Piracetam." *Clinical Neuropharmacology*, vol. 9, supple. 13. New York: Raven Press, 1986.

Moore, J.A.; C.S. Mellor; K.F. Standage; and H. Strong. "A Double-Blind Study of Electrosleep for Anxiety and Insomnia." *Biological Psychiatry* 10, no. 1: 59–63.

Murphree, H.B., et al. "The Stimulant Effect of 2-Diethylaminoethanlol (Deanol) in Human Volunteer Subjects." *Clinical Pharmacology and Therapeutics* 1 (1960): 303–10.

Murphy, Michael, *Golf in the Kingdom.* New York: Dell, 1972.

———. *The Future of the Body: Explorations into the Future Evolution of Human Nature.* Los Angeles: Tarcher, 1992.

Murphy, Michael, and Rhea White. *The Psychic Side of Sports.* London: Addison-Wesley, 1978.

Nandy, K. "Lipufuscinogenisis in Mice Early Treated with Centrophenoxine." *Mechanisms of Aging and Development* 8 (1978): 131–38.

———. "Aging Neurons and Pharmacological Agents." *Aging News*, vol. 21. New York: Raven Press, 1983.

Nandy, K., and G.H. Bourne. "Effect of Centrophenoxine on the Lipofuscin Pigments of the Neurons of Senile Guinea Pigs." *Nature* 210 (1966): 313–14.

Nandy, K., and F.H. Schneider. "Effects of Dihydroergotoxine Mesylate on Aging Neurons in vitro." *Gerontology* 24 (1978): 66–70.

Naranjo, Claudio, and Robert E. Ornstein. *On the Psychology of Meditation.* New York: Viking, 1971.

Neher, Andrew. "Auditory Driving Observed with Scalp Electrodes in Normal Subjects." *Electroencephalography and Clinical Neurophysiology* 13 (1961): 449–51.

"Neuron Regeneration in Lab Promising for Cancer, Aging." *Brain/Mind Bulletin* 1, no. 13 (1977).

Nickerson, V.J., and O.L. Wolthuis. "Effect of the Acquisition Enhancing Drug Piracetam on Rat Cerebral Energy Metabolism Comparison with Naftidrofuryl and Methamphetamine." *Biochemical Pharmacology* 35 (1976): 2241–44.

Nogaway, Tokuji, et al. "Changes in Amplitude of the EEG Induced by a Photic Stimulus." *Electroencephalography and Clinical Neurophysiology* 40 (1976): 78–88.

O'Leary, Daniel S., and Robert L. Heilbronner. "Flotation REST and Information Processing: A Reaction-Time Study." Paper presented at the first International Conference on REST and Self-Regulation, Denver, CO, March 17, 1983.

Oettinger, Leon. "The Use of Deanol in the Treatment of Disorders of Behavior in Children." *Journal of Pediatrics* 3 (1958): 671–75.

"Of Human Bonding: Social Attachment, Alienation." *Brain/Mind Bulletin* 5, no. 12 (1980).

Olds, James. "Pleasure Centers in the Brain." *Scientific American* 195 (1956): 105–16.

———. "The Central Nervous System and the Reinforcement of Behavior." *American Psychologist* 24 (1969): 707–19.

———. *Drives and Reinforcement: Behavioral Studies of Hypothalmic Functions.* New York: Raven Press, 1977.

Oliveros, J.C., et al. "Vasopressin in Amnesia." *Lancet*, January 7, 1978, 42.

Ornstein, Robert E. *On the Experience of Time.* New York: Penguin, 1969.

———. *The Psychology of Consciousness.* San Francisco: Freeman, 1972.

———. *The Amazing Brain.* Boston: Houghton Mifflin, 1984.

Ornstein, Robert E., ed. *The Nature of Human Consciousness.* New York: Viking, 1974.

Oster, Gerald. "Auditory Beats in the Brain." *Scientific American*, September 1973.

Ostrander, Sheila, and Lynn Scroeder with Nancy Ostrander. *Superlearning.* New York: Delacorte, 1979.

———. *Super-Memory: The Revolution.* New York: Caroll and Graf, 1991.

Osvaldo, Re. "2-Dimethyl aminoethanlo (Deanol): A Brief Review of Its Clinical Efficacy and Postulated Mechanism of Action." *Current Therapuetic Research* 16, no. 11 (1974): 1128–42.

Othmer, S.R. "EEG Biofeedback Training of Children with Attention Deficit Disorder, Conduct Disorder, and Learning Disability Problems: A Clinical Study." In John L. Carter (chair), Measurable Changes in Brain Functioning Related to Psychophysiological Self-Regulation Training (EMG, EEG and Audio Visual Stimulation). Symposium at 22nd Annual Meeting of the Association for Applied Psychophysiology and Biofeedback, Dallas, Texas 1991.

Otomo, E., et al. "Comparison of Vinpocetine with Ifenprodil Tartrate and Dihdroergotoxine Mesylate Treatment and Results of Long-term Treatment with Vinpocetine." *Current Therapeutic Research* 37, no. 5 (1985): 811–21.

Oyle, Irving, M.D. *The Healing Mind.* Millbrae, CA: Celestial Arts, 1979.

———. *The New American Medicine Show: Discovering the Healing Connection.* Santa Cruz, CA: Unity Press, 1979.

Paasch, Hope. "Wet Behind the Ears, but Learning Fast: Study Shows Floating Good for Students." Texas A&M *Battalion*, August 12, 1982.

"Pain: Placebo Effect Linked to Endorphins." *Science News*, September 2, 1978.

Patterson, Margaret, M.D. *Getting Off the Hook.* London: Harold Shaw Publishers, 1983.

Peacock, Samuel M. "Regional Frequency Sensitivity of the EEG to Photic Stimulation as Shown by Epoch Averaging." *Electroencephalography and Clinical Neurophysiology* 34 (1973): 71–76.

Pearson, D., and S. Shaw. *Life Extension*. New York: Warner Books, 1982.

Pelletier, Kenneth R. *Mind as Healer, Mind as Slayer*. New York: Delacorte, 1977.

———. *Toward a Science of Consciousness*. New York: Delacorte, 1978.

———. *Longevity*. New York: Delacorte, 1981.

Pelton, Ross, and T.C. Pelton. *Mind Food and Smart Pills: A Sourcebook for the Vitamins, Herbs, and Drugs That Can Increase Intelligence, Improve Memory, and Prevent Aging*. New York: Doubleday, 1989.

Penfield, Wilder. *The Mystery of the Mind*. Princeton, NJ: Princeton University Press, 1975.

Peniston, E.G., and P.J. Kulkowski. "Alpha-Theta Brainwave Training and B-endorphin Levels in Alcoholics." *Alcoholism* 13 (1989): 271–79.

"People Can Outgrow Low IQ." *Brain/Mind Bulletin* 7, no. 15 (1982).

Persinger, M.A. *ELF and VLF Electromagnetic Field Effects*. New York: Plenum, 1974.

Pert, Candace. "Neuropeptides and Their Receptors: A Psychosomatic Network." *The Journal of Immunology*, 135:2 (1985) 820–26.

Petrenko, E.T. "Effects of Flashes on Spectral Composition of Brain Potentials and Biomechanical Efficiency of Equilibrium." *Human Physiology* 8 (1982): 64–68.

Pfeiffer, Carl C., et al. "Stimulant Effect of 2-Dimethyl-1-aminoethanol: Possible Precursor of Brain Acetylcholine." *Science* 126 (1957): 610–11.

Pfurtscheller, Gert; Pierre Buser; Fernando H. Lopes da Silva; and Hellmuth Petche. *Rhythmic EEG Activities and Cortical Functioning*. Amsterdam: Elsevier/North Holland Biomedical Press, 1980.

Physiological Psychology: Readings from Scientific American. San Francisco: Freeman, 1971.

Pines, Maya. *The Brain Changers: Scientists and the New Mind Control*. New York: Harcourt Brace Jovanovich, 1973.

Pomeranz, B. "Brain's Opiates at Work in Acupuncture." *New Scientist* 6 (1977): 12–13.

"Pre-Birth Memories Appear to Have Lasting Effect." *Brain/Mind Bulletin* 7, no. 5 (1982).

Presman, A.S. *Electromagnetic Fields and Life*. New York: Plenum, 1970.

Prigogine, Ilya. *From Being to Becoming*. San Francisco: Freeman, 1980.

"Prigogine's Science of Becoming." *Brain/Mind Bulletin* 4, no. 13 (1979).

Prigogine, Ilya, and Isabelle Stengers. *Order Out of Chaos: Man's New Dialogue with Nature*. New York: Bantam, 1984.

Rao, Dodda B., and John R. Norris. "A Double-Blind Investigation of Hydergine in the Treatment of Cerebrovascular Insufficiency in the Elderly." *Johns Hopkins Medical Journal* 130 (1971): 317–23.

"Rats Can't Learn Without Aid of Norepinephrine." *Brain/Mind Bulletin* 4, no. 13 (1979).

Regan, D. "Some Characteristics of Average Steady-State and Transient Responses Evoked by Modulated Light." *Electroencephalography and Clinical Neurophysiology* 20 (1966): 238–48.

Restak, Richard M., M.D. *The Brain: The Last Frontier*. New York: Doubleday, 1979.

Reston, James, Jr. "Mission to a Mind." *Omni*, July 1984.

Reznick, O. "The Psychoactive Properties of Diphenylhydantoin: Experiences with Prisoners and Juvenile Delinquents." *International Journal of Neuropsychiatry* 3 (1967): 30–48.

Richardson, A., and F. McAndrew. "The Effects of Photic Stimulation and Private Self-Consciousness on the Complexity of Visual Imagination Imagery." *British Journal of Psychology* 81 (1990): 381–94.

Rider, M.S. "The Effect of Music, Imagery, and Relaxation on Adrenal Corticosteroids and Re-Entrainment of Circadian Rhythms." *Journal of Music Therapy* 22, no. 1 (1985): 46–58.

———. "Entrainment Mechanisms Are Involved in Pain Reduction, Muscle Relaxation, and Music-Guided Imagery." *Journal of Music Therapy* 22, no. 4 (1985): 183–92.

Riga, S., and D. Riga "Effects of Centrophenoxine on the Lipofuscin Pigments of the Nervous System of Old Rats." *Brain Research* 72 (1974): 265–75.

Robbins, Anthony. *Unlimited Power*. New York: Fawcett, 1986.

Rogers, M., D. Dubey, and P. Reich. "The Influence of the Psyche and the Brain on Immunity and Disease Susceptibility: A Critical Review." *Psychosomatic Medicine* 41 (1979): 147–64.

Rosenblatt, Seymour, M.D., and Reynolds Dodson. *Beyond Valium: The Brave New World of Psychochemistry*. New York: Putnam, 1981.

Rosenthal, Saul H. "Electrosleep: A Double-Blind Clinical Study." *Biological Psychiatry* 4, no. 2 (1972): 179–85.

———. "Alterations in Serum Thyroxine with Cerebral Electrotherapy (Electrosleep)." *Archives of General Psychiatry* 28 (1973): 28–29.

Rosenthal, Saul H., and Norman L. Wulfsohn. "Electrosleep, A Clinical Trial." *American Journal of Psychiatry* 127, no. 4 (1970): 533–34.

———. "Electrosleep: A Preliminary Communication." *Journal of Nervous and Mental Disease* 151, no. 2 (1970): 146–51.

———. "Studies of Electrosleep with Active and Simulated Treatment." *Current Therapeutic Research* 12, no. 3 (1970): 126–30.

Rosenzweig, Mark R. "Brain Changes in Response to Experience." *Scientific American*, February 1972.

———. "Experience, Memory, and the Brain." *American Psychologist*, April 1984.

Rosenzweig, Mark R., Edward L. Bennett, and Marian C. Diamond. "Effect of Differential Environments on Brain Anatomy and Brain Chemistry." In *Psychopathology of Mental Development*, ed. J. Zubin and G. Jervis. New York: Grune and Stratton, 1967.

Rossi, A.M.; P.E. Nathan; R.H. Harrison; and P. Solomon. "Operant Responding for Visual Stimuli During Sensory Deprivation: Effect of Meaningfulness." *Journal of Abnormal Psychology* 79 (1969): 188–93.

Rossi, Ernest Lawrence, Ph.D. *The Psychobiology of Mind-Body Healing*. New York: W.W. Norton, 1986.

Rossi, E.L., and David Mimmons, *The Twenty Minute Break* (L.A.: Tarcher, 1991).

Rossier, J., F.E. Bloom, and R. Guillemin. "Stimulation of Human Periaqueductal Gray for Pain Relief Increases Immunoreactive Beta-Endorphin in Ventricular Fluid." *Science*, January 19, 1979.

Routtenberg, Aryeh. "The Reward System of the Brain." *Scientific American*, November 1978.

Routtenberg, Aryeh, and Rebecca Santos-Anderson. "The Role of Prefrontal

Cortex in Intracranial Self-stimulation." In *Handbook of Psychopharmacology*, vol. 8, ed. Leslie L. Iversen, Susan D. Iversen, and Solomon H. Snyder. New York: Plenum, 1977.

Rubin, F. *Current Research in Hypnopaedia*. London: MacDonald, 1968.

———. "Learning and Sleep." *Nature* 226 (1970): 447.

Rugg, M.D., and A.M.J. Dickens. "Dissociation of Alpha and Theta Activity as a Function of Verbal and Visuospatial Tasks." *Electroencephalography and Clinical Neurophysiology* 53 (1982): 201–7.

Russell, H.L., and J.L. Carter. "EEG and Hemispheric Specific Biofeedback." Paper presented at the 13th annual meeting of the Biofeedback Society of America, Chicago, 1982.

———. "Cognitive and Behavioral Changes in Learning Disabled Children Following the Use of Audio-Visual Stimulation: The Trinity Project." Paper presented at the 16th annual meeting of the Biofeedback Society of Texas, Dallas, 1990.

———. "The Effects of Cognitive Task on Brain Function as Indicated by Brain Mapping: Normal vs. Dysfunctional Groups." Paper presented at the 16th annual meeting of the Biofeedback Society of Texas, Dallas, 1990.

Russell, H.L.; J.L. Carter; M.A. Desai; and N. Wang. "Some New and Old Approaches in Stroke and Closed Head Injury Rehabilitation: EEG and EMG Biofeedback and Traditional Chinese Medicine." Symposium at the 14th annual meeting of the Biofeedback Society of Texas, San Antonio, 1988.

Russell, Peter. *The Brain Book*. New York: Hawthorn, 1979.

———. *The Global Brain: Speculations on the Evolutionary Leap to Planetary Consciousness*. Los Angeles: Tarcher, 1983.

Ryan, Joseph J., and Gary T. Souheaver. "Effects of Transcerebral Electrotherapy (Electrosleep) on State Anxiety According to Suggestibility Levels." *Biological Psychiatry* 11, no. 2 (1976): 233–37.

———. "The Role of Sleep in Electrosleep Therapy for Anxiety." *Diseases of the Nervous System* 38, no. 7 (1977): 515–17.

Sagan, Carl. *Dragons of Eden*. New York: Random House, 1977.

Salk, L. "The Role of the Heartbeat in the Relations Between Mother and Infant." *Scientific American*, March 1973.

Samuels, Mike, M.D., and Nancy Samuels. *Seeing with the Mind's Eye*. New York: Random House, 1975.

San Martini, P.; R. Venturinni; G.A. Zapponi; and A. Loizzo. "Interaction Between Intermittent Photic Stimulation and Auditory Stimulation on the Human EEG." *Neurophysiology* 5 (1979): 201–6.

Satterfield, J.H. "Response to Stimulant Drug Treatment in Hyperactive Children: Prediction from EEG and Neurological Findings." *Journal of Autism and Childhood Schizophrenia*, no. 1 (1973): 36–48.

Satterfield, J.H., and M.E. Dawson. "Electrodermal Correlates of Hyperactivity in Children." *Psychophysiology* vol. 8 (1971): 191–7.

Sausa, Alan De, and P.C. Choudbury. "A Psychometric Evaluation of Electrosleep." *Indian Journal of Psychiatry* 17 (1975): 133–37.

Schacter, D.L. "EEG Theta Waves and Psychological Phenomena: A Review and Analysis." *Biological Psychology* 5 (1977): 47–82.

Schmeck, Harold M., Jr. "The Biology of Fear and Anxiety: Evidence Points to Chemical Triggers." *New York Times*, September 7, 1982.

———. "Addict's Brain: Chemistry Holds Hope for Answers." *New York Times*, January 25, 1983.

———. "Explosion of Data on Brain Cell Reveals Its Great Complexity." *New York Times*, March 6, 1984.

———. "Study Says Smile May Indeed Be an Umbrella." *New York Times*, September 9, 1983.

———. "Domination Is Linked to Chemical in the Brain." *New York Times*, September 27, 1983.

Schmitt, Richard, et al. "Cranial Electrotherapy Stimulation of Cognitive Brain Dysfunction in Chemical Dependence." *Journal of Clinical Psychiatry* 45, no. 2 (1984).

———. "Cranial Electrotherapy Stimulation as a Treatment for Anxiety in Chemically Dependent Persons." *Clinical and Experiemental Research* 10, no. 2 (March–April 1986).

Schul, Bill D. *Conceptual Discussion of Work Plans*. Faber, VA: Monroe Institute of Applied Sciences, n.d.

———. "Effects of Audio Signals on Brainwaves." Faber, VA: Monroe Institute of Applied Sciences, n.d.

Schultz, Duane P. *Sensory Restriction: Effects on Behavior*. New York: Academic Press, 1965.

Schultz, Johannes. "The Clinical Importance of 'Inward Seeing' in Autogenic Training." *British Journal of Medical Hypnotism* 11 (1960): 26–28.

Schultz, Johannes, and Wolfgang Luthe. *Autogenic Training: A Psychophysiological Approach in Psychotherapy*. New York: Grune and Stratton, 1959.

"Self-Organizing Brain Models Cooperative Action." *Brain/Mind Bulletin* 9, no. 17 (1984).

Selye, Hans, M.D. *The Stress of Life*, rev. ed. New York: McGraw-Hill, 1976.

Shafi, Mahammad, M.D. "Meditation and Prevention of Drug Abuse." *American Journal of Psychiatry* 132 (1975): 942–45.

Shafi, Mahammad, M.D., R. Lavely, and R. Jaffe. "Meditation and Marijuana." *American Journal of Psychiatry* 131 (1974): 60–63.

Shealy, C. Norman. "Summary Effects of the Lumatron upon Neurochemicals." The Shealy Institute, ms., 1993.

Shealy, C. Norman, et al. "Depression—A Diagnostic Neurochemical Profile and Therapy with Cranial Electrical Stimulation (CES)." *Journal of Neurological and Orthopedic Medicine and Surgery* 10, no. 4 (1989): 301–3.

Silverman, Lloyd. "Unconscious Symbiotic Fantasy: A Ubiquitous Therapeutic Agent." *International Journal of Psychoanalytic Psychotherapy* 7 (1978–79): 568.

Silverman, Lloyd, F.M. Lachmann, and R.H. Milich. *The Search for Oneness*. New York: International Universities Press, 1982.

Simonton, O. Carl, and Stephanie Simonton. "Belief Systems and Management of the Emotional Aspects of Malignancy." *Journal of Transpersonal Psychology* 7 (1975): 29–47.

Simonton, O., Carl Stephanie Matthews-Simonton, and J. Creighton. *Getting Well Again*. Los Angeles: Tarcher, 1978.

Singh, Baldev; G.S. Chhina; B.K. Anand; M.S. Bopari; and J.S. Neld. "Sleep and Consciousness Mechanism with Special Reference to Electrosleep." *Armed Forces Medical Review* (New Dehli) 27 no. 3 (1971): 292–97.

Sitaram, N., H. Weingartner, and J.C. Gillin. "Choline: Selective Enhancement of Serial Learning and Encoding of Low Imagery Words in Man." *Life Sciences* 22 (1978): 1555–60.

———. "Human Serial Learning: Enhancement with Arecholine and Choline and Impairment with Scopolamine Correlate with Performance on Placebo." *Science* 201 (1978): 274–76.

Sittenfeld, P., T. Budzynski, and J. Stoyva. "Differential Shaping of EEG Theta Rhythms." *Biofeedback and Self-Regulation* 1 (1976): 31–45.

Sjolund, B.H., and M.B.E. Eriksson "Electroacupuncture and Endogenous Morphines." *Lancet* 2 (1976): 1085.

Smith, Adam. *Powers of the Mind.* New York: Random House, 1975.

Smith, Anthony. *The Mind.* New York: Viking, 1984.

Smith, Ray B. "Confirming Evidence of an Effective Treatment for Brain Dysfunction in Alcoholic Patients." *Journal of Nervous and Mental Disease* (November 1981).

Smith, Ray B.; A.E. Burgess; V.J. Guinee; and L.C. Relfsnider; "A Curvilinear Relationship Between Alcohol Withdrawal Tremor and Personality." *Journal of Clinical Psychology* 35, no. 1 (January 1979): 199–203.

Smith, Ray B., and Eleanor Day. "The Effects of Cerebral Electrotherapy on Short-Term Memory Impairment in Alcoholic Patients." *International Journal of Addictions* 12, no. 4 (1977): 575–62.

Smith, Ray B., and Lois O'Neil. "Electrosleep in the Management of Alcoholism." *Biological Psychiatry* 10, no. 6 (1975): 675–80.

Smith, Ray B., and Frank N. Shiromoto. "The Use of Cranial Electrotherapy Stimulation to Block Fear Perception in Phobic Patients," unpublished manuscript.

Smith, Ray B., and Richard Tyson. "The Use of Transcranial Electrical Stimulation in the Treatment of Cocaine and/or Polysubstance Abuse." *American Journal of Psychiatry* February 1991.

Smith, W.L., and J.B. Lowrey "The Effects of Diphenylhyantoin on Cognitive Functions in Man." *Drugs, Development and Cerebral Function* (1972): 334–51.

———. "The Effects of Diphenylhyantoin on Mental Abilities in the Elderly." *Journal of the American Geriatrics Society* 23, no. 5 (1975): 207–11.

"Smuggling Drugs Across the Blood-Brain Barrier." *Science News,* January 2, 1982.

Snyder, Solomon H. "Opiate Receptors in the Brain." *New England Journal of Medicine* (1977).

———. "A Multiplicity of Opiate Receptors and Enkephalin Neuronal Systems." *Journal of Clinical Psychiatry* 43 (1982): 9–12.

Solomon, Philip; P.E. Kubzansky; P.H. Leiderman; J.H. Mendelson; R. Trumbull; and D. Wexler. *Sensory Deprivation: A Symposium Held at Harvard Medical School.* Cambridge: Harvard University Press, 1961.

Sommer, Robert. *The Mind's Eye.* New York: Delacorte, 1978.

Soulairac, A., H. Hossard, and A. Virel. "The Effect of Electronically Induced Alpha Rhythm on Anxiety States." *Annales Medico-Psychologiques* 2 (1977): 704–11.

Spiegel, Rene, et al. "A Controlled Long-Term Study with Ergoloid Mesylates (Hydergine) in Healthy, Elderly Volunteers: Results After Three Years." *Journal of the Geriatrics Society* 31, no. 9 (1983): 549–55.

"Spinning Therapy Calms Hyperactivity, Accelerates Physical Development." *Brain/Mind Bulletin* 5, no. 20 (1980).

Springer, Sally P., and Georg Deutsch. *Left Brain, Right Brain*. San Francisco: Freeman, 1981.

Squire, Larry R., and Hasker Davis. "The Pharmacology of Memory: A Neurobiological Perspective." In *Annual Review of Pharmacy and Toxicology, 1981*. Palo Alto, CA: Annual Reviews, 1981.

Staib, A., and D.N. Logan. "Hypnotic Stimulation of Breast Growth." *American Journal of Clinical Hypnosis* 19 (1977): 201.

Standing, Lionel. "Learning 10,000 Pictures." *Quarterly Journal of Experimental Psychology* 25: 207–22

Stanley, John M., William D. Francis, and Heidi Berres. "The Effects of Flotation REST on Cognitive Tasks." Paper presented at the first International Conference on REST and Self-Regulation, Denver, CO, March 17, 1983.

Starr, Douglas. "Brain Drugs." *Omni*, February 1983.

Stegink, A.J. "The Clinical Use of Piracetam, a New Nootropic Drug." *Arzneimittelgorschung* 22, no. 6 (1972): 975–77.

Stein, et al. "Memory Enhancement by Central Administration of Norepinephrine." *Brain Research* 84 (1975): 329–35.

Sterman, M.B., and L. Friar. "Suppression of Seizures in an Epileptic Following Sensorimotor EEG Biofeedback Training." *Electroencephalography and Clinical Neurophysiology* 33 (1972): 89–95.

Sterman, M.B., and L.R. Mac Donald. "Effects of Central Cortical EEG Feedback Training on Seizure Incidence in Poorly Controlled Epileptics." *Epilepsia* 19 (1978): 207–22.

Sterman, M.B., L.R. Mac Donald, and R.K. Stone. Biofeedback Training on the Sensorimotor Electroencephalographic Rhythm in Man: Effects on Epilepsy." *Epilepsia* 15 (1974): 395–416.

Stevens, Charles F. "The Neuron." *Scientific American*, September 1979.

Stone, Pat. "Altered States of Consciousness." *Mother Earth News*, March/April 1983.

Storfer, Miles David. *A Readers Guide to Brain Research Activities and Their Potential*. New York: Foundation for Brain Research, 1982.

———. *Brain Research: Our Journey Has Begun*. New York: Foundation for Brain Research, 1984.

———. *Intelligence and Giftedness: The Contributions of Heredity and Early Environment*. San Francisco: Jossey-Bass, 1990.

Stoyva, J.M. "Biofeedback Techniques and the Conditions for Hallucinatory Activity." In *The Psychophysiology of Thinking*, ed. F.J. McGuigan and R. Schoonnover. New York: Academic Press, 1973.

"Stress Held Factor in IQ Scores." *New York Times*, May 31, 1983.

Stroebel, Charles F., M.D. *QR: The Quieting Reflex*. New York: Putnam, 1982.

Subhan, Z., and I. Hindmarch. "Psychopharmacological Effects of Vinpocetine in Normal Healthy Volunteers." *European Journal of Clinical Pharmacology* 28 (1985): 567–71.

Suedfeld, Peter. "The Benefits of Boredom: Sensory Deprivation Reconsidered." *American Scientist* 63 (1975): 60–69.

———. "The Clinical Relevance of Reduced Sensory Stimulation." *Canadian Psychological Review* 16 (1975): 88–103.

———. "Using Environmental Restriction to Initiate Long-term Behavioral Change." In *Behavioral Self-management: Strategies, Techniques, Outcomes*, ed. R.B. Stuart. New York: Brunner/Mazel, 1977.

———. *Restricted Environmental Stimulation: Research and Clinical Applications*. New York: Wiley, 1980.

———. "REST: Technique, Treatment and Transcendence." Paper presented at the first International Conference on REST and Self-Regulation, Denver, CO, March 17, 1983.

Suedfeld, Peter, and J.A. Best. "Satiation and Sensory Deprivation Combined in Smoking Therapy: Some Case Studies and Unexpected Side Effects." *International Journal of Addiction* 12 (1977): 337–59.

Suedfeld, Peter, and R.D. Hare. "Sensory Deprivation in the Treatment of Snake Phobia: Behavioral Self-Report and Physiological Effects." *Behavioral Therapy* 8 (1977): 240–50.

Suedfeld, Peter, et al. (Eds.). *Restricted Environmental Stimulation: Theoretical and Empirical Developments in Flotation REST*. New York: Springer-Verlag, 1990.

Suinn, Richard M. "Body Thinking: Psychology for Olympic Champs." *Psychology Today*, July 1976.

Svyandosch, A. "The Assimilation and Memorization of Speech During Natural Sleep." In *Current Research in Hypnopaedia*, ed. F. Rubin. London: MacDonald, 1968.

Swedenborg, E. *Rational Psychology*. Philadelphia: Swedenborg Scientific Association, 1950.

"Synchro-energizer: Report No. 1." ms., Biofeedback Institute of Denver.

Tallman, John F., et al. "Receptors of the Age of Anxiety: Pharmacology of the Benzodiazepines." *Science* 207 (1980): 274.

Tansey, M.A. "Righting the Rhythms of Reason: EEG Biofeedback Training as a Therapeutic Modality in a Clinical Office Setting." *Medical Psychotherapy* 3 (1990): 57–68.

Tart, Charles T., ed. *Altered States of Consciousness*. New York: Doubleday, 1972.

Taylor, Gordon Rattray. *The Natural History of the Mind*. New York: Dutton, 1979.

Thomas, Norman R., et al. "The Effect of Repetitive Audiovisual Stimulation on Skeletomotor and Vasomotor Activity in Low Hypnotizable TMJ Subjects in Hypnosis." In *Proceedings of the 1987 European Congress on Psychosomtaic Disease*. New York: Oxford, 1990.

Taylor, Thomas E. "Learning Studies for Higher Cognitive Levels in a Short-Term Sensory Isolation Environment." Paper presented at the first International Conference on REST and Self-Regulation, Denver, CO, March 17, 1983.

Taylor, Thomas E., Margaret Hansen, et al. "A Study of EEG as an Indicator of Changes in Cognitive Level of Understanding in a Sensory Isolation Environment." ms., Dept. of Chemistry, Texas A & M University, 1982.

Tomarken, A.J., R.J. Davidson, and J.B. Henriques. "Resting Frontal Brain Asymmetry Predicts Affective Responses to Films." *Journal of Personality and Social Psychology* 59 (1990): 791–801.

Tomatis, Alfred. *The Conscious Ear*. Barington, NY: Station Hill Press, 1991.

Townsend, R.E. "A Device for Generation and Presentation of Modulated

Light Stimuli." *Electroencephalography and Clinical Neurophysiology* 34 (1973): 97–99.

Tsubokawa, T.; T. Yamamoto; Y. Katayama; T. Hirayama; S. Maejima; and T. Moriya. "Deep Brain Stimulation in a Persistent Vegetative State: Follow-up Results and Criteria for Selection of Candidates." *Brain Injury* 4, no. 4 (1990): 315–27.

Tucker, D.M. "Lateral Brain Function, Emotion, and Conceptualization." *Psychological Bulletin* 89 (1981): 19–46.

Turner, John W. "Hormones and REST and Self-Regulation." Paper presented at the first International Conference on REST and Self-Regulation, Denver, CO, March 18, 1983.

Turner, John W., and Thomas H. Fine (eds.). *Restricted Environmental Stimulation: Research and Commentary.* Toledo: Medical College of Ohio, 1992.

Turner, John, et al. "Effect of Wet and Dry Flotation REST on Blood Pressure and Plasma Cortisol." Paper presented at the fourth International Conference of the International REST Investigators Society, Seattle, WA, 1990.

Van der Tweel, L.H., and H.F.E. Verduyn Lunel. "Human Visual Responses to Sinusoidally Modulated Light." *Electroencephalography and Clinical Neurophysiology* 18 (1965): 587–98.

Vincent, George, et al. "The Effects of Aniracetam (Ro-13-5057) on the Enhancement and Protection of Memory." *Annals of the New York Academy of Sciences,* 244 (1985): 489–91.

Vogel, William; Donald M. Broverman; Edward Klaiber; and Karoly J. Kun. "EEG Response to Photic Stimulation as a Function of Cognitive Style." *Electroencephalography and Clinical Neurophysiology* 27 (1969): 186–90.

Walford, Roy L., M.D. *Maximum Life Span.* New York: Norton, 1983.

Walkup, Lewis E. "Creativity in Science Through Visualization." *Perceptual and Motor Skills* 221 (1965): 35–41.

Walsh, Roger. *Toward an Ecology of Brain.* Jamaica, NY: SP Medical and Scientific Books, 1982.

Walter, V.J., and W.G. Walter. "The Central Effects of Rhythmic Sensory Stimulation." *Electroencephalography and Clinical Neurophysiology* 1 (1949): 57–86.

Watson, Lyall. *Lifetide: The Biology of the Unconscious.* New York: Simon and Schuster, 1979.

Wauquier, Albert, and Edmund T. Rolls. *Brain Stimulation Reward.* Amsterdam: North Holland Publishing Co., 1976.

Weil, Andrew. *The Natural Mind.* Boston: Houghton Mifflin, 1972.

Weil, C., ed. "Pharmacology and Clinical Pharmacology of Hydergine." In *Handbook of Experimental Pharmacology.* New York: Springer-Verlag, 1978.

Weintraub, Pamela, ed. *The Omni Interviews.* New York: Ticknor and Fields, 1984.

Weiss, Marc F. "The Treatment of Insomnia Through the Use of Electrosleep: An EEG Study." *Journal of Nervous and Mental Disease* 157, no. 2 (1973): 108–20.

West, Michael A. "Meditation and the EEG." *Psychological Medicine* 10 (1980): 369–75.

Wickramsekera, I.E. *Clinical Behavioral Medicine: Some Concepts and Procedures.* New York: Plenum Press, 1988.

Wickramsekera, Ian. "Sensory Restriction and Self-Hypnosis as Potentiators of Self-Regulation," Paper presented at the first International Conference on REST and Self-Regulation, Denver, CO, March 18, 1983.

Willard, R.D. "Breast Enlargement Through Visual Imagery and Hypnosis." *American Journal of Clinical Hypnosis* 19 (1977): 195.

Williams, J.E. "Stimulation of Breast Growth by Hypnosis." *Journal of Sex Research* 10 (1974): 316–24.

Williams, J.T., and W. Zieglgansberger. "Neurons in the Frontal Cortex of the Rat Carry Multiple Opiate Receptors." *Brain Research* 226 (1981): 304–8.

Williams, Paul, and Michael West. "EEG Responses to Photic Stimulation in Persons Experienced at Meditation." *Electroencephalography and Clinical Neurophysiology* 39 (1975): 519–22.

Wilsher, Colin R., et al. "Piracetam and Dyslexia: Effect on Reading Tests." *Journal of Clinical Psychopharmacology* 7, no. 4 (1987): 230–37.

Wise, Steven P., and Miles Herkenham. "Opiate Receptor Distribution in the Cerebral Cortex of the Rhesus Monkey." *Science* 218 (1982): 387–89.

Witelson, Sandra. "Sex and Single Hemisphere: Specialization of the Right Hemisphere for Spatial Processing." *Science* 193 (1976): 425–26.

Wolpe, J. *The Practice of Behavior Therapy.* New York: Pergamon, 1969.

Woolfolk, Robert L., and Frank C. Richardon. *Stress, Sanity, and Survival.* New York: Monarch, 1978.

Wurtman, Richard, et al. *The Medical and Biological Effects of Light.* New York: The New York Academy of Sciences, 1985.

Wurtman, R.J., et al. "Piracetam Diminishes Hippocampal Acetylcholine Levels in Rats." *Life Science* 28 (1981): 1091–93.

Yaguchi, Kiyoshi, and Shinkura Iwahara. "Temporal Sequence of Frequency Specific and Non-Specific Effects of Flickering Lights upon the Occipital Electrical Activity in Man." *Brain Research* 107 (1976): 27–38.

Yesavage, Jerome A., et al. "Dihydroergotoxine: 6-Mg versus 3-Mg Dosage in the Treatment of Senile Dementia—Prelimary Report." *Journal of the American Geriatrics Society* 27, no. 2 (1979): 80–82.

Yoshikawa, Masami, et al. "A Dose-Response Study with Dihydroergotoxine Mesylate in Cerebrovascular Disturbances." *Journal of the American Geriatrics Society* 31, no. 1 (1983): 1–7.

Young, J.Z. *Programs of the Brain.* Oxford: Oxford University Press, 1978.

Zaidel, Eran. "Unilateral Auditory Language Comprehension on the Token Test Following Cerebral Commissurotomy and Hemispherectomy." *Neuropsychologia* 15 (1977): 1–18.

Zubeck, J.P., ed. *Sensory Deprivation: Fifteen Years of Research.* New York: Appleton-Century-Crofts, 1969.

Zuckerman, M. *Sensation Seeking: Beyond the Optimal Level Arousal.* Hillsdale, NJ: Lawrence Erlbaum Associates, 1979.

All of the devices described in this book are commercially available. There are also many commercial or medical facilities, such as brain-mind gyms, flotation centers, stress reduction centers, pain clinics, health clubs, and so on, where it is possible to have a session or a series of sessions with some of the devices. I conduct Megabrain Workshops in which participants have an opportunity to have hands-on experience with a variety of these tools. Special corporate Megabrain Workshops teach participants how to use mind technology for reducing stress, enhancing creativity, and improving the quality of the workplace.

Megabrain Report: The Journal of Mind Technology features reports on the continuing research and development in the area of mind machines, interviews with scientists and inventors, a "consumers' guide" to investigate and explore the effects (and effectiveness) of the growing array of mind-expansion devices, and a section of letters and reports from users and experimenters around the world that is a forum for communication, knowledge-sharing, free-wheeling speculation, and shared inspiration for a large and growing network of people.

In addition, I now write *The Hutchison Guide*, a free consumers' guide to consciousness technology. In this publication I provide up-to-date, in depth information about the brain machines I've found to be the best—those that show strong evidence they're effective, fairly priced, and of high quality. This regularly updated consumers' guide is part of a publication called *Tools for Exploration*, which ordinarily sells for $5 a copy. However, it will be provided free of charge to readers of this book. Call 1-800-456-9887 and be sure to mention *Mega Brain Power*.

To obtain a copy of my previous book, *Megabrain: New Tools and Techniques for Brain Growth and Mind Expansion*, please go to your local bookstore or order by calling Ballantine, toll-free, 1-800-733-3000 to use your major credit card.

For information about where the Megabrain devices may be used or purchased, about locations of workshops, to subscribe to *Megabrain Report*, or to receive your free guide to mind technology write to:

MICHAEL HUTCHISON
P.O. Box 2659
Sausalito, CA 94966–9998
U.S.A.
1-800-456-9887

Trademarked items included in this publication:

Tapes:
Hypo-Peripharal Processing™ tapes
Paraliminal™ tapes
Hemi-Sync™ tapes
Mega Brain Zones
Silent Stim™

Light-Sound machines:
The MindsEye Synergizer™
The MindLab DLS™
The MindLab DLS with PolySync™
Photosonix Galaxy™
The D.A.V.I.D. 2001™
The D.A.V.I.D. Paradise™
The D.A.V.I.D Paradise Jr.™
The Mind Gear™ SLX

Light and color devices:
Verilux™ full spectrum fluorescents
The Stress Shield™
The Lumatron™

Motion Systems:
The Symmetron™
The Integrative Motion System™

Sound Tables
The Genesis™
The Vibrasound™
Discovery™ Sound Table
PSI™ Sound Table
Somatron™

Other
Biocircuits™
Motivaidor™

Biofeedback devices:
Antense®
The Sedona Method®

INDEX

ABOUT THE AUTHOR

MICHAEL HUTCHISON's writings exploring the interplay between science and culture, information and power, have included *The Book of Floating*, *Megabrain*, and most recently, *The Anatomy of Sex and Power: An Investigation of Mind-Body Politics*. His fiction has been awarded the James Michener Prize; his nonfiction and poetry have appeared in *Esquire*, *The Village Voice*, *Outside*, *The Partisan Review*, *Playboy*, and numerous other magazines and newspapers.